Hither Shore

Interdisciplinary Journal
on Modern Fantasy Literature

Jahrbuch der
Deutschen Tolkien Gesellschaft e. V.

Tolkien and Romanticism

Tolkien und Romantik

Interdisziplinäres Seminar der DTG
23.-25. April 2010, Jena

Herausgegeben von:
Thomas Fornet-Ponse (Gesamtleitung),
Marcel Bülles, Thomas Honegger,
Rainer Nagel, Alexandra Velten,
Frank Weinreich

SCRIPTORIUM OXONIAE

Bibliografische Information der Deutschen Bibliothek

Die Deutsche Bibliothek verzeichnet diese Publikation in der Deutschen Nationalbibliografie; detaillierte bibliografische Daten sind im Internet über http://dnb.ddb.de abrufbar.

ISBN 978-3-9810612-5-3

Hither Shore, DTG-Jahrbuch 2010
veröffentlicht im Verlag »Scriptorium Oxoniae«
Deutsche Tolkien Gesellschaft e. V. (DTG)
E-Mail: info@tolkiengesellschaft.de
Scriptorium Oxoniae im Atelier für Textaufgaben e. K.
Brehmstraße 50 · D-40239 Düsseldorf
E-Mail: rayermann@scriptorium-oxoniae.de
Hither Shore, Gesamtleitung: Thomas Fornet-Ponse
Graurheindorfer Straße 64 · D-53111 Bonn
E-Mail: hither-shore@tolkiengesellschaft.de
Vorschläge für Beiträge in deutscher oder englischer Sprache (inklusive Exposé von ca. 100 Wörtern) werden erbeten an o.g. Adresse.

Alle Rechte verbleiben beim Autor des jeweiligen Einzelbeitrags. Es gilt als vereinbart, dass ein Autor seinen Beitrag innerhalb der nächsten 18 Monate nach Erscheinen dieser *Hither-Shore*-Ausgabe nicht anderweitig veröffentlichen darf.

Abwicklung: Susanne A. Rayermann, Düsseldorf
Layout/Design: Kathrin Bondzio, Solingen
Umschlagillustration: Anke Eißmann, Herborn
Druck und Vertrieb: Books on Demand, Norderstedt

Alle Rechte vorbehalten.

Inhalt

Preface 6
Vorwort 7

Tolkien Seminar 2010

Stars Above a Dark Tor: Tolkien and Romanticism 8
Anna E. Slack (Cambridge)

Romanticism, Symbolism, and Onomastics in
Tolkien's *Legendarium* 18
Annie Birks (Angers)

Mittelerde als Ausdruck romantischer Kreativität
und Sehnsucht 32
Oliver Bidlo (Essen)

'The past is another country' – Romanticism, Tolkien,
and the Middle Ages 48
Thomas Honegger (Jena)

Disenchanted with their Age: Keats's, Morris's, and
Tolkien's Great Escape 60
Marie-Noëlle Biemer (Frankfurt)

Celtic Influences and the Quest of National Identity 76
Doreen Triebel (Jena)

J.R.R. Tolkien und die romantische Nostalgie 94
Julian T.M. Eilmann (Aachen)

'There and back again' – a Romantic Walk?
Eine kritische Betrachtung von J.R.R. Tolkiens *The Hobbit*
aus dem Blickwinkel der Romantik 110
Thomas Scholz (Frankfurt)

Outer and Inner Landscapes in Tolkien:
Between Wordsworth, Coleridge, and Dostoevskij 120
Emanuele Rimoli (Roma), Guglielmo Spirito (Assisi)

'Secondary Belief': Tolkien and
the Revision of Romantic Notion of Poetic Faith 138
Eduardo Segura (Granada)

Beauty, Perfection, Sublime Terror.
Some Thoughts on the Influence of E. Burke's
A Philosophical Enquiry into the Sublime and Beautiful
on Tolkien's Creation of Middle-earth 152
Stefanie Schult (Greifswald)

Reading Tolkien's Work in the Light of
Hugo's Notions of the Sublime and the Grotesque 162
Marguerite Mouton (Paris)

Tolkien, Newman und das Oxford Movement 172
Thomas Fornet-Ponse (Bonn)

Tolkien, the Philistine, and the Politics of Creativity 188
Martin G.E. Sternberg (Bonn)

Falsche Harmonie oder: Darf man
nach Auschwitz noch vom Auenland träumen? 204
Fabian Geier (Bamberg)

Zusammenfassungen der englischen Beiträge 222

Summaries of the German Essays 229

Reviews / Rezensionen

Lothar Mikos, Susanne Eichner, Elizabeth Prommer, Michael Wedel:
Die »*Herr der Ringe*«-Trilogie – Attraktion und Faszination eines populärkulturellen Phänomens 234

Cécile van Zon (ed.): Tolkien in Poetry and Song 238

Isabelle Pantin: Tolkien et ses légendes.
Une expérience en fiction 239

Elizabeth Solopova: Languages, Myths and History.
An Introduction to the Linguistic and Literary Background
of J.R.R. Tolkien's Fiction 241

Steve Walker: The Power of Tolkien's Prose:
Middle-Earth's Magical Style 242

Fastitocalon. Studies in Fantasticism Ancient to Modern.
Vol I-1 (2010): Immortals and the Undead 244

Heidi Steimel and Friedhelm Schneidewind (eds.):
Music in Middle-earth 246

Martha Sammons: War of the Fantasy Worlds:
C.S. Lewis and J.R.R. Tolkien on Art and Imagination 251

Note

Publishing about Tolkien: Polemic Musings about New
Developments by an Old Hand in the Business 254
Thomas Honegger (Jena)

Über die Autorinnen und Autoren 258
About our Authors 262

Siglen-Liste 266

Index 268

Preface

April 2010 saw the seventh seminar of the German Tolkien Society, again organised in coordination with Thomas Honegger. With the experience of six conferences under our belt, and at a location we already knew – what could go wrong? Actually, a lot more than we imagined. Due to the eruption of the volcano Eyjafjallajökull and the resulting restrictions on air traffic, several of our originally scheduled speakers were prevented from presenting their ideas in person. The large number of remaining presentations, however, clearly shows the huge interest with which quite diverse disciplines have corresponded to the topic *Tolkien and Romanticism*. Indeed, had it not been for those cancellations, this would have been the seminar with the largest number of presentations so far. At least we are able to present two of these cancelled papers in this volume: those by Eduardo Segura and by Anna Slack.

As reading this book will immediately show, there is anything but scientific consensus on Tolkien's position regarding Romanticism – which already justifies our choice of topic in retrospect. A seminar at the end of which more questions are left unanswered as could be expected beforehand is certainly not a seminar held in vain! The differences within the scholastic community do not only come about because of different choices in text selection, but can also been seen in survey articles covering a larger body of texts. More importantly, though, they arise because there is not yet any generally accepted definition of what exactly is to be understood by the term Romanticism. This leads to the application of rather diverse concepts of Romanticism. Accordingly, it is quite possible to see Tolkien as an author in the Romantic tradition, due to his use of motives and certain characteristics. However, it is equally possible to present other aspects of his works as clearly non-Romantic. In addition, there is occasionally even vehement dissent about interpreting one particular element – such as Tolkien's recourse to the Middle Ages. Hence, the Middle Ages will be the overall topic of our next seminar, allowing us to seamlessly blend from this one to its successor.

In addition to the numerous papers from the seminar that shed a highly varied light on the dimensions of Tolkien's works, this volume also contains a few detailed reviews of current scientific studies as well as a short contribution by Thomas Honegger pointing out a problematic development in the field of secondary literature.

Finally, we would like to thank everyone involved in the success of the seminar and the creation of this newest volume of out yearbook: First of all, Prof. Dr. Thomas Honegger and his staff at Friedrich Schiller University, Jena; then *Walking Tree Publishers* and the *Association Modernités mediévales* for their friendly support; and of course also all contributors and our publisher's team Susanne A. Rayermann and Kathrin Bondzio.

Thomas Fornet-Ponse

Vorwort

Das »verflixte siebte Jahr«? In gewissem Sinne mag dies auf das im April 2010 in Jena in bewährter Zusammenarbeit mit Thomas Honegger durchgeführte 7. Tolkien Seminar der Deutschen Tolkien Gesellschaft zutreffen, dessen Vorträge die Grundlage dieses Bandes bilden. Denn aufgrund des Ausbruchs des Vulkans Eyafjallajökull und der dadurch verursachten Einschränkungen des Flugverkehrs war es mehreren der ursprünglich geplanten Referenten und Referentinnen verwehrt, ihre Thesen persönlich vorzustellen. Die hohe Zahl der verbliebenen Vorträge zeigt deutlich, auf welch großes Interesse das Thema *Tolkien und die Romantik* in ganz unterschiedlichen Disziplinen gestoßen ist – tatsächlich wäre es ohne Ausfälle das Seminar mit den bisher meisten Beiträgen gewesen. Zumindest zwei der nicht gehaltenen Beiträge liegen mit denjenigen Eduardo Seguras und Anna Slacks in diesem Band vor.

Wie sich bei der Lektüre schnell zeigen wird, besteht hinsichtlich der Nähe Tolkiens zur Romantik alles andere als ein Forschungskonsens – womit die Themenwahl sich auch im Rückblick als im höchsten Maße berechtigt erwiesen hat. Ein Seminar, an dessen Ende mehr Fragen offen sind als zu Beginn vermutet, hat gewiss nicht vergebens stattgefunden. Denn die Differenzen innerhalb der Forschergemeinde verdanken sich weniger einer unterschiedlichen Auswahl untersuchter Texte, da sie auch zwischen den ein größeres Textkorpus betrachtenden Artikeln bestehen. Vielmehr sind sie auch auf eine bis heute fehlende allgemein akzeptierte Definition dessen zurückzuführen, was unter Romantik genau zu verstehen ist, so dass recht unterschiedliche Romantikverständnisse verwendet werden konnten. Dementsprechend kann Tolkien einerseits anhand von Motiven und Charakteristika in die Tradition der Romantik gestellt werden, andererseits werden andere Aspekte seines Werkes als nicht romantisch herausgestellt. Darüber hinaus besteht zuweilen sogar im Blick auf das gleiche Element ein vehementer Dissens – genannt sei hier nur Tolkiens Rekurs auf das Mittelalter, weswegen sich das Thema des 8. Tolkien Seminars organisch an das vergangene anschließt.

Neben den zahlreichen und ganz unterschiedliche Dimensionen des Werkes Tolkiens untersuchenden Seminarbeiträgen enthält diese Ausgabe wiederum einige ausführliche Rezensionen zu aktuellen Forschungsarbeiten sowie einen kurzen Beitrag Thomas Honeggers, in dem dieser auf eine problematische Entwicklung im Feld der Sekundärliteratur aufmerksam macht.

Schließlich sei noch den verschiedenen am Erfolg des Seminars und dem Zustandekommen des aktuellen Jahrbuchs beteiligten Personen herzlich gedankt: Prof. Dr. Thomas Honegger und seinem Team von der Friedrich-Schiller-Universität Jena, dem Verlag *Walking Tree Publishers* und der *Association Modernités médiévales* für die freundliche Unterstützung sowie natürlich wie immer allen Beitragenden, den Mitgliedern des Board of Editors und Susanne A. Rayermann und Kathrin Bondzio vom *Scriptorium Oxoniae*. *Thomas Fornet-Ponse*

Stars Above a Dark Tor: Tolkien and Romanticism

Anna E. Slack (Cambridge)

> The beauty of it smote his heart... and hope returned to him.
> (LotR 957)

Imagine an English Romantic poet. What kind of picture comes to mind? Perhaps an indolent young man, quill in hand, ambling through the countryside? Or something much wilder – a visionary poet with wind-driven hair?

Out of barbaric curiosity, I tested this same question on some of my students. Their responses ranged from 'Some wet guy with flowing hair, moping in a field writing' to just two words: 'Oh God!' The latter student was not enamoured with English and its great literary heritage (and ambushing them in the lunch queue probably didn't help).

What my students' answers do suggest is that the Romantics are commonly misunderstood; the passing of two centuries sometimes blinds us to what is most fundamental about them.

The Romantics were radicals, thinking and writing about as far outside the contemporary box as it was possible for poets and writers in their time to go. Anti-establishmentarianism could have been their middle name. In every sphere – philosophical, ideological, political, religious and literary – these 18th century bad boys represented a threat to the establishment. These were the kind of men that sweet old ladies would shake their heads at. Worse than bad and ugly – they were considered mad and dangerous to know.

Why? The Romantic Movement created a profound shift in the West's attitudes to art and human creativity. Classical purity was formal and stiff-necked, and stifling neo-classical imitation seemed to repress the glory of the human spirit. This was not, to use a delightful English idiom, the Romantics' 'cup of tea'. Going entirely against the grain of contemporary literary thought, they turned inwards to unleash their innermost capacities of self-expression, exulting in the spontaneity and originality of their individual imaginations.

It was a Promethean exploit. In fact, we might take the story of Prometheus as a good symbol for what the Romantics were trying to achieve – they were wresting back the fire of the human spirit – imagination – for the use of all mankind. Unlike its classical counterpart, however, this Romantic Prometheus is released – just as he is in Shelley's closet drama *Prometheus Unbound*.

Imagination is the presiding spirit of the Romantic Movement. It was the visionary capacity that allowed the Romantic pen to strike back to a realm of myth and legend so as to capture the transcendence of nature and sheer presentness of human existence. More even than presiding spirit, imagination was the Romantics' very lifeblood, and it ran throughout Europe.

The Wild, the Improbable, the Fanciful: England's Romantics

Asked to name the six key figures of English Romanticism, any good student of English Literature will list William Blake, William Wordsworth, Samuel Taylor Coleridge, John Keats, Percy Bysshe Shelley and Lord Byron as the guilty parties. These poets range from the truly visionary to the revolutionary and the outright tragic. They were all prolific writers – any one of them might claim Ozymandias' infamous words: 'look on my works, ye mighty, and despair'. Tigers, albatrosses, daffodils and Grecian urns had perhaps never before enjoyed such notoriety as these poets gave them. And, although they may have differed in opinion on some details, the heart of their theories of poetry was the same: everything resided in the crucial role of the imagination.

William Blake perhaps put it most clearly when he wrote: 'This world of imagination is the world of eternity' (Keynes 639). Indeed, for Coleridge, imagination was 'the living Power and prime Agent of all human Perception... a repetition in the finite mind of the eternal act of creation in the infinite I AM' (Shawcross I. 202). More personably than his co-Romantics, Keats wrote: 'I am certain of nothing but the holiness of the heart's affections and the truth of the imagination' (Letter to Benjamin Bailey).

This is what we might, with hindsight, call a eucatastrophic vision of literature. However it is expressed the essential sentiment is the same: there is something about imagination that transcends human experience and puts it back in touch with higher, eternal truths. The city of London, reviled by Blake as a place where 'soldiers' sighs / Run in blood down palace walls' (Willmott 38) is mystically redeemed in its reconnection to the glories of creation when Wordsworth finds its smokeless morning sleep as much a thing of splendour as the Edenic first light on valley, rock and hill.

This is linguistically and ideologically powerful stuff. But the Romantic imagination entailed far more than lounging about on London bridges writing sonnets. This notion of imagination was all-encompassing. For the Romantics, imagination meant breaking away from the classical unities of form and structure; spurning the trappings of rationalism in favour of the feeling of individual experience; and rejecting the rapidly expanding grind of urban life so as to return to man's true setting – nature, free from the 'mind-forged manacles' of a mechanistic view of life. It was an ideal vision of the world in so far as it was rooted entirely in ideas.

Needless to say, the Romantics were not very high up on Locke and Newton's Christmas card lists. Romanticism was an 'all or nothing' affair. You could not be half-hearted in this line of literature.

Transposing these ideals of imagination from mind to paper might seem a daunting prospect. But these poets were nonplussed by the challenge. They saw themselves as inheritors of the great romances, those 'wild, improbable... fanciful' tales that were 'full of wild scenery' (Coleridge I. 352). Imagination was the key – and these writers used it to unlock new styles and types of literature.

Imagination: The Divine Vision

It is by now clear that in order to grasp the Romantics we need to grapple with the idea of imagination. The OED defines it, rather dryly, as 'the faculty or action of forming ideas or mental images'. Imagination is a concept that, from our earliest childhoods, is set in stern opposition to reality. Tolkien himself acknowledges this in *On Fairy-Stories*, where he explores how fantastical literature can be condemned as escapist and juvenile. This trend goes back at least as far as Plato's theory of forms – imagination here is considered as a step too far from the true nature of things, leading to the expulsion of poets from the Republic.

Even today, imagination is seemingly divorced from any redemptive creative wellspring – its places are the nursery or the business board room. Phrases like 'he has an over-active imagination' or 'you're just imagining things' point to a certain distrust of this human faculty.

For Blake, imagination was 'the divine vision', one that enabled you to see 'a world in a grain of sand' (Keynes 118). Tolkien would go on to make this same connection, both in *Mythopoeia* (where he writes to C.S. Lewis that 'we make still by the law in which we're made') and *On Fairy-Stories*. For Tolkien, as for the Romantics, the process of sub-creation – a divinely ordained imagining of other worlds – is not only innately but vitally human, connecting us to creation itself in a way that few other processes are capable of doing.

In many ways, we can view Tolkien's minor work *Leaf by Niggle* as a deeply personal and thinly-veiled allegorical dialectic exploring this very issue. Niggle spends as much of his life as he can working on his painting of a tree, but it is only after he leaves the purgatorial Workhouse and goes on to Niggle's Country that the truer nature of his painting is revealed:

> A great green shadow came between him and the sun. Niggle looked up and fell off his bicycle.
> Before him stood *the* Tree, his Tree, finished. If you could say that of a tree that was alive, its leaves opening, its branches growing and bending in the wind that Niggle had so often felt or guessed, and so often failed to catch. He gazed at the Tree, and slowly lifted his arms and opened them wide.
> 'It's a gift!' he said. He was referring to his art, and also to the result; but he was using the word quite literally.
>
> (LN 136, emphasis mine)

Tolkien clearly aligns himself here with what we might call a Romantic mode of imagination. If we take Niggle's tree as an allegorical expression of the role of imagination in art, then it is a gift, to be used wisely (as the rest of Niggle's tale clearly shows). But the tree is only truly finished once its mimetic quality – the way in which its artistry mirrors something definitive and eternal – is revealed. The art brings us a step closer to the high, eternal form. In this way, Tolkien's view of imagination assimilates and inverts Plato's theory of forms:

> 'Niggle's Picture!' said Parish in astonishment. 'Did you think of all this, Niggle? I never knew you were so clever. Why didn't you tell me?'
> 'He tried to tell you, long ago,' said the man, 'but you would not look. He had only got canvas and paint in those days, and you wanted to mend your roof with them. This is what you and your wife used to call Niggle's Nonsense...'
> 'But it did not look like this then, not real,' said Parish.
> 'No, it was only a glimpse then,' said the man; 'but you might have caught the glimpse, if you had ever thought it worth while to try.' (LN 141)

As for the Romantics, imagination is a gift, a divine vision, a sub-creative act that can reconnect man to the divine. Rather than removing us from the true nature of things Tolkien argues that it can offer us a heart-shattering glimpse of them. It was an idea that would find academic crystallisation in his concept of eucatastrophe. Pursuing the creative impulse grants us a glimpse of eternity – in Niggle's case, 'an introduction to the Mountains'. C.S. Lewis called the same 'glimpsing' experience 'Joy'. Blake, with his accustomed visionary vigour, likens that moment of transcendent clarity to 'Hold[ing] infinity in the palm of your hand / and eternity in an hour' (Keynes 118).

Painting Niggle's Tree: Imagination in Action

Imagination is the envisioning of something beyond reality, something which perhaps offers a glimpse of eternity. So far so good – but how do you get a transcendent experience neatly down onto an obliging bit of paper?

The Romantics almost invariably turned to poetry. The choice is an obvious one – it could be argued that few other literary forms offer the writer such an intense vehicle of expression, replete as it is with the subtleties of rhythm, diction and imagery. Poetry is an ancient and aural art, one that forces the listener or reader to open their own imagination to the writer's vocalised vision. Take, for example, the hypnotic power of William Blake's *The Tiger* – a poem which is itself concerned with sub-creation:

> Tiger, Tiger, burning bright
> In the forests of the night:
> What immortal hand or eye
> Could frame thy fearful symmetry? ...
>
> When the stars threw down their spears,
> And watered Heaven with their tears,
> Did he smile his work to see?
> Did he who made the lamb make thee? ...
>
> (Wilmott 34)

The tight rhymes and relentless rhythm of Blake's poem convey a sense of awe and urgency in a way that perhaps no prose can. This visionary lyric assaults the senses, forcing an imaginative response in its arresting language and questioning of the reader – we cannot evade it. Blake's choice of poetic form and structure are exact.

Of course, Tolkien's works are not renowned for their poetry – although one can (and I would!) argue for the astonishing, eucatastrophic power of Sam's song in Cirith Ungol or the almost unbearable poignancy of *Bilbo's Last Song*. But that is not to say that we must bar Tolkien from his Romantic heritage on account of his choice of form; we often have a special reverence for poetry, tending to view it as the highest form of literary expression. At times that is well deserved. But we should not forget that our word poetry derives, after all, from the Greek verb *poiein*, to create – and if Tolkien does anything, he creates. The power of poetry perhaps lies in the way that it can linguistically and musically spark the imagination. If that is the case, then Tolkien's prose is at times as poetic as the most startling or breath-taking passages of the Romantic canon:

> And in that very moment, away behind in some courtyard of the City, a cock crowed. Shrill and clear he crowed, recking nothing of wizardry or war, welcoming only the morning that in the sky far above the shadows of death was coming with the dawn. And as if in answer there came from far away another note. Horns, horns, horns. In dark Mindolluin's sides they dimly echoed. Great horns of the North wildly blowing. Rohan had come at last. (LotR 861)

Tolkien's choice and use of language here is every bit as deliberate as that of his Romantic forbears. He weaves together semantic patterns, chosen details and literary allusions to create a moment of eucatastrophe. Tolkien's choice of prose, we might argue, serves as a foil to such moments of lyrical or visionary clarity. In this, perhaps he goes a step further than the Romantics; while they focussed on keeping their sense of imagination in overdrive, Tolkien's prose more closely mimics the experience of reality: our lives are not overflowing with this kind of imaginative, eucatastrophic clarity – what Virginia Woolfe would call 'moments of being'. A prosaic exposition of an imaginary world therefore allows us to integrate more fully with its mundane experience and its moments of being – something that poetry does not always permit us.

Tolkien's prose is littered with such instances; almost invariably, he ties that sense of 'poetry' to the experience of eucatastrophe, as in this example from *The Two Towers*:

> 'Look, Sam!' [Frodo] cried, startled into speech. 'Look! The king has got a crown again!'
> The eyes were hollow and the carven beard was broken, but about the high stern forehead there was a coronal of silver and gold. A trailing plant with flowers like small white stars had bound itself across the brows as if in reverence for the fallen king, and in the crevices of his stony hair yellow stonecrop gleamed.
> 'They cannot conquer forever!' said Frodo. And then suddenly the *brief glimpse* was gone. The sun dipped and vanished, and as if at the shuttering of a lamp, black night fell.
> (LotR 727, emphasis mine)

This second passage is perhaps less spine-tingling than the first coming, as it does, not on a field of battle but really just in a field – but the power of imagination and its culmination in eucatastrophic glimpses of something beyond us is nevertheless outspoken. We are presented first with a microcosmic, personal experience of the power of imagination in Frodo's response to the natural world. In fact, his experience is so over-powering that it startles our troubled hobbit hero to speech, the verbs *cried* and *startled* strongly implying a moment of transcendence before we reach its verbal expression in 'The king has got a crown again!'. It is in the imagining of a crown – expressed delicately but evocatively in Tolkien's detailed attention to the natural world, where the flowers become 'small white stars' – that we are led to the moment of clarity: 'they cannot conquer forever'. Like a true Romantic, Tolkien turns to the natural world and infuses it with a sense of the eternal so as to express the power of the imagination to lesson us in eternal things. But Tolkien is at pains to show the temporal nature of this experience: Frodo's 'brief glimpse' is gone as suddenly as it appeared, and a more prosaic diction (with the vanishing sun compared to a shuttered lamp) reinforces our sense that everyday experience always truncates the moments in which our imaginations are liberated to glimpse beyond it. The juxtaposition is heart-rending – but it is chiefly achieved through creative mastery of natural details.

As *The Lord of the Rings* nears its end, Tolkien's engagement with the natural world becomes a *tour de force* of pathetic fallacy. The road to Mordor becomes somewhat of a physical representation of Frodo's and Sam's emotional and spiritual journey, heightening our sense of their exhaustion and nigh despair. Against this framework, Tolkien sets the scene for another moment of transcendent imagination:

> The land seemed full of creaking and cracking and sly noises, but there was no sound of voice or of foot. Far above Ephel Duath in the West the night-sky was still dim and pale. There, peeping among the cloud-wrack above a dark tor high up in the mountains, Sam saw a white star twinkle for a while. The beauty of it smote his heart, as he looked up out of the forsaken land, and hope returned to him. For like a shaft, clear and cold, the thought pierced him that in the end the Shadow was only a small and passing thing: there was light and high beauty for ever beyond its reach.
> (LotR 957)

C.M. Bowra once wrote that: 'The Romantics... explore[d]... the world of the spirit... each of them believed in an order of things which is not that which we see and know... They wished to penetrate to an abiding reality... [and] were convinced that, though visible things are the instruments by which we view this reality, they are not everything and have indeed little significance unless they are related to some embracing and sustaining power' (Bowra 9). In this passage, Tolkien does just that.

The artistry and the setting of the natural world have again become the vehicle for a powerful epiphany of imagination. Tolkien's language here oscillates, in a way that is delightfully appropriate to Samwise, between the touching tones of the everyday ('peeping', 'twinkle for a while') to the high and poetic modes of romance ('smote', 'forsaken'). Sam is aware both of the transience of the piercing star and the permanence of the idea it represents in his imagination. Tolkien perfectly captures the essence of a moment of divine vision as it occurs, not in the Romantic imagination, but in human experience – and, vitally, this linking of reality and the eternal leads to eucatastrophic renewal: hope returns to Sam so that 'his own fate, and even his master's, ceased to trouble him'.

The twinkling white star in every way indicates to us an embracing and sustaining power. This very Romantic capacity of using the natural world to capture the essence of spiritual moments is evident throughout Tolkien's work. The same imagination that conjures up wild worlds uses the very fabric of those worlds to transmit hope and imagination as best it can.

Shelob's Lair: An Aside on Tolkien and the Gothic

Of course, the Romantic imagination did not simply conjure up instances of revelatory clarity. The movement was experiential and so also indulged in the sensuous and the nightmarish. The idealism of the Romantics gave rise to the thrills of the gothic – literature so radical that it was deemed unsuitable for women. While many of these works – such as *Frankenstein* or *Wuthering Heights* – are now considered among the classics of world literature, they were sensational and unpredictable. The link between the monstrous and the world of Romance may well seem evident to us – knights were fighting dragons long before Spenser's Redcrosse knight encountered Errour in her den or Gawain ventured to the Green Chapel – but the radical nature of the Romantics produced an equally radical version of the monstrous. For some, the gothic quickly became viewed as a distasteful literary expression of excess, calculated to thrill and little else.

And here is another place where Tolkien differs from his Romantic and Gothic forbears: he wrote that 'every romance that takes things seriously must have a warp of fear and horror, if however remotely or representatively it is to resemble reality, and not the merest escapism.' (L 120) While acknowledging the integral link between romance and horror Tolkien's focus is still clearly that of resembling reality. In the same letter, he adds about the horror he has attempted in his own novel: 'But I have failed if it does not seem possible that mere mundane hobbits could cope with such things. I think that there is no horror conceivable that such creatures cannot surmount, by grace (here appearing in mythological forms) combined with a refusal of their nature and reason at the last pinch to compromise or submit' (L 120).

For Tolkien, the purpose of fear and horror is to both render the world of the imagination more life-like, and to produce a platform for the outworking of grace. This is perhaps seen nowhere as clearly as in Shelob's lair:

> In a few steps they were in utter and impenetrable dark... Here the air was still, stagnant, heavy, and sound fell dead... As they thrust forward they felt things brush against their heads, or against their hands, long tentacles or hanging growths perhaps. ... and still the stench grew.
> ... from behind them came a sound, startling and horrible in the heavy padded silence: a gurgling, bubbling noise, and a long venomous hiss. They wheeled round, but nothing could be seen. Still as stones they stood, staring, waiting for they did not know what.
> ... Then, as he stood, darkness about him and a blackness of despair and anger in his heart, it seemed to [Sam] that he saw a light: a light in his mind, almost unbearably bright at first, as a sun-ray to the eyes of one long hidden in a windowless pit...
> The bubbling hiss drew nearer, and there was a creaking as of some great jointed thing that moved with slow purpose on the dark. A reek came on before it. 'Master, master!' cried Sam, and the life and urgency came back into his voice. 'The Lady's gift! The star-glass!' ...
> 'The star-glass?' muttered Frodo, as one answering out of sleep, hardly comprehending. 'Why, yes! Why had I forgotten it? A light when all other lights go out! And now indeed light alone can help us.' (LotR 744ff)

Tolkien does not stint in building up the horror of Shelob's lair and is masterful in his execution of suspense. But where Peter Jackson unashamedly turns to the tropes of the horror-film (itself a genre drawing heavily on the gothic) Tolkien keeps the narrative details concrete and sense-focussed, drawing his readers into the lair itself. Like Frodo and Sam, we are left with only our senses of touch, sound and smell – literal and metaphorical sight only returns with the memory of Galadriel and the use of the star-glass. It is Galadriel's gift – that of light in the darkness – which acts as the grace that permits the hobbits to surmount the horror of Shelob's lair.

Keeping his focus on overcoming horror rather than allowing it to overwhelm the narrative sets Tolkien apart from those who first followed in the steps of the Romantics.

The Great Instrument for the Moral Good

Shelley once wrote that the imagination was 'the great instrument for the moral good'. Although their interpretation of moral was not necessarily uniform the statement is summative of much that the Romantics strove to achieve. Imagination was a tool to enrich human experience.

Tolkien undeniably lived and wrote in the tail of the Romantics' visionary comet, and his work has traits in common. But in Tolkien's case, 'moral' good would perhaps be better read as spiritual good – for him, imagination is a pathway to the integration of the world around us with the world beyond us. It is when the two are imaginatively connected, allowing us through one to catch a glimpse of the other – when we, as Tolkien puts it, escape and then return to the world able to see green as green again – that imagination has served its highest purpose. He strove to unify the realms of experience and 'being' in a way that encompassed the eternal but enriched, rather than cast aside, the temporal. Standing at the threshold between imagination and faith, Tolkien's romanticism truly is a kind of divine vision.

Bibliography

Bowra, C.M. *The Romantic Imagination*. London: Oxford University Press, 1976.

Carpenter, Humphrey (Ed.). *The Letters of J.R.R. Tolkien*. London: HarperCollins, 1995

Coleridge, Ernest Hartley (Ed.). *Letters of Samuel Taylor Coleridge*. London: 1895

Keynes, Geoffrey (Ed.). *Poetry and Prose of William Blake*. London: 1939

Wilmott, Richard (Ed.). *William Blake: Songs of Innocence and of Experience*. Oxford: Oxford University Press, 2001

Shawcross, J. (Ed.). *Coleridge: Biographia Literaria*. Oxford: 1907

Tolkien, J.R.R. *The Lord of the Rings*. London: HarperCollins, 1995

Quotation from Keats's letter to Benjamin Bailey on Nov 22nd 1817: http://www.john-keats.com/briefe/221117.htm

Romanticism, Symbolism and Onomastics in Tolkien's *Legendarium*
Annie Birks (Angers)

Introduction

Edwin Berry Burgum once wrote in the *Kenyon Review* (1941): "He who seeks to define Romanticism is entering a hazardous occupation which has claimed many victims". Indeed this many-faceted, broadly-spanned and long-lived artistic movement is notoriously complex to define (cf. Furst 6). The American philosopher A.O. Lovejoy (1873-1962) even argued that it would be more appropriate to speak of Romanticisms instead of Romanticism (cf. Beer xi).

When one thinks of Tolkien's *Legendarium*, the association with Romanticism might not instantly spring to mind, but if one considers the consensual pointers of the genre, there is no denying that sensibility ranks among the first. And if one seeks to explore Professor Tolkien's motives behind the unfolding of his *Legendarium*, there is again no denying that his self-avowed extreme sensitivity to words and languages is not only a pointer but also lies at the root of his entire writing process. Such visceral fascination with the beauty and musicality of words can be found in the etymology and symbolism of personal and place names throughout the history of Middle-earth.

As a contribution to the study of Romanticism in Tolkien's works, this paper will examine some of the most commonly accepted characteristics of this complex movement that find an echo in the author's onomastic sub-creation and the latter's subsequent relation to some of the characters, places and objects in Middle-earth.

An Intimate Fusion of Sensitivity and Imagination

Let us first expand on the background of our initial reflections. As is explained in the author's *Letters* and the official biography, Tolkien's *Legendarium* was born from his emotional encounter with two lines of the Anglo-Saxon religious poem *The Crist of Cynewulf*, and more particularly with a name – Earendel:

> Eala Earendel engla beorhtast
> Ofer middangeard monnum sended.[1]

---
1 Hail Earendel, brightest of angels / Above middle-earth sent unto men. (Cf. Carpenter 72)

Upon discovering these lines, Tolkien said: "I felt a curious thrill" and added "as if something had stirred in me, half wakened from sleep. There was something very remote and strange and beautiful behind those words, if I could grasp it, far beyond ancient English." (Cf. Carpenter 72)

This purely subjective, sensory response to the Old English lines echoes William Wordsworth's response to nature upon revisiting the banks of the River Wye near Tintern Abbey:

> Therefore am I still
> A lover of the meadows and the woods,
> And mountains; and of all that we behold
> From this green earth; of all the mighty world
> Of eye and ear, both what they half-create,
> And what perceive; well pleased to recognize
> In nature and the language of the sense,
> The anchor of my purest thoughts…
> *The Lyrical Ballads* (cf. Bewley 152)

Indeed intense emotion awakens the poet's creative impulse; it stimulates and directs his imaginary vision. In the same manner, sensibility and imagination in Tolkien merged in an intimate fusion.

Just as he later set out to discover what lay behind the word Hobbit after he once wrote "In a hole in the ground, there lived a Hobbit", Tolkien, as a true explorer, tried to find out who Earendel could be. He came to the conclusion that, on the one hand, Earendel was a Mariner journeying across the world before his ship became a star and that, on the other hand, the "nonsense fairy language" that he, Tolkien, as a passionate philologist had been working on for a while, was the language spoken by the fairies or Elves the Mariner had come across.[2] The Old English name Earendel took on an Elvish hue under Tolkien's pen and became Eärendil. Etymology came into play, conferring the meaning "Lover of the sea" to the name Eärendil – composed of the noun "eär" which stems from the Common Eldarin "ayar", "sea", and the element or verbal base "dil", 'to love, be devoted to", a suffix often found in the Elvish onomasticon (L 386).

Thus, unlike most stories in literature, Tolkien's narratives unfolded from names. As he himself put it: "To me a name comes first and the story follows". His passion for languages and words dating back to his childhood and his invention of languages which he called his "secret vice" explain why he once dubbed *The Lord of the Rings* "an essay in 'linguistic aesthetic'" (L 143). His numerous onomastic sub-creations give us an overview of the manifold interlocking strands underlying his fiction and indeed testify to his extreme sensitivity.

---

2   The Anglo-Saxon word "Earendel" meant "ray of light" and was applied sometimes to the morning-star (L 150).

Nonetheless, not only did Tolkien develop his long-lasting "secret vice" by further elaborating languages which eventually became "embodied in a history" (LR 341), but his passion for words and philological skills revealed a great power of imagination, a poetic sensitivity, a love of beauty and nature which do not fail to evoke some of the broad-ranging aspects that shaped Romanticism.

An Interpenetration of Beauty and Nature

Without indulging in what Tolkien called "private amusements" (L 380) on the part of some investigators brandishing theories and fancies concerning hidden linguistic equations which most irritated him, let us now consider the onomasticon of some of the races of Middle-earth. Amid the corpus of names which gave expression to his "personal linguistic 'aesthetic' or taste" (L 380), the Elvish compositions in Quenya and Sindarin represent a fertile field for our study. Their construction, based on pre-existing languages, do contain as might be expected "analyzable meanings" which are – as Tolkien insisted – solely relevant to the *Legendarium* (apart from the case of Eärendil) (cf. L 380).

Being "cursed by acute sensibility" in the matter of onomastics (L 144), the sub-creator portrayed the First-Born (the Elves) as lovers of the beauty of the world which they could bring to full bloom with their "aesthetic and creative faculties" and their sense of perfection and delicacy (L 176; 147). Their names and the names of places related to their race often echo these features and highlight their communion with Middle-earth.

Water

The Quenya toponym Cuiviénen, referring to the lake, beside whose waters they awoke, bears witness to the interpenetration of the Elves with their natural milieu – a major characteristic of the early Romantics like Wordsworth and Coleridge, and later Lord Byron, who sought to commune with nature. The meaning of this toponym, "Water of awakening" ("cuivië", "awakening" and "nen", "water") (S 388), cannot but conjure up fitting connotations for these Elder Children of Ilúvatar.

Water is well-known as the source of all potentialities in existence. It is associated with birth, the feminine principle, the universal womb and fertility. It is also equated with benediction and spiritual refreshment when materialized in drops of dew (cf. Cooper 188).

The Constellations

As water is also the liquid counterpart of light, it is perfectly relevant that the Elves are connected with the stars even though the reason is historically justified:

the first things their eyes beheld upon awakening were the constellations Varda fashioned for them with the silver dews from the vats of Telperion, the White Tree of Valinor (S 55 pp). Hence their reverence to this sublime Valië.³ When the Vala Oromë the Hunter discovered these "marvelous and unforeseen" beings he gave them the Quenya name of Eldar, ("People of the stars") (S 57). Later this name was restricted to the Three Kindreds of Elves who passed Oversea (cf. L 281).

The prefix "el", ("star"), finds many resonances in the history of Middle-earth: for example, in the name of Eärendil's son, Elrond, which means "Star-dome/vault". Tolkien explained that "rondō" was a primitive Elvish word for "cavern" and thus justified the etymology of the name. Indeed Elrond and his brother Elros were found as infants in a cave at the mouths of the river Sirion by the sons of Fëanor (cf. L 282). More precisely, according to Tolkien, "rond" in Sindarin and "rondo" in Quenya come from "rono", that is "to arch over, roof in" and could be applied both to natural and to artificial structures (WJ 414). In Common Eldarin, "rondo" referred to a "vaulted or arched roof, as seen from below (and usually not visible from the outside)" or to "a large hall or chamber so roofed" (WJ 414).

The two components of the name interestingly reflect the protecting role performed by this Elven-lord in Middle-earth. In the first syllable, the stars evoke the presence of the divinity, the eternal, the undying, hope (like Eärendil, his father, shining in the sky as a star). In the second syllable, the reference to a vault symbolizes the meeting place between heaven and earth (cf. Cooper 184).

Elrond's realm is known under several names: "Imladris" ("Deep dale of the cleft") in Sindarin, "Karningul" ("Cut valley") in general Westron; Rivendell (Cloven-dell) in English (cf. Lobdell 191). The reference to a valley evokes life, fertility and more specifically the sheltering feminine aspect, which reinforces the characteristics of this Elven-Refuge (cf. Cooper 184).

In one of his letters, Tolkien points out that Elrond symbolizes ancient wisdom and his House symbolizes Lore: "The preservation in reverent memory of all tradition concerning the good, wise, and beautiful" (L 153). It is no coincidence that both Thorin and his companions on their "quest of the Dragon-gold" (L 159) and later Frodo together with the other members of the fellowship – after escaping from imminent evil – start their journey by a visit to Elrond's home-like refuge. From there, the heroes depart "in a wholly new direction: to go and face it [evil] at its source" (L 153).

Such symbolic interpretation of Tolkien's star-related onomasticon echoes these lines from Wordsworth's sonnet *The Stars Are Mansions Built by Nature's Hand* (cf. Morley 579):

> The stars are mansions built by Nature's hand,
> And, haply, there the spirits of the blest
> Dwell, clothed in radiance, their immortal vest;

---

3 Feminine form of Vala.

Huge Ocean shows, within his yellow strand,
A habitation marvelously planned,
For life to occupy in love and rest;
All that we see--is dome, or vault, or nest,
Or fortress, reared at Nature's sage command.
Glad thought for every season! ...
Abodes where self-disturbance hath no part.

Among other names composed with the syllable "el", is Nam Elmoth, "Valley of star-dusk", the forest in East Beleriand where the Elven-Lord Elwë Singollo/ Thingol first saw the Maia Melian. This toponym is highly appropriate as the name of a meeting place for these two characters, as the notion of dusk or twilight adds uncertainty and ambivalence to the symbolism of the valley and the star (cf. Cooper 182).

While wandering in the forest, Elwë fell under "the enchantment of Beauty" as he heard Melian sing (cf. Helms 50). Back in Aman, it was said that

> There were none more beautiful than Melian, nor more wise, nor more skilled in songs of enchantment ... the Valar would leave their works, and the birds of Valinor their mirth, ... the bells of Valmar were silent and the fountains ceased to flow, when at the mingling of the lights Melian sang in Lórien. Nightingales went always with her, and she taught them their song ...   (S 64)

It comes as no surprise when one discovers that her name in Quenya means "Love-gift". However, if Elwë's relationship with Melian bears much fruit – among which the birth of their daughter Lúthien Tinuviel – Elwë falls under another spell which causes his ruin: that of the Silmarils. His unhealthy desire for the jewels puts him under the curse of Mandos and brings many woes. The two names he bears underline the ambivalence of his development. Elwë in Quenya means "Star-man", to which is adjoined "Singollo", Greycloak, an old form of the Sindarin name Thingol (cf. LR 355, 398).

The prefix "el" is not only a component in Elvish names but it is also found in references to places and characters related to the Eldar. Such is the case of the above-mentioned Valië Varda who is given by the Elves the Sindarin epithets "Elbereth" and "Elentári", ("Star-queen"); not to mention the names of men whose friendships or connections with the Elves grant them this honour: the great mariner Elendil[4], meaning "Star-lover" and therefore "Elf-friend" in Quenya; Elros, Elrond's brother, "Star-glitter" (WJ 414) or "Star-foam" (S 394) as justified by the tale of the two babes in the cavern, for if Elrond was hidden

---

4   Father of Isildur and Anárion.

at the far end of the cave, Elros was found "dabbling in the water" (L 282); their mother, Elwing, "Star-spray", so named because of the waterfall of Lanthir Lamath at her birthplace; finally, let us cite Elessar (Elf-stone), Aragorn's name as King, referring to the great emerald brooch Arwen had given him.

Trees

As a synthesis of heaven, earth and water, comes the tree, also the symbol of dynamic life (as opposed to the static life of the stone). Such is the reference underlying the name of the Elves who live in Lothlórien with Lady Galadriel: the Galadrim (in Sindarin, "Tree-people").

Although it is easy to wrongly render the etymology of Lady Galadriel as being Tree-Lady, her association with Trees is undeniable. Her wooden realm, where the magnificent Mallorn ("Gold-trees" in Sindarin) grow, bears a most appropriate name.

Although she was banned from Aman by the Valar and was therefore one of the exiles, the motive of this Noldorin princess was unstained (L 431): she had not left the Undying Lands to lend support to her cousin Fëanor but rather to discover Middle-earth and fulfill her dream of governing her own realm there. Hence the name of her kingdom in Quenya: Lórien, "Dream-land", which refers both to the real name and the dwelling of the Vala Irmo, the Master of visions and dreams in Valinor. The addition of "Loth", meaning "Flower" or "Blossom" in Sindarin, is rather telling.

Even though her dream to recreate the beauty of Valinor in Middle-earth materialized, she realized that the destiny of the Elvish race was not what she had expected. Her ordeals and outstanding behaviour as a "penitent" in Middle-earth freed her from the illusions which retained her. Her name – a sindarinized version of Alátriel or Altáriel in Quenya – means "Maiden crowned with a glittering garland/with gleaming hair" (L 423, 428; Noel 108), as a reference to her golden hair. Traditionally the garland does not only conjure up dedication, holiness, honour, distinction for a hero and most significantly a happy fate, but it is also equated with the notion of binding and linking (cf. Cooper 72). A most fitting connotation, as the original meaning of the word atonement could infer, at-one-ment, she is finally re-united and reconciled to her Fate (cf. Birks 308).

If we look even closer into the names related to the Lady of the Golden Wood, we learn that the original name of Lórien was Laurenlindórinan[5] ("Land of the Valley of the Singing Gold") which links her directly to Laurelin ("Song of Gold"), the Golden Tree of Valinor. Her return to the Blessed Realms echoes the symbolism of regeneration associated to the Tree of Life that grows in Paradise (cf. Cooper 176).

---

5   Gold-song-land-valley.

References to trees can be traced in Tolkien's onomasticon, which comes as no surprise as it is well known that he was a lover of trees. In the Elvish repertoire, it would be appropriate to note the name of the Woodland Elf Legolas, Sindarin for "Green leaf". The reference is fitting as it usually depicts hope, revival and renewal. Legolas's friendship with Gimli embodies the renewal of the relationship between Elves and Dwarves.

Birds

Further echoes of the Romantics' interest in nature can be identified in the Elvish Onomasticon. Such is the case of Alqualondë, the name of the unfortunate City and Port in Eldamar which underwent the first slaying of Elves by Elves. The toponym means "Haven of the Swans" owing to the form of the ships harbored there. If the swan is generally regarded as the bird of life, it also represents purity in Christian mythology, and the dying swan denotes martyrdom (cf. Cooper 164). Again the etymological tool eloquently expresses the underlying themes of the story.

Although on a much more tragic level, one could parallel the kinslaying in Alqualondë – as symbolized by the massacre of the swans and followed by the curse of Mandos which befalls the instigators – with the shooting of the albatross and the subsequent fate of the eponymous character in Samuel Taylor Coleridge's *Rime of the Ancient Mariner*.

Another name related to birds is that of Thingol and Melian's daughter, the above-mentioned Eldarin Princess, Lúthien Tinuviel, which means "Blossom nightingale". The epithet Tinuviel was first given to her by Beren, the man she weds, to evoke the beauty and the perfection of her singing. The poet John Keats dedicated an Ode to this bird illustrating, among other themes, the fragility of life as opposed to the immortality of the nightingale's song. Often associated with love, the nightingale traditionally highlights the close link between love and death (cf. Chevalier 826). Without a doubt, the beautiful tale of Lúthien and Beren bears such resonances. As a reflection of her mother's vocal endowments, Lúthien's voice is thus described at the outset of the tale:

> There came a time near dawn on the eve of spring, and Lúthien danced upon a green hill; and suddenly she began to sing. Keen, heart-piercing was her song as the song of the lark that rises from the gates of night and pours its voice among the dying stars, seeing the sun behind the walls of the world; and the song of Lúthien released the bonds of winter, and the frozen waters spoke, and flowers sprang from the cold earth where her feet had passed.
> (S 198)

Lúthien is therefore associated with a lark when Beren first sees her and the scene is imbued with promising happiness. Often opposed to the lament of the nightingale, the song of the lark is filled with joy.[6] This bird is also well-known for quickly ascending very high above the ground and suddenly dropping head-first. Owing to its successive ascents and descents, the lark usually symbolizes the union between heaven and earth and stands as a mediator. This is a most adequate comparison to illustrate Luthian's part in Beren's fate. The following lines from Percy Shelley's poem *To a Skylark* could be quoted in praise of this "most beautiful of all the Children of Ilúvatar":

> Teach us, sprite or bird, / What sweet thoughts are thine:
> I have never heard / Praise of love or wine
> That panted forth a flood of rapture so divine.
>
> (Cf. Bewley 846)

Nostalgia : A Yearning for Past Beauty

As a corollary to the Elves' attraction to the beauty of nature, comes their desire to immortalize it. Hence their reluctance to change and their desire to arrest time and transient beauty. All the more so, as their lifespan overlaps the centuries and imposes on them the sordidness of the dark lords' ill-doings, whether it be Morgoth's or Sauron's. Alphonse de Lamartine, a pioneer of French Romanticism, expresses such feelings in one of his most famous poems *Le Lac* (cf. Chassang 102):

> Ô temps ! suspends ton vol, et vous, heures propices !
> Suspendez votre cours:
> Laissez-nous savourer les rapides délices
> Des plus beaux de nos jours ![7]

This yearning for past beauty can be regarded as the motive of their fall (cf. L 148). The Elves are prepared to wage war to keep things as they were. Although

---

6   References to these two emblematic birds are recurrent in Romantic poetry. In *Visions of the Daughters of Albion*, William Blake evokes them together with the eagle, a bird endowed with a paramount part in Tolkien's Middle-earth: "The nightingale has done lamenting, The lark does rustle in the ripe corn, and the Eagle returns, From nightly prey, and lifts his golden beak to the pure east; Shaking the dust from his immortal points to awake, The sun that sleeps too long" (cf. Ostriker 198).

7   "O time, suspend your flight! And you, happy hours / Suspend your race: / Let us savour the fleet delights / Of our fairest days!" [www.consolatio.com/2007/12/lamartine-man-h.html (17.09.2010)]

there might be nothing essentially wrong with wanting to build kingdoms which resemble Valinor in Middle-earth, their desire to "arrest change" can be viewed as discordant (cf. L 197).

The whole process starts with the Noldorin prince Fëanor, son of Míriel and Finwë, who captures the light of the Two Trees of Valinor in his Silmarilli[8], ("Radiance of pure light") (L 148) and disobeys the Powers of the West to recover these three jewels from Melkor and his companion Ungoliant.

This mightiest of the Noldor, whose name means "Spirit of fire", is entirely ruled by his emotions and his highly egotistical quest leads to terrible woes throughout the history of Middle-earth. As an ambivalent symbol, fire can "restore primordial purity by burning away the dross", but it can also devour and destroy the soul (cf. Cooper 67). It can be either divine or demonic. Fëanor's fire is manifested first as a powerful source of energy and creative inspiration which finally gives way to a terrible consuming determination guided by hatred, vengeance and covetous desire. The etymology of Fëanor's name is a good illustration of Shelley's view of poetry as expressed in his essay In Defense of Poetry: "Feeling and passion are best painted in, and roused by... figurative language" (cf. Goodson 17).

Through his blasphemous oath which involves his seven sons and descendants, Fëanor is ensnared in a web of destiny, symbolized by Ungoliant, who is both named and depicted as a great spider.

By refusing to listen to the Valar, his decision places him under the sway of Melkor, ("He who arises in Might"). In the history of Middle-earth, it appears that all creatures refusing to place themselves under the influence of Ilúvatar run the risk of exposing themselves to "the law of evil". As Shippey rightly points out, wouldn't Morgoth, "The Black Enemy", be what he claims to be when he declares himself as "the master of the fates of Arda" (cf. Shippey 234)? In which case, he is the master of all those who turn away from their creator.

Such could have been the fate of the Elven smith Celebrimbor who forged the three Rings with a view to arresting change and healing the wounds caused by malice in Middle-earth. Interestingly the name of this Noldorin Elf – in Quenya: Telperinquar; in Sindarin: Celebrimbor – means "Hand of silver" or "Silver fist". One cannot but think of the eponymous hero of Smith of Wootton Major who exercised the same trade and wore a silver star on his brow. The choice of this particular metal is rather revealing.

If gold conjures up incorruptibility, purity and perfection, silver, although a highly valuable metal, can oxidize and requires constant care. Just as one might wonder what Smith of Wootton Major shall do with the silver star in the Realm of Faerie, one might also wonder what Celebrimbor's "silver hand" will achieve in Eregion ("Holly-region" in Sindarin). Both Smith and Celebrimbor

---

8   Tolkien uses the verb "imprison".

are prone to nostalgia: returning to the land of Faerie at the end of the story for one and preserving the beauty of the past for the other. The ambivalence of this metal seems to point towards ambivalence of choices, as though its value and that of the characters associated with it, required constant cleaning and polishing, lest they deteriorate.

If Laurelin, the elder Tree of Valinor, is associated with gold, Telperion, the younger one, bears a reference to silver in its name. And if gold traditionally – and in the *Legendarium* – is associated with the sun, silver is linked to the moon. This association of symbols sheds light on Isildur's name which means "Lover of the Moon".[9] This Dúnadan of Númenor has, at one stage, a crucial choice to make.

Contrary to what is found in traditional legends, Tolkien did not intend to identify the Sun shining on Middle-earth as a divine symbol; rather it represents "a second-best thing" for its light is derived from Telperion, the Tree of Gold, after it was sullied by the enemy (which is also the case of the Moon). Tolkien equates the "world under the Sun" with "a fallen world", "a dislocated imperfect vision" (L 148). It should be noted that the Silmarilli which Fëanor and his followers attempt to recover contain the "light before the Sun" (L 149).

With regards to Celebrimbor, Tolkien himself stressed that the Three Rings remained unsullied for they were not created to dominate or usurp power (cf. L 236). The purity of his intentions was rewarded by the moment of lucidity during which the Elven smith became aware of Sauron's perfidy and rescued them from his control.

It is most appropriate that, at the end of the Third Age, the Three Rings leave Middle-earth for the Blessed Realms. Like their possessors Gandalf, Galadriel and Elrond, whose natural powers they have enhanced, the Three Rings have served their purpose (cf. L 152).

The red Ring of fire Narya not only helped Gandalf rekindle the hearts but it also identifies his association with fire. His descent into the fire of Moria obviously underlines the purification and regenerative process he went through; his contribution to the War of the Ring is fuelled not only by inspiration and enlightenment but also by power, strength and energy, all these being attributes of fire (cf. Cooper 66 pp). His deeds echo Jesus's assertion in *Luke* 12:49 "I have come to bring fire on the earth". It is indeed when Gandalf sets foot on the shore of Middle-earth that Cirdan, the shipwright, secretly hands him Narya.

---

9   There is an abundance of references to the moon in Romantic poetry. For example, in *The Cloud*, Percy Shelley writes: "That orbèd maiden, with white fire laden / Whom mortals call the moon" (cf. Quigley 180). There is a connection between the moon and silver in William Butler Yeats' *Song of Wandering Aengus*: "And pluck till time and times are done / The silver apples of the moon/ The golden apples of the sun" (cf. *The Oxford Dictionary of Quotations*).

Galadriel's white Ring of water, Nenya, and Vilya, Elrond's blue Ring of air, the "mightiest of the Three" (SD 111), indeed helped the Elves to preserve "the memory of the beauty of old" and maintain "enchanted enclaves of peace where time seems to stand still and decay is restrained, a semblance of the bliss of the True West" (L 157). Galadriel's association with water highlights her change of ontological plane and Elrond's association with air confirms his presence as a tangible symbol of invisible life, intermediary between heaven and earth (cf. Chevalier 19).

Conclusion

When referring to Tolkien's works, Romanticism is hardly the first genre that comes to mind. They are rather viewed as works of heroic fantasy and stories of adventure. The spontaneous reluctance to link Tolkien to Romanticism is no doubt due to the connotation of the adjective "romantic" which commonly conjures up excessive sentimentality, self-deluding idealism or subjective approaches to reality, a most simplistic description of this many-faceted literary genre.

Indeed as this brief study has attempted to point out, Tolkien's onomasticon contains Romantic features related to great unifying concepts such as aesthetics, nature or nostalgia. These features appear to be mainly traced in the Elvish repertoire. The names of men tend to reflect their occupation, power or status[10]; the names of Hobbits often underline their personal characteristics[11]. Elvish names unveil a sensitive poetic approach which, as Shelley put it, conveys "the expression of imagination" (cf. Goodson 14) and supersedes more traditional modes of fiction as a touchstone to life. They open up levels of understanding the reader is not necessarily aware of. They no doubt contribute to "the recovery of *the magic of everyday life*", a concept dear to Tolkien and formulated as such by the American philosopher Charles Larmore about the aim of the Romantic poet in *Romantic Legacy* (cf. Eldridge 3).

However it is interesting to note that, in Tolkien's works, some of the darker characters are those who succumb to what could appear to be the sirens of excessive Romanticism. Such is the case of Fëanor or such could have been the case of Celebrimbor. Among the Men, Denethor's name,[12] which means "Water torrent", on the one hand heralds a life-giving process and on the other hand foreshadows the potentiality of a dangerous effusion of water which can sweep

---

10 An example would be the Rohirrim ("Masters of horses") whose names were often linked to their passion for horses.
11 Frodo: OE *fród*, "wise, prudent, sage", *freoda*, "protector, defender", *freodo*, " peace, security"; Samwise: OE *sam*, *wís*, "half wise"; Hamfast, OE, "stay-at-home" ... (Noel 20).
12 A name first born by a Noldorin Elf.

away or drown. This is a most fitting name for a Steward of Gondor who listened to his overwhelming fears and wallows in self-indulgence instead of listening to his reason – in spite of Gandalf's enlightenment. However characters who attach too much importance to mere reason, a feature which is often opposed to Romanticism, are not granted a brighter fate. Such is the case of Saruman ("Crafty man" in Old English) whose fallacious argumentation leads him to join the "New Power" which is rising, with a view to restoring "Knowledge, Rule" and "Order" (LotR I 339 pp).

Throughout the history of Middle-earth the characters are brought to battle between their emotions and their reason. The path between the two is not easy to tread. Aragorn's name, which in Sindarin means "Royal Tree", magnificently reflects the role of the character as a link between heaven and earth. He stands as a paragon of courage, patience and measure.

Finally, these observations in Tolkien's works highlight another crucial factor of Romanticism which is commonly defined as the right to be free in one's mode of expression. There is no denying that Tolkien's *Legendarium*, and more particularly his onomasticon, can be viewed as being as much of a genuine testimonial to literary liberalism as were in their days the *Lyrical Ballads* of Wordsworth and Coleridge.

Bibliography

Beer, John. *Questioning Romanticism*. London: The Johns Hopkins University Press, 1995

Bewley, Marius. *The English Romantic Poets*. New York: The Modern Library, 1970

Birks, Annie. *La Rétribution dans l'œuvre de J.R.R. Tolkien*, doctoral thesis, 2007. Paris IV – Sorbonne

Carpenter, Humphrey (Ed.). *The Letters of J.R.R. Tolkien*. London: Allen & Unwin, 1981

---. *J.R.R. Tolkien: A Biography*. London: Allen & Unwin, 1978

Chassang, Arsène and Charles Senninger. *Recueil de textes littéraires français, XIXe siècle*. Paris: Hachette, 1966

Chevalier, Jean, Gheerbrant, Alain. *Dictionnaire des Symboles*. Paris: Robert Laffont, 1982

Cooper, J.C. *An Illustrated Encyclopaedia of Traditional Symbols*. London: Thames and Hudson, 1978

Eldrige, Richard. *The Persistence of Romanticism*. Cambridge: CUP, 2001

Forster, Robert. *The Complete Guide to Middle-Earth*. London: HarperCollins, 2001

Furst, Lilian. *Romanticism*. London: Methuen & Co, 1979

Goodson, A.C. "Romantic Theory and the Critique of Language". *Questioning Romanticism*, Ed. John Beer. London: The Johns Hopkins University Press, 1995

Helms, Randel. *Myth, Magic and Meaning in Tolkien's World*. London: Thames and Hudson, 1976

Lobdell, Jared. *A Tolkien Compass*, La Salle: Open Court, 1975

Morley, John. *The Complete Poetical Works of William Wordsworth*. London: Macmillan, 1905

Noel, Ruth. *The Languages of Tolkien's Middle-earth*. Boston: Houghton Mifflin Company, 1980

Ostriker, Alicia (Ed.). *William Blake The Complete Poems*. New York: Penguin Books, 1981

Quigly, Isabel (Ed.). *Shelley: Poems*, London: Penguin Poetry Library, 1985

Shippey, Tom. *The Road to Middle-earth*. London: HarperCollins, 1992

Tolkien, J.R.R., *The Fellowship of the Ring*. London: HarperCollins, 1993

---. *The Silmarillion*. Ed. Christopher Tolkien. London: Allen & Unwin, 1979

---. *The Lost Road and Other Writings. The History of Middle-earth V.* Ed. Christopher Tolkien. London: Allen & Unwin, 2002

---. *Sauron Defeated. The History of Middle-earth IX.* Ed. Christopher Tolkien. London: Allen & Unwin, 2002

---. *Morgoth's Ring. The History of Middle-earth X.* Ed. Christopher Tolkien. London: HarperCollins, 2002

---. *The War of the Jewels. The History of Middle-earth XI.* Ed. Christopher Tolkien. London: Allen & Unwin, 2002

The Oxford Dictionary of Quotations. London: Guild Publishing, 1985

Mittelerde als Ausdruck romantischer Kreativität und Sehnsucht
Oliver Bidlo (Essen)

Einleitung

Dieser Aufsatz möchte die Begriffe »Kreativität« und »Sehnsucht« im Umkreis von Tolkiens Welt Mittelerde näher beleuchten und in einen besonderen Bezug setzen. Dabei ist die Folie, vor der sich diese Aspekte abspielen, die Romantik und die ebenfalls im weiteren Verlauf – zumindest fragmentarisch – darzustellende Grundhaltung Tolkiens als Romantiker. Die beiden Begriffe »Kreativität« und »Sehnsucht« können als eine Matrix des romantischen Denkens verstanden werden. Und diese Matrix, das Schöpfen aus einer Sehnsucht heraus, zeigt sich auch bei Tolkien und seinem schriftstellerischen Wirken: Die Welt Mittelerde ist die geronnene Form dieses romantischen Prozesses, der auf dem Zusammenspiel von »Kreativität« und »Sehnsucht« fußt.

Aus diesem Grund herrscht auch eine besondere Beziehung zwischen Autor und Werk, der man mit einer reinen werkimmanenten Betrachtungsweise oder einer biographischen Analyse nicht wirklich beikommt. Man erblickt dann nur Einzelaspekte, nicht aber das, was sich zwischen beiden abspielt. Daher sind meine Betrachtungen auch gekennzeichnet durch den Sprung von Werk zum Autor und umgekehrt, werden werkimmanente und biographische Aspekte herangezogen, um diesen Bereich des *Zwischen* deutlicher zu machen.

Nun vorab: Es gab eine Geistesströmung bzw. Epoche, die man mit dem Namen »Romantik« bezeichnet. Soweit sind sich die meisten Gelehrten, Forscher und Literaturwissenschaftler einig. Dennoch suggeriert ein solcher Epochenbegriff eine Einheitlichkeit – sowohl thematisch als auch stilistisch –, die es so nicht gibt. Daher bilden bereits der Begriff und seine Vieldeutigkeit eine Kernthematik der Romantik-Forschung (vgl. Schmitz-Emans 7).

Aus diesem Grund fällt es schwer, die Romantik genau ein- oder abzugrenzen. Tut man es dennoch, bietet sich darüber hinaus immer die Möglichkeit des folgenden Gegenargumentes: Wenn man nicht genau sagt, was die Romantik ist, kann man dann nicht alles darunter subsumieren? Und wenn man umgekehrt so vieles zur Romantik zählt, lässt sich dann nicht nahezu jede Literatur *irgendwie* der Romantik zuzählen? Wird aber der Gegenstand dadurch nicht beliebig? Ist es also nicht eine berechtigte Kritik, dass, wenn die Romantik so vielfältig ist, man ihr fast alles unterschieben kann und damit auch in Tolkiens vielschichtigem Werk zwangsläufig romantische Versatzstücke finden muss?

Sagt man wiederum, was genau man unter der Romantik versteht oder was genau diese einschließt, grenzt man ganz viele nichtgesagte Aspekte an den Randbereichen zu anderen Geistesströmungen aus – was wiederum den Kritikpunkt der Unschärfe mit sich bringt. Hier zeigt sich ein Paradoxon: Je enger man fokussiert, je deutlicher man versucht, den Begriff der Romantik ins Visier zu nehmen, desto unschärfer wird das Bild, das man von ihr bekommt. Aus der Physik kennt man das Phänomen übrigens spätestens durch die Heisenberg'sche Unschärferelation.

Ich möchte – ohne hier ausführlicher darauf einzugehen – auf das Problem des Definierens einer Sache im Allgemeinen und der Definition, was Romantik sei, im Besonderen hinweisen. Definitionen haben meist nur eine begrenzte Gültigkeit und Halbwertszeit oder werden letztlich kaum geteilt, sodass sie nur bedingt intersubjektive Gültigkeit erlangen. Hinsichtlich der Romantik ergibt sich ein eigentümliches Bild. Manche suchen nach einem wesenhaften Kern, andere nach festzusetzenden Jahreszahlen, andere geben einen gewissen Kopf, Künstler oder Literaten an, mit dem die Romantik beginnt, oder durch den sie sich besonders ausdrückt. Letztlich kann man die Romantik – so wie viele Epochenbegriffe – als ein heuristisches Konstrukt verstehen und mit diesem operieren.

Ein weiterer Weg, um nun ein Werk als romantisch zu identifizieren, ist: Man sucht und markiert zunächst wiederkehrende Einzelaspekte in den Beschreibungen, was Romantik und romantisch sei, und weist diese dann als typisch romantisch aus. Findet man solche in dem zu untersuchenden Text – in unserem Falle Tolkiens Texte zu Mittelerde –, bis eine kritische Menge[1] überschritten ist, kann man den Text als einen romantischen verstehen.

Ich werde zu zeigen versuchen, dass Tolkien nicht nur geschickt romantische Einzelaspekte verarbeitet hat, sondern diese Einzelaspekte *Auswurf* und Ergebnis seiner romantischen Haltung sind. Zunächst sollen also einige Sätze zu Tolkien und zur Romantik vorgebracht werden. Danach werden die beiden Begriffe »Sehnsucht« und »Kreativität« aus der Sicht der Romantik dargelegt, wird ihren Ausläufern in geronnener Form bei Tolkien nachgespürt und sie werden an einigen Beispielen deutlich gemacht. Neben der »Sehnsucht« ist es besonders der Begriff der »Kreativität«, der die Romantik als Geistesströmung und -haltung kennzeichnet und dort eine besondere Rolle spielt.

Bei genauer Betrachtung beider Begriffe zeigt sich, dass sie in der Romantik *wesentlich* zusammenhängen. Die Kreativität entspringt nämlich der Sehn-

---

1 Man kann zunächst offen lassen, wie groß eine solche kritische Menge ist oder sein muss, bzw. dies dem Leser überlassen, ob eine solche kritische Menge für ihn – oder konsensustheoretisch – innerhalb einer Gruppe erreicht wurde.

sucht nach einem unbefangenen und sich frei entfaltenden Phantasieren. Die Phantasie, die in ihrer kreativen Ausgestaltung die Kunst der Zweitschöpfung verwirklicht, rückt Tolkien, wie auch die Romantiker zuvor, in den Mittelpunkt. »Die Phantasie (in diesem Sinne, der das Phantasiegebilde mit einschließt) erscheint mir nicht als eine niedere, sondern als eine höhere Form der Kunst, ja, als diejenige Form, welche der Reinheit am nächsten kommt, und daher (wenn gelungen) die stärkste« (BB 50). Es ist die Sehnsucht nach Zauberkraft, Magie und Drachen und der Wunsch, »diese Kräfte in der Welt außerhalb unseres Geistes zu gebrauchen« (BB 29), die die Phantasie kreativ befeuert und eine neue Form, eine *Kreatur*, eine Zweitschöpfung hervorbringt. »Doch in einer solchen ›Phantasie‹, wie man dies nennt, wird neue Form geschaffen; das Feienwerk [sic] beginnt, und der Mensch wird zum Zweitschöpfer« (BB 29).

In Tolkiens Idee der Schöpfung und der Ausgestaltung Mittelerdes drückt sich der romantische Prozess der Schöpfermacht, der Sprache und Sehnsucht nach der Ausgestaltung einer der Phantasie entspringenden Welt aus. Im romantischen Denken wollte der Dichter gerade nicht die Wirklichkeit abbilden oder wiedergeben, sondern durch seine eigene Kreativität – durch seine Schöpferkraft –, angetrieben von einer nach innen gerichteten Sehnsucht, eine neue Welt schöpfen.

Eine solche Welt steht in Opposition zur rationalistisch ausgestalteten Wirklichkeit, wie man sie zu Zeiten der Romantik überwinden wollte, aber auch zu Tolkiens Lebzeiten mit ihrer sich ausbreitenden Industrialisierung entdecken kann. Der Bedeutungsgehalt des Neuen und Schöpferischen findet sich auch im englischen Begriff der Kreativität, *creativity*, der die Fähigkeit beschreibt, Neues zu schaffen.

Dabei zeigt sich im Zusammenhang mit Tolkien, dass es nicht nur romantische Einzelaspekte innerhalb Mittelerdes gibt. Tatsächlich findet sich eine Vielzahl von Versatzstücken romantischen Denkens unmittelbar in den Zeilen z.B. des *Herrn der Ringe* oder des *Silmarillion*. Wichtiger als diese werkimmanente Sichtweise – obgleich wichtiger Teil davon – ist das Wechselspiel zwischen Autor, Werk und Leser, aus dem heraus sich eine Welt konstituiert, die als Ergebnis eines romantischen Kreativitätsprozesses verstanden werden muss, der wiederum auf die romantische Grundhaltung des Autors zurückgeführt werden kann.

Ich wiederhole mich: Damit ist gemeint, dass der Autor nicht zwangsläufig romantische Einzelaspekte und -elemente bewusst innerhalb seiner Geschichte verankert haben muss, das hat – wie sich zeigen wird – Tolkien augenscheinlich getan, sondern dass die Gesamtkonzeption Mittelerdes – lassen wir Mittelerde mit dem Schöpfungsmythos im *Silmarillion* beginnen – *durch* die erwähnte romantische Grundhaltung des Autors in ihrer Ausgestaltung Ergebnis eines romantischen Prozesses ist. Werfen wir dafür zunächst einen fokussierten Blick auf die Romantik.

Die Romantik

Die Geistesströmung der Romantik war ein vielschichtiges Phänomen in der ersten Hälfte des 19. Jahrhunderts. Es sind gewöhnlich die Jahrzehnte zwischen 1790 und 1840, die als Zentrum dieser Geisteshaltung gesehen werden. Wiederholt wird eine Dreigliederung der Romantik vorgenommen – zumindest für den deutschsprachigen Raum – in eine Früh-, Hoch- und Spätromantik. Das Besondere der Frühromantik (1790er Jahre) liegt in ihrer theoretischen und philosophischen Grundierung und einer ästhetischen Programmatik. In der Hochromantik (Beginn des 19. Jh.) liegt der Schwerpunkt des romantischen Denkens und Arbeitens im Bereich des Historischen, Mythologischen, der Sammlung und Auseinandersetzung mit Märchen. Die Spätromantik (Beginn: 1820er Jahre) setzte sich verstärkt mit der Religion und der menschlichen Psyche auseinander und bildete diese Themen in Romane, Volks- und Kunstmärchen ab.

Die Romantik gilt als die letzte, ganz Europa umfassende geistige Bewegung und hatte eine universale und tiefgreifende Bedeutung. Ihre territoriale Ausdehnung erfasste nicht nur alle Teile Europas mit Ausnahme der Türkei, sondern auch den amerikanischen Kontinent. Sie hatte nicht nur Einfluss auf die Literatur im Allgemeinen oder die Lyrik im Besonderen, sondern auch auf die Musik, die bildenden Künste in den verschiedenartigsten Ausprägungen, auf das soziale Denken und das Geschichtsverständnis.

Wortgeschichtlich stammt »Romantik« von dem altfranzösischen Wurzelwort *romanz*, das die romanische Volkssprache im Gegensatz zur Gelehrtensprache Latein bezeichnete. Dichtungen und Erzählungen in der Volkssprache nannte man *romance* – später wurde daraus der Roman –, und diese hatten meist Abenteuer- und Rittergeschichten zum Gegenstand. Und bald wurde das Adjektiv *romantisch* im Sinne von romanhaft, phantasievoll oder abenteuerlich gebraucht. Wortgeschichtlich hat sich dergestalt im Laufe der Zeit eine Reihe von Inhalten auf diesen Begriff gelegt. Man kann allerdings konstatieren, dass es sich dabei immer um eine Art Gegenbegriff und -entwurf gehandelt hat.

Es gibt bedeutende romantische Aspekte, auf die ich gleich noch kurz zu sprechen kommen werde. Nicht alle findet man überall dort, wo man von Romantik spricht. Aber in Kombination mit anderen Einzelheiten, z.B. dem schwer fassbaren Zeitgeist, also einer geistigen Atmosphäre, die vorherrschte, den politischen Verhältnissen oder emanzipatorischen Absetzbewegungen zur Klassik und der Antike erwächst eine Haltung zum Subjekt, zur Natur oder zur Gesellschaft, die eine romantische genannt werden kann. Und diese Haltung drückt sich dann durch gewisse wiederkehrende Einzelaspekte oder Motive aus wie z.B. Sehnsucht, Wandermotiv, Hinwendung zum Mittelalter usw.

Durch den Einfluss deutscher Autoren auf die anderen europäischen Länder kommt Deutschland eine wichtige Rolle in der europäischen Romantik zu.

Friedrich Schlegels 116. *Athenaeum-Fragment* verdichtet wesentliche Aspekte der Kunst-, Lebens- und Weltauffassung der Romantik:

> Die romantische Poesie ist eine progressive Universalpoesie. Ihre Bestimmung ist nicht bloß, alle getrennten Gattungen der Poesie zu vereinigen und die Poesie mit der Philosophie und Rhetorik in Berührung zu setzen. Sie will und soll auch Poesie und Prosa, Genialität und Kritik, Kunstpoesie und Naturpoesie bald mischen, bald verschmelzen, die Poesie lebendig und gesellig und das Leben und die Gesellschaft poetisch machen, den Witz poetisieren und die Formen der Kunst mit gediegenem Bildungsstoff jeder Art anfüllen und sättigen und durch die Schwingungen des Humors beseelen. Sie umfaßt alles, was nur poetisch ist, vom größten, wieder mehrere Systeme in sich enthaltenden Systeme der Kunst bis zu dem Seufzer, dem Kuß, den das dichtende Kind aushaucht in kunstlosem Gesang. (Schlegel 182)

Ein Ursprung der Romantik liegt in England. Wichtige Namen – die sogenannten »Big Six« (Reinfandt 33) – der englischen Romantik waren William Wordsworth, Samuel Taylor Coleridge, William Blake als erste Generation und Percy Shelley, John Keats und George Gordon Lord Byron als zweite Generation. Innerhalb der bildenden Künste waren es besonders John Constable und William Turner, die atmosphärische Naturbilder und Landschaften entwarfen, die die Romantik geprägt haben. Hauptmerkmal englischer romantischer Bilder wurden jene entworfenen und gemalten Landschaften, welche mit romantischen Gefühlen hoch aufgeladen wurden.

Allgemeine und wiederkehrende Motive und Aspekte der Romantik waren nun die Opposition gegen die Aufklärung – vor allem in der Frühromantik –, eine Sehnsucht nach Gott und Natur, eine Gegenwartskritik, die den Menschen als eine Maschine verstand – besonders in der Spätromantik – und einen nur auf den Verstand, Kausalität und Ordnung zielenden Geist.

Will man schlagwortartig wesentliche Elemente benennen, um die die Romantik und das romantische Denken kreisen, kann man auf folgende Begriffe kommen:
- Träume
- Gefühl
- Phantasie
- Geheimnis
- Sehnsucht

Die Sehnsucht selbst hat ihrem romantischen Wesen nach nicht ein eindeutiges Ziel, sondern blieb in gewissem Maße unbestimmt und richtete sich auf fremde, andere Welten und Länder, die Natur, Gott und den Tod. Sie soll eine gewisse Unerreichbarkeit und eine nicht enden wollende Suche widerspiegeln, so wie die blaue Blume Novalis' als romantisches Symbol dieser Sehnsucht. Auch auf die Vergangenheit richtete sich die Sehnsucht der Romantiker, so besonders auf das Mittelalter oder auf die Kindheit als zurückliegende Lebensphase. Der romantische Kindheitsmythos sah in Kindern und der Kindheit das Reine, Göttliche, die noch unverbrauchte Potentialität des Lebens und die große Kraft der Phantasie, die in den Augen der Romantiker bei Erwachsenen bereits verloren gegangen war (vgl. Baader 417).[2]

Tolkien und die Romantik

Ich habe in verschiedenen Vorträgen – die nicht nur, aber in einiger Hinsicht auf meinem Buch *Sehnsucht nach Mittelerde?* gründen – nachgezeichnet, dass Tolkien eine Geisteshaltung innehatte, die man als eine Romantische bezeichnen kann: Was zeichnet eine solche Geisteshaltung aus, ohne hier bereits auf die beiden noch zu besprechenden Begriffe »Kreativität« und »Sehnsucht« einzugehen? Hierzu zunächst einige Beispiele.

Tolkien und sein Werk um die Welt Mittelerde stehen in verschiedener Art und Weise in Verbindung mit der epochalen Geistesströmung der Romantik. Man kann die Verbindung beispielsweise in der Liebesbeziehung zwischen Arwen und Aragorn, Beren und Lúthien, die beide ein Widerhall von Tolkiens eigener Liebe zu seiner Frau Edith sind, oder in der Betonung der Freundschaft erkennen. Viele der Grundpfeiler und Überzeugungen im Denken J.R.R. Tolkiens finden sich in und entspringen dem romantischen Gedankengut. Tatsächlich finden sich so viele Überschneidungen, dass man wohl mit Recht davon ausgehen darf, dass Tolkien ein Romantiker war.

In der Romantik sowie bei Tolkien findet sich beispielsweise die tiefe christliche Überzeugung, gepaart mit einer Hinwendung, Wiederbelebung und Neuentwicklung des Mythos auf der Basis alter Sagen und Legenden. Gerade die Wiederbelebung des Mythos war für die Romantiker ein wesentliches Anliegen. Der Mythos wurde verstanden als Weltschleier, er behielt in der romantischen Auffassung das Rätsel- und Schleierhafte, während die Zeit vor der Romantik den Mythos noch zu häufig allegorisch fasste. »Wenn man so will, bedeutet die Wiederbelebung des Mythos in der Romantik die Emanzipation des Mythos. Es ist die Emanzipation von der mythosfremden, rationalen Verwendung und

---

2 Tolkien hat sich in seinem Essay *Über Märchen* in diesem Zusammenhang auch mit Kindern und ihrem Verhältnis zu Märchen und solchen Erzählungen geäußert und verwies darauf, dass Märchen seiner Ansicht nach nicht eigens Kindern zugedacht werden sollten (vgl. BB 46).

Deutung im Sinn der Allegorie« (Koopmann 167). Aber auch der Neuentwurf einer Mythologie war den Romantikern wichtig und galt als ein Ziel. Ihre neumythopoetischen Schöpfungskonzeptionen galten ihnen als Ausdruck der Opposition zu den zeitgenössischen abstrakt konstruierten Gotteskonzeptionen der Philosophie. Die Nähe des *Silmarillion* als Tolkiens Entwurf eines Schöpfungsmythos zu diesem Punkt der Romantik ist unverkennbar (ausführlicher Bidlo, *Sehnsucht* 76f). Tolkiens Werk steht in mannigfacher Hinsicht in Verbindung mit dem Begriff des Mythos und der Mythologie. Denn als Schöpfer der Sekundärwelt Mittelerde griff er selbst auf vielerlei Mythen, Legenden und Sagen zurück, um daraus eine eigene und selbstständige Mythologie zu entwerfen. Und er widmete seinem Heimatland England diese mythopoetische Schöpfung.

> Lachen Sie nicht! Es gab aber eine Zeit (seither bin ich längst kleinlauter geworden), da hatte ich im Sinn, eine Sammlung von mehr oder weniger zusammenhängenden Legenden zu schaffen, die von den großen, kosmogonischen bis hin zum *romantischen Märchen* [Hervorhebung O.B.] reichen sollten – die größeren auf den kleineren gründend, in Berührung mit der Erde, die kleineren um den Glanz des weiten Hintergrundes bereichert – ein Werk, das ich einfach England widmen könnte, meinem Lande. Es sollte den Ton und Charakter besitzen, den ich wünschte, ein wenig kühl und klar, an unsere ›Luft‹ erinnernd (Klima und Boden des Nordwestens, das heißt Englands und der hiesigen Teile Europas, nicht Italiens oder der Ägäis, noch weniger des Ostens), und indem es (wenn ich das zu leisten vermochte) die helle, entrückte Schönheit besitzen sollte, die manche ›keltisch‹ nennen (obwohl sie sich in echten altkeltischen Dingen nur selten findet), sollte es ›erhaben‹ sein, vom Niedrigen gereinigt und dem erwachseneren Geist eines lange in Poesie gewiegten Landes gemäß. Ich wollte manche der großen Erzählungen ganz ausführen, für viele andere dagegen nur ihren Ort im Zusammenhang bestimmen und es bei Skizzen belassen. Die Zyklen sollten zu einem majestätischen Ganzen verbunden sein und doch für andere Geister und Hände Raum lassen, die Farbe, Musik und Drama hinzutun konnten. Absurd!
>
> (zit. n. Carpenter 122)

Gerade der letzte Satz unterstreicht nochmals die Offenheit, die Tolkien in seinem Werk mit angelegt hat, um für andere »Hände Raum« zu lassen.

In der Romantik und bei Tolkien findet man die Überzeugung der Wichtigkeit einer Geschichtlichkeit, um seinen Platz innerhalb dieser Geschichte einsehen zu können. Im *Herrn der Ringe*, aber auch in den weiteren Werken rund um Mittelerde spielen Genealogien und vergangene Geschichten eines Volkes eine wichtige Rolle, oft wird auf die verschiedenen Zeitalter verwiesen. Und die ganze Tiefe und Bedeutung des Ringes wird innerhalb der Erzählung selbst nur durch die geschichtliche Darstellung für die Protagonisten (und für die Leser) deutlich. Weitere zusammenfallende Aspekte bei beiden – der Romantik und Tolkien – können stichwortartig subsumiert werden:

- ein Bevorzugen des Mittelalters und einer mittelalterlichen Atmosphäre (man denke hier auch an den romantischen Ruinenkult)
- ein vehementes Stemmen gegen ein zu rasches Voranschreiten einer oft sinnlosen Mechanisierung und Industrialisierung der Welt (man denke aufseiten Tolkiens und des *Herrn der Ringe* z.B. an Saruman und die brennenden Schlote von Isengart) und der damit einhergehenden Zerstörung der Natur
- die tiefe Liebe und Hinwendung zur Natur und der Schöpfung
- der Hang zur Phantasie, ja sogar das Hervorheben der Phantasie und des Gefühls im Gegensatz zum reinen Verstandesdenken und in diesem Zusammenhang die betonte Stellung des Märchens und seiner Bedeutung[3]

All jene Punkte, die die Romantik zu dem machen, was sie ist, finden sich ebenfalls als exaltierte Überzeugungen bei Tolkien selbst und in vielen seiner Werke. Nun ist eine Reihe von den genannten Aspekten mittelalterlichen Ursprungs. Und in der Tat spielt das Mittelalter bzw. so etwas wie eine mittelalterliche »Atmosphäre« in Tolkiens *Herr der Ringe* eine nicht unerhebliche Rolle, zumal Tolkien selbst Mediävist und Philologe war und eine Vielzahl von mittelalterlichen Quellen verwendet hat. Das ist zu Recht oft betont worden und führt dann zu der Frage und der postwendenden Antwort: »Sind Mediävisten die ›besseren‹ Leser von Tolkiens Werk? Meine Antwort ist ein qualifiziertes *Ja*« (Honegger 50).

Die Kenntnis mittelalterlicher Literatur hilft ohne Zweifel, die verschiedenen Tiefenschichten der Texte um Mittelerde aufzuspüren und nachzuzeichnen (allgemein Bidlo, *Mythos*). Ob sich dadurch zwangsläufig ein tieferes Verständnis für das Werk und seiner Bedeutung für den Autor *und* den Leser ergibt, bleibt aber unbestimmt. Denn ohne den romantischen Bedeutungs- und Bezugsrahmen des Werkes bleibt auch die Kenntnis der mittelalterlichen Quellen *leblos* und führt nicht zu einem tieferen Verständnis, sondern verliert sich in faktischem Wissen über es. Betrachtet man zudem die Art und Weise, wie mittelalterliche Aspekte dort dargestellt und implementiert sind, zeigt sich, dass im *Herrn der*

---

3 Für Tolkiens Verständnis der Phantasie und ihrer Wichtigkeit und der Bedeutung des Märchens vgl. Tolkien 1982.

Ringe eine – wenn man so will – Mittelalterrezeption aus romantischer Perspektive erfolgt. Es ist keine authentische Mittelalterdarstellung, sondern eine romantisch und phantastisch aufgeladene Darstellung des Mittelalters und von Geschichte. Es dient hier wie dort als Projektionsfläche für Sehnsüchte und für die Möglichkeit zur Wiederherstellung einer verloren geglaubten Harmonie und Weltordnung. Diese Harmonie – das Goldene Zeitalter – erkannten vor allem die Hochromantiker im Mittelalter.

Im *Herrn der Ringe* bricht für Mittelerde und das Auenland das Goldene Zeitalter dann im vierten Zeitalter an, das durch Frodos Aufgabenerfüllung eingeläutet wird. In Anlehnung an das o.g. Zitat lässt sich dann sagen: Die emotionale Tiefe und Bedeutung der Tolkientexte um die Welt Mittelerde sind von einem romantisch geschulten Leser – und das umschließt das Wissen um mittelalterliche Quellen – besser zu erfassen.

Sehnsucht und Kreativität in der Romantik, bei Tolkien und in seiner Welt Mittelerde

In der Romantik will der Dichter die Wirklichkeit nicht einfach nachahmen, sondern sie durch seine eigene Kreativität neu erschaffen. Dieser Prozess des Schaffens ist in doppelter Hinsicht in der Romantik *eigenartig*. Zum einen geht es nicht darum, dass die erschaffene Wirklichkeit eine Kopie oder originalgetreue Wiedergabe der herkömmlichen Wirklichkeit sei. Zum anderen herrschte das Bewusstsein vor, dass der kreative Prozess der Schöpfung nie vollendet sein kann, sondern sich fortlaufend weiterschreibt. Wichtige Motive sind hier der Auszug und Aufbruch in die Ferne, die Suche nach dem eigenen Ich, aber auch das Aufeinanderprallen verschiedener Wertvorstellungen, welches sich aus der Wanderung ins Neue und Unbekannte ergibt. Zudem gehören die Hinwendung zum Wunderbaren und die Sehnsucht nach dem Geheimnis zu diesen Aspekten.

Kreativität und Sehnsucht finden ihren Ausdruck und kulminieren zugleich in dem Begriff des Aufbruchs und damit des Reisens, der die o.g. Aspekte einschließt. Das Reisemotiv, »auf zu neuen Ufern«, enthält beides: die Sehnsucht und die Kreativität, als Haltung der Möglichkeit, Neues auf sich wirken zu lassen und dadurch selbst eine Veränderung des eigenen Ichs möglich zu machen. Man erfindet sich, man schöpft sich neu durch den Aufbruch, durch eine Reise.

Frodos Auszug aus dem Auenland und sein Weg nach Mordor hat natürlich den Stil einer mittelalterlichen Queste. Aber die mittelalterliche Queste diente nicht unerheblich dem romantischen Wandermotiv als Vorlage. Und ein wichtiger Unterschied ist, dass im romantischen Wandermotiv nicht ein Held oder Ritter auszieht, um Ruhm und Ehre auf seiner Heldenreise zu erwerben, sondern oft ein einfacher Wanderer, der in die Fremde gezogen und gestoßen wird, und sich auf eine aufgezwungene Wanderung begibt. Das Neue – Erfahrungen, Wissen, Sichtweisen –, das während der Reise erworben wird, muss in die alten Vorstellungen integriert werden.

Im romantischen Wandermotiv ist der Wanderer, der sich durch die unberührte Natur gleich einer Märchenwelt bewegt, zwischen Heim- und Fernweh hin und her gerissen, und während seiner Wanderung wird er häufig mit dem christlichen Mittelalter konfrontiert. Man benötigt nicht viel Phantasie, um dies auch als Folie des *Hobbit* und später des *Herrn der Ringe* zu verstehen. Auch hier gilt mein Hinweis: Nicht dieser Aspekt allein macht aus dem *Hobbit* oder dem *Herrn der Ringe* ein romantisches Buch. Aber er trägt als ein Einzelaspekt dazu bei, auf die romantische Grundhaltung Tolkiens rückzuschließen, die wiederum das daraus entstandene Werk als ein romantisches mit ausweist.

Die Sehnsucht steht in vielerlei Hinsicht in Verbindung zu Tolkiens Werk. Zum Beispiel findet man sie »materialisiert« bei den Elben, die von einem tiefen Fernweh ergriffen werden, wenn sie Möwen oder das Meer erblicken und ihre Sehnsucht immer bei sich tragen. Es zieht sie über das Meer. Weiterhin steht die Sehnsucht auch für die Beschreibung einer Seite Tolkiens, die sich aus seiner Biographie ergibt. Bemerkt sei hier das lange Warten, bis er endlich seine große Liebe Edith heiraten konnte, es waren beinahe sieben Jahre (1909-1916). Tolkien erinnerte sich oft daran, wie er mit seiner Frau auf dem Lande spazieren ging. Und auf den Streifzügen durch einen schönen Wald tanzte und sang sie für ihn. Diese Begebenheit sollte später als Vorlage für die Liebe und Geschichte von Lúthien und Beren und Arwen und Aragorn dienen.

Zudem lebte Tolkien zur Zeit der Neoromantik, einer Zeit, in der das romantische Gedankengut wieder aufkam – die Betonung des Phantastischen, Märchenhaften und die Neigung zur Verwendung von Symbolen – und sich neu in Literatur und Kunst ausdrückte. Niederschlag findet das z.B. in der Kunstrichtung des Jugendstils, die übrigens auch bei Tolkien ihren Eingang gefunden hat, z.B. in der Kunst der Elben, dem Schmuck oder mancher Architektur oder auch in Tolkiens eigener Kunst. Die Opposition zur sich immer weiter ausbreitenden Industrialisierung zur Zeit Tolkiens ist eine Reminiszenz an die Überbetonung des Verstandes zuungunsten der Phantasie und des Träumens, gegen die sich die Romantik wandte.

An einem kurz besprochenen Bild-Beispiel möchte ich erläutern, wie auch die romantische Kunst gewisse Beschreibungen im *Herrn der Ringe* beeinflusst hat. Tolkiens ausdrucksstarke, bildhafte Sprache und Beschreibung wurden von vielen Künstlern und Malern als Inspirationsquelle aufgenommen. Die folgende Passage aus dem *Herrn der Ringe* wurde z.B. von Tad Nasmith in seinem Bild *Riders at the Ford* nach dieser Beschreibung gemalt:

> In diesem Augenblick erhob sich ein Brausen und Tosen: ein
> Rauschen von lauten Wassern, die viele Steine mit sich reißen.
> Undeutlich sah Frodo, wie der Fluß unter ihm stieg und eine
> ganze Reiterschar von Wellen das Flußbett herunterkam. Weiße
> Flammen schienen auf ihren Kämmen zu flackern, und halb bildete sich Frodo ein, inmitten des Wassers weiße Reiter auf weißen
> Pferden mit schäumenden Mähnen zu erkennen. (HdR I 259)

Nimmt man die Beschreibungen von Tolkien und das dazu gemalte Bild von Nasmith, kommt man schnell überein, dass das Bild eine nahe am Text erstellte visuelle Umsetzung ist. Nur liegt dieser Passage – und damit unweigerlich auch dem Bild von Nasmith – ein anderes Bild zugrunde, das Tolkien bewusst oder unbewusst als Vorlage für diese bildhafte Beschreibung genutzt hat.

Das Bild, von dem ich spreche, nennt sich *Die Rosse des Neptun* oder auch *Die Pferde Neptuns* und stammt von Walter Crane. Und Walter Crane wiederum war zusammen mit William Morris und Dante Gabriel Rossetti einer der wichtigsten Mitglieder der Arts and Crafts Bewegung, die Wegbereiter des Jungendstils war und romantische Ideen aufnahm. Von einigen wurde er sogar als der wahre Vater des Art nouveau bzw. des Jugendstils angesehen. Und hinsichtlich des Einflusses von William Morris auf den *Herrn der Ringe* bzw. einzelner Szenen äußerte sich Tolkien einmal in einem Brief an Professor L.W. Forster vom 31. Dezember 1960 wie folgt:

> *Der Herr der Ringe* wurde eigentlich, als eine Sache für sich,
> um 1937 angefangen und war schon bis zum Gasthaus in Bree
> gekommen, bevor der Schatten des zweiten Krieges fiel... Die
> Totensümpfe und die Zugänge zum Morannon haben etwas von
> Nordfrankreich nach der Schlacht an der Somme. Mehr aber haben
> sie von William Morris und seinen Hunnen und Römern, etwa in
> *The House of the Wolfing* oder *The Roots of the Mountains*.
> (B 397)

Tolkien stammt derart aus einer politischen und gesellschaftlichen »Großwetterlage«, die – über die Arts-and-Crafts-Bewegung, der Neoromantik und des Jugendstils – romantisch geprägt war, die ihn beeinflusst und geprägt und darüber Eingang in sein Werk gefunden hat.

Aber auch wenn man den Blick weg von biographischen oder textimmanenten Aspekten nimmt und auf die Rezipienten von Tolkiens Werken rund um Mittelerde richtet, zeigen sich die Offenheit seiner Werke und seine Sehnsucht bildende Kraft. Tolkiens phantastische Schöpfung erweckt auch in den Leserinnen und Lesern ein tiefes Gefühl von Sehnsucht. Und Tolkiens Werke sind meines Erachtens auch deshalb so erfolgreich, weil sie eine gewisse Unbestimmtheit in sich tragen und Raum für den Leser und dessen Phantasie und Vorstellung lassen.

Ohne an dieser Stelle ausführlich auf rezeptionsästhetische Aspekte einzugehen (hierzu Bidlo, *Pfade*) sei betont, dass aus rezeptionsästhetischen bzw. wirkungsästhetischen Gesichtspunkten sich ein Text erst im Lesevorgang generiert und aktualisiert, d.h. in der Interaktion zwischen Werk und Leser. Aus diesem Grund liegt die Bedeutung eines Textes nicht allein im Text, sondern *zwischen* Leser und Text. Literarische Texte wandeln sich je nach ihrem Rezeptionsumfeld, in welchem sie aktualisiert werden. Das wiederum kann erklären, warum sich unterschiedliche Interpretationen eines Werkes bilden können und es nicht nur *eine* gültige ausweist. Aber neben der Interpretation, was die Erzählung möglicherweise bedeutet, zeigt Tolkien selbst auf, dass es eine weitere Ebene gewisser Texte – hier Märchen – gibt.

> [D]ann bleibt immer noch eines, das allzuoft vergessen wird, nämlich die Wirkung, die diese alten Stoffe in den Geschichten, so wie sie sind, *jetzt* hervorrufen... [D]er wichtigste Eindruck aber, den diese Erzählung in meiner Erinnerung hinterlassen hat, war nicht der des Schönen oder Grauenhaften, sondern der Anhauch einer Ferne, eines tiefen Zeitenabgrundes. (BB 36)

Tolkien weist hier schon – ohne sie beim Namen zu nennen – auf die Sehnsucht hin, die letztlich im Zentrum der menschlichen Kreativität in Form des Menschen als Zweitschöpfers (vgl. BB 41) steht. Denn die Sehnsucht ist ein bewundernswertes, aber auch melancholisches und schmerzhaftes Streben, das in vielfältiger Art und Weise das tiefe Wesen des *Herrn der Ringe* und der Welt Mittelerde offenlegt. Und Sehnsucht nimmt auch einen bedeutungsvollen Rang in Tolkiens Denken über die Bedeutung menschlicher, schöpferischer Kunst ein. Über Ausflüge in seiner Kindheit in das Reich der Phantasie und der Märchenwelt schreibt er selbst:

> Aber ich kann mich nicht daran erinnern, daß meine Freude an einer Geschichte jemals von dem Glauben abhängig gewesen wäre, daß dergleichen im ›wirklichen Leben‹ geschehen könne oder geschehen sei. Offensichtlich ging es in den Märchen nicht in erster Linie um das Mögliche, sondern um das Erwünschte. Wenn sie das *Verlangen* [Hervorhebung im Original] weckten und es befriedigten, nachdem sie es oft bis zur Unerträglichkeit angestachelt hatten, waren sie gelungen... Phantasie, das Erschaffen oder Erspähen anderer Welten, war das Herzstück des Verlangens nach dem Elbenreich. Ich verlangte nach den Drachen mit einer tiefen Sehnsucht. (BB 44f)

Betrachten wir in diesem Zusammenhang kurz den Begriff der *Kreativität*. Es wurde nach dem lateinischen Wort *creare* gebildet. Dieses Wort tauchte ursprünglich fast ausschließlich in der Theologie auf. Die Fähigkeit, schöpfen und erschaffen zu können, sprach man nur dem Creator, dem Schöpfer-Gott zu. Aber die Menschen sind nach der Lehre des Alten Testaments auch ein Bild Gottes. So ist es verständlich, dass im christlichen Abendland die Nachahmung jener göttlichen Fähigkeit eine besondere Bedeutung gewann. Zunächst übertrug sich diese göttliche Tugend des Schöpferischen auf einen besonderen Menschentypus, auf das Genie oder eben besondere Menschen. Aber letztlich ist jedem Menschen der Schöpferdrang inhärent, der auf einer im Menschen verankerten Sehnsucht fußt.

Wo findet man den Kreativitätsbegriff im *Herrn der Ringe* oder darüber hinaus? Vielleicht ausdrücklich nicht, aber im Sinne der Kreatur, des Geschöpften und des Entworfenen. Das Entworfene ist das Hinausgeschleuderte. Wohin wird und woher wurde es geschleudert? Das Geschöpf ist hier das durch den Autor Geschöpfte, es ist entworfen, hinausgeschleudert und zwar aus der Phantasie und Sehnsucht des Autors hinaus in die Welt außerhalb des Geistes des Autors. Mittelerde selbst ist eine geschöpfte, eine kreierte Welt, erschaffen durch die subkreative Kunst Tolkiens. Tolkien selbst wies auf die Sehnsucht hin, aus der viele Elbengeschichten geboren sind. »Im Herzen vieler von Menschenhand geschaffener Elbengeschichten findet sich offen und verhüllt, rein oder beigemischt, das Verlangen nach einem lebendigen, wahrgewordenen Zweitschöpfertum... Aus diesem Verlangen sind die Elben geschaffen« (BB 55).

Durch die Entgrenzung des eigenen Ichs, eben durch das Entwerfen, das Hinausschleudern einer neuen, anderen Welt bzw. durch einen Entwurf derselben sollte sich der Mensch in der Romantik von konventionellen Ketten befreien, die Ketten des eigenen Seins sprengen, die eigenen Grenzen verschieben. Die Innerlichkeit rückte in den Mittelpunkt der Kunst, denn nur dort ist der Mensch in der Lage, Gottes Schöpfung zu erkennen. Das Gefühl der Schöpfungskraft ist eines der zentralen Motive der Romantik. Und dabei ist das dort entworfene Kunstwerk nie vollkommen eine Widerspiegelung der göttlichen Wirklichkeit der Welt, sondern nur ein Hintasten. Daher zeigen das Fragmentarische und verschiedene Brüche den Prozess der Entwicklung an, jedoch auch die selbstkritische Distanz des Dichters.

Der Dichter innerhalb der Romantik kommentiert sein eigenes Werk, schreibt es weiter, korrigiert und amüsiert sich auch teilweise selbst darüber oder tritt hinter diesem zurück, externalisiert es und trifft auf es erneut wie auf eine von ihm unabhängige Schöpfung. Und bei Tolkien wird die Schöpfung, das Ergebnis des kreativen Aktes, ein *Auswurf* der Phantasie. Phantasie und Kreativität sind hier kaum mehr zu trennen. Sie sind ein kraftvoller *Strudel* im menschlichen Denken, der Neues erschafft. »Die schöpferische Phantasie dagegen, weil sie in der Hauptsache auf etwas anderes ausgeht (das Erschaffen von Neuem)« (BB 59).

Die Offenheit von Tolkiens Werk im Allgemeinen und des *Herrn der Ringe* im Besonderen drückt sich besonders durch seine intertextuelle Anlage aus. Tolkiens Werke, zumal *Der Herr der Ringe*, sind im hohen Maße von Intertextualität gekennzeichnet, was so viel meint, als dass bewusste und unbewusste Bezüge auf andere Geschichten, Mythen oder Erzählungen verarbeitet sind. Literatur besteht in einem großen Maße aus dem Kombinieren von alten Motiven.

Schneidewind betont zu Recht: »Die Kunst des Schreibens besteht zu einem nicht unerheblichen Teil darin, Ideen und Motive neu zu verbinden und darzustellen. Was immer man genau unter phantastischer Literatur und Fantasy versteht, eines zeichnet diese stets aus: So gut wie immer finden wir darin Topoi oder Motive aus älteren Mythen« (Schneidewind 9). Tolkien weist in einer Fußnote selbst darauf hin, dass Mythen, zumal die großen Erzählungen, aus unzähligen Fäden ge- und verwoben sind, und weist ihnen emergente Eigenschaften zu. »Das Bild ist größer als die Summe der Fäden, aus denen es besteht, und wird durch sie nicht erklärt. Hier liegt die Schwäche, die der analytischen (oder ›wissenschaftlichen‹) Methode innewohnt: Sie findet vieles über Dinge heraus, die in Erzählungen vorkommen, aber wenig oder nichts über deren Wirkung in einer bestimmten Erzählung« (BB 28).

Innerhalb der Romantik galt das Unabgeschlossene und Offene des romantischen Kunstwerkes als eine wichtige Grundlage dafür, dass der Leser zum Weiterdenken des Werkes animiert wird. Und dadurch wiederum leitet der Leser einen nicht enden wollenden Prozess des Werkes selbst ein. Es endet nicht auf der letzten Seite, sondern bietet eine Reihe von Anknüpfungs- und Fortsetzungspunkten. Auf Tolkien bezogen sind dies zum einen die Intertextualität und zum anderen seine im Text angelegten Verweise z.B. auf frühere Zeiten, Genealogien oder Geschichten eines Volkes und der mitunter fragmentarische Stil im Rahmen dieser Verweise, die eine Offenheit im Werk selbst erzeugen.

Tolkien wollte Anknüpfungspunkte in seinem Werk setzen – Raum »für andere Geister und Hände« lassen (vgl. Carpenter 122) –, sodass die Geschichten fortgeschrieben und -gedacht werden können. Und zumindest sein Werk rund um Mittelerde besitzt eine innere Verweisungsstruktur aufgrund der verschiedenen Zeitalter, auf die sich bezogen wird. So weist der *Herr der Ringe* oder der *Hobbit* hinaus auf das *Silmarillion*. Und schaut man auf das Ende des *Herrn der Ringe* – oder auf die im Text nur fragmentarisch und unvollendet gelassenen Geschichten –, seien es die letzten Zeilen des letzten Bandes oder die Anhänge, wird deutlich, dass das Werk offen gehalten ist zum Weiterdenken durch den Leser.

Literatur innerhalb der Romantik verbindet die Wirklichkeit und die Phantasie zu einem Werdensprozess, der nie vollkommen fertig sein kann. Und dieses Motiv lässt sich deutlich bei Tolkien wiederfinden.

Abschluss

Tolkiens Zweitschöpfung – der deutsch-jüdische Kulturphilosoph Martin Buber sprach einmal von einem dem Menschen inhärenten Urhebertrieb (vgl. Buber 17) – ist ein Kreiertes, etwas Entworfenes, das durch die Kreativität und Phantasie des Autors geschaffen wurde. Der Antrieb dieser Kreativität ist die Sehnsucht, die durch das Werk eine materielle Form erhält. Sehnsucht und Kreativität gab es natürlich nicht erst seit der Romantik, sondern sie sind beständiger Teil der Menschheit. Aber in der Romantik sind beide Begriffe in der oben dargestellten Weise miteinander verknüpft, sind so aufeinander bezogen und stehen im Zentrum des romantischen Denkens.

Der Einfluss romantischen Denkens bei Tolkien ist derart nicht mehr nur durch das Suchen, Auffinden und die Addition bestimmter romantischer Einzelaspekte nachspürbar, sondern Tolkiens Mittelerdewerk selbst muss als Ergebnis und Entwurf einer romantischen Geisteshaltung verstanden werden, ohne dass unterschiedliche und andere Einflüsse, die sich ohne Zweifel in hohem Maße in den Werken Tolkiens wiederfinden, dadurch ausgegrenzt werden oder nicht integrierbar sind. Es gibt somit eine fundierte romantische Lesart von Tolkiens Mittelerde-Werken im Allgemeinen und des *Herrn der Ringe* im Besonderen.

Bibliographie

Baader, Meike Sophia. »Der romantische Kindheitsmythos und seine Kontinuitäten in der Pädagogik und in der Kindheitsforschung«. *Zeitschrift für Erziehungswissenschaft* 7 (3/2004): 416-430

Bidlo, Oliver. *Mythos Mittelerde. Über Hobbits, Helden und Geschichte in Tolkiens Welt.* Essen: BoD, 2002

---. *Sehnsucht nach Mittelerde?.* Essen: BoD, 2003

---. »Verbotene Pfade nach Mittelerde?«. *Hither Shore* 1 (2004): 25-35

Buber, Martin. *Reden über die Erziehung.* Heidelberg: L. Schneider, 1998

Carpenter, Humphrey. *J.R.R. Tolkien. Eine Biographie.* Stuttgart: Klett-Cotta, 1979

Honegger, Thomas. »Die *interpretatio mediaevalia* von Tolkiens Werk«. *Hither Shore* 1 (2004): 37-51

Koopmann, Helmut. *Mythos und Mythologie in der Literatur des 19. Jahrhunderts.* Frankfurt am Main: Klostermann, 1979

Reinfandt, Christoph. *Englische Romantik. Eine Einführung.* Berlin: Erich Schmidt Verlag, 2008

Schlegel, Friedrich. *Fragmente. Athenäums-Fragmente.* Kritische Friedrich-Schlegel-Ausgabe. Herausgegeben von Ernst Behler. Bd. 2. München/Paderborn/Wien: Schöningh, 1967

Schmitz-Evans, Monika. *Einführung in die Literatur der Romantik.* Darmstadt: Wissenschaftliche Buchgesellschaft, 2004

Schneidewind, Friedhelm. *Mythologie und phantastische Literatur.* Essen: Oldib Verlag, 2008

Tolkien, John Ronald Reuel. *Baum und Blatt.* Stuttgart: Klett-Cotta, 1982

---. *Briefe.* Ausgewählt und herausgegeben von Humphrey Carpenter mit der Hilfe von Christopher Tolkien. Stuttgart: Klett-Cotta, 1991

---. *Der Herr der Ringe.* Band 1. Stuttgart: Klett-Cotta, 1997

'The past is another country' – Romanticism, Tolkien, and the Middle Ages

Thomas Honegger (Jena)

> Hobbits are an unobtrusive but very ancient people,
> more numerous formerly than they are today;
> for they love peace and quiet and good tilled earth:
> a well-ordered and well-farmed countryside was their favourite haunt.
> They do not and did not understand or like machines
> more complicated than a forge-bellows, a water-mill, or a hand-loom,
> though they were skilful with tools.
> (LotR Prologue 1)

Introduction

The Shire, a timeless idyll, may not be the most obvious place to look for the Middle Ages, or for elements of Romanticism in Tolkien. We know that it is, according to Tolkien himself, an idealised version of rural England around the time of Queen Victoria's Diamond Jubilee (i.e. 20 June 1897; L 230). Yet its idyllic rural and provincial qualities are exactly the elements that link it with the idealised 'conceptual' Middle Ages – which stand for a time before the cataclysmic events of the French Revolution (1789) in the case of the Romantics, and the worst excesses of industrialisation and mechanised warfare (late 19th, first half of the 20th century) in the case of Tolkien. He and his generation, and before him the Romantics, were both 'reacting' to events and large-scale developments that questioned and threatened the culture and society in which they had grown up. They were, of course, reacting differently, not least since the French Revolution and the ensuing wars in Europe cannot be compared to the industrial revolution and World War I – and yet both the Romantics and Tolkien chose to look back towards a lost Golden Age rather than forward towards a Golden Age to come. Interestingly, it is not classical antiquity or any other historical period they are turning to but the Middle Ages.[1]

In the case of the Romantics, however, it is not so much the 'historical' Middle Ages that fascinated them but the ideals and clichés projected onto this era – whether by their medieval ancestors themselves or by later writers (cf.

---

1 The (possible) reasons why most Romantics chose the Middle Ages are manifold and cannot always be established with certainty. For many it was, at least at first, a rebellion against conventional history and learning. See Alexander 1-23 and Chandler 12-51 for a general overview.

Alexander 1-64). These 'conceptual' and idealised Middle Ages are characterised by a pre-Reformation unity and spirituality (cf. Novalis, *Christenheit*), a clearly structured (feudal and paternal) estate society, a (more or less clearly) identifiable national character, and by personalised political and professional relationships.[2] It is therefore no surprise that these idealised Middle Ages often became the desired 'homelands' for the poets and writers who were increasingly alienated by the excesses of the Enlightenment and not least the French Revolution with its radical egalitarianism, anti-clericalism and rationalism.

In the following, I am going to look at two examples of these 'conceptual' and 'Romantic' Middle Ages as found in Novalis's *Heinrich von Ofterdingen* (1802) and in Sir Walter Scott's *Ivanhoe* (1819).[3] The events in both books are set towards the end of the 12th century,[4] i.e. in the high Middle Ages, and the action takes place within a clearly identified geographical framework – Germany in the case of Novalis, whose Heinrich travels from Eisenach in Thuringia to Augsburg in Bavaria, and England in the case of Sir Walter Scott, especially the area around Sheffield. The foci of these two works are, however, rather different. Novalis's text can be best classified as a *Bildungsroman*, i.e. a text focussing on the intellectual or spiritual development of an individual protagonist, namely the eponymous character Heinrich. Scott's work, by contrast, is not so much concerned with Ivanhoe or Richard Lionheart (or Robin Hood, who also makes an appearance) but with the origin and development of the English nation. Indeed, Scott's main protagonist is 'England the Nation' and his theme is the making of this nation from the often conflicting and disparate elements of the Anglo-Saxon and Norman parts of the population.[5]

Novalis and Scott thus depict medieval societies in radically different situations. Novalis uses a stable and internally peaceful estate-society as the backdrop for the exploration of the development of Heinrich as an artist-poet, whereas Scott presents us a society in crisis and at a crucial stage of its development towards becoming a unified nation. These differences in the medieval societies depicted are not essential ones but only situational – and the re-establishment

---

2   See Chandler 1-11. I consciously exclude the tradition of the dark 'Gothic' Middle Ages as found in the numerous works of Gothic fiction.
3   Lobdell (9) writes: "The pivotal figure among the British Romantics is probably Sir Walter Scott, to whom we are principally indebted not so much for the romance of history as for the historical romance." He (ibid.) also explicitly mentions Novalis as bringing to us (together with Coleridge) the Romantic archetype who speaks to us out of a universal past.
4   Ivanhoe is set in ca. 1194, the time of King Richard Lionheart's return from the crusades and his captivity in the castles of Dürnstein (modern Austria) and Trifels (modern Germany), whereas Heinrich von Ofterdingen (chapter 5) meets Duke Friedrich III von Zolre (died 1201) who lives as a hermit in a cave.
5   The Celtic element, extensively treated in Scott's other novels, has, in this context, been omitted.

of the rightful order towards the end of *Ivanhoe* gives us a society rather similar to that hinted at in *Heinrich von Ofterdingen*.

What, then, are the characteristics of a medieval society, as found in the works of these two Romantic authors? We could characterise the 'Romantic' view of the Middle Ages with the following keywords:

- post-Roman-Empire
- pre-Reformation
- holistic or coherent view of the world
- largely pre-technological and pre-science
- personal and hierarchical relationships

Whether the historical Middle Ages actually fulfilled all those categories is more than debatable. The important point is that the Romantics – and to some extent even the people living in the Middle Ages themselves – believed that they did, that they lived in the time after the downfall of the Roman Empire, that their society and world is one that is structured and governed by a unifying and holistic principle. Tolkien's Middle-earth, as we encounter it in *The Hobbit* and *The Lord of the Rings*, and I specifically exclude his other writings, seems to partake in this 'Romantic' view of times past.[6] In the following I am going to discuss briefly each point and, in the end, present a concluding assessment of Tolkien's use of the 'topos of the Middle Ages'.

Post-Roman-Empire

We find throughout the Middle Ages (i.e. from the Fall of Rome in AD 476 onwards) a striving towards the re-establishment of the former empire. Charlemagne (AD 742-814) and his successors were thus seen not so much as establishing a new realm but rather as working towards a 'restoratio/renovatio imperii', the restoration of the former glory. The existence of the 'Heilige Römische Reich Deutscher Nation' (Holy Roman Empire of the German Nation, AD 962-1806), which lasted nine centuries, illustrates the tenacity of this idea. The Romantics such as Novalis or Scott were thus looking back towards a reformed and Christian – and no longer Mediterranean – post-Roman empire. The old order of classical antiquity had been lost but a new imperial force had established itself with the coronation of Charlemagne in AD 800. And, what is more, an empire that – in the case of Novalis – was yet in existence (at least in theory) or – in the case of Scott – was still within living memory.

---

6   Lobdell (12) writes that the "springs of Romantic Medievalism are one of the origins of the stream of 'Tolkienian' fantasy."

The situation towards the end of the Third Age, i.e. the time-frame for *The Hobbit* and *The Lord of the Rings*, is comparable to the early European Middle Ages (i.e. between AD 500 to 750) rather than to the later centuries. The Númenorian empire had collapsed and only Gondor still survives, though it, too, comes increasingly under pressure from the enemy hordes out of the east. Aragorn's 'return' to the long-vacant throne of Gondor and his re-establishment of the former double-empire of Gondor and Arnor is reminiscent of Charlemagne's achievement, who re-united the territories of modern-day Germany and Italy, and the coronation by the hand of Gandalf may be an (intended) parallel to Charlemagne's coronation by Pope Leo III.

Pre-Reformation / Holistic or Coherent View of the World

I have conflated the next two points, i.e. pre-Reformation society and the holistic or coherent view of the world, since they are closely connected. The Reformation and thus the loss of a unified religious doctrine in Western Europe are considered as one of the decisive events that mark the end of the Middle Ages. The time before this break with ancient tradition was therefore often seen as a time of European unity and coherence – with the Islamic countries as 'the Other'. After the Reformation the internal differences became too great to be bridged and the 'religious Other' was as much found in one's own country as in the exotic lands of the East.

Novalis's Heinrich, then, lives in a world where the Christian Catholic religion is part of society's very fabric and the 'religious Other' makes an appearance only in the figure of the Muslim captive Zulima. Religion in Heinrich's world seems to represent less ideology than culture and civilization and is much more tolerant and accommodating towards the brand of nature-mysticism that occurs frequently in this work. In this Novalis is closer to Tolkien than Scott – maybe because the former two are Catholics, whereas the latter is a Protestant.[7]

The world of *Ivanhoe* is, of course, a Catholic one – Scott is too much of a historian to depict it otherwise. And yet it is not the 'exotic' figures of the Jews (Isaac and Rebecca) or the Saracen servants of the Templar Knight Brian de Bois-Guilbert who provide the contrasting elements but rather the 'proto-Anglicans' Ivanhoe and Richard Lionheart himself – or, if one stretches things a bit, even the 'Friar Tuck' figure (the Holy Clerk of Copmanhurst), who could be seen as an 'Anglican monk'. All of them are (favourably) contrasted with the

---

7   Scott no doubt worshipped in the Anglican Church when he was resident in England, but he must have been brought up in the Church of Scotland, which is considerably more Calvinistic.

either corrupt or fanatical members of the Knights Templars, who represent everything a God-fearing Anglican Protestant abhors and associates with Papism. The final dissolution of the Templars' headquarters at Templestowe could therefore be seen as a premonition of the dissolution of the monasteries under Henry VIII. Scott's depiction of internal, religiously motivated tensions within medieval society is certainly more realistic – yet his motivation for deviating from the ideal of a unified and harmonious Catholic society is clearly connected to his aim of exploring the constitutive elements of the English nation. In this he joins a long tradition of English historians who, ever since the break from Rome under Henry VIII, have tried to prove the original independence of an English-speaking Church. The medieval society Scott presents is already divided and the pre-Reformation unity is nothing but a superficial veneer.

Tolkien, as I have mentioned before, is more in line with Novalis – not least because he does not put religion into the foreground but weaves it invisibly into the very fabric of his tales. As he himself pointed out (L 172), *The Lord of the Rings* is a Catholic tale – even more so since he removed all (or almost all) overt references to religious rituals and organised religion. The underlying ethos, often more felt than consciously noticed, is that of a coherent and harmonious metaphysical view of the world – a world that is indeed 'catholic' in the sense of the word as 'all embracing, comprehensive'.

In this all three authors are in agreement: their worlds are not yet secularised and the great divorce between matter and spirit has not yet taken place.[8] The religious framework, even if it has come under pressure and begins to show some cracks, still constitutes the all-encompassing frame responsible for the overall cohesion of things. Linked to this is a second characteristic shared by the worlds of all three authors: their pre-technological and pre-science status.

Pre-Technological and Pre-Science

alking about technology and science, we have first to make clear that the distance between the Middle Ages and Novalis and Scott on the one hand, and Tolkien on the other, is not the same. Novalis and Scott were both living in a world that had been removed from the Middle Ages by the Enlightenment and the effects of the scientific revolution. Yet, they were not affected by the later effects of large-scale industrialisation both in production and warfare – developments that made a lasting impression on Tolkien and which found their imaginative representations in his descriptions of Mordor, Isengard and Saruman/Sharky's attempted destruction of the Shire. Tolkien's own world is doubly

---

8   See Lewis's classical study *The Discarded Image* for a very readable and knowledgeable introduction to the medieval view of the world.

removed from the Middle Ages – once by the 'scientific turn' and once more by the large-scale 'technological turn'.[9] Novalis and Scott had merely to revert to a time before the Enlightenment – their 'natural world' was still more or less in an unbroken line that reached back to the Middle Ages and was, as such, 'pre-technological' even if not pre-scientific. As a consequence, the difference between their fictional medieval worlds and their own contemporary societies is predominantly one of 'outlook' and not of large-scale physical change, and (modern) technology and (large-scale) industrialisation are simply absent from their fictional frameworks because these developments had not yet made an impact on the world of their authors. There is no contrast between the 'pre-industrialised' landscape and the one marred by pollution and exploitation of the natural resources – in contrast to Tolkien's Middle-earth where the opposition is prominent. Tolkien was aware of the destructive potential of modern technology and his description of a pre-technological world is a conscious choice, creating thus a contrast to his post-technological reality.

I am not going to discuss the Romantic topos of the appreciation of 'untamed nature', simply because the texts by Novalis and Scott do not present nature in this way. Nature, be it the greenwood of the outlaws or the generic 'outdoors' of other episodes, merely provides the backdrop to the events that take centre stage. It would therefore be misguided to talk about 'the Romantic view of nature' in such a context. Tolkien's view, then, is clearly medieval.[10] Nature untamed or unguarded is not appreciated per se and, moreover, has a tendency to go bad (cf. Old Man Willow). It is the well-tended garden, the tilled earth and the well-managed forest that characterises the ideal landscape of the Shire. Nature, according to Tolkien, comes into her own through a symbiotic relationship with elf, man, hobbit, or dwarf – who thus participate in the sub-creation of the Valar.[11] Tolkien is also clearly pre- or even anti-scientific.

As Dirk Vanderbeke has shown, traditional lore is valued more than newly acquired knowledge – which, once again, is a very medieval concept[12] and finds expression in medieval scholarship in the prominent position of the *auctores*. Gandalf, finally, puts the anti-scientific stance into authoritative form in his warning to Saruman: "And he that breaks a thing to find out what it is has left the path of wisdom." (LotR II, ii, 259).

---

9 The Middle Ages were, of course, not entirely devoid of technology (nor of science). There existed proto-industrial water mills that ground not only flour but were also used to work iron. We even have a short alliterative Middle English poem (no. 132 in Duncan 178-79) whose author complains about the ceaseless noise from a nearby smithy.
10 See Dickerson and Evans for an in-depth discussion of Tolkien's attitude towards nature.
11 See, for example, Gimli's enthusiastic description of the Caves of Aglarond beneath Helm's Deep in Rohan and how the dwarves would 'tend' them so that the full potential of their natural beauty would be realised (LotR III, viii, 547).
12 See also Rebecca's traditional medical lore in *Ivanhoe*.

Hand in hand with this critical stance towards scientific and technological progress goes an un-alienated relationship with nature and places so that an almost symbiotic union with one's dwelling place is a clear indication of moral soundness (cf. Honegger, "Bag End"). Romantic nationalistic ideas may show a similar appreciation of 'Heimat' (though it is often called 'Vaterland' – which is probably not a valid Tolkienian category),[13] but neither *Ivanhoe* nor *Heinrich von Ofterdingen* provides any instances of this.

What we do find, however, is an example of a pre-industrialised, non-alienated, almost symbiotic relationship between man and nature in Novalis's portrait and account of the miner ('Bergmann'). The old miner's description[14] of how he was initiated into the guild of miners and how he learned and practised the craft (or, one is almost tempted to say, art) is strongly reminiscent of Gimli's enthusiastic praise of dwarvish 'mining'. Novalis has, of course, first-hand experience in this field (he worked as 'supervisor of mines' from 1796 on), and he was familiar with the harsh reality of mining. And yet he transforms the miner's work into a sort of mystic quest for the treasures of the earth and links it with pantheistic ideas. Miner and the earth enter into a symbiotic, almost loving relationship. The contrast to the life-sapping, alienating realities of industrialised mining could hardly be greater, and working below ground becomes for Novalis's miner an all-encompassing way of life. It may be no coincidence that the miner's tale reads more like a successful individuation in the Jungian sense rather than a capitalist success story. The key to personal fulfilment, as Novalis, and also Tolkien and Scott, suggest, lies in the 'personalisation' of one's relationship with society and nature – which brings us to our last point.

Personal and Hierarchical Relationships

Pre-modern societies were predominantly personal and hierarchical. I do not want to deny individual attempts to the contrary (the Peasants' Revolt of 1381 in England or the 17th century Levellers come to mind), but the larger picture is that of a society whose members stand to each other in a hierarchical and personal relationship. These social realities have given rise to theoretical concepts that try to stabilise and justify the existing structures. Most widespread is the presumably Indo-European (Dumézil) division of society into farmer, priest, and warrior, which received its medieval form at the latest in 10th century England (cf. Powell). The Anglo-Saxon clergyman Ælfric of Eynsham, in an appendix to the Maccabees homily, develops the classic model of the three

---

13 For Tolkien's view of politics and nationalism, see his letters 52 and 53 (L 63-66).
14 See chapter 5 in Novalis's *Heinrich von Ofterdingen* (especially pages 63-75).

estates, i.e. *laboratores, oratores* and *bellatores*. These three estates live and work in close harmony and fulfil complementary functions. The *laboratores* are responsible for covering the basic necessities of life, i.e. food, clothing, shelter, whereas the *oratores* are charged with the duty to establish and keep up a harmonious relationship with God. The *bellatores*, finally, defend the other members of society against all forms of aggression from within or without. All three authors base their depiction of society on this model.

Novalis, to proceed chronologically, is probably the one who consciously exploits the audience's familiarity with the pre-French Revolution (at least theoretically) harmonious co-existence of the different estates. The artistic, poetic and personal development of his main protagonist Heinrich, who comes from a family of craftsmen and merchants, takes place against an only vaguely sketched backdrop of the medieval estate society. Novalis actually does what many modern authors of fantasy do: by using familiar elements and recurring popular stereotypes he is able to evoke an entire world by means of a few simple strokes.

Scott, on the other hand, is not interested in the development of an individual, but of late 12th century society in its entirety. He therefore focuses on the social interaction between the different elements of this society. We have basically three parts. First, the traditional Anglo-Saxon society as represented by the household of Cedric of Rotherwood. It is characterised by inherited social hierarchies that allow upward mobility (the swineherd and thrall Gurth becomes, in the end, a landed freeman). The relationship between the hierarchically different people is one of personal loyalty. Thus, the thrall and fool Wamba gladly runs the risk of getting hanged in order to save his master Cedric – an act which is not so much motivated by a sense of duty but by a feeling of loyalty and filial love. This archaic society of paternal hierarchy is contrasted with and opposed to the basically mercenary feudal structure of the Norman nobility as represented by Prince John and his cronies. Their main motivation is no longer the unconditional personal affection and loyalty between the members of society but primarily personal gain. The outlaws in the great greenwood may be seen as the third element. Living outside soci-ety, they nevertheless practice a kind of natural justice under the leadership of Locksley (aka Robin Hood). Scott does not advocate an egalitarian society, and even if obvious wrongs and abuses of the system have to be fixed, it has to be done in the correct way. To cite just one example: the renegade Norman nobles have taken Ivanhoe, his father and some other people prisoner and keep them at the castle of Torquilstone. The outlaws want to storm the castle and free the prisoners – and pay back the Norman knights for years of oppression and cruelty. The description of the storming of the castle must have reminded Scott's original audience of the storming of the Bastille during the French Revolution. The English, however, do it differently. The outlaws are actually led in their attack by the Black Knight, i.e. king Richard

Lionheart himself, who has just returned from abroad. In the French context, the storming of the Bastille constituted a radical break with the old order; in *Ivanhoe* the storming of castle Torquilstone marks the re-establishment of the feudal hierarchy in an 'improved' form. The solution Scott advocates is therefore not 'Liberté, Égalité, Fraternité' but a paternally governed estate society. For him, the ideal is the fusion of the originally disparate Anglo-Saxon and Norman elements under a new form of patriotic royal leadership characterised by loyalty and affection – to England and the King!

Tolkien's world is in many aspects rather similar to Scott's medieval England. The societies of the Shire, of Rohan and of Gondor, are all hierarchical and personal. It is the 'modern' and centralised state of Sauron that is hierarchical yet utterly impersonal. The orc-officer does not ask for the name, but for the soldier's number (LotR VI, ii, 931) – I do not think any of Gondor's or Rohan's soldiers would even dream of getting a number! The establishment of the personal yet hierarchical relationship in the societies of the Shire, Rohan, and Gondor can be seen most clearly in the relationship between Frodo and Sam, Théoden and Merry, and Denethor and Pippin respectively. All three 'subordinate' hobbits enter into a service-relationship with a person in a superior position, and the way it is done is telling. Sam unceremoniously and stubbornly attaches himself to Frodo – there is simply no question that he will follow him through thick and thin. No ceremony is needed to ratify this strongest of links.

The model for such a relationship, as Mark Hooker has shown, is that between officer and his batman – a relationship Tolkien himself witnessed and valued during his service in the trenches of the Somme. The bond between Théoden and Merry may be best characterised as 'paternalistic'. Merry's feelings for Théoden are comparable to that of a son for his father, and the ceremony which marks Merry's acceptance as a warrior of Rohan is simple yet touching (LotR V, ii, 777). Compared to this, the Gondorian oath of fealty between Denethor and Pippin (LotR V, i, 756), which is reminiscent of the oath of fealty in the feudal system of the high Middle Ages, strikes the reader as formal and impersonal.

Conclusion

The last point mentioned, i.e. Tolkien's multiple views of personal hierarchical relationships in different cultures, is characteristic for his use of 'the Middle Ages'. Tolkien and the two Romantic authors discussed share the use of what I would like to call 'conceptual' Middle Ages, i.e. a time characterised by being pre-Reformation, pre-French Revolution, and – in the case of Tolkien especially relevant – pre-Industrial Revolution and pre-WW I. Novalis and Scott react to the atrocities of the French Revolution and contrast the radical egalitarianism of the new government with an idealised paternal 'ancient regime'. Tolkien, by contrast, writes primarily in reaction to the technological and industrial developments and the rise of the new absolutistic ideologies of communism and fascism. He thus shares a common line of vision with the Romantic authors, i.e. backwards.

His starting point of view, however, is not primarily 'post-French-Revolution' but 'post-Industrial-Revolution' and 'post-WW I'. Furthermore, he possesses, as a medievalist, an intimate knowledge of medieval literature and history – which makes him reluctant to reduce the one thousand years of the Middle Ages to a simple cipher or stereotype. And unlike Scott, who is writing 'historical romance' and has therefore to avoid anachronisms and historical inaccuracies that are too obvious, Tolkien is free to sub-create his own Middle Ages – which are not called 'Middle Ages' anyway. Tolkien, to some extent, can have his cake and eat it: Middle-earth at the end of the Third Age offers the heroic-Germanic Middle Ages in Rohan (cf. Honegger, "Rohirrim"), the 'imperial' Middle Ages in Gondor, and the prototypically idyllic 'Middle Ages' in the Shire. Scott's depiction of a surviving Anglo-Saxon element in the late 12th century is a structurally necessary anachronism and we are willing to suspend our critical historical disbelief.

Tolkien's synchronic anachronisms, however, would not really work in a real-world historical framework – Gondor and Rohan, yes, but not Gondor and Rohan and the Shire. Yet, in Middle-earth, they do so beautifully – at least for me and many other readers. Furthermore, Tolkien actually reverses the Romantic line of vision with the creation of the Shire. It is a 'post-Medieval' society that has developed out of the 'Middle Ages' without suffering the destructive effects of the cataclysms of a French or an Industrial Revolution – maybe even without a Norman Conquest.

Tolkien is thus not so much a Romantic dreaming of a time long past, but a medievalist dreaming of an organic and harmonious continuation of transformed and 'purified' Middle Ages as found in the Shire.

Bibliography

Alexander, Michael. *Medievalism. The Middle Ages in Modern England*. New Haven/London: Yale University Press, 2007

Chandler, Alice. *A Dream of Order. The Medieval Ideal in Nineteenth-Century Literature*. London: Routledge & Kegan Paul, 1971

Dickerson, Matthew and Jonathan Evans. *Ents, Elves, and Eriador. The Environmental Vision of J.R.R. Tolkien*. Lexington, KT.: The University Press of Kentucky, 2006

Duncan, Thomas G. (ed.). *Medieval English Lyrics 1200-1400*. London: Penguin, 1995

Honegger, Thomas. "From Bag End to Lórien: The Creation of a Literary World." *News from the Shire and Beyond – Studies on Tolkien*. (Cormarë Series 1). Eds. Peter Buchs and Thomas Honegger. Zurich/Berne: Walking Tree Publishers, 1997. 48-67

---. "(Heroic) Fantasy and the Middle Ages – Strange Bedfellows or an Ideal Cast?" *Médiévalisme. Modernité du Moyen Âge*. Ed. Vincent Ferré. Paris: L'Harmattan, 2010, 61-71

---. "The Rohirrim: 'Anglo-Saxons on Horseback'? An Inquiry into Tolkien's Use of Sources." *Tolkien and the Study of His Sources: Critical Essays*. Ed. Jason Fisher. Jefferson, NC: McFarland, 2011

Hooker, Mark T. "Frodo's Batman." *Tolkien Studies* 1 (2004): 125-136

Lewis, Clive Staples. *The Discarded Image*. Cambridge: Cambridge University Press, 1964

Lobdell, Jared. *The Rise of Tolkienian Fantasy*. Chicago and La Salle, Illinois: Open Court, 2005

Novalis (Georg Friedrich Philipp Freiherr von Hardenberg). *Heinrich von Ofterdingen*. 1802. Frankfurt/Leipzig: Insel, 1982

---. *Die Christenheit oder Europa. Ein Fragment*. 1802. Stuttgart: Reclam, 1991

Powell, Timothy E. "The 'Three Orders' of Society in Anglo-Saxon England." *Anglo-Saxon England* 23 (1994): 103-132

Scott, Sir Walther. *Ivanhoe*. 1819. Ware, Hertfordshire: Wordsworth Classics, 1995

Tolkien, John Ronald Reuel. *The Lord of the Rings*. 1954/55. (50th anniversary one-volume edition). Boston/New York: Houghton Mifflin Company, 2004

---. *The Letters of J.R.R. Tolkien*. Ed. Humphrey Carpenter (with the assistance of Christopher Tolkien). 1981. Boston/New York: Houghton Mifflin, 2000

Vanderbeke, Dirk. "Language, Lore and Learning in *The Lord of the Rings*." *Reconsidering Tolkien*. (Cormarë Series 8). Ed. Thomas Honegger. Zurich/Berne: Walking Tree Publishers, 2005. 129-151

Disenchanted with their Age: Keats's, Morris's, and Tolkien's Great Escape

Marie-Noëlle Biemer (Frankfurt/Main)

Introduction

Since the advent of the gothic novel, authors of the fantastic have been taxed with the accusation of writing so much escapist drool. The academic discussion thus usually focuses on why escapism is good or bad for the reader and society in general (and possibly also the author) and where the authors escape *to*. The paper in hand takes a closer look at what three particular authors actual-ly escaped *from* and some similarities that can be found in the execution of their subject matter.

The authors have been chosen as representatives of their time, starting with John Keats (1795-1821) who, as a Romantic, was one of the first to be subjected to the criticism of turning to things wholly irrelevant to contemporary society.[1] The last in line is the so-called founder of modern fantasy, J.R.R. Tolkien (1892-1973). The natural link between these two seems to be William Morris (1834-1896) as his works were heavily influenced by Keats and who, in turn, left a lasting impression on Tolkien. The allegation is self-professed by both the later authors. In a letter to Cowden Clarke, Morris speaks of "Keats for whom I have such a boundless admiration, and whom I venture to call one of my masters" (Colvin). Tolkien writes from the front in 1914 to Edith Bratt: "I am trying to turn one of the stories ... into a short story somewhat on the lines of Morris' romances with chunks of poetry in between" (L 7). Besides common criticism of their works, their literary output shows similar motifs, moods, and a richness of mythological backdrop.

Escapism

To start with a tangible definition of escapism, we take a look at what *Wikipedia* has to say on the subject: "Escapism is mental diversion by means of entertainment or recreation, as an 'escape' from the perceived unpleasant or banal aspects of daily life." The first part of the definition includes the neutral

---

1 Though his alleged "death through criticism" (Byron comments on Keats's death in *Don Juan*: "Strange that the mind, that very fiery particle, / Should let itself be snuffed out by an article," [Colvin]) is certainly exaggerated.

facts; the second part then goes on to the psychological aspect of the word: "It can also be used as a term to define the actions people take to try to help relieve persisting feelings of depression or general sadness."[2]

In social and literary criticism the term has mostly been used with its negative connotation, as a flight from what is real – on the premise that not living in total scientific clarity all the time is something dangerous. Romantics as well as authors of modern fantasy have thus been criticised for descending into the irrational, mysticism and nostalgia. Michael Moorcock even accuses J.R.R. Tolkien of cowardice in the face of reality as he does not address the social grievances of his time directly (cf. Moorcock). Which poses the question: Does more explicitness really lead to better literature?

Though fantasy today has found its way into the academic circle – you are holding a prime example in your hand – there still seems to be some topicality in calling for a defence of escapist literature and its descendants: In January 2010, the Dungeons & Dragons role-playing game was banned in Wisconsin prisons because it allegedly "leads to gang behaviour and fantasies about escape" (Schwartz), i.e. lets inmates actually escape their dreary everyday life through the imagination. Prof. Ilya Somin, an associate professor of law, aptly replies: "Should prisons ban 'The Count of Monte Cristo' on the grounds that it might encourage escape attempts?" (ibid.)[3]. The topical discussion definitely reminds us of Tolkien's take on escapism and prisons:

> Why should a man be scorned, if, finding himself in prison he tries to get out and home? Or if, when he cannot do so, he thinks and talks about other topics than jailers and prison-walls? ... [C]ritics ... are confusing, not always by sincere error, the Escape of the Prisoner with the Flight of the Deserter. (FS 148)

Our three authors sought different ways to escape what they perceived as a dreary reality. We here concentrate on their literary achievements, but they were all also quite accomplished artists (cf. e.g. Keats's drawing of the Sosibios vase, Tolkien's illustrations of *The Hobbit*, Morris's painting *Queen Guenevere*). Especially William Morris's artistic escape went much further than that, as we will see later. The disaffection with their times was foremost linked to a decline of society's values, an increasing industrialisation, scientific progress, and the ensuing consequences for nature and the countryside.

---

2 *Wikipedia* unfortunately does not cite any reference but the given definition is certainly a good starting point for the following discussion.
3 I would like to thank Timothy Miller for pointing this discussion out to me.

Disenchanted States

In a time when the wonders of nature were disenchanted by men of science, Keats turned the other way. He was an apprentice doctor till 1814 but never finished his medical studies. Instead, with the help of his patron Leigh Hunt, he turned to the study of literature. Hunt also helped him to publish his first collection of poetry (called *Poems*) in 1817. He was not only criticised as an escapist, but was also branded a "Cockney poet" for his simple diction and colloquialisms (cf. Rossetti 84).

For Keats, two main reasons why he was more than disenchanted with his age can be identified. The end of his short life was plagued by tuberculosis, an illness that had already claimed the lives of his mother and brother Tom. His declining health often led to melancholy fits and a deep desire, especially during the last months that he spent in Rome, to escape to another world: "[W]hen misfortunes are so real we are glad enough to escape them, and the thought of them" (Keats, *To George and Georgiana*) that desire becomes more than legitimate.

The other factor creating a need for Keats to turn to the fantastic was the progression of the Industrial Revolution. As a Londoner, he would have experienced the explosion of the city's population first hand, as well as the pollution associated with the masses and the growing number of factories. In 1818 he thus moved to Hampstead, then considered a "country retreat away from the bustle and smoke of London, with fresh air and water" (Camden Council).

As an avid traveller, first out of interest and then mainly for health reasons, Keats could contrast the great outdoors and the city. On a visit to the Lake District, where he met William Wordsworth, he found a new tendency that made him fear for the wholesomeness of the countryside not only in terms of environmental pollution:

> The disfigurement I mean is the miasma of London. I do suppose it contaminated with bucks and soldiers, and women of fashion- and hat-band ignorance. The border inhabitants are quite out of keeping with the romance about them, from a continual intercourse with London rank and fashion. (Keats, *To Michael Straight*)

Keats here witnesses a loss of traditional country values that are supplanted by the fashions from the big city.

William Morris's qualms with his times were also linked to a still growing Industrialisation and the values that were disseminated at the time. Morris sees everything being tainted by a market value (cf. Tompson 18) that does not necessarily correspond with his aesthetic and intellectual evaluation of the same object. He mourned the indiscriminate demolition of old buildings to make room for modern housing: "I was born in Walthamstow ... a suburban village on the edge of Epping Forest, and once a pleasant place enough, but now terribly cocknified and choked up by the jerry-builder" (ibid. 2). The sentiment is very similarly expressed by Carpenter writing about Tolkien's loss of the countryside of his childhood: "[Birmingham's views] of almost unbroken rooftops with the factory chimneys beyond. The green countryside was just visible in the distance, but it now belonged to a remote past that could not be regained" (Carpenter, *Biography* 52).

Morris furthermore condemned the blind belief in progress as preached by the dialectics, for instance. The dialectics thought that through a communication of opposites a consensus could be reached that necessarily led to something better. This ongoing progress was to ultimately result in perfection (cf. Bidlo 59). This ideal process does not only jar with Morris's view of the world: Bidlo ascertains the introduction of a habitual disaffection with one's present and questions the embrace of the future as the only thing worth striving for while forgetting the present (cf. ibid. 60f).

Of Tolkien we know that he was deeply rooted in the countryside around Sarehole Mill, where he spent formative years of his childhood. He developed a strong relationship with his natural surroundings: "There was a willow hanging over the mill-pool and I learned to climb it ... One day they cut it down. They didn't do anything with it: The log just lay there. I never forgot that" (Carpenter, *Biography* 39). Tolkien also lamented the urbanisation of the place when he returned to it later in life and cultivated a deep-rooted suspicion of modern technology, especially of cars and airplanes. He likened his surroundings to corresponding settings from his own mythology: "... the spirit of 'Isengard', if not of Mordor, is of course always cropping up. The present design of destroying Oxford in order to accommodate motor-cars is a case" (L 235). The "aeroplane of war ... is the real villain ... My sentiments are more or less those that Frodo would have had if he discovered some Hobbits learning to ride Nazgûl-birds, 'for the liberation of the Shire'" (ibid. 115).

Though all three were writers accused of escapist tendencies, they still shared a common belief in art as something that should convey morals – but not moralise. Maybe the subtler approach, without the openly didactic message found in many of their respective contemporaries, led to this misconception. Patrick Curry, for example, states about Middle-earth that it is a place of escape, but with a certain twist: "[H]ere, at least, a reader may take refuge from a world where ... humanity has swollen to become everything, and the measure of everything" (Curry 61). The sub-creation is thus distinctly different from the real world – and it has been developed intentionally so in order to show some sort of an alternative.

Julian Eilmann, in his article *The Minstrel's War: Song and Power in J.R.R. Tolkien's Middle-earth*[4], demonstrates the case in Tolkien's poems very well. The creators of "words of power", i.e. enchanters, such as Lúthien singing in front of Morgoth or Morgoth himself changing Ilúvatar's theme during the creation, prove their worth by either adhering to a certain code of conduct or not. They are shown as bearing a responsibility to those who listen to their words, just as any sub-creator has a responsibility to his audience/readers (cf. Eilmann 81ff).

Keats sees a true poet charged with a greater mission as well, as "... being a great Poet – or one of those beings who are privileged to wear out their Lives in the pursuit of Honor" (Keats, *To Benjamin Haydon*), though he does not fancy himself as belonging to that group.

In a lecture on *The English Pre-Raphaelites*, Morris aptly summarises our authors' outlook on life and art:

> When an artist has really a very keen sense of beauty, I venture to think that he can not literally represent an event that takes place in modern life. He must add something or other to qualify or soften the ugliness and sordidness of the surroundings of life in our generation. That is not only the case with pictures ... it is the case also in literature. (Thompson 56)

The dissatisfaction with their times led Keats, as a representative of the late Romantic movement, to turn towards formerly unsuitable topics, such as the fantastic or the gothic and give his stories grand mythological or medieval backdrops. Morris wrote five prose romances[5] in medieval style late in life that could be classed amongst the first fantasy novels. Tolkien was not only declared the founder of modern fantasy, he also gave us a theoretical and still topical background on fantasy (and escapism) in his 1937 lecture *On Fairy-Stories*.[6] In their works, they all offer alternative views of the world, show a new perspective and mirror reality in an unexpected way instead of openly criticising the grievances of their times through more realistic approaches, as e.g. practised by Dickens during Morris's lifetime.

---

4   Published in German: Der Sängerkrieg: Gesang und Gewalt in J.R.R. Tolkiens Mittelerde
5   *The Story of the Glittering Plain* (1891), *The Wood Beyond the World* (1894), *The Water of the Wondrous Isles* (1895), *The Well at the World's End* (1896), and *The Sundering Flood* (1897) (I purposely exclude the two pseudo-histories, *The House of the Wolflings* [1888] and *The Roots of the Mountains* [1889], as they are not set in wholly fictional storyscapes).
6   Published in 1947.

Changing "Escapist" Approaches

We thus see different and changing forms of escapist literature, rooted in the time it was written in, but also linked to the predilection of the particular author. The poets of the early Romantic Movement still wanted to change reality through their art. They had seen that it was actually possible to influence politics through mere scribbling, as the French Revolution was supported and propagated by many Romantic writers in England. They were called "English Jacobins" and included, for instance, Samuel Taylor Coleridge, William Hazlitt, and Charles Lamb (cf. Ruston 88).

In another example for a close connection between Romantic literature and its time, Byron was implicated in a tribunal for treason of the leaders of a Nottinghamshire uprising in 1817. The most charismatic of the leaders, Jeremiah Brandreth, was compared to one of Byron's heroes by the defence:

> I have ... found him so wonderfully depicted by a noble poet of our time, and one of the greatest geniuses of any age that I shall take the liberty of now reading that prophetic description. It will perfectly bring before you his character, and even his appearance, the commanding qualities of his powerful but uncultivated mind, and the nature of his influence over those that he seduced to outrage.
>
> [The defender] proceeded to quote to the court some thirty lines of *The Corsair*.
>
> (Butler 319)

The Romantics' contribution definitely had an impact on public opinion. Keats must already be counted amongst those Romantics who were disillusioned by the tyrannical regime that followed in the wake of the French Revolution and ongoing social woes of his own country (cf. Ruston 95). Yet he still thought that his writing could make a difference. In a letter to his patron in 1817, Keats wrote: "These last two day[s] however I have felt more confident – I have asked myself so often why I should be a Poet more than other Men, – seeing how great a thing it is, – how great things are to be gained by it" (Keats, *To Leigh Hunt*). The Romantics' "escape" into a fantastic world can thus be seen as a rebellion against the *Zeitgeist* with the definite intention to change reality.

William Morris started out as a post-Romantic idealist. He grew up in Walthamstow, in prosperous middle-class society, playing fairy tales and knight in a toy suit of armour (cf. Thompson 3f). His first works (what Thompson calls his "first revolution") thus consisted of poetry that built worlds within worlds, whose values were distinct from a hated modern civilization (cf. ibid. 76). As

Morris became older and wiser, realisation hit that poetry alone would not change reality. He decided to become a Socialist and tried to change workers' fate through his commitment to the Socialist cause (for example in the Democratic Federation or later in the Socialist League). He wrote pamphlets, which he printed in his own publishing house Kelmscott Press, and held lectures for those organisations (cf. ibid. 276ff). Apart from that, he also founded the Society for the Protection of Ancient Buildings in 1877 to stop the indiscriminate demolition of historic buildings (cf. ibid. 228), thus actively working against a loss of architectural tradition. Morris' artistic examination of his time went well beyond the scope of literature. He was an active member of the Pre-Raphaelite Brotherhood and the Exhibition Society, both groups of artisans who rebelled against artistic conventions of their times and who propagated beauty and aesthetics in all aspects of life (cf. ibid. 557). He founded his own company (Morris & Co.) in order to realise the designs of furniture, tapestries, cloth, tiles, stained-glass windows etc. that he and his partners (amongst them Edward Burne-Jones, Dante Gabriel Rossetti, Ford Madox Brown, and Philip Webb) thought up (cf. Clutton-Brock 66). He thus facilitated an escape from drab modern times through offering aesthetically pleasing products made by artisans instead of labourers exploited by mass production for the whole domestic sphere – admittedly only affordable by the well-to-do, though. Late in life, he wrote his five prose romances in medieval style which tend to a rather nostalgic and sentimental look on a past heroic age. His artistry thus developed from an idealistic Romantic revolutionary, via a pragmatic entrepreneur and theoretician, to a misty-eyed venerator of a forlorn golden age – the last stage of which is particularly open to criticism of escapist tendencies.

J.R.R. Tolkien wrote fantasy without any claim that he wanted to change the world through his writing. Yet his "message" to, for example, respect nature and be suspicious of progress at all costs still reached many people, such as the environmental movement of the 1960s and 1970s in the US. A Greenpeace activist, returning from a protest at the nuclear test site on the Mururoa Atoll, records some striking parallels:

> I had been reading 'The Lord of the Rings'. I could not avoid thinking of parallels between our own little fellowship and the long journey of the Hobbits into the volcano-haunted land of Mordor, home of the Dark Lord who lived in his fortress surrounded by fierce armies, his Evil Eye scanning, scanning, scanning for intruders. (Cf. Kehr 91)

Though this message is not conveyed in a moralising tale, one can see a definite trend in *The Lord of the Rings*, away from anything magical, from fantasy towards reality (e.g. with the departure of the Istari and Elves) and an assignment for the reader (as especially reflected in the Hobbits as focal characters) to finish the story themselves, to continue the "good work" (cf. ibid. 20f). It is thus a tale with applicable story elements that can be transferred into the real world. Tolkien's famous words about allegory and applicability exactly support his argument:

> I cordially dislike allegory in all its manifestations, and have always done so since I grew old and wary enough to detect its presence ... I think that many confuse 'applicability' with 'allegory'; but the one resides in the freedom of the reader, the other in the purposed domination of the author.   (LotR I xviii)

Tolkien's fantastic heroes show a certain morale, embody certain ideals that can be applied to reality. His take on escapist literature was therefore always linked to a certain responsibility towards his own surroundings (cf. also Eilmann above).

In his essay *On Fairy-Stories* Tolkien gives us a theoretical backdrop to the escapist discussion by elaborating on his own concept of escape in fantastic stories. It is always linked with the terms consolation and recovery. The first is an "imaginative satisfaction of ancient desires" (FS 153) (ranging from basic hunger to immortality) as well as a "fleeting glimpse of Joy" (ibid.) (in the happy ending or eucatastrophe). This joy can lead to a "glimpse of the underlying reality of truth" (ibid. 155) that lets the reader recover an alternative or clearer view of the world (cf. ibid. 146). According to Tolkien, fantasy stories help to regain that distance with which one can see the wonders of the world again. The escape into another world is thus no cowardly act but an active way to mirror reality.

Moods and Motifs

Apart from the biographical evidence that these three authors share when it comes to a dissatisfaction with their times, we see many parallels in their works, especially when it comes to mood and motif. All these similarities are particularly linked to the so-called "Romantic escape". We here take a look at the three most striking, which I subsume under the categories "Golden Age / Fall from Grace", "Industry vs. Nature", and "Faërie".

Looking back at a Golden Age when everything was better than it is now was severely criticised as anti-progressive and nostalgia for nostalgia's sake, i.e. without any significance for the present or the future.[7] This yearning for the

---

7   Bob Dixon, for example, observes: "The effect of this kind of literature, as with tract literature, is to divert people from the here and now and persuade them that it's not possible to do anything about the problems of the world" (Dixon 149).

past could be conveyed through different forms. We see a look at one's own time through the eyes of an idealised heroic age, for example, in Keats's *On First Looking into Chapman's Homer*:

> Much have I travell'd in the realms of gold,
> And many goodly states and kingdoms seen;
> (Keats, *Homer* 602)

Morris expresses a yearning for past (and lost) skills in *The Sundering Flood*: "[A sword] of beauteous and wondrous fashion, such as no smith may work now" (72). Both techniques of remembering a lost time can be found in Tolkien as well. Legolas exclaims: "Alas for us all! And for all that walk the world in these after-days" (LotR I 497), reflecting on the Golden Ages we can read about in the *Ainulindalë* – when the Gods still walked Middle-earth – or even the *Quenta Silmarillion* – when the Noldor were engaged in high heroics and daring feats. The first of these tales is also concerned with the Fall from Grace; a direct descent into darker days through the actions of the rogue Vala Melkor. That the skills of the past are lost is lamented, for example, by Gimli in *The Fellowship of the Ring* when he sings *Durin's Song* in Moria:

> There hammer on the anvil smote,
> There chisel clove, and graver wrote;
> There forged was blade, and bound was hilt;
> The delver mined, the mason built.
> There beryl, pearl, and opal pale,
> And metal wrought like fishes' mail,
> Buckler and corset, axe and sword
> And shining spears were laid in hoard.
>
> Unwearied then were Durin's folk;
> Beneath the mountains music woke:
> The harpers harped, the minstrels sang,
> And at the gates the trumpets rang.
>
> The world is grey, the mountains old,
> The forge's fire is ashen-cold;
> No harp is wrung, no hammer falls:
> The darkness dwells in Durin's halls... (LotR I 415f)

This nostalgic view of the past should not be seen wholly critically, though. People have an innate need for tradition, a longing to know their roots in order to understand their present, a starting point to develop a meaningful future (cf. Bidlo 86). Apart from that, a rich historical or mythical backdrop is also a literary device to give a poem or a story an inherent depth.

A second key motif that can be found in all three author's writings can be termed "Industry vs. Nature". It also encompasses the tensions between the city vs. the countryside, technology and rationality vs. tradition and mysticism. The Romantics rebelled against the Enlightenment that started to disseminate around the late 17th century. It tried to rationally explain all the wonders of nature, thus stripping it of its mystical and mythological roots. The progressing scientific development certainly led to improvements in many sectors, but also entailed environmental pollution, a loss of quality of life for many labourers, and a loss of tradition. Everything that seemed wondrous and magical suddenly had a rational explanation (cf. Ruston 23ff).

Throughout Keats's *Ode to a Nightingale*, we find a landscape beset with nature. The opening stanza differs in perspective, though. The narrator gives his introduction from a grey and desolate place – most certainly associated with age, but also equivalent to a dreary place bereft of all magic:

> Fade far away, dissolve, and quite forget
> What thou among the leaves hast never known,
> The weariness, the fever, and the fret
> Here, where men sit and hear each other groan;
> Where palsy shakes a few, sad, last gray hairs,
> Where youth grows pale, and spectre-thin, and dies;
> Where but to think is to be full of sorrow
> And leaden-eyed despairs;
> Where Beauty cannot keep her lustrous eyes,
> Or new Love pine at them beyond to-morrow.
> (Keats, *Nightingale* 605)

These dreary places can also be formed by a dark companion of industrialisation: war. It brings forth many inventions that are sold as progress, but are then used for something dreadful, as in the Land of the Tower in Morris's *The Well at the World's End*, for example:

> [It is] the lonesomest of deserts. I deem indeed that it was once one of the fairest of lands, with castles and cots and homesteads all about, and fair people no few, busy with many matters amongst them ... [T]here are many tales about of the wars and miseries that turned this land into a desert. (Morris, *Well* 187)

In Tolkien's *The Lord of the Rings*, we find the embodiment of technological progress without any care for its negative impacts in the character of Saruman.[8]

---

[8] Sauron is another candidate, of course, but Saruman, who is actually interacting with the protagonists, presents the apter choicer. The very roots of his name (Mercian *saru = device, design, contrivance, art) certainly point in that direction (cf. Shippey 153).

The former leader of the Istari, originally sent out to care for Middle-earth and its inhabitants, falls from grace through his fascination with power and progress. He uses his inventions mainly to wage war on his neighbours and defiles his home in Isengard as well as the bordering Fangorn forest. He loses all respect for the creation around him:

> [Saruman] has a mind of metal and wheels; and he does not care for growing things, except as far as they serve him for the moment ... There is always smoke rising from Isengard these days.
> (LotR II 84f)

Treebeard curses him for actually killing his friends (cf. ibid. 85) which goes far beyond an accusation for environmental pollution. Tolkien here follows the Romantic tradition of seeing nature as something beyond the merely physical and rational. He does not only facilitate a communication with certain animals[9] or externalise nature's spirit in humanoid races such as the Elves but ensouls even the trees.

The character of Saruman furthermore incorporates an allusion to "real world" science, viz. Newton's refraction of light with a prism. The wizard, as the leader of his clan, is initially called Saruman the White. When Mithrandir returns to Middle-earth as Gandalf the White and the new leader of the Istari, the treacherous Saruman of Many Colours emerges: "For I am Saruman the Wise, Saruman Ring-Maker, Saruman of Many Colours! ... and the white light can be broken" (LotR I 339). Incidentally, the negative connotation of Newton's refraction of light is also taken up by Keats in his poem *Lamia*:

> Philosophy will clip an Angel's wings,
> Conquer all mysteries by rule and line,
> Empty the haunted air, and gnomed mine–
> Unweave a rainbow, as it erewhile made   (Keats, *Lamia*)

The philosopher Apollonius here unravels the secret of the beautiful Lamia, who tricks Lycius into marriage with fairy glimmers with which she disguises her real appearance (a serpent) and creates an illusion of a palace filled with treasure.[10] Though Lamia is, of course, a dangerous creature, a melancholy is conveyed by the poem that laments the denouement of the bride and the loss of all her hopes of happiness. The fairy magic is dispersed by the powers

---

9   E.g. Huan the great wolfhound in *The Silmarillion* (cf. S 208).
10 A haunting music, sole perhaps and lone / Supportress of the faery-roof, made moan (Keats, *Lamia*).

of observation of the rational mind; the fascination of the rainbow has been broken by a banal explanation.

This brings us to the third great similarity of motif (and mood) in the three authors' works: they all engage in travels to "Faërie". Some of their heroes encounter a Faërie-woman and come away changed:

> I met a lady in the meads,
> Full beautiful — a faery's child,
> Her hair was long, her foot was light,
> And her eyes were wild ...
>
> She took me to her elfin grot,
> And there she wept, and sigh'd fill sore,
> And there I shut her wild wild eyes
> With kisses four ...
>
> I saw pale kings and princes too,
> Pale warriors, death-pale were they all;
> They cried — 'La Belle Dame sans Merci
> Hath thee in thrall!' (Keats, *Dame* 613f)

> And now once more the thought came on him, that the Maid was one of the fays, or of some race even mightier; and it came on him now not as erst, with half fear and whole desire, but with a bitter oppression of dread, of loss and misery; so that he began to fear that she had but won his love to leave him and forget him for a new-comer, after the wont of fay-women, as old tales tell.
> (Morris, *Wood* 95)

> [Galadriel was] grave and beautiful ... clad fully in white; and the hair of the Lady was of deep gold ... no sign of age was upon [her], unless it were in the depths of [her] eyes. (LotR I 465)

> Few escape her nets, they say. (LotR II 30)

In all authors' works, we get a glimpse of Faërie as a beautiful but perilous realm peopled with strong elfin women. They are not dangerous because they are inherently evil, but because their enchantment and beauty wreaks havoc with mere mortals who are just not fit to travel through Faërie. It is a popular motif that can be found in medieval romances such as the one about Thomas

Erceldoune or Ogier le Danois and the ballads and folktales derived from the romances (e.g. *Thomas the Rhymer*) (cf. Acland).

Another phenomenon any mortal in Faërie experiences is a displacement in time. When the Fellowship leaves Lothlórien, they realise that what they thought was a months-long stay was actually only four weeks (cf. LotR III 462). It is said that the power of Galadriel's ring has halted or slowed time within the borders of Lórien. Other travellers in Faërie like, for example, Ogier le Danois think they only spend 20 years away from home to find on their return that 200 years have passed (cf. Acland note 14).

Taking a closer look at the otherworldly experience of Faërie and the mood that is created, we find two very similar scenes in Keats's *The Song of the Indian Maid* and Tolkien's *The Hobbit*:

> And as I sat, over the light blue hills
> There came a noise of revellers: the rills
> Into the wide stream came of purple hue —
> 'Twas Bacchus and his crew!
> The earnest trumpet spake, and silver thrills
> From kissing cymbals made a merry din —
> 'Twas Bacchus and his kin!
> Like to a moving vintage down they came,
> Crown'd with green leaves, and faces all on flame;
> All madly dancing through the pleasant valley,
> To scare thee, Melancholy! (Keats, *Indian Maid* 603)

> The feast that they now saw was greater and more magnificent than before; and at the head of a long line of feasters sat a woodland king with a crown of leaves upon his golden hair ... The elvish folk were passing bowls from hand to hand and across the fires, and some were harping and many were singing. Their gloaming hair was twined with flowers; green and white gems glinted on their collars and their belts; and their faces and their songs were filled with mirth. (H 150)

Though revelling Baccantae are surely of another calibre than Thranduil and his elves feasting in the woods, the main issue – that of the onlooker left behind with a sense of melancholy wonder and loss as the pervading mood – merits a comparison. Experiences in Faërie generally tend to be transient, difficult to grasp, like a will o'the wisp. All three authors thus take recourse on popular folklore conceptions of Faërie that became increasingly popular during the Romantic Movement (cf. Ruston 61).

Conclusion: Escapism Revisited

s early as 1814, E.T.A. Hoffmann was convinced that fantastic literature does indeed have bearings on everyday life:

> Favourable reader, while you are in the faery region of glorious wonders, where both rapture and horror may be evoked; where the goddess of earnestness herself will waft her veil aside and show her countenance ... while you are in this region which the spirit lays open to us in dreams, make an effort to recognize the well-known forms which hover around you in fitful brightness even in ordinary life. You will then find that this glorious kingdom lies much closer at hand than you ever supposed.
>
> (Hoffmann 18)

After looking into the works and lives of Keats, Morris, and Tolkien, it is difficult to see their sub-creations merely as a way to escape a dreary reality. There is another function in the escape into a fantastic world different from what we perceive as real, and that is the intensification of the real through a mythological backdrop. The new perspective makes it possible to visualise "things underneath the surface", to externalise thoughts and images that could otherwise only be conveyed through dreams, to mirror reality in an unrealistic fashion.

W. Courthope, one of Keats's critics who did not come to any favourable conclusion about the poet's works sees the true power of poetry and its relevance to posterity in the direct relation that it bears to social and political activities of its period (cf. Colvin). Keats wrote poems during the Romantic period when literature was still a lot more intertwined with society. Morris certainly cared for his times and proved his concern by becoming a Socialist and using his artistic genius to influence almost all spheres of life. Tolkien wrote applicable fiction that was, for example, termed the "epic of the Green Movement" (Flieger 147) by a BBC commentator. Their works, though seemingly far removed from their respective realities, mirror their attitude to their times. For each individual, and clustered together as representatives of their period, I hope to have shown that our three authors' re-awakening of the imagination to nature and romance[11] was in fact a direct response to their times.

For "[w]e need ... to clean our windows; so that the things seen clearly may be freed from the drab blur of triteness or familiarity" (FS 146).

---

11 On a re-enchantment of the world, as Kehr puts it in his work on nature and ecology in *The Lord of the Rings*.

Bibliography

Acland, Abigail. "Thomas Rhymer". *Tam Lin Balladry*, 1997
http://tam-lin.org/texts/Thomas.html (08-16-2010)

Bidlo, Oliver. *Sehnsucht nach Mittelerde?* Norderstedt: Books on Demand, 2003

Butler, Marilyn. "The Orientalism of Byron's Giaour". *Three Oriental Tales*.
Ed. Alan Richardson. Boston: Houghton Mifflin, 2002

Camden Council. "Camden's History"
http://www.camden.gov.uk/ccm/content/leisure/local-history/camdens-history.en
(05-04-2010)

Carpenter, Humphrey. *J.R.R.Tolkien: A Biography*. London: HarperCollins, 2002

---. Ed. *The Letters of J.R.R. Tolkien*. London: HarperCollins, 1995

Clutton-Brock, Arthur. *William Morris*. New York: Parkstone, 2007

Colvin, Sidney. *John Keats: His Life and Poetry, His Friends, Critics and After-Fame*, 1917
http://englishhistory.net/keats/colvinkeats.html (04-30-2010)

Curry, Patrick. *Defending Middle-earth. Tolkien: Myth and Modernity*. London: HarperCollins, 1998

Dixon, Bob. *Catching Them Young*. Vol. 2: *Political Ideas in Children's Fiction*. London: Pluto, 1978

Eilmann, Julian. "Der Sängerkrieg: Gesang und Gewalt in J.R.R. Tolkiens Mittelerde". *Hither Shore* 6 (2010): 70-84

Flieger, Verlyn. "Taking the Part of Trees. Eco-Conflict in Middle-Earth". *J.R.R. Tolkien and His Literary Resonances. Views of Middle-earth*. Eds. George Clark & Daniel Timmons. Westport: Greenwood Press, 2000

Hoffmann, E.T.A. "The Golden Flower Pot". *The Best Tales of Hoffmann*. Translated by Thomas Carlyle. Mineolar, NY: Dover, 1967, 1-70

Keats, John. 'La Belle Dame Sans Merci'. *The New Oxford Book of English Verse*. Ed. Helen Gardner. Oxford: Oxford UP, 1997, 613-614

---. 'Lamia'. *The Poetical Works of John Keats*. London: Macmillan, 1884
http://www.bartleby.com/126/37.html (08-27-2010)

---. 'Ode to a Nightingale'. *The New Oxford Book of English Verse*. Ed. Helen Gardner. Oxford: Oxford UP, 1997, 605-607

---. 'On First Looking Into Chapman's Homer'. *The New Oxford Book of English Verse*. Ed. Helen Gardner. Oxford: Oxford UP, 1997, 602

---. 'The Song of the Indian Maid'. *The New Oxford Book of English Verse*. Ed. Helen Gardner. Oxford: Oxford UP, 1997, 602-605

---. 'To Benjamin Robert Haydon, 10-11 May 1817'. *John Keats: Selected Letters*.
http://englishhistory.net/keats/letters.html (05-10-2010)

---. 'To George and Georgiana Keats, September 1819'. *John Keats: Selected Letters*.
http://englishhistory.net/keats/letters.html (05-04-2010)

---. 'To Leigh Hunt, 10 May 1817'. *John Keats: Selected Letters*.
http://englishhistory.net/keats/letters.html (05-25-2010)

---. 'To Michael Straight, 25-27 June 1818'. *John Keats: Selected Letters*.
http://englishhistory.net/keats/letters.html (05-10-2010)

Kehr, Eike. *Die wiederbezauberte Welt. Natur und Ökologie in Tolkiens "The Lord of the Rings"*. Schriftenreihe und Materialien der Phantastischen Bibliothek Wetzlar, Band 79. Wetzlar, 2003

Moorcock, Michael. "Epic Pooh". *Revolution SF* http://www.revolutionsf.com/article.php?id=953 (04-15-2010)

Morris, William. *The Sundering Flood*. Holicong: Wildside, 2001

---. *The Well at the World's End*. New York: Ballantine, 1970

---. *The Wood Beyond the World*. Holicong: Wildside, 2001

Rossetti, William Michael. *The Life of John Keats*. Adamant Media Corporation, 2005

Ruston, Sharon. *Romanticism*. London: Continuum, 2007

Schwartz, John. "Dungeons & Dragons Prison Ban Upheld". *New York Times* http://www.nytimes.com/2010/01/27/us/27dungeons.html (04-15-2010)

Shippey, Tom A. *The Road to Middle-earth*. London: HarperCollins, 1992

Thompson, E.A. *William Morris: Romantic to Revolutionary*. New York: Pantheon, 1976

Tolkien, J.R.R. "On Fairy-Stories". *The Monsters and the Critics and Other Essays*. Ed. Christopher Tolkien. London: HarperCollins, 1997, 109-161

---. *The Fellowship of the Ring. Being the First Part of The Lord of the Rings*. London: HarperCollins, 1999

---. *The Two Towers. Being the Second Part of The Lord of the Rings*. London: HarperCollins, 1999

---. *The Return of the King. Being the Third Part of The Lord of the Rings*. London: HarperCollins, 1999

---. *The Hobbit*. London: HarperCollins, 1990

---. *The Silmarillion*. Ed. Christopher Tolkien. London: HarperCollins, 1994

Wikipedia. "Escapism" http://en.wikipedia.org/wiki/Escapism (05-04-2010)

Celtic Influences and the Quest of National Identity

Doreen Triebel (Jena)

he period in which Tolkien created his literary œuvre was one of far reaching social and cultural changes that prompted a need for redefinition in various aspects of society and were, inter alia, reflected in contemporary art, music, architecture, theology, social structures and literature. In the latter field, modernist authors, such as Virginia Woolf, James Joyce, H.G. Wells and D.H. Lawrence experimented with notions of plot, innovative subjects and new narrative techniques in order to question the postulates of the previous époque and to explore the nature of humanity as well as the inner worlds of their characters. Like several of his contemporaries Tolkien was famously skeptical of industrial progress, materialism and what he called "slavery" to the "recognition of fact" (FS 55); but in contrast to most other writers of the same period, his creative gaze was not primarily directed towards the future or the present but towards an ancient Anglo-Celtic past.

He was, however, by no means the only post-medieval author to be considerably influenced by Celtic literature and traditions. A revived interest in folk tales, folklore, folk art and music, which went hand in hand with a heightened feeling of nationalism, was a substantial aspect of the Romantic Movement in the late 18th and 19th centuries and it continued to influence various fields far beyond that period. However, just like Tolkien, writers in the era of Romanticism were faced with a vast and sometimes rather confusing scholarly and literary treatment of the Celtic world, which is inextricably intertwined with notions of national identity.

The Meaning of 'Celtic'

ne of the most controversial issues has certainly been the definition of the term 'Celtic' as such, i.e. the level of inclusiveness or exclusiveness of the ethnic category. Since the 19th century it has become commonplace to regard the Celtic and the Anglo-Saxon histories and cultures as quite distinct from one another. In fact English, meaning Anglo-Saxon, nationalism was to a large degree based on the supposedly binary opposition with the Celts. However, that has not always been the case. In fact, as Colin Kidd points out,

> cultural historians have revealed the origins of the modern duality of Celt and Saxon: the twin influences of romanticism and racialism forged the modern myth of the Celt, and contributed to the

> emergence of related phenomena such as the ideology of pan-Celtic nationalism. The opposition of the pragmatic, freedom-loving Teuton and the mystical, sentimental but improvident Celt was not a feature of early modern ethnic stereotyping. This romantic conception of the Celt took shape gradually, beginning with the Ossianic vogue of the late eighteenth century, and culminated in the vision of the high-minded Celt peddled by Matthew Arnold. In the interim the romantic Celt had been appropriated by Teutonic racialists as the hapless antithesis of the vigorous and prosperous Saxon. (Kidd, *Identities* 185)

Tolkien refers to that idea and the stereotypes that go along with it in his 1955 lecture *English and Welsh*, where he concludes:

> In [the modern myth] Celts and Teutons are primeval and immutable creatures... fixed not only in shape but in innate and mutual hostility, and endowed even in the mists of antiquity, as ever since, with the peculiarities of mind and temper which can be still observed in the Irish or the Welsh on the one hand and the English on the other: the wild incalculable poetic Celt, full of vague and misty imaginations and the Saxon, solid and practical when not under the influence of beer. Unlike most myths this myth seems to have no value at all. (EW 171f)

However, that view was a decidedly modern one. Up to and including the 18th century the national identities of the different countries that we commonly refer to as Celtic today were dominated by ongoing patriotic debates concerning "inconsistencies between different national origin myths, questions of imperial suzerainty and regnal autonomy within the British Isles and matters of national honour" (Kidd, *Identities* 186, cf. Trevor-Roper and Leersoon). Moreover, scholars did not clearly distinguish between Celts and Germans until Thomas Percy published his edited version of Paul-Henri Mallet's *Northern Antiquities* in 1770 and even then there were still some inconsistencies in the construction of a pre-romantic Celtic identity and numerous instances of confusion (cf. Kidd, *Past* 187).

On the one hand the peoples we refer to as Celtic today were equated with the Gauls in the early modern period and on the other hand Celt was, together with Scyth, used as an umbrella term for many different ethnic groups, which evoked the idea that most tribes in Western Europe originated from them and caused some ethnological conflations with the equally wide and vague concept of the Scythes (cf. ibid. 189, Johnson and Stillingfleet 38). Research into the works of classical geographers and historians as well as medieval chroniclers further complicated modern ethnic classifications and, as Kidd points out, the term Celt did not acquire its present meaning[1] before the late 20th century when the category's boundaries became less inclusive as well as less vague.

The Celts possessed a rich mythology, which on the British Isles preceded classical, Anglo-Saxon or Norman influences and was driven close to extinction by the different invaders. Nonetheless, Celtic culture, languages and stories survived and became an important influence on later literary époques, culminating in a revived interest in Celticism during the Romantic age and at the turn of the 20th century. Incorporating the almost forgotten folk ballads into the literary creations of these periods was a means of preserving an ancient heritage but there was more to the appeal of the Celtic folk tale tradition than just artistic reasons or cultural-historical interests. Particularly Romantic authors, who deliberately drew on the old Celtic tales that date back to a Britain before the Roman Conquest and less from the more recent classical tradition or literary fairy tales, also made an ideological statement directed against the Roman invaders (cf. Gallant 4).

The fascination for a pre-Christian Briton society during the Romantic era coincided with an increasing nationalistic identification with the native peoples of the British Isles. As Christine Gallant points out, "Celtic Scholars of this earlier period held that the British Celtic culture predated the classical one of ancient Greece and Rome; and they fervently believed that the Celtic culture was superior to it too" (ibid. 10, cf. Doyle 22-25). This predilection for the ancient history and culture of the Celts also went hand in hand with a sympathy for the English colonies on the Celtic fringes and, as Gallant adds, "it pointed to an anti-monarchism" (Gallant 10). Celticism was used as a tool in the ideological construction of Britain. For the English, turning to a time before Roman, Anglo-Saxon or Norman invaders left their marks on the British Isles was a form of nostalgic patriotism. It was even more so for the descendants of the Celts for whom a remembrance of their rich heritage was a means of keeping up their self-worth as a people while they were increasingly pushed towards the north-western fringes of Europe and systematically devalued, even dehumanised as the primitive Other[2] by arriving colonizers.

---

1   Today Celtic usually refers to the cultures and languages of Ireland, Scotland, Wales, Cornwall, the Isle of Man and Brittany, which have been recognized as Celtic nations or territories by the Celtic League, an organization concerned with common interests of the people in these areas ("The Celtic League," 15-01-2010: http://www.celticleague.net/).
2   As Murrey Pittcock (20-29) points out, the Scots had contunially been depicted as violent and sexually disordered savages, the Irish as brainless and primitive and the Welsh as humourusly stupid liars or thieves.

Romantic Authors and Celticism

One of the first literary works of European Romanticism to incorporate Celtic themes was also one of the most disputed ones. Between 1760 and 1763 the Scottish poet James Macpherson published what he claimed to be translations of an originally Scottish Gaelic cycle of poems written by a 3rd century bard named Ossian, son of Fingal, and preserved mostly in the oral tradition. Despite immediate debates surrounding the authenticity of the texts, they generated considerable excitement, quickly gained international popularity and inspired numerous European writers, such as Blake, Coleridge, Wordsworth, Byron, Scott, Cesarotti, Herder and Goethe. Modern literary criticism has tended to marginalize Macpherson and to play down the importance of his work for the Romantic Movement[3], although, as Jerome MacGann has emphasised, "*Ossian's* influence on the late 18th century eclipsed all others" (McGann 33).

Despite criticism from various quarters, the most eminent of which was Dr. Samuel Johnson[4], Macpherson insisted on the existence of ancient sources on which his texts are based, although he never presented them to the public. Yet, not until almost two centuries after their publication has a scholar undertaken a largely successful attempt to rehabilitate Macpherson's work. In *The Gaelic Sources of Macpherson's "Ossian"* (1952) Derick Thomson, one of few remaining native Scots Gaelic speakers, provided an overview of the sources available at the time and identified the oral material that Macpherson used in the construction of the poems. Thus, the author cannot without controversies be accused of having attempted to hoax the literary public but it has become quite clear that his Ossianic poems are no mere translation of ancient texts. What he did is take up themes and concepts from Gaelic tales and creatively engage with the material, which he subsequently weaved into new literary creations. He adapted and re-appropriated the material and reconstructed it to fit the Zeitgeist of the Romantic present he was writing in.

In doing so he on the one hand satisfied British needs for a national literary tradition, which was partly comparable but significantly distinct from classical poetry (Maclachlan 235), and on the other hand he provided an important source for contemporary notions of the Celtic. In fact, Macpherson's adaptation of the Celtic material to the Romantic era probably reveals more about the latter than it does about the ancient time that inspired him in this creative process.

Macpherson's works were published in a time of cultural and political change, breeding a profound uncertainty regarding national identity, especially on the

---

3   See Moore, Response for a comprehensive discussion of the critical response to Macpherson's Ossianic poems.
4   See Samuel Johnson's *A Journey to the Western Islands of Scotland* (1775).

British Isles. After centuries of English colonial ventures into its neighbouring countries, the Union of the (English and Scottish) Crowns under James I, the Personal Rule of Charles I, which brought England, Scotland and Ireland under the same monarchy, and a succession of interconnected conflicts culminating in the Wars of the Three Kingdoms in the mid 17th century, the United Kingdom, comprised of England, Wales and Scotland, was established in 1707 and extended to include Ireland in 1801.

Thus, when Macpherson started to undertake his investigations into the largely lost Scottish Gaelic poetry and to publish his works, the Acts of Union and the effects of English Imperialism on the Celtic fringe were still fresh in the national memory of his native country and his compatriots embraced the epic that allegedly proved the existence of an ancient Scottish literary tradition seemingly on a par with classical mythology (cf. Kidd, *Past* 220). Aware of the effects of commerce and Anglicization on the Highlands and still valuing their traditional ideals (cf. Porter 399), Macpherson turned his attention to Scotland's secluded areas, which were deemed to be largely unspoiled by any of these influences.

From there he set out to collect and preserve tales that were threatened to fall into oblivion. In reconstructing the culture and worldview of the ancient Celtic inhabitants he aimed to "purify and simplify the Scottish past, liberating the true national history from beneath a palimpsest of Irish cultural Imperialism and Romish priestcraft" (Kidd, *Past* 232), as Irish and Roman legends were available and presumably reliable sources of information about early Britain (cf. ibid. 231). Indeed, his alleged discovery had significant implications for questions concerning British nationalism. Like many other Romantic authors Macpherson idealized the Celtic periphery and particularly its rural regions for their physical and ideological distance from urban areas as well as the effects of the British Empire. However, as Tim Fulford points out,

> [Macpherson's poems] offered a sentimental admiration for a Gaelic past rather than an angry indictment of present English colonialism or an urgent advocacy of change... Yet, they laid the foundation for more radical writing, which brought their Romantic anti-colonialism into the context of present-day nationalist struggles. (Fulford 180)

What appealed to 18th-century readers was not just their importance for historiography and nationalism but the "extravagant nobility of the supposedly primitive warriors in the poems and the deep cast of melancholy thrown over their mighty speech and actions" (Maclachlan 836), because, as Maclachlan adds, "[h]ere seemed to be firm evidence of the natural moral superiority of a people unaffected by the sophistication of modern civilization" (ibid.). Inspired by Celtic art and culture Macpherson created an epic that reflected and fortified the spirit of the era with its wistful tone and its nostalgic portrayal of a mythic race of ancient Highlanders, which was governed by natural principles of intuition, feeling and heroism. In doing so he provided his contemporaries with a supposedly ancient embodiment of Romantic ideals.

Yet, although Macpherson attempted to connect the Ossianic epics primarily with his native country and to obscure their Irish roots (cf. Thomson 23f), his writings did not only fuel Scottish Romantic nationalism. In Ireland reports about Irish origins[5] of the epic and the conclusion that Macpherson had reinterpreted Irish literature and significant figures of Irish history and mythology as Scottish lead the first critics to refute his poems and their claims about Irish history rather than analyze them as serious pieces of literature (Mac Craith 92). Furthermore, many Irish writers and historians at the time were trying to counter the idea of a romantically primitive Irish culture, because this stereotype, which was still held by many people in Britain, was frequently used as a justification for English colonial politics in Ireland. In "Irish Re-Creations of the Gaelic Past: The Challenge of Macpherson's Ossian" O'Halloran thus points out,

> for... Irish Catholic historical tradition, the notion of an exclusively oral medium of communication undermined their portrayal of early Ireland as a sophisticated, aristocratic and, above all, literate society, and it had thus to be attacked as part of the British tendency to depict the Irish as barbaric.   (O'Halloran 77)

Only later has the value of the poems for Ireland and its Gaelic poetry been openly acknowledged and attempts been undertaken to reclaim Ossian's poems as Irish (cf. ibid. 78-84). The subsequent pervasion of late 18th century Irish historical[6] and literary[7] writing by the bardic tales of Ossian reflected the extent to which Macpherson's poetry had become part of Irish national identity in spite of the initial rejection (cf. ibid. 84-86). As O'Halloran further argues, examples like Charlotte Brooke's *Reliques of Irish Poetry* show how Irish literati started to use the ancient Celtic tales and their Romantic reconstructions to foster better understanding between Ireland and Britain and started to consider Macpherson's Celtic-based poetry as a potent weapon against a colonial stereotype, portraying the Irish as barbaric (cf. ibid. 87-89).

---

5   The tales on which his Ossianic poetry is based are indeed Irish and the heroes Fingal and Ossian have been revealed to be versions of Fionn Mac Cumhal and Oissín as they appear in the pre-Christian Irish oral tradition (cf. O'Halloran 74).
6   See e.g. Joseph Walker's *Historical Memoirs of the Irish Bards, Interspersed with Anecdotes of, and Occasional Observations on the Music of Ireland; Also, an Historical and Descriptive Account of the Musical Instruments of the Ancient Irish, and an Appendix Containing Several Biographical and Other Papers With Select Irish Melodies.*
7   See e.g. Charlotte Brooke's *Reliques of Irish Poetry.*

The Romantic reconstructions of a rural idyll, Celtic culture and the notion of the Celts as a mythic, spiritual and mournful people prone to gloomy broodings and sentimental melancholy wielded considerable influence over many contemporary writers, not only from the Celtic periphery but also from the national core, England, where these ideas had great impact on the concept of Romantic nationalism. Although William Wordsworth did not openly acknowledge his indebtedness to Macpherson's poetry, his works contain explicit references to Ossian, images and phrases that are evocative of the epic and very similar representations of nature, which is one of the most important motifs in his writings.[8] What is, however, more significant is that he was also heavily influenced by Celtic art, culture and most notably the landscape at large. Wordsworth traveled to Wales[9] and the deep impression that these visits made on him are reflected, for example, in *The Prelude* and most notably in the ascent of Snowdon in the final book. The narrator describes his experience of the sublime night landscape in which even the "least sensitive, see, hear, perceive, / And cannot choose but feel" (*The Prelude*, Book XIV, ll. 85-86). Although transcending time and space the "glorious faculty, / That higher minds bear with them as their own" (ibid. Book XIV, ll.89-90), i.e. the imagination or creative power, which he feels in that moment, is deliberately connected with the North Wales landscape.

Furthermore, the narrator's admiration for the Celts' and other peoples' will to freedom and independence, as demonstrated in an unflinching resistance to colonial oppression, goes so far that he praises William Wallace who led a resistance against the English during the Scottish Wars of Independence (cf. ibid. Book I, ll.214-220) and, when he finds himself in a Welsh village church, he even rejoices at the thought of the army of the British Empire being defeated in battle against the French Republic (cf. ibid.: Book X, ll.282-289). Wordsworth frequently used heroic figures incarnating his conception of liberty, thereby drawing on bardic and druidic tales, especially for his poems *To the Clouds*, *An Evening Walk,* and his series of *Ecclesiastical Sonnets* (cf. Watson 97). For Wordsworth Wales was an inspiring country and, as Watson adds:

> Above all, perhaps, it was different – Welsh, Celtic: North Wales was the land of the druids, priests of an ancient religion and culture; it was the land where the bards had defied the tyranny of the English conquest, and been put to death because they were the guardians of national identity and feeling.   (Cf. ibid. 101)

By emphasising the Celtic elements, most notably the landscape, Wordsworth attempted to promote his ideals of 'National Independence and Liberty', which,

---

8 For a more detailed discussion of Macpherson's influence on Wordsworth see: Moore, *Debt*.
9 For a deeper insight into his visits to Wales and their impact on his writing see: Watson.

comparable to Macpherson's works, necessarily implies criticism of English *colonial* policy.

John Keats was similarly inspired by things Celtic and he was notably in line with Tolkien in preferring older and more primitive folk-fairy lore over the literary fairy-tradition, which had a major influence on Shakespeare or Spenser in the Renaissance (Briggs, *Encyclopedia* 167 and Gallant 3). It is well-known that Keats was particularly inspired by Sir Walter Scott's oeuvre, particularly *The Minstrelsy of the Scottish Border*, which was not only rich in Celtic motifs and references but also provided background information, in the form of introductory essays, about the folk beliefs underlying the ancient Gaelic tales Scott used as source material. Similar to Wordsworth or Scott, Keats's fascination for the Celtic countries prompted him to undertake a walking tour through Northern England, Scotland and parts of Ireland, which had a lasting influence on his poetry. Although motifs taken from classical culture, which was by many still valued above the rites and beliefs of the native Britons, figure prominently in his poetry and were long regarded as his sole inspiration, Keats's works show a strong affinity for Britain's pre-Roman period (cf. Gallant 5).

The Celtic influences on his poetry become obvious, for instance, in his portrayal of the Titans in *Hyperion* and *The Fall of Hyperion: A Dream*[10], which is notably influenced by the theories of Edward Davies, a Welsh writer and Celtic antiquarian who established a connection between the Titans, the British Druids and ultimately the Celtic bards, while maintaining that their history did not go back to the classical world, as was commonly assumed, but that they were essentially British (cf. ibid. 30-33). The poem depicts the Titans', or if we follow that interpretation, the Celtic Druids' downfall and the coming into power of the Olympians, i.e. the Roman invaders of Britain and, as Christine Gallant emphasizes, "[i]t is permeated with contemporary Ossianism and its powerful nostalgia for the ancient times when the Celts prevailed on the British Isles" (ibid. 72).

Several of Keats's depictions of faeries, especially in his earlier poetry, might share some attributes with the often diminutive creatures we find in Shakespeare's or Spenser's works but at the same time they notably differ from these, thereby revealing Keats's indebtedness to the folk tale tradition, on which he, just like Tolkien, drew more and more as he matured in his writing. The fairies of folklore are often depicted as malignant or at least as having a double morality; on the one hand they can be alluring, exalted, sinister and dangerous but on the other hand they are in general not wholly evil or hostile towards men without any reason (cf. Briggs, *People* 151-161).

Although Keats's earlier works, e.g. *Calidore: A Fragment* or *Imitation of Spenser*, might offer a faint glimpse of this ancient concept of fairies, the crea-

---

10 In Book I, l. 135 of Hyperion, for example, Keats directly refers to Saturn's locks as "druid" and in Book II, ll. 34-35 he associates some of the Titans with "a dismal cirque / Of Druid stones".

tures we encounter here are diminutive and quite harmless. In that they are more reminiscent of Shakespeare and Spenser than they are of ancient Celtic mythology but Keats incorporates some partly sinister folkloric allusions not to be found in the works of the Renaissance poets (Gallant 42).[11] Similarly, as Christine Gallant points out, within *Endymion* "there is a running Celtic counterpoint to [the] overtly displayed classical mythology which subverts the dominance of classicism" and she adds that "within the poem are increasing echoes of [Edward] Davies's ideas about the Druid and their disciples the Bards" (ibid. 46). In *Endymion* Keats deliberately diverges from classical themes, emphasises the superiority of the "Muse of [his] native land" (*Endymion*, Book IV, l.1) to its classical equivalent, and invokes the familiar Celtic motif of a mortal being enchanted by the fairy queen and lured away to the otherworld (cf. Gallant 46-62).

Although *Endymion* has been regarded as merely escapist (cf. Caudwell 120), Daniel Watkins has pointed out that, "[i]t is a poem that displays the disintegration of public hope and social possibility and at the same time seeks an alternative possibility of value in the mind and in transcendental redemptive powers" (Watkins 37f). As he further argues, the escapist tendency of *Endymion* is precisely what reveals the author's critical stance towards contemporary politics and social relations. In other words, Keats uses the otherworldly qualities of the Celtic in order to pass criticism on the political and social circumstances of his time and indeed the opening lines of Book III express an open revolt against royal and aristocratic authority as well as the social inequality of his time.

The most obvious references to Celticism, however, appear in Keats's faery[12] poems of 1819, among which we can find *La Belle Dame Sans Merci* and *Lamia*. The first one thematically echoes *Endymion* in incorporating the familiar story of a mortal man lured away by an unearthly beautiful faery and, just like in numerous Celtic folk tales, the poem presents a rather sinister, potentially dangerous view of the otherworld and its inhabitants, an aspect that clearly distinguishes the poem from the works of the Renaissance and also Keats's earlier writings. Similarly, the titular heroine of *Lamia*, despite being a creature well-known from Greek mythology, is associated with Celtic folklore and it is made quite clear that she belongs to the "faery broods" mentioned at the

---

11 In Calidore: A Fragment Keats, for instance, mentions certain plants or animals that were commonly associated with hauntings and fairies (cf. Gallant 42). For a more comprehensive analysis of the folkloric motifs in this poem, see: ibid. 42-44.
12 It is quite noteworthy that Keats, just like Tolkien, prefers the older spelling 'faery' over the contemporary 'fairy'.

beginning of the poem (*Endymion*, Book I, l.1)[13]. The character is repeatedly connected with faery motifs and Keats notably refrains from alluding to the habit of devouring children, which is typical of Lamias in Greek mythology. She is unable to shapeshift but in general her powers seem to be greater than those of Hermes, one of the twelve Olympians, who, for instance, has to ask her for help in the search of his 'sweet nymph' and is tricked into transforming Lamia from her serpent form into that of a fair young women (cf. Gallant 118-119). Furthermore, it is remarkable that after Lycius learns about the true nature of his bride, he does not turn to her in scorn but to his old teacher, a sophist, whom he accuses of "unlawful magic and enticing lies" (*Endymion*, Book II, l.286), even going so far as to refer to him as a "demon" (ibid. Book II, l.289), thereby emphasising the superior power of the Celtic over the classical.

In incorporating motifs from Celtic folklore, even though sometimes conflated with classical ones, and giving them priority over those from the literary fairy tale tradition and more significantly, those familiar from Roman and Greek mythology, Keats and other Romantic authors did not only make an artistic statement but also a political one. Following, among others, Thomas Gray and Macpherson with his Ossianic nostalgia for an ancient past, many Romantic writers joined the Celtic Revival, which put a strong nationalistic emphasis on a pre-Norman, pre-Saxon and pre-Roman era and culture and predated a later one which took place predominantly in 19th and 20th century Ireland, Britain and Central Europe.

Tolkien and Celticism

This movement was very influential on Tolkien, who similar to Keats increasingly drew on Celtic mythology as his idea of Faery, the realm of fairy-stories, widened and deepened. However, Tolkien's attitude towards things Celtic was not without contradictions. On the one hand he vehemently refused the idea that his tales show any such influences and emphasises that he "feel[s] for them a certain distaste: largely for their unreason. They have bright colour, but are like a broken stained glass window reassembled without design. They are in fact 'mad'..." (L 26). On the other hand he admired the elusive beauty of Celtic languages, most notably Welsh. In his 1955 O'Donell lecture he called it "the language of Heaven" (EW 164) and emphasises that "Welsh is beautiful" (ibid. 189).

---

13 Gallant points out that, "[a]gain and again Keats uses the word 'fairy' to describe her, and motifs relating to the faery run through the story. 'King Oberon' who later disposed of the classical nymphs and fauns must be her king, too. She has the magical powers that faeries have, and she certainly acts in the mercurial way that we expect of faeries" (Gallant 118).

Tolkien lamented the lack of a mythology for his country, a literary heritage that, just like the tales collected by the brothers Grimm in Germany or Elias Lönnrot's *Kalevala* in Finland, could provide the foundation of a feeling of national identity that is decidedly distinct from a British one. In a letter to Milton Waldman he wrote:

> There was Greek, and Celtic, and Romance, Germanic, Scandinavian, and Finnish (which greatly affected me); but nothing English, save impoverished chap-book stuff. Of course there was and is all the Arthurian world, but powerful as it is, it is imperfectly naturalized, associated with the soil of Britain but not with English; and does not replace what I felt to be missing. (L 144)

He established a clear contrast between the Celtic literary heritage and what he undertook to create, a body of connected stories that trace back first and foremost to purely English roots (cf. ibid.). As this passage makes clear, Tolkien had a strong sense of national identity but it appears like he did not associate this feeling of Englishness with the Celtic past, the Roman conquest of Britain or the Norman invaders, but with the arrival of Angles, Saxons and Jutes on British soil and the ensuing formation of Anglo-Saxon kingdoms. In a letter to his son Christopher, Tolkien is quite clear about his conviction that these Germanic tribes are the ancestors of the English people. After having browsed through Stenton's *Anglo-Saxon England* he writes, "I'd give a bit for a time-machine. But of course... it is the things of racial and linguistic significance that attract me and stick in my memory. Still, I hope one day you'll be able (if you wish) to delve into this intriguing story of the origins of our peculiar people" (ibid. 108).

He felt an intense fascination with Old English philology and that interest is not only reflected in his academic career but also in his literary creations. In the *Book of Lost Tales*, for example, we find the character Ælfwine or Eriol, who comes from the region that was notably also the native soil of the Angles before they came to Britain (cf. LT 2 295 and Honegger 4). After the death of his wife he leaves his sons Hengest and Horsa, who later become powerful chieftains, and travels to Tol Eressëa where he marries an elvish woman and adopts the name 'Angol'. It is, of course, no coincidence that his sons bear the names of the legendary brothers who were the leaders of the Germanic tribes that invaded England in the 5th century A.D. and, as Tolkien points out, "Thus it is through Eriol and his sons the *Engle* (i.e. the English) have the true tradition of the fairies, of whom the *Íras* and the *Wéalas* (the Irish and Welsh) tell garbled things" and his son comments that this is how "a specifically English fairy-lore is born, and one more true than anything to be found in Celtic lands" (LT 2 295). Tolkien attempted to write an Elvish history that is clearly distinct from the Celtic tales about fairies and that could become the beginning of a mythology, which he felt his country lacked. Nevertheless, Celtic motifs found their way into his stories (cf. Fimi).

His juvenile writings, e.g. the poems *Goblin Feet* or *The Little House of Lost Play: Mar Vanwa Tyaliéva*, show a strong affiliation with the concept of fairies prevalent in the Victorian age, in which these beings were generally depicted as insect-like creatures with butterfly wings that were mostly light-hearted, playful, sometimes also melancholy, often mischievous but on the whole not seriously threatening. The portrayal of elves in these early works and the realms they inhabit differs widely from his later ones, in which Faery is not only presented as a place evoking an image of Paradise, beautiful and enchanting, but also as a state that is, just like its denizens, characterised by sublimity and in which every visitor or intruder, in spite of the imposing experience, is aware of the presence of a darker, perilous side. Despite his asserted dislike for things Celtic he was well-versed in Celtic studies[14] and he discovered therein a slightly different, more absorbing, mystical representation of Faery.

One of the most notable attributes of this heaven world of the ancient Celts was that it was not situated in some vague, unknown and distant region, as equivalent places in other literary traditions, but on our earth, although sometimes located underground or more frequently, as for instance Hy-Brazil, in the midst of the Atlantic Ocean (cf. Evans-Wentz 334). Similar motifs reoccur in Breton lays like *Sir Orfeo* which, in spite of being derived from classical sources, portrays a fairy kingdom that is hardly reminiscent of the Greek Hades and more consistent with Celtic fairy-lore. Fascinated by these works and their mystical fairyland Tolkien abandoned previous ideas of an otherworld reachable through dreams, as it is in *The Little House of Lost Play: Mar Vanwa Tyaliéva*, or any similar way and placed his otherworld either in dense forests as in *The Lord of the Rings* and *Smith of Wootton Major* or made it accessible by means of a western sea voyage as in *Imram* or the Undying Lands of *The Silmarillion*.

The Celtic fairy realm, just like Tolkien's otherworld is inhabited not only by one race but by a diversity of creatures, for "[i]n it alike – gods, Tuatha De Danann, fairies, demons, shades, and every sort of disembodied spirits – find their abode..." (ibid. 336). Tolkien went even further when he claimed that Faery does not only hold elves, fays, dwarves, witches, or dragons but also the sun, the moon, and the earth with all things upon it, including men when enchanted (cf. FS 9). He considers Faery to be more than just a place in his fictional universe. Deliberately using an ambiguous term, he points out

---

14 Tolkien studied Celtic languages and had a quite intimate knowledge of stories composed in Welsh (EW). In 1925 he published a scholarly edition of *Sir Gawain and the Green Knight* together with E.V. Gordon and he also tried his hand at writing poetry dealing with Celtic themes, e.g. *The Lay of Aotrou and Itroun*.

that it is the "*state* in which fairies have their being" (ibid., emphasis added), meaning that it does not only denote a physically existent land but also the feeling of enchantment people experience in an encounter with the allures of the wondrous realm. The Celtic otherworld in its different occurrences was mostly regarded as more than merely a land of the dead but, as exemplified by the Welsh Annwn or the Arthurian Avalon, it was a place where mortals were often believed to go after their death. In the same way, in Tolkien's works the spirit or fëa of immortal Elves whose physical existence, hroa, has ceased go to the Halls of Mandos, located in Aman, whence they are allowed go anywhere in the Undying Lands to reside there until they can return to the world of the living by way of some kind of reincarnation.[15] It is furthermore indicated that likewise deceased humans also go to Mandos's Houses of the Dead, before they, however, finally leave the world forever (cf. S 117). If, however, a mortal sought to enter the Celtic fairyland before the appointed hour, he often needed some kind of passport. This idea reappears in the fay star of *Smith of Wootton Major*, which allows the protagonist to enter the wondrous realm and protects him from lesser evils.

Another theme common to Celtic mythology was that of fairy women crossing the Atlantic in magic boats in order to lure away mortal men through love for them and to take them back to their own realm (Evans-Wentz 334).[16] However, if the humans finally returned to their own world, they often had to find out that, while only some months seemed to have gone by in the fairy realm, in the mortal lands decades or even centuries might have passed, leaving them estranged from their home country and without family or friends. Frequently they were not even able to return to the fairy realm and not belonging to either of the worlds they were condemned to lead the lonely life of a hermit. The same fate overtakes Keats's unnamed knight in *La Belle Dame sans Merci*, who after the encounter with the mysterious fairy, is left "alone and palely loitering" (ll. 2 and 47) on "the cold hill's side" (l. 44). These stories apparently captivated Tolkien so much that the core elements found their way into his own 'trapped mortal' poems, *Ides Ælfscýne* and *Ofer Wídne Garsecg*, and the loss of access to Faery became one of the most important issues for many of his fictional characters; the fellowship in *The Lord of the Rings* after their sojourn in Lórien, Bilbo, Smith, and the protagonist of *The Sea-bell*. Moreover, the notion of a different time scheme in the Celtic fairyland reoccurs in Tolkien's works as one of the most striking and mystical qualities of the perilous realm.

---

15 For Tolkien's elaborations on the idea of Elven rebirth, see "Of Death and the Severance of Fëa and Hrondo" (MR 217-219) and "Of Re-Birth and Other Dooms of Those That Go to Mandos" (ibid. 220-225).
16 For an extensive discussion of various stories involving human captives in different fairylands, see: Briggs, *People* 104-117.

Although the two fairyland poems *Kôr* and *The Shores Faëry*, with its first representation of Valinor were written only some months after *Goblin Feet* and *You and Me / and the Cottage of Lost Play*, they already show obvious qualities of the ancient Celtic otherworld tales. For these poems Tolkien shifted into a different register, which in turn had a strong impact on the notion of the fairy realm depicted therein. It is no longer the home of playful little fairies but anticipates the grandeur of the, however here unnamed, even unmentioned elven folk, as represented in the subsequent works, and the enchanting sublimity of the otherworld they inhabit.

The subsequent works, like *The Happy Mariners*, *A Song of Aryador*, and especially *Kortirion Among the Trees* show that by autumn 1915 Tolkien had largely rid himself of the Victorian imageries and reached back to an older fantasy tradition, which inspired him to create works that already foreshadow the lures of enchantment evoked by the fairy realms of *The Lord of the Rings* or *Smith of Wootton Major*. Faery in his writings began to develop into a prototypical land, an archetype of the natural world as becomes obvious especially in the depiction of the two most perfected fairy realms, Lothlórien and the wondrous land described in his last short story. These realms represent a place of nature, timeless beauty, regeneration, and enchantment.

Moreover, as Tolkien's concept of the elven realm changed he discovered its dark and perilous side. This development can already be seen in the premature representation of the fairyland in *The Hobbit* and when he gave his Andrew Lang lecture shortly after the publication of his children's book, he was already very well aware that, "Faëry is a perilous land, and in it are pitfalls for the unwary and dungeons for the overbold" (FS 3). In contrast to the fairy realms of Victorian literature but also of Tolkien's very early works, this Otherworld is not only a place of goodness and wonder but also of ever-present danger.

However, not only the realm of Faery was heavily influenced by Celtic elements; also for the history of its inhabitants Tolkien drew on Irish mythology. As Dimitra Fimi has pointed out, the history of the Noldor and their arrival on the shores of Middle-earth closely resembles the invasion of Ireland by the semi-divine Túatha Dé Danann, as recounted in the *Lebor Gabála Érenn*, *The Book of Invasions* (cf. Fimi). Just like this collection of tales gives an account of the mythical origins of the Irish people, in *The Book of Lost Tales* and other works Tolkien attempted to provide the English with a similar history in order to promote a feeling of national identity. However, the fact that he models the earliest stories of his supposedly purely English elves and their lands on Irish creation myths is very significant and it seems to undermine his objective.

Furthermore, in creating Sindarin, the language of his Grey-elves, Tolkien deliberately drew on Welsh and explains that "it seems to fit the rather 'Celtic' type of legends and stories told of its speakers" (L 176). Akin to many Romantic writers Tolkien incorporated Celtic motifs in his literary works and the nostalgic, wistful nature of the elves, especially those who dwell in his most elaborate Faery realms within the borders of mortal lands, Lothlórien or the perilous realm roamed by Smith of Wooton Major, is clearly influenced by a Romantic conception of these mythical beings and particularly reminiscent of the tone prevalent in the Ossianic poems.

However, in contrast to Macpherson, Wordsworth or Keats, whose works expressed an anti-colonialist attitude, Tolkien's use of familiar motifs from Celtic mythology does not imply criticism, however subtle, of his mother country. Rather, his incorporation of these elements, which seems to run counter to the initial idea of the elves and their lands as purely Anglo-Saxon, suggests that, in spite of frequent assertions that his feeling of national identity is exclusively associated with his Englishness, he felt more British than he was probably aware of. That sentiment already found expression in his 1955 O'Donnell lecture, in which he explains the merits of Welsh and emphasises that, "Welsh is of this soil, this island, the senior language of the men of Britain" (EW 189). In a similar vein he goes on to distinguish between the first learned language, the language of custom, and a person's native language, an individual's linguistic predilection. For Tolkien this native language was the one that he first encountered on coal-trucks and station signs, the one that "pierced [his] linguistic heart" (ibid. 192) – Welsh. He was immediately drawn to it and convinced that:

> [His] pleasure in the linguistic style, though it may have an individual colouring, would not, therefore be expected to be peculiar to [himself] among the English. It is not. It is present in many of them... it may be stirred by contacts no nearer than the names in Arthurian romance that echo faintly the Celtic patterns of their origin; or it may with more opportunity become vividly aware... we are all still 'British' at heart. It is the native language to which in unexploded desire we would still go home. (ibid. 194)

Just like the inherent connection he felt with the Celtic language, Tolkien's literary works and more precisely the Celtic elements pervading them, show that he was, as he held most of his fellow countrymen to be, 'British at heart'. As Tolkien was more and more drawn to the Celtic, be it in the form of language or literature, he began to question and eventually to overcome the idea of a binary opposition between English and Celtic. As a result, his work, which began as a 'mythology for England' gradually turned into a mythology for Britain.

Bibliography

Briggs, Katharine M. *Encyclopedia of Fairies: Hobgoblins, Brownies, Bogies, and Other Supernatural Creatures*. New York: Pantheon Books, 1976

---. *The Vanishing People: Fairy Lore and Legends*. New York: Pantheon Books, 1978

Carpenter, Humphrey (Ed. with assistance of Christopher Tolkien). *The Letters of J.R.R. Tolkien*. London: HarperCollins, 2006

Caudwell, Christopher. "The Bourgeois Illusion and English Romantic Poetry". *Romanticism: Points of View*. Eds. Robert F. Gleckner and Gerald E. Enscoe. Detroit: Prentice-Hall, 1970, 108-124

Evans-Wentz, Walter Y. *The Fairy-Faith in Celtic Countries*. New York: Carol Publishing, 1994

Fimi, Dimitra. "'Mad' Elves and 'Elusive Beauty': Some Celtic Strands of Tolkien's Mythology". *Folklore* Vol. 117, No. 2 (2006): 156-170

Fulford, Timothy. "Poetry, Periphery and Empire". *The Cambridge Companion to British Romantic Poetry*. Eds. James Chandler and Maureen N. McLane. Cambridge: Cambridge UP, 2008, 178-194

Gallant, Christine. *Keats and Romantic Celticism*. Basingstoke/New York: Palgrave Macmillan, 2005

Honegger, Thomas. "ÆLfwine (Old English "Elf-Friend")". *J.R.R. Tolkien Encyclopedia: Scholarship and Critical Assessment*. Ed. Michael D.C. Drout. New York/Abingdon: Routledge, 2007, 4-5

Johnson, James W. "The Scythian: His Rise and Fall". *Journal of the History of Ideas*, Vol. 20, No. 2 (1959): 250-257

Kidd, Colin. *Subverting Scotland's Past: Scottish Whig Historians and the Creation of an Anglo-British Identity, 1689-c.1830*. Cambridge: Cambridge UP, 1993

---. *British Identities Before Nationalism: Ethnicity and Nationhood in the Atlantic World, 1600-1800*. Cambridge: Cambridge UP, 1999

Leersoon, Joseph Th. *Mere Irish and Fior-Ghael: Studies in the Idea of Irish Nationality, Its Development and Literary Expression Prior to the Nineteenth Century*. Amsterdam/Philadelphia: John Benjamins, 1986

Mac Craith, Mícheál. "'We know all these poems': The Irish Response to Ossian". *The Reception of Ossian in Europe*. Ed. Howard Gaskill. London/New York: Thoemmes Continuum, 2004, 91-108

Maclachlan, Christopher. "Ossian". Encyclopedia of the Romantic Era: 1760-1850. Ed. Christopher John Murrey. London: Taylor & Francis Books, 2004, 835-837

McGann, Jerome. *The Poetics of Sensibility: A Revolution in Literary Style*. Oxford: Clarendon Press, 1996

Moore, Daffydd R. "The Critical Response to Ossian's Romantic Bequest". *English Romanticism and the Celtic World*. Eds. Gerard Carruthers and Alan Rawes. Cambridge: Cambridge UP, 2003, 38-53

Moore, John R. "Wordsworth's Unacknowledged Debt to Macpherson's Ossian". *PMLA*, Vol. 40, No. 2 (1925): 362-378

O'Halloran, Clare. "Irish Re-Creations of the Gaelic Past: The Challenge of Macpherson's Ossian". *Past and Present* 124 (1989): 69-95

Pittcock, Murphey. *Celtic Identity and the British Image*. Manchester: Manchester UP, 1999

Porter, James. "'Bring Me the Head of James Macpherson': The Execution of Ossian and the Wellsprings of Folkloristic Discourse". *The Journal of American Folklore*, Vol. 114, No. 454 (2001): 396-435

Stillingfleet, Edward. *Origines Britannicae; or The Antiquities of the British Churches*, London: M. Flesher for Henry Mortlock, 1685

Thomson, Derick S. "James Macpherson: The Gaelic Dimension". *From Gaelic to Romantic: Ossianic Translations*. Eds. Fiona Stafford and Howard Gaskill. Amsterdam/Atlanta: Rodopi, 1998, 17-26

Tolkien, John R.R. *The Book of Lost Tales Part II. The History of Middle-earth II*. Ed. Christopher Tolkien. New York: Ballantine Books/Del Rey, 1984

---. *Morgoth's Ring. The History of Middle-earth X*. Ed. Christopher Tolkien. London: HarperCollins, 1994

---. *The Silmarillion*. Ed. Christopher Tolkien. London: HarperCollins, 1999

---. "On Fairy-Stories". *Tree and Leaf: Including the Poem "Mythopoeia"; "The Homecoming of Beorhtnoth: Beorhthelm's Son"*. London: HarperCollins, 2001, 3-81

---. "English and Welsh". *The Monsters and the Critics and Other Essays*. London: HarperCollins, 2006, 162-197

Trevor-Roper, Hugh R. *George Buchanan and the Ancient Scottish Constitution*. The English Historical Review: Supplement 3. London: Longmans, 1966

Watkins, Daniel P. *Keats's Poetry and the Politics of the Imagination*. Toronto/London: Associated UP, 1989

Watson, John R. "Wordsworth, North Wales and the Celtic Landscape". *English Romanticism and the Celtic World*. Eds. Gerard Carruthers and Alan Rawes. Cambridge: Cambridge UP, 2003, 85-102

J.R.R. Tolkien und die romantische Nostalgie

Julian Tim Morton Eilmann (Aachen)

Der Aufsatztitel macht bereits deutlich, worum es im Folgenden gehen soll: um spezifische inhaltliche Gemeinsamkeiten zwischen J.R.R. Tolkien und der Romantik in Bezug auf den Topos der Nostalgie. Bevor ich meine Thesen zur Traditionslinie zwischen Tolkien und der Romantik erläutere, ist es mir jedoch wichtig, in einer Vorbemerkung grundlegend auf das Oberthema des Tolkien Seminars 2010 einzugehen, denn für mich ist es erstaunlich, dass der Bezug zwischen Tolkien und der Romantik als Seminarthema ausgewählt wurde. Noch erstaunlicher ist es, dass eine so große Zahl an Tolkien-Forschern dieses Thema offensichtlich begierig aufgegriffen hat. Es scheint demnach ein immenses Forschungsinteresse am Romantikbezug Tolkiens zu bestehen. Fast entsteht der Eindruck, als hätte die Gemeinschaft der Tolkien-Wissenschaftler nur darauf gewartet, dass das scheinbar so wichtige Romantikthema endlich einmal auf der Tagesordnung steht. Die Begeisterung für die Romantik erscheint mir umso verwunderlicher, als, soweit ich die einschlägige Tolkien-Forschung dahingehend überblicke, in den vergangenen Jahrzehnten lediglich ein paar vorsichtige Äußerungen in diese Richtung formuliert wurden. Die Begriffe *Romantik* oder *romantisch* sind somit sicherlich keine Termini, die im Vokabular der Tolkienistik wiederholt auftauchen.

War Tolkien also ein Romantiker? Eine Beantwortung dieser Frage wurde mit dem Seminar bekanntlich versucht. Die bemerkenswert kontroverse Diskussion auf der Tagung hat jedoch gezeigt, dass sich bei dieser Frage verschiedene konträre Forschungspositionen gegenüberstehen. Während manche Diskutanten einen Romantikbezug im Werke Tolkiens für fragwürdig halten, da sich vor dem Hintergrund des von ihnen gewählten Romantikbegriffs keine inhaltlichen Bezüge herstellen lassen, plädieren andere Tolkien-Forscher dafür, dass sich bei spezifischen literarischen und poetologischen Einzelaspekten durchaus sinnvolle Traditionslinien zwischen Tolkien und der Romantik nachweisen lassen. Der vorliegende Aufsatz ist aufseiten der letztgenannten Position zu verorten, bin ich doch nach langjähriger Auseinandersetzung mit Tolkiens Werk und der deutschen Romantik tatsächlich davon überzeugt, dass sich wesentliche Berührungspunkte mit der Epoche der Romantik nachweisen lassen.

Wichtig ist nur, was durch die streitbare Seminardiskussion noch einmal sehr deutlich wurde, dass man sich jeweils bewusst macht, wovon man spricht, wenn man den Begriff *Romantik* auf Tolkiens Schriften anwendet. Wenn im Folgenden von der Romantik gesprochen wird, dann beziehe ich mich geistesgeschichtlich explizit auf jene Epoche der deutschen Literaturgeschichte, die vonseiten der Germanistik traditionell unter dem Begriff Romantik bekannt ist: die Zeit von 1790 bis ca. 1850.[1] Dass ich mich ausdrücklich auf zentrale inhalt-liche und poetologische Aspekte der *deutschen Romantik* beziehe, erscheint mir als eine wichtige Vorbemerkung, da die Epoche der Romantik zwar ein gesamteuropäisches Phänomen darstellt, jedoch hat sich die Romantik in jedem Land unterschiedlich ausgeprägt.

Weiterhin soll es im Folgenden nicht darum gehen, eine Vielzahl verschiedener epochentypischer Merkmale der Romantik zu benennen, um diese im Werke Tolkiens nachzuweisen. Angesichts der Vielschichtigkeit des Romantikbegriffs und der Tatsache, dass sich eine vollständige Übereinstimmung zwischen der romantischen Dichtungstheorie und Tolkien sicherlich nicht nachweisen lässt, erscheint ein solches Vorgehen wenig sinnvoll. Vielmehr soll meine Studie aufzeigen, dass sich hinsichtlich eines für die deutsche Romantik bedeutsamen Motivs, der *romantischen Nostalgie*, durchaus Parallelen aufzeigen lassen. Ich gehe davon aus, dass der Vergleich des nostalgischen Vergangenheitsbezugs in der romantischen Dichtung mit dem Werke Tolkiens uns dabei helfen kann, Tolkiens literarisches Werk besser zu verstehen.

Noch eine weitere terminologische Vorbemerkung: Bei der Behandlung der romantischen Nostalgie im Kontext der Romantik ist es unumgänglich, auch auf die *romantische Sehnsucht* einzugehen, sind die Begriffe Nostalgie und Sehnsucht in der Romantik doch unmittelbar aufeinander bezogen, wie noch deutlich werden wird. Leider muss ich hier aus Platzgründen die Diskussion mancher aufschlussreicher Aspekte ausklammern, auf die ich unter der gewählten Fragestellung gerne eingegangen wäre. Deshalb werde ich im Folgen-den nur die Leitlinien meiner Forschungen zur romantischen Nostalgie bei Tolkien vorstellen (Ergänzungen können möglicherweise im Rahmen eines Varia-Artikels vorgelegt werden).

Bevor ich näher darauf eingehe, was wir uns unter romantischer Nostalgie vorzustellen haben, zunächst zur besseren inhaltlichen Orientierung ein kurzer Überblick über die in Tolkiens Werk nachweisbaren Formen der Nostalgie.

Drei Formen der Nostalgie in Tolkiens Werk

Der Topos der romantischen Nostalgie ist in Tolkiens Werk in drei Formen verankert. Zuerst finden sich in Tolkiens Texten an verschiedenen Stellen Hinweise auf eine Form des Heimwehs, die ich als örtlich-gebundenes, gegenwartsbezogenes Heimweh bezeichnen möchte. Bei dieser Form der Nost-

---

1 Zur ›Frage nach dem Ort der Romantik‹ in der Literaturgeschichte und der grundsätzlichen Problematik solcher literaturhistorischer Periodisierungsversuche vgl. Segeberg 31ff.

algie handelte sich um das, was man sich auch im Alltagsleben unter Heimweh vorstellen wird, eben die ausgeprägte und mitunter auch quälende Sehnsucht eines von der Heimat räumlich entfernten Individuums, das sich danach sehnt, nach Hause zurückzukehren (vgl. Gerschmann 934).

Darüber hinaus ist die Nostalgie in Tolkiens Werk jedoch nicht nur im räumlichen Sinne auf einen Heimatort gerichtet. Nostalgie in Tolkiens Werk hat auch eine ausgeprägte zeitliche Dimension, d.h. wir haben es mit einem Heimweh zu tun, das sich auf eine glanzvolle poetische Vergangenheit richtet, die mit einer prosaischen Gegenwart kontrastiert wird. Wie wir sehen werden, wird auf diese Weise im Sinne der Romantik ein Gegensatz zwischen einer poetischen Vergangenheit, die man auch als Goldenes Zeitalter bezeichnen könnte, und einer im Vergleich dazu blassen und prosaischen Gegenwart hergestellt. Wichtig im Hinblick auf Tolkiens Mittelerde ist, dass an einem solchen nostalgischen Vergangenheitsbezug auch handfeste politische Hoffnungen und Forderungen geknüpft sein können.

Beide Formen der Nostalgie mit ihrer Raum- und Zeitdimension laufen in Tolkiens Werk in einer dritten Nostalgie-Form zusammen, die ich als existentielles Heimweh bezeichnen möchte. Wie deutlich werden wird, handelt es sich hierbei um eine transzendente Sehnsucht des sterblichen Subjekts, ein Heimweh, das in den Kreisen der Welt nicht gestillt werden kann und das sich als eine Erinnerung an eine verlorene spirituelle Heimat manifestiert. Dies ist der Punkt, an dem die Verbindungen zwischen Tolkien und zentralen Konzepten der deutschen Romantik besonders deutlich werden.

Romantische Nostalgie und Sehnsucht

Kommen wir nun zum Begriff der romantischen Nostalgie und Sehnsucht. Was hat es hiermit auf sich und warum sind diese Termini für ein Verständnis romantischen Denkens entscheidend? Der Begriff Nostalgie selbst leitet sich ab von den griechischen Wörtern *nóstos* (Rückkehr, Heimkehr) und *álgos* (Schmerz, Trauer). Als individuelles wie kollektives Phänomen ist Nostalgie im alltäglichen Sprachgebrauch die Sehnsucht »nach der Vergangenheit, die als schöner u. besser als die Gegenwart u. Zukunft betrachtet wird« (Wahrig 862). Historisch lassen sich die Spuren nostalgischen Denkens in der europäischen Geistesgeschichte auf vielfältige Weise verfolgen. So tritt die Nostalgie bereits in der antiken Sehnsucht nach dem Goldenen Zeitalter auf, eine Vorstellung, die im Abendland griechischen Ursprungs ist und zuerst bei Hesiod literarischen Niederschlag gefunden hat, sich aber auch in der Überlieferung fast aller Kulturkreise nachweisen lässt. Darüber hinaus spielt die Idee eines verlorenen Urzustandes u.a. in der christlichen Elegie des Paradieses eine große Rolle. Im engeren Sinn, als diffuse Sehnsucht nach Zuständen der Vergangenheit, stellt das

»Kunstwort« (Gerschmann 934) *Nostalgie* allerdings ein Phänomen der Neuzeit dar. Als medizinischer Befund bezeichnete er ursprünglich das Heimweh bei Schweizer Söldnern, von dem man meinte, dass es sich in körperlichen Symptomen äußere und sogar zum Tod führen könne, die so genannte Schweizerkrankheit (vgl. ebd.). Im 19. Jahrhundert lässt sich schließlich eine semantische Verschiebung erkennen, die die Nostalgie weitgehend von pathologisierenden Konnotationen befreit und zu einer rein psychischen Befindlichkeit macht.

Wodurch ist jedoch die spezifisch romantische Nostalgie geprägt? Um diese Frage zu beantworten, muss man sich den poetologischen Angelpunkt der romantischen Weltanschauung vor Augen führen – einen Gedanken, den, wie vielleicht kein anderer, der Dichter Joseph von Eichendorff in seinem Gedicht *Wünschelruthe* poetisch zum Ausdruck gebracht hat. Nicht ohne Grund ist Eichendorffs vielzitierter Vierzeiler zu einer Art poetologischer Kernformel der deutschen Romantik geworden:

> Schläft ein Lied in allen Dingen,
> Die da träumen fort und fort,
> Und die Welt hebt an zu singen,
> Triffst Du nur das Zauberwort.
>
> (Eichendorff I/1 121)

Eichendorffs kurzes Gedicht hat es wahrlich in sich: Ein poetischer Zauber – ein Lied – schlummert tief verborgen in den Wesenheiten der uns umgebenden Welt. Wer sich dieses Zaubers bewusst ist und ihn erkennt, ist eine jener glücklichen Naturen, einer jener Romantiker, die um das Geheimnis des Daseins wissen (vgl. Eilmann, *Song* 167). Sowie der Dürstende mit einer Wünschelrute das Lebenselixier Wasser ausfindig machen kann, so soll das poetische Gemüt durch seine künstlerische Begabung die Welt zum Singen bringen und so zum Kern der Wirklichkeit vorstoßen (ebd.).

An dieser Stelle kommt der romantische Nostalgiebegriff ins Spiel, denn die Romantik geht weiterhin davon aus, dass der Mensch in früheren Zeiten – in einem Poetischen Zeitalter – einen viel unmittelbareren Zugang zu den Dingen gehabt und so das schlafende Lied zum Klingen gebracht habe. Mit der ihm eigenen dichterischen Sprachgewalt hat der Romantiker Novalis die romantische Nostalgie in seinem Romanfragment *Heinrich von Ofterdingen* ausgedrückt. Darin hat der Titelheld gleich zu Beginn des Romans eine Art poetisches Erweckungserlebnis, nachdem er im Traum die blaue Blume erblickt hat, jenes visionäre Bild, das als Symbol der romantischen Poesie schlechthin in die Literaturgeschichte eingegangen ist.

In dieser Erweckungsszene ahnt Heinrich jenen verlorenen Urzustand, als dem Menschen die Welt noch nicht als großes Rätsel sondern wie ein offenes Buch gegenüberstand:

> Ich hörte einst von alten Zeiten reden; wie da die Tiere und Bäume und Felsen mit den Menschen gesprochen hätten. Mir ist gerade so, als wollten sie allaugenblicklich anfangen, und als könnte ich es ihnen ansehen, was sie mir sagen wollten. Es muß noch viel Worte geben, die ich nicht weiß: wüßte ich mehr, so könnte ich viel besser alles begreifen.
>
> (Novalis I 195)

Im zweiten Romankapitel erfährt Heinrich von einigen Kaufleuten, mit denen er von zuhause aus in die ihm unbekannte Welt aufbricht, von jenen mythischen »alten Zeiten«, in denen das Subjekt der mannigfaltigen Welt noch nicht fremd gegenüberstand. Da in dieser Textpassage der Gedanke der romantischen Nostalgie in großer Klarheit formuliert ist, soll diese längere Stelle vollständig zitiert werden:

> In alten Zeiten muß die ganze Natur lebendiger und sinnvoller gewesen sein, als heutzutage. Wirkungen, die jetzt kaum noch die Tiere zu bemerken scheinen, und die Menschen eigentlich allein noch empfinden und genießen, bewegten damals leblose Körper; und so war es möglich, daß kunstreiche Menschen allein Dinge möglich machten und Erscheinungen hervorbrachten, die uns jetzt völlig unglaublich und fabelhaft dünken. So sollen vor uralten Zeiten ... Dichter gewesen sein, die durch den seltsamen Klang wunderbarer Werkzeuge das geheime Leben der Wälder, die in den Stämmen verborgenen Geister aufgeweckt, in wüsten, verödeten Gegenden den toten Pflanzensamen erregt, und blühende Gärten hervorgerufen, grausame Tiere gezähmt und verwilderte Menschen zu Ordnung und Sitte gewöhnt..., reißende Flüsse in milde Gewässer verwandelt, und selbst die totesten Steine in regelmäßige tanzende Bewegungen hingerissen haben. Sie [die Künstler] sollen zugleich Wahrsager und Priester, Gesetzgeber und Ärzte gewesen sein, indem selbst die höhern Wesen durch ihre zauberische Kunst herabgezogen worden sind, und sie in den Geheimnissen der Zukunft unterrichtet, das Ebenmaß und die natürliche Einrichtung aller Dinge, auch die innern Tugenden und Heilkräfte der Zahlen, Gewächse und aller Kreaturen, ihnen offenbart... Seltsam ist nur hierbei, daß zwar diese schönen Spuren, zum Andenken der Gegenwart jener wohltätigen Menschen, geblieben sind, aber entweder ihre Kunst, oder jene zarte Gefühligkeit der Natur verloren gegangen ist. (ebd. 210f)

Wichtig für unser Verständnis der romantischen Nostalgie ist nun, dass aus diesen Vorstellungen die Hoffnung abgeleitet wird, den verlorenen Einheitszustand, in dem die Trennung zwischen Mensch, Natur und Welt aufgehoben ist, mithilfe der Poesie wiederherzustellen. Das Ziel der nostalgischen Sehnsucht der Romantiker ist demnach die ›Wiederverzauberung der Welt‹. Dabei wird die romantische Nostalgie gleichzeitig zu einer in die Vergangenheit projizierten Utopie. Verfolgen wir vor dem Hintergrund dieser Kenntnisse zum Topos der romantischen Nostalgie die verschiedenen Formen der Nostalgie in Tolkiens Werk.

Die Heimat als Sehnsuchtsort: Das irdische gegenwartsbezogene Heimweh

Auf diejenige Form des Heimwehs, die ich eingangs als *örtlich-gebundenes, gegenwartsbezogenes Heimweh* bezeichnet habe, möchte ich nur kurz eingehen. Denn dieser Aspekt spielt für die spezifisch romantische Nostalgie nur eine untergeordnete Rolle. Auf die Sehnsucht, nach Hause zurückzukehren, wird in Tolkiens Romanen an vielen Stellen eingegangen. Dass es dabei gerade die heimatbewussten Hobbits sind, die ihrem Heimweh Ausdruck verleihen, wird uns nicht weiter erstaunen. Stellvertretend für den Leser, der zusammen mit den Hobbits Stück für Stück die anfangs unbekannte Welt Mittelerde kennen lernt, fungiert das Auenland als Sinnbild für das wohlgeordnete bürgerliche Zuhause, das angesichts der zunehmenden Gefahren der Reise nur noch an Reiz gewinnt:

> If the dwarves asked him [Bilbo] what he was doing he answered: ›You said sitting on the doorstep and thinking could be my job, not to mention getting inside, so I am sitting and thinking.‹ But I am afraid he was not much thinking of his job, but of what lay beyond the blue distance, the quiet Western Land and the Hill and his hobbit-hole under it. (H 193)

> Now they could look back over the lands they had left, laid out behind them far below. Far, far away in the West, where things were blue and faint, Bilbo knew there lay his own country of safe and comfortable things, and his little hobbit-hole... ›The summer is getting on down below,‹ thought Bilbo, ›and haymaking is going on and picnics.‹ (ebd. 53)

Die Fokussierung auf die verlassene Heimat kontrastiert im Falle der Hobbits mit den Erfahrungen von Entbehrung, Leid und Tod. Dass die Heimat hier stark beschönigt wird, ist als psychologisches Phänomen im Handlungszusammenhang durchaus nachvollziehbar. Insbesondere Frodo und Sam schaffen sich im Angesicht des allgegenwärtigen Schreckens auf ihrem Weg zum Schicksalsberg das geistige Konstrukt einer paradiesischen heimatlichen Idylle. Ein solcher nostalgischer Sehnsuchtsort wird entsprechend mit unbeschwerter friedlicher Harmonie assoziiert. Diese Form des Heimwehs ist zwar für den Handlungsverlauf wichtig, motiviert sie doch die Protagonisten auf ihrem beschwerlichen Weg; für meine Fragestellung ist diese Art der Nostalgie jedoch nicht von ausschlaggebender Bedeutung, so dass ich an dieser Stelle nicht weiter darauf eingehen möchte.

Die historische Nostalgie

Im Kontext der Romantik erscheint hingegen die zweite Form nostalgischer Sehnsucht als weitaus interessanter: Ich möchte sie als *historische Nostalgie* bezeichnen. Wie bereits deutlich wurde, handelt es sich hierbei um einen nostalgischen Gestus, der sich auf eine poetische Vergangenheit richtet, die mit einer prosaischen Gegenwart kontrastiert wird. Einen solchen wehmütigen Vergangenheitsbezug hat Tolkien im *Herrn der Ringe* u.a. in Gimlis Lied zum Ausdruck gebracht. Schauen wir uns dieses Lied also genauer an. Das von Gimli in den Tiefen Morias angestimmte Lied kann als Ausdruck nostalgischer Erinnerung verstanden werden, da darin ein Gegensatz zwischen einer glorifizierten Vergangenheit und einer wenig ruhmreichen Gegenwart konstruiert wird. So preist Gimli in seinem Gesang das untergegangene Reich des legendären Zwergenherrschers Durin und beklagt, dass von dieser ehemaligen Prachtentfaltung in der Gegenwart des Sängers und seiner Zuhörer nichts mehr übrig sei. Dieser Kontrast der Zeitebenen (damals und heute) ist im gesamten sechsstrophigen Lied präsent. Eine Rahmungsfunktion hat dabei jeweils der erste Vers in der ersten und letzten Strophe. Darin heißt es einerseits über die idealisierte Vergangenheit: »The world was young, the mountains green« (LotR 308), während andererseits die Gegenwart des Sängers bei gleichem Satzbau mit gegenteiligen Adjektiven beschrieben wird: »The world is grey, the mountains old« (ebd.). Der Jugend und dem lebendigen Grün des Damals stehen das Alter und das blasse Grau des Jetzt gegenüber. Mittelerde zu Durins Zeiten präsentiert sich gewissermaßen als eine Welt vor dem Fall (»In Elder Days before the fall« ebd.), eine Welt, in der metaphorisch gesprochen der Mond noch fleckenlos schien. Diese ›unbefleckte‹ Vergangenheit wird mit zahlreichen positiv konnotierten Begriffen charakterisiert: young, green, no stain, fair, tall, mighty, golden, silver, power, light, sun, undimmed, bright (vgl. ebd.). Demgegenüber beschreiben Begriffe wie grey, old, ashen-cold, darkness, shadow (vgl. ebd.) die Gegenwart als negativ, glanzlos und dunkel. Das untergegangene Zwergenreich hingegen erscheint als eine Gesellschaft, in der alle sozialen Gruppen mit ihrem geschäftigen und sinnvollen Treiben Hand in Hand einem gemeinsamen Ziel zugearbeitet haben:

> There chisel clove, and graver wrote;
> There forged was blade, and bound was hilt;
> The delver mined, the mason built.
> Unwearied then were Durin's folk;
> Beneath the mountains music woke:
> The harpers harped, the minstrels sang,
> And at the gates the trumpets rang. (ebd.)

Durins Zeit mit all ihrer schillernden Größe und Kunst erscheint gewissermaßen als ein Goldenes Zeitalter des Glücks und der Pracht. Charakteristisch für diese »Elder Days« (ebd.) sind denn auch »mighty kings« (ebd.), ein starkes Königtum, das von den Zwergen des Dritten Zeitalters gerade schmerzlich vermisst wird. Wichtig für unsere Fragestellung ist, dass diese Form der historischen Nostalgie als eine Anklage an die als ungenügend empfundene Gegenwart zu verstehen ist. Gimlis Lied hat also eine eindeutige Appellfunktion, die vergangene Größe wiederzuerlangen. In der Person Durins manifestiert sich in diesem Sinne auch die politische Dimension eines solchen nostalgischen Vergangenheitsbezuges. Der Verlust von Durins Zeit wird eben nicht lediglich beklagt; vielmehr artikuliert sich in Gimlis Lied ein gegenwartsbezogener Herrschaftsanspruch, verkündet doch bezeichnenderweise der letzte Vers des Liedes mit der Formulierung »Till Durin wakes again from sleep« (ebd. 309) die Gewissheit, dass der poetisch verklärte König einst zurückkehren wird.

Für ein Verständnis des nostalgischen Gehalts dieses Liedes verdient auch der Ort Beachtung, an dem es angestimmt wird: Gimli singt das Lied gerade an jenem Ort, der ehemals die Macht und Glorie der Zwerge manifestierte. Auf diesen Kontrast zwischen dem Verfall der Gegenwart und dem Glanz vergangener Zeiten macht denn auch Gimli aufmerksam: »These are not holes. This is the great realm and city of the Dwarrowdelf. And of old it was not darksome, but full of light and splendour, as is still remembered in our songs« (ebd. 307). Der Gegensatz zwischen dem gefährlichen Moria und der prächtigen Zwergenstadt von einst wird durch die Intonation des Liedes am historischen Ort noch verstärkt. So bleibt es Gimlis Zuhörern und dem Leser überlassen, die »many-pillared halls of stone« (ebd. 308) in ihrer Vorstellung zu bevölkern und mit Leben zu erfüllen.

Diese Form der historischen Nostalgie steht in Tradition romantischen Denkens, spielt die nostalgische Erinnerung an ein verlorenes Goldenes bzw. Poetisches Zeitalter doch auch in der Weltanschauung der Romantik eine wichtige Rolle. Bekanntlich haben die Romantiker das Goldene Zeitalter nicht mehr, wie seit der Renaissance üblich, in der Antike sondern im Mittelalter verankert (vgl. Schwering 545f). In seiner Schrift *Die Christenheit oder Europa* hat Novalis vor dem Hintergrund der Französischen Revolution die romantische Sehnsucht nach einem glorifizierten Mittelalter auf den Punkt gebracht. Während den Romantikern das Europa Ende des 18. Jahrhunderts als eine Zeit der politisch-religiösen Zerrissenheit erscheint, wird das Mittelalter mit einer starken christlichen Einheitskirche als eine Zeit geschildert, in der der »Sinn des Unsichtbaren« (Novalis III 507), wie es Novalis formuliert, noch erfahrbar war. Mit allen Farben der Sehnsucht wird diese ursprüngliche Verbundenheit der Menschen untereinander und mit Gott geschildert:

> Es waren schöne glänzende Zeiten, wo Europa ein christliches Land war, wo *Eine* Christenheit diesen menschlich gestalteten Welttheil bewohnte; *Ein* großes gemeinschaftliches Interesse verband die entlegensten Provinzen dieses weiten geistlichen Reichs. – Ohne große weltliche Besitzthümer lenkte und vereinigte *Ein* Oberhaupt, die großen politischen Kräfte. – ... Jedes Glied dieser Gesellschaft wurde allenthalben geehrt, und wenn die gemeinen Leute Trost oder Hülfe, Schutz oder Rath bei ihm suchten, und gerne dafür seine mannigfaltigen Bedürfnisse reichlich versorgten, so fand es auch bei den Mächtigeren Schutz, Ansehn und Gehör, und alle pflegten diese auserwählten, mit wunderbaren Kräften ausgerüsteten Männer, wie Kinder des Himmels, deren Gegenwart und Zuneigung mannigfachen Segen verbreitete. Kindliches Zutrauen knüpfte die Menschen an ihre Verkündigungen. – Wie heiter konnte jedermann sein irdisches Tagewerk vollbringen, da ihm durch diese heilige Menschen eine sichere Zukunft bereitet, und jeder Fehltritt durch sie vergeben... wurde. (ebd.)

Wichtig für ein Verständnis der historischen Nostalgie ist, dass aus einer solchen wehmütigen Verklärung einer imaginierten Vergangenheit die Hoffnung abgeleitet wird, dieses Zeitalter der Einheit in der Zukunft wiederzuerlangen. Auf weitere Beispiele der historischen Nostalgie in Tolkiens Werk muss ich hier verzichten, um den Rahmen des Aufsatzes nicht zu sprengen. Es soll lediglich erwähnt werden, dass der nostalgische Rückbezug auf eine verlorene politische Größe auch für Repräsentanten anderer Völker, insbesondere die Menschen, von großer Bedeutung ist. Für den zukünftigen König Aragorn wird beispielsweise die Wiederherstellung eines ehemaligen historischen Herrschaftszustandes zum treibenden Handlungsimpuls und im Text des *Herrn der Ringe* demnach vielfach mit rhetorischem oder lyrischem Pathos beschworen.

Poetisches Zeitalter – Prosaische Zeitalter

Festzuhalten ist, dass durch die Sehnsucht nach einer vergangenen heroisch-poetischen Epoche, wie sie etwa in Gimlis Lied zum Ausdruck kommt, die Gegenwart in gewisser Weise prosaisch wird. Der Topos der romantischen Nostalgie ist demnach auch in Tolkiens Werk aufs Engste mit einer Gegenüberstellung zwischen einem Poetischen Zeitalter (der Vergangenheit) und einem Prosaischen Zeitalter (der Gegenwart) verbunden. Es ist dabei charakteristisch für ein solches nostalgisches Denken, dass Poesie, Größe und Glanz immer in der Vergangenheit gesucht und in der Gegenwart schmerzlich vermisst werden. In Mittelerde des Dritten Zeitalters erscheint denn auch die Vergangenheit, deren Spuren in den ehrfürchtig zitierten Liedern und Gedichten, in den Ruinen verlorener Königreiche auffindbar sind, oder wie sie von den letzten Vertretern legendärer Völker verkörpert wird (Ents, Elben), als märchenhafter als die Gegenwart.

Manchen Leser mag dies auf den ersten Blick erstaunen, denn aus heutiger moderner Sicht ist Mittelerde so, wie es sich im *Hobbit* und im *Herrn der Ringe* präsentiert, selbstverständlich ein phantastisches Märchenland. Aber dennoch: Aus Sicht der Protagonisten ist der Schimmer einer historisch-poetischen Wirklichkeit stets gegenwärtig. Wenn Aragorn den Hobbits auf der Wetterspitze einen Ausschnitt des Liedes von Beren und Lúthien vorsingt, dann wird die zeitliche Ferne zwischen der Gegenwart des Dritten Zeitalters und der märchenhaften Vorzeit Lúthiens und Berens erahnbar (vgl. Eilmann, *Lieder* 249). Auf diese Weise entsteht ein Kontrast zwischen der prosaischen Situation der Hobbits und der von Sam sehnlichst erwünschten »tale of the old days... a tale about the Elves before the Fading time« (LotR 187). Auch die letzten in Mittelerde lebenden Repräsentanten von nahezu legendären Völkern (Ents, Elben oder auch die Drúedain), die ehemals Mittelerde bevölkerten und nun beinahe in Vergessenheit geraten sind und den meisten nur aus Erzählungen bekannt sind, verbinden die prosaische Gegenwart mit einem märchenhafteren Zeitalter. Die Tatsache, dass die Eldar, die die poetische Vergangenheit in besonderem Maße verkörpern, im Dritten Zeitalter im Schwinden begriffen sind, verstärkt dabei noch die ehrfürchtige Haltung, die gegenüber den Elben als Vertretern eines Poetischen Zeitalters eingenommen wird.

Handelt es sich beim Dritten Zeitalter demnach um eine Zeit des Übergangs, in der alter Glanz noch präsent und vorhanden, aber bereits im Schwinden begriffen ist, so stellt das Vierte Zeitalter eine entzauberte Welt dar, die schließlich mehr und mehr der prosaischen Wirklichkeit des Lesers gleichen wird. Über das Vierte Zeitalter hat uns Tolkien nur wenige Hinweise hinterlassen. Dennoch finden sich im *Herrn der Ringe* und im *Silmarillion* Hinweise darauf (vgl. LotR 949f u. S 366), dass die Wunder und die Poesie, die Mittelerde noch im Dritten Zeitalter charakterisieren, im Vierten Zeitalter nahezu gänzlich aus der Welt verschwunden sein werden und man sich ihrer höchstens noch mit Wehmut erinnert. Der Übergang von einem Poetischen zu einem Prosaischen Zeitalter wird dann abgeschlossen sein.[2] Mit dem Vergehen der »Elder Days« (LotR 308), was wie gesagt am deutlichsten durch das Schwinden der Elben verkörpert wird, bleibt die wehmütige Erinnerung an das, was einst schön und glanzvoll war, als ein Modus der nostalgischen Vergangenheitsvergegenwärtigung.

Kortirion among the trees

In seinem Gedicht *Kortirion among the trees* hat Tolkien diesen Prozess des Schwindens der Poesie und den damit verbundenen nostalgischen Gestus literarisch kunstvoll verarbeitet. Das gesamte Gedicht stellt eine elegische Klage dar und ist geprägt von einer ausgeprägten Sehnsucht nach einer verlorenen poetischen Zeit, die in der Gegenwart des lyrischen Ichs nur erahnbar ist. Inhaltlich geht es um die Stadt Kortirion im Zentrum der Insel Tol Eressea in einem frühen Stadium von Tolkiens Mythologie. In der ersten Fassung des Gedichts beklagt das lyrische Ich (offensichtlich ein Mensch) die Leere des verlassenen Koritirions: eine verblassende Stadt (»fading town« LT I 33), in der eine alte Erinnerung (»old memory« ebd.) zwar noch an den ehemaligen Glanz erinnert, in der aber auch die Erinnerung bereits im Schwinden begriffen ist, sodass ein gänzlicher Verlust, ein vollständiges Vergessen als Gefahr aufscheint. Eine regelrechte Handlung gibt es in dem Gedicht nicht. In *Kortirion among the trees* herrscht die lyrische Stimmungsbeschreibung vor.

Zentral für die vorliegende Fragestellung ist, dass in Tolkiens *Kortirion*-Gedicht der Übergang von einem Poetischen zu einem Prosaischen Zeitalter und die damit verbundene nostalgische Sehnsucht sehr deutlich Gestalt nimmt.

---

2 Als Repräsentant eines solchen Prosaischen Zeitalters ist insbesondere Saruman anzusehen, der sich die Welt mit seinen Maschinenträumen und rationalistischen Prinzipien unterwerfen möchte. Saruman verleiht dem Bewusstsein einer historischen Zeitenwende in seiner Auseinandersetzung mit Gandalf Ausdruck, wobei er aus der Erkenntnis der historischen Umbruchssituation einen persönlichen Machtanspruch generiert: »The Elder Days are gone. The Middle Days are passing. The Younger Days are beginning. The time of the Elves is over, but our time is at hand: the world of Men, which we must rule« (LotR 252).

In den vier Strophen des Gedichts beklagt das lyrische Ich immer wieder den drohenden Verlust der überirdischen Schönheit, die der Ort Kortirion letztlich manifestiert. Beispielhaft sei hierfür der Beginn der zweiten Strophe zitiert, in der das lyrische Ich seine Eindrücke davon schildert, wie die »Lonely Companies« der »holy people of an elder day« (ebd. 34) manchmal noch innerhalb Kortirions gesehen werden und die Stadt mit ihrem magischem Glanz erfüllen:

> Thou art the inmost province of the fading isle
> Where linger yet the Lonely Companies
> Still undespairing here they slowly file
> Along thy paths with solemn harmonies
> The holy people of an elder day
> Immortal Elves that singing fair and fey
> Of vanished things that were and could be yet
> Pass like a wind among the rustling trees
> A wave of bowing grass and we forget
> Their tender voices like wind-shaken bells
> Of flowers their gleaming hair like golden asphodels.
> (ebd.)

Dass für die Elben die Adjektive *holy* und *solemn*, heilig und feierlich, gewählt werden, ist in diesem Zusammenhang kein Zufall. Denn der heilige, feierliche Glanz, mit dem die elbische Gegenwart das verlassene Kortirion erfüllt, erscheint aus der Perspektive der Sterblichen eben als jene im wahrsten Sinne des Wortes übermenschliche Schönheit, deren Verlust offensichtlich nicht aufzuhalten ist, aber tief betrauert wird. Als heiliges Volk der Alten Tage, das von schönen Dingen singt, die einst waren und wieder sein könnten, repräsentieren die Elben hier wahrhaftig die »Elder Days« (LotR 308), ein Poetisches Zeitalter.

Untersucht man die verwendete Wortwahl des Gedichts, dann wird ersichtlich, dass Tolkien auf wenige Wortfelder zurückgreift, um die intendierte elegische und nostalgische Stimmung beim Leser hervorzurufen: So lauschen wir im Gedicht »wistful songs«, sehnsuchtsvollen Liedern, und einer »sad and haunting magic note«, einer schwermütigen und quälenden Zaubermelodie. Auch ertönt »a long sad whisper and lament« (LT I 34), ein langes trauriges Flüstern und Klagen. Schließlich hallt das Echo milder Klänge voller Traurigkeit, »mellow sounds of sadness echoing« (ebd. 35). Allein der Begriff *fading* wird im Gedicht sechs Mal verwendet und verweist so darauf, dass das Schwinden, der Verlust eines poetischen Daseinszustands als das Leitmotiv des Gedichts anzusehen ist. Formulierungen dieser Art, in denen aus der Sicht eines Sterblichen nostalgischer Trauer Ausdruck verliehen wird, kontrastieren das prosaische Jetzt mit einem poetischen Damals, in dem die ehemaligen Bewohner Kortirions dieses mit Glanz, Schönheit und Musik erfüllten. Auf die beiden anderen Fassungen des Gedichts soll an dieser Stelle nicht weiter eingegangen werden, da der nostalgische Gestus der ersten Fassung auch dort die Stimmung des gesamten Gedichts prägt.

Existentielles Heimweh in Mittelerde

Neben den bereits behandelten zwei Formen der innerweltlichen Nostalgie ist im Werke Tolkiens noch eine weitere Ausprägung der Nostalgie von Bedeutung, die ich die als *existentielles Heimweh* bezeichnen möchte und die in deutlichem Bezug zur Romantik steht. Was jedoch haben wir uns unter existentiellem Heimweh in Tolkiens Mittelerde vorzustellen? Es handelt es um ein Gefühl bzw. ein Wesensmerkmal, das insbesondere für die Menschen als Gattungswesen charakteristisch ist. In dem posthum veröffentlichen Text *Athrabeth Finrod ah Andreth* finden wir den Gedanken eines existentiellen Heimwehs, das die Menschen in Tolkiens Kosmos plagt, am deutlichsten formuliert. Geschildert wird ein Dialog zwischen dem Elben Finrod und der Menschenfrau Andreth, in dem die beiden die unterschiedlichen Schicksale ihrer Rassen diskutieren und insbesondere zur Frage der Unsterblichkeit Stellung nehmen.

Entscheidend für unser Verständnis des existentiellen Heimwehs bei Tolkien sind einige Ausführungen Finrods zum Wesen des Menschen. So beobachtet Finrod bei den Menschen ein unterschwelliges Gefühl, in Arda unbehaust und nicht heimisch zu sein, ein Gefühl, das die Menschen spüren und die Elben erkennen können: »Of this then we are certain without debate, or else all our wisdom is vain: ... we see clearly that the *fëar* of Men are not, as are ours, confinded to Arda, nor is Arda their home« (MR 315). Die Menschen haben nach dieser Einschätzung ihre Heimat *nicht* in Arda. Dieses grundlegende Wesensmerkmal des Menschen ist für Finrod die Begründung für eine spezifische Art des Menschen, den Dingen in der Welt zu begegnen:

> Each of our kindreds perceives Arda differently, and appraises its beauties in different mode and degree. How shall I say it? To me the difference seems like that between one who visits a strange country, and abides there a while (but need not), and one who has lived in that land always (and must). To the former all thing that he sees are new and strange, and in that degree loveable. To the other all things are familiar, the only things that are, his own, and in that degree precious. (ebd.)

Aufgrund dieser besonderen Art, die Dinge als Fremder anzuschauen, bezeichnen die Elben die Menschen als Gäste in Arda (vgl. ebd.). Und diese besondere Art der Anschauung ist es auch, die für unsere Fragestellung so interessant ist. Wodurch ist der charakteristische Weltzugang der Menschen nach Finrod weiter gekennzeichnet?

> But do you know that the Eldar say of Men that they look for no thing for itself; that they study it, it is to discover something else: that they love it, it is only (so it seems) because it reminds them of some other dearer thing? Yet with what is this comparison? Where are these other things? We are both, Elves and Men, in Arda and of Arda; and such knowledge as Men have is derived from Arda (or so it would appear). Whence then comes this memory that ye have with you, even before ye begin to learn? (ebd. 316)

Finrod analysiert hier, von seinem (beschränkten elbischen) Standpunkt aus, das existentielle Heimweh des Menschen in Tolkiens Mittelerde. Der Mensch sucht in den Dingen Ardas im Gegensatz zum Elben immer etwas anderes. Er blickt die Dinge an und sieht sie eigentlich gar nicht als das, was sie sind. Die Dinge so, wie sie sind oder wie sie den Elben erscheinen, interessieren ihn nicht. Der Mensch schaut durch die Objekte gleichsam hindurch. Für ihn sind die Dinge Symbole für etwas anderes, etwas Schönes, etwas, an das sich der Mensch durch den Anblick der Welt wehmütig erinnert fühlt, was er jedoch nicht genau benennen kann. Der Mensch besitzt demnach eine nostalgische Erinnerung an eine Heimat, die nicht in den Kreisen der Welt liegt und die durch die Begegnung mit den Dingen geweckt wird.

Dem liegt der Gedanke der Zeichenhaftigkeit der Welt zugrunde, wonach die Dingwelt nur das Überzeitliche widerspiegelt oder durchschimmern lässt. In diesem Sinne fragt Finrod: »Or is there somewhere else a world of which all things we see, all things that either Elves or Men know, are only tokens or reminders?« (ebd. 318). Alle Dinge sind demnach nur Zeichen (tokens) und eine Mahnung bzw. Erinnerung (reminders). Neben anderen philosophisch-religiösen Systemen, auf die man an dieser Stelle sicherlich eingehen könnte (z.B. Platons Ideenlehre), ist ein solches Ungenügen an der Dingwelt doch auch eindeutig in der romantischen Weltanschauung verwurzelt. Auch für den Romantiker sind die Dinge Sinnbilder. Sinnbilder für was? Der Romantiker würde sagen: Für das schlummernde Lied, für das Absolute oder Göttliche in allen Dingen. Novalis spricht in diesem Zusammenhang von Hieroglyphen oder Chiffren, die in der Natur aufscheinen und uns als eine halb bekannte Zeichenschrift den eigentlichen Charakter der Dinge ahnen lassen. So erkennt der Mensch in allem

> ... Figuren, die zu jener großen Chiffernschrift zu gehören scheinen, die man überall, auf Flügeln, Eierschalen, in Wolken, im Schnee, in Kristallen und in Steinbildungen, auf gefrierenden Wassern, im Innern und Äußern der Gebirge, der Pflanzen, der Tiere, der Menschen, in den Lichtern des Himmels, auf berührten und gestri-

chenen Scheiben von Pech und Glas, in den Feilspänen um den
Magnet her, und sonderbaren Konjunkturen des Zufalls erblickt.
In ihnen ahndet man den Schlüssel dieser Wunderschrift... allein
die Ahndung will sich selbst in keine feste Form fügen, und scheint
kein höherer Schlüssel werden zu wollen. (Novalis I 79)

Finrods Einschätzung des Menschen als ein Wesen, das die Dinge ansieht, ihre Schönheit schätzen und lieben kann, weil sie Zeichen und Symbol für etwas Höheres sind, ist eine durch und durch romantische Weltanschauung. Ein Mensch, der der Welt so begegnet, wartet auf ein Zeichen, das den Schleier vor den Dingen hebt und das Eigentliche offenbart, auf das alle Dinge nur verweisen. Dieser Gedankengang findet in der *Athrabeth* seine finale Schlussfolgerung in den Worten Finrods, wenn er den Zustand der Menschen am Ende aller Zeiten, in »Arda Remade«, als eine Heimkehr schildert: »But ye, ye would then be at home, looking at all things intently, as your own« (MR 319). Das existentielle Heimweh des Menschen wäre dann überwunden und es wäre nicht mehr vonnöten, ständig aufs Neue zu versuchen, die Zeichensprache der Natur zu entschlüsseln, da der Mensch den Dingen dann nicht mehr als Fremder gegenüberstände.

Zusammenfassung

Fassen wir die Ergebnisse zusammen. Der Topos der romantischen Nostalgie ist in Tolkiens Werk in drei Formen verankert. Das örtlich-gebundene, gegenwartsbezogene Heimweh bezieht sich auf die Sehnsucht eines von der Heimat entfernten Individuums, nach Hause zurückzukehren. Durch Formen historischer Nostalgie in Tolkiens Werk kann – im Sinne der Romantik – ein Kontrast zwischen einer glanzvollen poetischen Vergangenheit und einer im Vergleich dazu prosaischen Gegenwart hergestellt werden. An eine solche nostalgische Vergangenheitsverklärung können darüber hinaus politische Hoffnungen und Forderungen gebunden sein. Die Sehnsucht nach einem poetischen, von den Elben verkörperten Zeitalter hat sich bei Tolkien u.a. in seinem bisher wenig beachteten *Kortirion*-Gedichten niedergeschlagen.

Insbesondere die dritte Form der Nostalgie in Tolkiens Werk, das existentielle Heimweh des Menschen, weist Bezüge zur romantischen Weltanschauung auf. Der Gedanke einer existentiellen Heimatlosigkeit des Menschen in Arda, die Vorstellung, dass die Sinnenwelt dem Menschen als eine Zeichenschrift gegenübersteht, die ihn auf seine eigentliche Heimat verweist und eine nostalgische Sehnsucht weckt, sind allesamt Aspekte, die auch für die Romantik charakteristisch sind.

Bibliographie

Eichendorff, Joseph v. *Sämtliche Werke des Freiherrn Joseph von Eichendorff. Historisch-kritische Ausgabe*. Begr. Wilhelm Kosch u. August Sauer. Hg. Hermann Kunisch, Helmut Koopmann u.a. 18 Bde. Stuttgart: Max Niemeyer, 1993ff

Eilmann, Julian. »Lieder und Poesie als Teil der kulturellen Kommunikation Mittelerdes«. *Hither Shore* 3 (2006): 246-259

---. "Sleeps a song in things abounding. J.R.R. Tolkien and the German Romantic Tradition". *Music in Middle-earth*. Eds. Heidi Steimel and Friedhelm Schneidewind. Zurich/Jena: Walking Tree Publishers, 2010: 167-184

Gerschmann, Karl-Heinz. »Nostalgie«. *Historisches Wörterbuch der Philosophie*. Bd. 6. Hg. Joachim Ritter u. Karlfried Gründer. Darmstadt: WBG, 934-935

Novalis. *Schriften. Die Werke Friedrich von Hardenbergs*. 4 Bde. Hg. Paul Kluckhohn u. Richard Samuel. Stuttgart: Kohlhammer, 1960f

Schwering, Markus. »Romantische Geschichtsauffassung – Mittelalterbild und Europagedanke«. *Romantik-Handbuch*. Hg. Helmut Schanze. Stuttgart: Kröner, 1994, 541-555

Segeberg, Harro. »Phasen der Romantik«. *Romantik-Handbuch*. Hg. Helmut Schanze. Stuttgart: Kröner, 1994, 31-78

Tolkien, J.R.R: *The Hobbit or there and back again*. Boston/New York: Houghton Mifflin, 1996

---. *The Lord of the Rings*. London: HarperCollins, 1995

---. *The Book of Lost Tales*. Hg. Christopher Tolkien. (The History of Middle-earth I and II) London: HarperCollins, 2002

---. *Morgoth's Ring*. Hg. Christopher Tolkien (The History of Middle-earth X). London: HarperCollins, 2002

Wahrig, Gerhard, Hildegard Krämer u. Harald Zimmermann, Hg. *Brockhaus-Wahrig. Deutsches Wörterbuch*. Bd. 4. Wiesbaden: Brockhaus, 1982

'There and back again' – a Romantic Walk?
Eine kritische Betrachtung von J.R.R. Tolkiens *The Hobbit* aus dem Blickwinkel der Romantik
Thomas Scholz (Frankfurt)

Der Frage, ob Tolkiens Werk – in unserem Fall *The Hobbit*[1] – als (spät-) romantisch verstanden werden kann, können wir selbstverständlich nur nachgehen, wenn wir ein möglichst klares Verständnis davon haben, was wir unter dem Begriff *Romantik* verstehen. Den Paradigmenwechsel vom Neoklassizismus hin zu einer modernen Ästhetik, den Clifford Siskin als »The Lyric Turn« (Siskin 1ff) beschreibt, hat die Forschung seit ihren Anfängen jedoch derart mannigfaltig charakterisiert, dass bereits vor mehr als 80 Jahren eine eindeutige Definition schwierig wurde. »The word ›romantic‹ has come to mean so many things that, by itself, it means nothing. It has ceased to perform the function of a verbal sign«, konstatiert Arthur Lovejoy schon 1924 (Lovejoy 232). Diese Heterogenität beginnt bereits bei den Big Six der Romantik – William Blake, William Wordsworth, Samuel Taylor Coleridge, Lord Byron, Percy Shelley und John Keats, die lange Zeit wie die einzigen Vertreter dieser Epoche gehandelt wurden. Bereits ihre Texte können wir nicht unter »love, landscape & longing« zusammenfassen. Die Unterschiede werden noch größer, wenn wir den erweiterten englischen Romantik-Kanon und nicht hier nur die männlichen Autoren sondern auch ihre schreibenden Zeitgenossinnen betrachten. Vollkommen unübersichtlich wird es, wenn wir die Nationalliteraturen abgleichen und feststellen müssen, dass es zwischen deutscher, englischer und französischer Romantik ebenfalls deutliche Unterschiede gibt. Lovejoy plädiert daher für die Verwendung des Begriffs im Plural und möchte über *romanticisms* sprechen. Dieser Ansatz stellt einen Kompromiss dar zwischen der in den 1920ern herrschenden Erkenntnis, dass es »die eine« Romantik nicht gibt, und dem gleichzeitigen Wunsch, nicht auf den tradierten und in einigen Belangen durchaus praktischen Begriff zu verzichten. Ein solcher Mittelweg vereint zwar alle Erkenntnisse, lässt das Problem aber weiterhin bestehen.

Mittlerweile hat die Philologie diese Hürde durch einen legitimen Trick genommen. Die Kriterien für die Zugehörigkeit zur Romantik liegen nicht mehr allein im Text, sondern im Kontext seiner Entstehung. Die Romantik wird als Reaktion auf den historischen Umbruch der sozialen, wirtschaftlichen und politischen Gefüge in ihrer Epoche verstanden. So wird die Heterogenität der

---

1 Ich verstehe das Buch ausdrücklich als eigenständigen Text. Auch wenn oberflächliche Betrachtungen zu anderen Schlüssen kommen, legen sowohl seine historische Genese als auch die narratologischen Strukturen nahe, The Hobbit nicht als vierten Band von *The Lord of the Rings* zu verstehen.

Epoche programmatisch integriert, wie Christoph Bode 2005 konstatiert. »All this variety need not worry us, if we reconceptualise European Romanticism as a *set of responses*, highly differentiated and at times downright contradictory, to a historically specific *challenge*: the challenge of the ever-accellerating [sic] modernization of European society« (Bode 127).

Will man untersuchen, ob und auf welche Art der *Hobbit* mit einer derart definierten Romantik in Verbindung steht, sind zwei Ansätze notwendig. Zum einen müssen wir prüfen, ob Tolkiens Text auf ästhetischer oder inhaltlicher Ebene signifikante Gemeinsamkeiten mit den Texten aufweist, die wir der Romantik zuordnen. Zum anderen müssen wir feststellen, ob der *Hobbit*, Gemeinsamkeiten hin oder her, als eine weitere Reaktion auf den nach unserer Definition für die Romantik ursächlichen Wandel – oder seine Fortsetzung – zu lesen ist.[2]

Ausschließen können wir in aller Kürze eine Überschneidung des *Hobbit* mit den besonderen Merkmalen der christlichen Romantik. Den einzigen Verweis auf religiöse Konzepte liefert uns der sterbende Thorin. Er erwartet, in den *halls of waiting* bis zur Erneuerung der Welt an der Seite seiner Vorfahren zu sitzen (vgl. H 348). Nach zwei spärlichen Zeilen ist dieser Aspekt jedoch abgehandelt. Gandalfs christliche Konnotation hält erst im *Lord of the Rings* Einzug. Keine Religion, weder die christliche noch sonst eine, spielen im *Hobbit* eine Rolle.

Ebenfalls irrelevant sind die Konzepte romantischer Liebe. Kein Wunder: Im Text sucht man vergebens nach nur einem einzigen namentlich erwähnten weiblichen Charakter. Und auch die *queer studies* sind bislang auf der Suche nach amourösen Beziehungen nicht fündig geworden. Brenda Partridges Aufsatztitel *No Sex Please – We're Hobbits* ist nicht nur für den *Herrn der Ringe* sondern auch für den *Hobbit* programmatisch. Von romantischer Liebe, dem heutigen populärkulturellen Inbegriff der Romantik, findet sich keine Spur.

Ganz anders verhält es sich, wenn wir uns dem romantischen Topos der Natur zuwenden. Hier bietet der *Hobbit* grundsätzlich Material, so dass wir erstmals zu einem Vergleich ansetzen können. Zunächst jedoch ein Blick in die Romantik – genau genommen in Wordsworth's *Daffodiles*:

> I wandered lonely as a cloud
> That floats on high o'er vales and hills,
> When all at once I saw a crowd,
> A host, of golden daffodils;
> Beside the lake, beneath the trees,
> Fluttering and dancing in the breeze.

---

2   Ignorieren werde ich dabei ganz bewusst die Tatsache, dass der englische Roman für die Romantik nur eine untergeordnete Rolle spielt – nicht umsonst wird die Epoche oft als Phase der ›Krise‹ und ›Verwilderung‹ des Romans bezeichnet (vgl. Schlaeger 319-324). Salopp gesprochen »findet Romantik in der Lyrik statt«, und dorthin werde ich den Blick richten.

Continuous as the stars that shine
And twinkle on the Milky Way,
They stretched in never-ending line
Along the margin of the bay:
Ten thousand saw I at a glance,
Tossing their heads in a sprightly dance.

The waves beside them danced, but they
Out-did the sparkling waves in glee:
A poet could not but be gay,
In such a jocund company:
I gazed – and gazed – but little thought
What wealth the show to me had brought:

Beschränken wir unseren Blick fürs Erste auf die Strophen eins bis drei. Die erhabene Schönheit der einfachen Natur steht im Vordergrund, das Vermögen des Menschen, sich mit ihr in eine Verbindung zu setzen. Ein Blick in den *Hobbit* zeigt, dass Natur auch anders sein kann. »Not far ahead were dreary hills, rising higher and higher, dark with trees. On some of them were old castles with an evil look, as if they had been built by wicked people« (H 65). Auch der Weg durch die Berge, die in der Romantik der Inbegriff des Erhabenen sind, wird für die 14 Gefährten nicht besser.

»It was a hard path and a dangerous path, a crooked way and a lonely and a long« (H 101). Und auch der Wald scheidet als romantischer Topos aus. »The entrance to the path was like a sort of arch leading into a gloomy tunnel made by two great trees that leant together, too old and strangled with ivy and hung with lichen to bear more than a few blackened leaves« (H 191). Wenig romantisch und viel mehr neo-gothisch muten uns die Schilderungen an. Die Natur ist die Kulisse für Abenteuer, in der man besser mit einem Schwert gerüstet ist als dass man Narzissen beobachtet. Positiv aufgeladen sind die künstlichen Wohnorte von Hobbits, Elben und Zwergen und nicht die einsamen Wälder und gefährlichen Schluchten.

Trotz dieser widrigen Verhältnisse ist die Verbundenheit mit der Natur ein erstrebenswerter Zustand. Im Einklang mit ihr bewegen sich die Hobbits fast lautlos fort – der praktische Nutzen der Verbundenheit ist hier offensichtlich. Die Sprache der Tiere zu sprechen ist von großem Vorteil. Nicht nur in kriegerischen Auseinandersetzungen im Sinne Thorins, sondern auch in öko-romantischer Anbindung an Beorn und seine idyllische Tierkommune. Als *skinchanger* halb Mensch, halb Tier, verkörpert er perfekt die Symbiose mit der Natur und ist Teil von ihr. Nur durch ihn wird die Natur erhaben – wenn auch erst in der Schlacht.

But even with the eagles they were still outnumbered. In that last hour Beorn himself had appeared – no one knew how or where from. He came alone, and in bear's shape; and he seemed to have grown almost to a giant-size in his wrath. The roar of his voice was like drum and guns; and he tossed wolves and goblins from his path like straws and feathers. He fell upon their rear, and broke like a clap of thunder through the ring.

(H 349)

Dass die Natur nicht aus sich heraus erhaben ist, sondern erst im Kampf für die gerechte Sache ihre Größe offenbart, tritt an dieser Stelle symptomatisch für den gesamten Text zutage. Denn während die Romantik die Natur als solche für verehrungswürdig hält, herrscht im *Hobbit* eine andere Gewichtung. Hier ist die Vergangenheit per se ein erstrebenswerter Zustand, die enge Verbindung zur Natur ist ein ihr untergeordneter Bestandteil. Beorns übermenschliche Fähigkeiten und sein Verhältnis zu den Tieren entspringen seiner uralten Abstammung. *Orcrist* und *Glamdring* sind mächtige Waffen aus der Vergangenheit. Früher verstanden die Zwerge die Vögel leichter, die Hobbits waren größer, und die Elben marschierten schneller. Kurz und gut: Früher war alles besser. Gemeinsam hat die Fantasyliteratur mit der Romantik daher die Annahme, dass der aktuelle Zustand nicht der beste ist. Doch die Romantik propagiert eine fortlaufende Annäherung an den von ihr formulierten Idealzustand in einer Vorwärtsbewegung. Die Fantasy hingegen stemmt sich gegen den kontinuierlichen Verfall. Nach vorne geht es nur bergab – bergauf liegt hinter uns, im Mittelalter.

Doch nicht nur Tolkiens kontra-empirische Literatur nutzt das Mittelalter intensiv. Auch die Romantik bedient sich reichlich. John Keats' Gedicht *The Eve of Saint Agnes* (1820) ist ein prominentes Beispiel für die ritterliche Liebe, die die Romantiker hoch schätzten. Nicht zuletzt die Ordnung des Mittelalters, in der jeder Mensch einen fest angestammten Platz hatte, faszinierte die romantischen Dichter in ihrer Zeit der Umwälzungen. Im *Hobbit* jedoch ist die Vergangenheit mehr – sie ist superlativ. Die Helden waren größer, ihre Waffen gefährlicher, ihre Schätze prächtiger und auch ihre Gegner und die Niederlagen waren von übermenschlichen Ausmaßen. Der spektakuläre Untergang des Zwergenkönigreichs durch Smaugs Angriff und seine intradiegetische historiographische Tradierung (vgl. H 44f) sind dafür signifikant.

Unter dieser alles überragenden Vorzeit subsumiert Tolkien einiges, das in der Romantik an anderer Stelle zu finden ist. Beispielsweise die revolutionäre Stoßrichtung vieler romantischer Autoren. Die Französische Revolution inspirierte fast alle Romantiker. Lord Byron propagierte im Oberhaus liberales Gedankengut. Percy Shelleys Gedicht *The Mask of Anarchy* (veröffentlicht 1832) prangert nach dem Peterloo Massaker 1819 die Autoritäten »God, and King, and Law« an und fordert die Bevölkerung zum Widerstand auf. Und auch im *Hobbit* ist Widerstand gegen die politischen Herrscher zu finden.

> 'We will have King Bard!' the people near at hand shouted in replay. 'We have had enough of the old men and the money-counters!' And people further off took up the cry: 'Up the Bowman, and down with Moneybags,' till the clamour echoed along the shore.
> (H 310)

Hier legen die Bewohner der *Lake-town* jedoch – ganz im Gegensatz zu den Autoren der Romantik – recht mittelalterliche Maßstäbe an. Bard zeichnet sich sowohl durch seine königliche Abstammung als auch durch seine heroischen Taten in der Schlacht aus. Mit ihm soll ein rudimentär demokratisches System durch eine Monarchie ersetzt werden – ein Tausch, dem kein Romantiker zugestimmt hätte. Dafür hat wiederum ein ursprünglich sehr romantisches Versatzstück den Weg in die Mittelalterlichkeit Mittelerdes gefunden – auch wenn es heute oftmals in anderem Kontext gelesen wird.

> Out leapt the King under the Mountain, and his companions followed him. Hood and cloak were gone; they were in shining armour, and red light leapt from their eyes. In the gloom the great dwarf gleamed like gold in a dying fire.
>
> ...Wolf and rider fell or fled before them. Thorin wielded his axe with mighty strokes, and nothing seemed to harm him.
>
> 'To me! To me! Elves and Men! To me! O my kinsfolk!' he cried, and his voice shook like a horn in the valley.
>
> Down, heedless of order, rushed all the dwarves of Dain to his help. Down too came many of the Lake-men, for Bard could not restrain them; and out upon the other side came many of the spearmen of the elves.
> (H 343f)

Thorin kämpft mit dem Siegesheil des gerechten Königs, ganz nach mittelalterlicher Vorstellung. Daraus erwächst jedoch ein Zugriff auf das Kollektivsubjekt der Volksgemeinschaft (die hier sogar völkerübergreifend funktioniert). Auch wenn der Begriff im Nationalsozialismus nachträglich umbesetzt wurde und daher für uns heute in anderem Kontext steht, hat doch die Romantik die Vorstellung hervorgebracht, dass das von ihr so hoch bewertete Subjekt in einem Kollektiv aller Subjekte seinen Platz finden und zu einem Teil des größeren Ganzen werden kann (vgl. Reinfandt, bspw. 30 oder 94). Sich diesem Kollektiv in einem gerechten Kampf anzuschließen, unter der Führung eines von Natur aus rechtmäßigen Anführers, der dem Impuls des Augenblicks folgt, ist der Inbegriff der Romantik.

Doch wie steht es mit dem Auenland? Hier haben wir keine Mittelalterlichkeit sondern reine Neuzeit vorliegen – Tabak, Tee und das Postsystem sind nur die oberflächlichsten Anzeichen dafür (vgl. Scholz 40ff). Die Romantik des Vergangenen entfällt somit. Und auch sonst finden wir in den spärlichen Schilderungen, die dem Auenland im *Hobbit* vorbehalten sind, keine gewichtigen Anhaltspunkte für eine besondere Dominanz romantischer Aspekte. Gewiss ist die Hobbithöhle in einen Hügel eingebaut und somit eine gewisse Nähe zur Natur gegeben. Doch diese Symbiose ist in keiner Weise markiert – weder als idyllisch noch als ideal, noch als in irgendeiner anderen Art besonders.

Natürlich ist dem Auenland nicht viel Platz gewidmet, doch gerade hier wird potentiell romantisches Material quasi verschenkt. Es existiert zwar der von Hegel in seinen »Vorlesungen über die Ästhetik« (1835-1838) für das Romanhafte geforderte Konflikt zwischen »Individuen mit ihren subjektiven Zwecken« und der »feste[n], sichere[n] Ordnung der bürgerlichen Gesellschaft« (Hegel 219f). Doch dieser Konflikt wird quasi im Nachwort ausgetragen. Nach Bilbos Rückkehr ins Auenland werden die Probleme seiner Reintegration in die Gesellschaft und seine neue Position in derselben lediglich paraphrasiert (vgl. H 360ff).

Das Romantischste an unserem Helden ist seine Einfühlsamkeit. Sie lässt ihn den Schwerthieb gegen den wehrlosen Gollum nicht führen. Sie lässt ihn am Totenbett des sterbenden Thorin weinen. Und sie veranlasst ihn, beim Anblick seiner lang vermissten Heimat spontan ein Gedicht zu verfassen:

> Roads go ever ever on,
> Over rock and under tree,
> By caves where never sun has shone,
> By streams that never find the sea;
> Over snow by winter sown,
> And through the merry flowers of June,
> Over grass and over stone,
> And under mountains in the moon.
> Roads go ever ever on
> Under cloud and under star,
> Yet feet that wandering have gone
> Turn at last to home afar.
> Eyes that fire and sword have seen
> And horror in the halls of stone
> Look at last on meadows green
> And trees and hills they long have known.
>
> (H 359f)

Auf dieser metadiegetischen Ebene finden wir ein scheinbares Versatzstück der Romantik. »For all good Poetry«, so heißt es in dem von Wordsworth 1802 verfassten »Preface« der *Lyrical Ballads*, »is the spontaneous overflow of powerful feelings« (Wordsworth 62). Für Bilbos Gedicht ist dieses Kriterium gegeben. Doch Wordsworth fährt im »Preface« fort:

> Poems to which any value can be attached, were never produced on any variety of subjects but by a man who being possessed of more than unusual organic sensibility had also thought long and deeply. For our continued influxes of feeling are modified and directed by our thoughts. (ebd.)

Ein Blick in die letzte Strophe der *Daffodiles* untermauert das Wordsworth'sche Konzept:

> For oft, when on my couch I lie
> In vacant or in pensive mood,
> They flash upon that inward eye
> Which is the bliss of solitude;
> And then my heart with pleasure fills,
> And dances with the daffodils.

Erst die Reflexion in der vierten Strophe über die Emotion macht die subjektive Erfahrung allgemein zugänglich. Sie wird in eine Kunstform gegossen und somit »kulturell gebändigt« (Reinfandt 41), durch die Thematisierung des Verfahrens wird der Effekt noch verstärkt. Bilbos Eindrücke hingegen finden wir zwar in ein regelmäßiges Versschema gepresst, doch von einer Reflexion über den Prozess der subjektiven Wahrnehmung der Natur kann hier nicht die Rede sein. Ein essentielles Element romantischer Lyrik fehlt somit.

Auch in seiner Prosa verzichtet Tolkien weitgehend auf eine subjektive Perspektive, die doch für die Romantik so wichtig ist. Auch wenn der extradiegetische Erzähler sich einige Male in den Vordergrund drängt und durch Anknüpfungen an die Welt des intendierten Lesers Sachverhalte von Middle-earth erläutert, tritt dabei doch nie eine explizit subjektive Sichtweise zutage. Er bleibt unsere einzige Informationsquelle. Und auch Bilbos Einschätzungen sind zwar ex definitione subjektiv, doch geht ihnen dabei pikanterweise fast jegliche Subjektivität ab. Für Farah Mendlesohn ist dieser offensichtliche Widerspruch fester Bestandteil der Portal-Quest-Fantasy, zu der sie *The Hobbit* zählt, und somit leicht erklärbar: »The portal-quest-fantasy by its very nature needs to deny the possibility of a polysemic discourse in order to validate the ›quest‹. There can only be one understanding of the world: an understanding that validates the quest« (Mendlesohn 12f).

Die Welt, die der Erzähler uns präsentiert, darf in der Portal-Quest-Fantasy nicht hinterfragbar sein. Entweder wird sonst auch die *quest* hinterfragbar und die Wirkung des Textes somit vollkommen verändert, oder aber der so genannte *information download*, die Vermittlung der relevanten Fakten bezüglich der Sekundärwelt, wird deutlich gestört. Die Funktion des Verfassers als *sub-creator* im Sinne Tolkiens würde dadurch fast zwangsläufig torpediert. Seine Schöpfung wäre nicht mehr konsistent.

Dieses Problem in Bezug auf eine Verbindung von Fantasyliteratur und Romantik ist in einem ästhetischen Paradigma der romantischen Epoche angelegt, dass M.H. Abrams bereits 1953 in seinem Buch *The Mirror and the Lamp* anschaulich erläutert. Während die Kunst von der Antike Platons bis in Dr. Johnsons Zeit die Welt widerspiegeln wollte (Abrams 30ff), hat es sich die Romantik selbst zum Ziel gesetzt, die innere Welt des Subjekts wie eine Lampe zu erleuchten. Dieser Ansatz ist auch unproblematisch zu verfolgen, solange allen Beteiligten des Kommunikationsprozesses »Literatur« der jeweilige Bezugspunkt bekannt ist.[3] In anderen Worten: Eine Welt, deren Vorbild ich als Leser aus meiner Lebensrealität kenne, muss nicht gespiegelt werden, um sie zu erfassen. Ich kann mich ganz auf die Beleuchtung der inneren Welt einlassen. Handelt das Kunstwerk, also hier der Text, jedoch von einer Sekundärwelt, so kann ich nicht auf deren Spiegelung verzichten. Denn das gespiegelte Original ist unbekannt. Wir wüssten nichts über Mittelerde, wenn wir nicht Tolkiens Spiegelungen hätten. Hätte er sich darauf beschränkt, dass Innenleben seiner Charaktere zu beleuchten, wäre uns seine Sekundärwelt unzugänglich.

Ohne eine entsprechende erzählte Subjektivität kann es natürlich auch nicht ihre narrative Synthese mit der objektivierenden Darstellung geben. In dieser Verschmelzung spiegelt sich in der Romantik die Umwälzung der Lebenswelt im Ästhetischen wider, wird so zum künstlerischen Programm. Tolkien greift diesen ästhetischen Aspekt für den *Hobbit* nicht auf, kann ihn gar nicht aufgreifen, wenn man Mendlesohns Argumentation folgt. Während Jane Austen durch die erlebte Rede Erzählinstanz und Charakteraussage bewusst untrennbar miteinander vermengt und so deren Differenz überhaupt thematisiert, setzt Tolkien auf die direkte Rede. Die Unterschiede der erzählten Figuren und des Erzählers werden so marginalisiert.

Ziehen wir eine Zwischenbilanz: Auf der Ebene der *histoire* finden wir wenig Übereinstimmung mit der Romantik. Religion und Liebe spielen keine Rolle. Der Natur wird nicht die Bedeutung zugemessen, die sie in der Romantik erfährt. Nur die Vergangenheit wird, ebenso wie in der Romantik, überhöht.

---

3 An diesem Punkt vereinfache ich das komplexe Beziehungsgeflecht von empirischer Wirklichkeit und literarischer Realität sträflich. Eine angemessene Ausführung würde jedoch den hier gegebenen Rahmen sprengen.

Das jedoch in viel stärkerem Maße, als es für Keats & Co. typisch ist. Der *discourse* wiederum zeichnet sich noch weniger durch eine Überschneidung mit der Romantik aus. Die narrative Subjektivität wird nicht thematisiert, folglich auch nicht synthetisch integriert oder kulturell gebändigt. Die Verortung des Subjekts in der Gesellschaft, die die Romantik ästhetisch spiegelt, spielt in Tolkiens Text keine Rolle.

Wenn wir uns jedoch die Definition der Romantik als »a *set of responses*... to a historically specific *challenge*« (Bode 127) ins Gedächtnis rufen, drängt sich die Frage auf, ob Tolkien nicht etwa eine ebensolche Reaktion verfasst hat. Begeben wir uns daher für einen kurzen Exkurs aus der Literatur hinaus und in die Geschichte hinein, in die Lebenszeit Tolkiens.

Die »ever-accellerating modernization« Europas hat hier seit der Romantik nicht angehalten. Ganz im Gegenteil. Technische Neuerungen wie Telegraph, Telefon und Automobil halten Einzug ins alltägliche Leben. Die politischen Systeme ändern sich, ein allgemeines Wahlrecht für alle Erwachsenen über 21 Jahre wird in England schrittweise bis 1928 eingeführt. Die Weltwirtschaftskrise 1929 erschüttert als erste negative Folge der beginnenden Globalisierung die Welt. Und vor allem der Erste Weltkrieg hat seine Spuren im Britischen Empire hinterlassen, das zwar in jedem Weltkrieg auf der Gewinnerseite steht, seine Stellung als Weltmacht jedoch einbüßt.

Aus diesen Umständen eine subjektive Marginalisierung des Individuums abzuleiten, das Schwinden sozialer Verortung zu konstatieren und somit zu einem recht ähnlichen Befund zu kommen, wie er für die Romantik gemacht wurde, kann nicht schwer sein. *The Hobbit* könnte auf dieser Basis als literarische Reaktion auf seine Entstehungszeit gelesen werden, die ähnlichen Verwerfungen wie die Romantik unterworfen war.

Doch warum reagiert Tolkien weniger optimistisch als die Romantiker? Natürlich fehlt den Big Six die traumatisierende Weltkriegserfahrung. Doch gerade diese für Tolkien so oft als prägend eingestufte Erfahrung ist nicht der einzige mögliche Ursprung für die Abwesenheit des romantischen Optimismus. Vielmehr hat sich ein Teil der programmatischen Forderungen der Romantik erfüllt – das Wahlrecht ist der einfachste Beleg –, ohne dass ihre Kernfrage nach der Verortung des Subjekts beantwortet worden wäre. Von einer stabilen Verortung in der Gesellschaft kann zu Tolkiens Zeit wesentlich weniger die Rede sein als in der frühen Romantik. Eine Rückkehr zur Natur ist ferner denn je. Dass der *Hobbit* das Heil in eine exotische Vergangenheit projiziert, kann daher vielleicht als Hinweis darauf gelesen werden, dass eine romantische Alternative in der eigenen Realität subjektiv weiter entfernt zu sein scheint als die einer Sekundärwelt. Dass Tolkien nicht naiv einer eskapistischen Vision nachhängt, beweist wiederum die Portalfunktion des Auenlandes – sowohl als Ein- wie auch als Ausstieg in die mittelalterliche Welt von Mittelerde. Hier ist die Idylle klein und das Übel noch kleiner, von idealisierter Romantik ist man weit entfernt. Über diese wenig exotische Schwelle lässt sich Mittelerde gut betreten, und hier kann man sowohl den Leser und auch den Protagonisten getrost zurücklassen.

Fänden sich für diese Hypothesen ausreichend Anhaltspunkte, müsste *The Hobbit* tatsächlich als eine Fortführung der Romantik mit anderen Mitteln gelesen werden. Als romantisch im klassischen Sinne kann das Buch jedoch nur sehr bedingt gelesen werden.

Bibliographie:

Abrams, M.H. *The Mirror and the Lamp*. Oxford: Oxford University Press, 1953

Bode, Christoph. "Europe" *Romanticisms: An Oxford Guide*. Ed. Nicholas Roe. Oxford: Oxford University Press, 2005, 126-136

Farah Mendlesohn. *Rhetorics of Fantasy*. Middletown: Wesleyan University Press, 2008

Hegel, Georg Wilhelm Friedrich. »Vorlesung über die Ästhetik« (1835-1838). *Theorie-Werksausgabe*. Bd. 14. Frankfurt: Suhrkamp, 1970

Lovejoy, Arthur O. "On the Discrimination of Romanticisms". *Publications of the Modern Language Association of America* 39 (1924): 229-253

Partridge, Brenda. "No Sex Please – We're Hobbits: The Construction of Female Sexuality in *The Lord of the Rings*". *J.R.R. Tolkien: This Far Land*. Ed. Robert Giddings. London: Vision Press Limited, 1983, 179-197

Reinfandt, Christoph. *Englische Romantik*. Berlin: Erich Schmidt Verlag, 2008

Schlaeger, Jürgen. »Die Unwirtlichkeit des Wirklichen: Zur Wandlungsdynamik des englischen Romans im 18. Jahrhundert«. *Poetica* 25 (1993): 319-337

Scholz, Thomas. *Weit entfernte Wunder*. Frankfurt: Peter Lang Verlag, 2009

Siskin, Clifford. *The Historicity of Romantic Discourse*. New York/Oxford: Oxford University Press, 1988

Tolkien, J.R.R. *The Annotated Hobbit*. Ed. Douglas A. Anderson. Second edition, revised. London: HarperCollins, 2003

Wordsworth, William. *Lyrical ballads*. Harlow: Longman, 1992

Outer and Inner Landscapes in Tolkien: Between Wordsworth, Coleridge, and Dostoevskij

Emanuele Rimoli (Roma) / Guglielmo Spirito (Assisi)

The beauty of the earth is the first beauty. Millions of years before us the earth lived in wild elegance. Landscape is the first-born of creation. Sculpted with huge patience over millennia, landscape has enormous diversity of shape, presence and memory. There is poignancy in beholding the beauty of the landscape: often it feels as though it has been waiting for centuries for the recognition and witness of the human eye. In the ninth *Duino Elegy*, Rilke says:

> Perhaps we are here in order to say: house,
> bridge, fountain, gate, pitcher, fruit-tree, window...
> To say them more intensely than the Things themselves
> ever dreamed of existing.

Unable to penetrate the earth, light knows how to tease suggestions of depth from its surface. Where radiance falls, depths gather to the surface as to a window.

There is something in our clay nature that needs to continually experience the ancient, outer ease of the world. The earth is not only outside us; it is within. When we emerge from our offices, rooms and houses, outdoors we are also at home (cf. O'Donahue 32-37). Or perhaps not, if we are as forlorn as Merry at Harrowdale:

> He sat for a moment half dreaming, listening to the noise of water, the whisper of dark trees, the crack of stone, and the vast waiting silence that brooded behind all sound. He loved mountains, or he had loved the thought of them marching on the edge of stories brought from far away; but now he was borne down by the insupportable weight of Middle-earth. He longed to shut out the immensity in a quiet room by a fire.
>
> (LotR 822)

A Glimpse of a Vision

So it came to pass that we choose *Outer* and *Inner Landscapes* as the focus of our talk.[1] Our intention and aim is rather modest: simply to suggest a very few – amongst many – characteristics of J.R.R. Tolkien's literary sub-creation (with the consequent perception and description) of 'Inner and Outer Landscapes'. We do not intend to explore influences nor argue about forms and styles, but try to *recognize a glimpse of a vision*. 'Poetry which needs explanation is not worth reading', said Flannery O'Connor once. Prose either, we may say.

Those simple distinctive characteristics of Tolkien are better seen, we suggest, in comparison with some of the Romantics – English and Russian –, including a former admirer and follower of some of them – but who was not one of them: the great Fedor Dostoevskij.

Englishmen and Russians

We may have some justification for blending together such different authors as Russians and English, because we follow Clive Staples Lewis's statement in *The Four Loves:*

> For some people, perhaps especially for Englishmen and Russians, what we call 'the love of nature' is a permanent and serious sentiment...
> The nature-lovers whom I have in mind are not very much concerned with individual beautiful objects – trees, flowers and animals. An enthusiastic botanist is for them a dreadful companion on a ramble. He is always stopping to draw their attention to particulars. Nor are they looking for 'views' or landscapes. Wordsworth, their spokesman, strongly deprecates this. It leads to 'a comparison of scene with scene', makes you 'pamper' yourself with 'meagre novelties of colour and proportion'. While you are busying yourself with this critical and discriminating activity you lose what really matters

---

[1] The Romantics being our partners in reflection, and remembering Wordsworth's and Coleridge's friendship, we decided to give this talk together, for – as Coleridge wrote in his notebooks – 'the flames of two candles joined give a much stronger light than both of them separate' (Sisman 121).

– the 'moods of time and season', the 'spirit' of the place. And of course Wordsworth is right. That is why, if you love nature in his fashion, a landscape painter is (out of doors) an even worse companion than a botanist. (Lewis 22)

This is exactly the way Tolkien did *not* see things. Unlike Lewis, we can not find in Tolkien any real sympathy for Wordsworth. And he behaves rather as a 'botanist' while walking in the countryside, disliking the Lewis brothers' 'ruthless' speed, as he saw it (Carpenter, *Inklings* 210). We find a surprisingly identical way of seeing things in the great Russian theologian and martyr, Pavel Florenskij (cf. 4).

When Lewis said: 'Tollers, one of us should write a tale of time travel and the other should do space travel', Tolkien reminded his friend of a rather similar challenge well over a century before: Lord Byron, at Lake Geneva in 1816, had challenged Percy Shelley and Mary Shelley to write a ghost story... and Mary, a mere girl at the time, went on to write *Frankenstein*... (cf. Duriez 100)[2].

What came out of Tolkien's and Lewis's challenge are among the masterpieces of 20th century literature. Together with an Englishman then, we may also find a Russian who tells things from another angle. In the work of Dostoevskij, *places* and *spaces* are not predefined, but arise and grow along with the character: they are at his service. What characterizes them is that they are both *anthropological* and *anthropocentric* (cf. Catteau 540): places and spaces reveal the man, they are *for* humans. There is neither psychological dynamic of projection, nor shameless subjectivity. Rather it is the capacity, typically human (and here Dostoevskij reveals himself as a skilled creator/sub-creator), to respond with the inner being to the outer world: 'The more a person is excellent, the stronger, richer, deeper and more sophisticated is his ability to meet, answer, and so come back to himself' (Guardini 18, translation ER/GS).

Dostoevskij never seeks to explain the nature of human space, never to replace his characters in describing, telling, acting; he never imposes on his characters (or on the reader) his own idea of the world. Dostoevskij lets the world be the natural environment in which the characters pursue their freedom. The characters, dreadfully free – as real men – obtain it in and through the places they frequent.

---

2   Although we have not included Lord Byron in this paper, we may recall that he shared with Tolkien a great love for Venice. We would like to remember also Byron's love for the Armenians – beside the sinister novel by Schiller, *Geisterseher*, translated as *The Armenian, or The Ghost-seer*, to which he was addicted as a boy (cf. MacCarthy 318). In Venice he was guest of the *Armenian Monastery of the Mechitaristi Monks*, in *San Lazzaro* Island. We mention this, for April 24th is the anniversary of the Armenian Genocide perpetrated by the Ottomans in 1915, with almost one and a half million people murdered; genocide still denied by Turkey until this very day.

The novelist designs a *scenario* where the final verdict is given, but within this, the hero is free to converse with his own conscience and with those of others.

> 'With utter realism [I want] to find the man in man... They call me a psychologist; this is not true. I am merely a realist in the higher sense, that is, I portray all the depths of the human soul.'
> (Dostoevskij quoted in Crane 140)

Looking at his notes it should be noticed that unlike Tolstoy and Turgenev, Dostoevskij cares little about descriptions. In the notebooks of *Crime and Punishment*, for example, there are only brief notes, the brevity of which contrasts with the richness and number of records relating to Raskolnikov's timing or thoughts. In the completed work, however, the balance is restored, the elements relating to the area – topography, locations of action, *inner* and *outer* colours – occupy an important place, as much as the indicators of time.

We must conclude that in Dostoevskij, space is not given or represented from the beginning, but gradually drawn around the characters. Somehow, it seems that something quite different happens with Tolkien, at least if we recall when he wrote to his son Christopher (6 May 1944) about how Faramir came to be:

> A new character has come on the scene (I am sure I did not invent him, though I like him, but there he came walking into the woods of Ithilien): Faramir, the brother of Boromir. (L 79)

In this case, the character comes out from within the unfolding of the story, almost out of the landscape itself!

The structure of Dostoevskij's spaces is symphonic, progressively organized in an imperceptible and untiring accumulation of elements. The whole, as it is constituted, is not perceived except through time and as a memory that records brief, scattered and fleeting indications. The environment is constructed as the need arises, like a country that is discovered as you approach it, or like a city that we see 'built' at every turn.

All these data, contained in the perception of the hero, offer a very concrete picture to the reader of a landscape in which the existential force arises precisely from the gaze of others, not from feelings or thoughts – as is the case of the Romantics. The eyes of the fictional characters build the cities in Dostoevskij. Their perceptions, in fact, testify to and provide the space (Catteau 529). This method is surprisingly effective: the space, thus, acquires the value of existential presence (*Sitz im Leben*). Because this reality does not need to be shown or described as existing, it is simply there (Catteau 526). For instance:

Siberia. On the banks of a broad solitary river stands a town, one of
the administrative centres of Russia; in the town there is a fortress,
in the fortress there is a prison. In the prison the second-class
convict Rodion Raskolnikov has been confined for nine months.
Almost a year and a half has passed since his crime.
(Dostoevskij, *Delitto* 635, translation ER/GS)

The description is concise, a zoom in concentric circles, a climax that points to the character and his history – from a boundless space that is Siberia, the reader's attention, in a few lines, is focussed on the 'louse' Raskolnikov. After the first few lines, the final expression turns on the vitality of the narrative: there is the *topos* (or location) and there is the perception that something has happened and is still unfolding.

Wordsworth and Coleridge

Nineteen years after the first appearance of *Lyrical Ballads*, Coleridge in his *Biographia Literaria*, set out its broad thematic terms:

During the first year that Mr Wordsworth and I were neighbours, our conversations turned frequently on the two cardinal points of poetry, the power of exciting the sympathy of the reader by a faithful adherence to the truth of nature, and the power of giving the interest of novelty by modifying colours of the imagination.
(quoted by Blades 175)

This very much echoes Wordsworth's own view in the preface to *Lyrical Ballads* (cf. Blades 175). Romantic appreciation of landscape was highly subjective; it changed according to the writer's mood and state of mind, so that the external forms of nature are less important than the internal effects they have upon the mind. Coleridge followed his close friend to the Lake District, but after a while his scintillating notebooks entries about the landscape faded. His rural existence became a claustrophobic world of isolation, ill health and domestic unhappiness. As his imagination failed, so his perception of the landscape darkened, a process he articulated in his poem *Dejection, An Ode* (Hebron VII-IX).

Wordsworth is often credited with the rediscovery, even the reinvention, of nature. For him, it exerts a real and awesome presence. The landscape becomes interfused with something internal and intangible (cf. Blades 173.205; Hebron 17). His friend, the young critic William Hazlitt, who visited Wordsworth and Coleridge at Alfoxden, recalled the moment as a sort of epiphany for him:

> Wordsworth, looking out of the low, latticed window, said, 'How beautifully the sun sets on that yellow bank!' I thought within myself, 'With what eyes these poets see nature!' and ever after, when I saw the sun-set stream upon the objects facing it, conceived I had made a discovery, or thanked Mr Wordsworth for having made one for me! (Blades 185f)

Far are we, of course, from the sunset's description of Henneth Annun, in *The Window on the West*. Faramir's favourite spot lacks also the 'sense sublime' so present in Coleridge's *The Ancient Mariner*, though it has a more concrete, deeper radiance.

'I question, if there be a room in England which commands a view of Mountains & Lakes & Woods & Vales superior to that, in which I am now sitting', wrote Coleridge to Godwin from Greta Hall, adding pointedly, 'I say this, because it is destined for your Study, if you come' (Hebron 38). When he was not gazing from his window, Coleridge went exploring. C.S Lewis, J.R.R. Tolkien – and other friends – would love doing the same long walks, exploring the countryside (and the Inns along with it). Tolkien's own idea of a walk in the countryside involved frequent stops to examine plants or insects, and this irritated Lewis (cf. Carpenter, Inklings 57f).

Pushkin and Lermontov

Although living in a house seems to be as normal and natural as breathing, eating, or sleeping in a bed, it involves a complex reality, which can be observed in narratives of all cultures and ages. Domesticity has to do with the family, intimacy and a devotion to the home, as well as a sense of the house embodying – not only harbouring – these sentiments.

In Pushkin's work, for instance, we find the beginning of the Russian 'literature of the house', as in Lermontov we have the initiator of the 'literature of homelessness'. These tendencies complement each other (cf. van Baak 101).

For Pushkin, the utopian ideal behind this archetype is often illusory and unreliable, which makes the 'house' in his work a symbol of human life *par excellence,* whilst giving shape to the anguish and anxiety of his contemporaries.

This anxiety can be considered characteristic of late Romanticism (the Russian one) a kind of 'tamed Romanticism' (unlike the 'high' or 'absolute' Romanticism of Germany and England): uncertainty about the safety and stability of the way of life and even of the world-order. It is haunted by feelings of confusion and disarray. The craving for homeliness and close family ties; the 'flight' to the safe warmth and comfort of the domestic hearth and the idyllic garden; a modest utopianism, as when Evgenij in *The Bronze Horseman* dreams of 'a simple, humble shelter' (cf. van Baak 131-133). Not unlike Merry at Harrowdale!

'Houselessness' and Homelessness are prominent in Lermontov's work, which is not surprising when we consider that Lermontov's literary world is largely made up of Romantic heroes. We see it for example in *Mtsyri* (1839), probably one of the last true Romantic epic poems of Russian Romanticism:

> ... and I remembered my father's house, / The canyon where we lived, and / In the shade the village scattered around it; ... And I remembered our peaceful house / And at the fireplace in the evening / The long stories about / how people used to live in earlier days, / When the world was still more splendid   (van Baak 141)

In his most famous poem *I step out on to the road alone* (1841), he evokes the Romantic (and Lermontovian) leitmotiv of wandering, and thus implicitly of leaving one's home and being or becoming homeless:

> All alone I step out on to the road, / Through the haze the stone road glistens. / The night is silent... In the heavens there is solemnity and wonder! / The earth is asleep in blue radiance... / What causes my pain and suffering? / Do I hope for something? Do I regret something? ... I search for freedom and rest!
>
>   (van Baak 144)

If we recall here Bilbo's song *The Road goes ever on and on*, we may find a rather different set of feelings and vision of life and the world involved in it. We may say that landscape is a *'remembered landscape'* – for Lermontov and the Russians –, while it is more a *'walked across landscape'* for Tolkien.

Tolkien: The House of Tom Bombadil

It would be better if we allowed the texts to speak for themselves. So we have chosen a few examples of inner landscapes, regarding a House, a Barrow and an Inn, taken from *The Fellowship of the Ring*, but have also brought Dostoevskij into our fellowship as well.

We may now move on to the arrival at Tom Bombadil's house:

> The path... wound up on the top of a grassy knoll, now grey under the pale starry night; and there, still high above them on a further slope, they saw the twinkling lights of a house... Suddenly a wide

> yellow beam flowed out brightly from a door that was opened...
> They all hurried forward ... the hobbits stood upon the threshold,
> and a golden light was all about them.
> The four hobbits stepped over the wide stone threshold, and stood
> still, blinking. They were in a long low room, filled with the light
> of lamps swinging from the beams of the roof; and on the table of
> dark polished wood stood many candles, tall and yellow, burning
> brightly. (LotR 137)

And after being welcomed by Lady Goldberry ('Let us shut out the night! Fear nothing! For tonight you are under the roof of Tom Bombadil'), Frodo

> stood as he had at times stood enchanted by fair elven-voices; but
> the spell that was now laid upon him was different: less keen and
> lofty was the light, but deeper and nearer to mortal heart.
> (LotR 137f)

When they left and went on, as we know, they were trapped by the fog on the Barrow-Downs.

> [Frodo] for a moment could recall nothing except a sense of dread.
> Then suddenly he knew that he was imprisoned, caught hopelessly;
> he was in a barrow...

> Suddenly a song began: a cold murmur, rising and falling. The
> voice seemed far away and immeasurably dreary, sometimes high
> in the air and thin, sometimes like a moan from the ground out
> of the formless stream of sad but horrible sounds, strings of words
> would now and again shape themselves: grim, hard, cold words...
> The night was railing against the morning of which it was bereaved,
> and the cold was cursing the warmth for which it hungered.

To Frodo *came the memory of the house down under the Hill, and of Tom singing* and he called to him for help:

> By water, wood and hill, by the reed and willow,
> By fire, sun and moon, harken now and hear us! ...
> There was a loud rumbling sound, as of stones rolling and falling,
> and suddenly light streamed in, real light, the plain light of day
> ... and there was Tom's head (hat, feather, and all) framed against
> the light of the sun rising red behind him.
> (LotR 155-157)

There are even much darker landscapes in Imlad Morgul and in the Stairs of Cirith Ungol – in Shelob's Lair –, as the darkening of Frodo's mind and soul unfolds within him while getting nearer to the Nameless Land.

Dostoevskij: Notes from the Underground

Only Dostoevskij can match those dark descriptions. Being almost exclusively an urban author, he describes the dramatic (demonic) forces at work in the modern impersonal city and in the inner labyrinths of the human heart and mind. This is clear from his early work (as *Poor Folk*, 1846), still influenced by Gogol and the European Romantics.[3]

A good example is given by *Notes from the Underground*, witch inaugurates the period of the great novels of Dostoevskij. Here everything is in the hands and in the eyes of the protagonist, he projects into space his feeling of deep internal stagnation, of self-loathing, and colours the external reality with the dirty shades of his soul, steeped up to rot in the mud of his underground existence: 'In unutterable anguish I went to the window, opened the movable pane and looked out into the troubled darkness of the thickly falling wet snow' (Dostoevskij, *Memorie* 883, translation ER/GS). It is enough for him to think about death, the offense and the duel, and the whole surrounding landscape takes on a funeral air.

> The wet snow was falling in big flakes; I unbuttoned myself, regardless of it. I forgot everything else, for I had finally decided on the slap, and felt with horror that it was going to happen NOW, AT ONCE, and that NO FORCE COULD STOP IT. The deserted street lamps gleamed sullenly in the snowy darkness like torches at a funeral. (899)

After his tormenting adventure with the gullible Liza, the man of the Underground has a start. He launches himself in pursuit of her to, perhaps, mend the outrage that he has inflicted on her. He questions the landscape, looking at it he watches himself as in a mirror, and the surrounding space responds to his mute question.

> It was a still night and the snow was coming down in masses and falling almost perpendicularly, covering the pavement and

---

[3] Also in the late works it is possible to find romantic characters: Prince Myshkin (*The Idiot*, 1868), for example, is very elvish-like.

the empty street as though with a pillow. There was no one in the street, no sound was to be heard. The street lamps gave a disconsolate and useless glimmer. I ran two hundred paces to the cross-roads and stopped short... I longed for that, my whole breast was being rent to pieces, and never, never shall I recall that minute with indifference... I stood in the snow, gazing into the troubled darkness and pondered this. (945)

Tolkien: At The Prancing Pony

When the four Hobbits arrived at Bree, Sam was finding his first sight of Men and their tall houses quite enough, indeed too much for the dark end of a tiring day. He pictured black horses standing all saddled in the shadows of the inn yard, and Black Riders peering out of dark upper windows.

Soothing Sam's reluctance to get into The Prancing Pony Inn – he wanted to ask for hospitality among hobbit-folk: 'It would be more homelike'–, Frodo answered:

> 'What's wrong with the inn?' said Frodo. 'Tom Bombadil recommended it. I expect it's homelike enough inside'. After a while, they were washed and in the middle of good deep mugs of beer when Mr. Butterbur and Nob came in again. In a twinkling the table was laid. There was hot soup. Cold meats, a blackberry tart, new loaves, slabs of butter, and a half ripe cheese: good plain food, as good as the Shire could show, and homelike enough to dispel the last of Sam's misgivings (already much relieved by the excellence of the beer).
> (LotR 168-170)

In common: Love and Preservation of Landscape

There is, perhaps, one point in which the Romantics and Tolkien would have agreed upon without difficulty: the deep love and desire to *preserve* the landscape untouched by 'progress'.

> Sweet is the lore which Nature brings;
> Our meddling intellect
> Misshapes the beauteous forms of things;
> – We murder to dissect.

> Enough of science and of art;
> Close up these barren leaves;
> Come forth, and bring with you a heart
> That watches and receives.

John Blades comments on these stanza of the *Lyric Ballads*: 'art' as a artifice, deceit (Blades 189). May we not recognize the voice and the deeds of Saruman – or Sharkey – here, both around Orthanc and in the Shire?

The charm of what *was*, depended upon what was *not*. Wordsworth singles out an example of offensive architecture: the circular Villa on Belle Island, on Lake Windermere. The house was strongly disliked by Dorothy Wordsworth when she crossed by the ferry in June 1802:

> It is neither one thing nor another-neither natural nor wholly cultivated & artificial which it was before, & that great house! Mercy upon us! If it could be concealed it would be well for all who are not pained to see the pleasantest of earthly spots deformed by man. But it cannot be covered. Even the tallest of our old oak trees would not reach the top of it.
>
> (quoted by Hebron 155)

Wordsworth's attempts to prevent the railway from extending into the Lake District, were unsuccessful. The line was opened in September 1846 and in April 1847 – three years before Wordsworth's death – it was extended to its present terminus.

Man's destruction of the landscape moved Tolkien to profound anger, as we may read in his anguished description of a return to his childhood landscape of Sarehole Mill in 1933:

> I pass over the pangs to me of passing through Hall Green – become a huge tram-ridden meaningless suburb, where I actually lost my way – and eventually down what is left of beloved lanes of childhood, and past the very gate of our cottage, now in the midst of a sea of new red-brick... How I envy those whose precious early scenery has not been exposed to such violent and peculiarly hideous change.
>
> (Carpenter, *Tolkien* 169f)

Later in life, he would see a new road that had been driven across the corner of a field and cry, 'There goes the last of England's arable!' (Carpenter, *Tolkien* 170).

The End of Similarities:
Frodo & the Inner Consistency of Reality

But, many would agree perhaps, that after their *attention* for *watching* and *seeing* nature and their common love for preservation of unmarred landscapes ends all real similitude between the Romantics' sensibility and Tolkien's. As Gerard Manley Hopkins said in his poem *God's Grandeur*:

> Generations have trod, have trod, have trod;
> And all is seared with trade; bleared, smeared with toil;
> And wears man's smudge and shares man's smell: the soil
> Is bare now, nor can foot feel, being shod.
>
> And, for all this, nature is never spent;
> There lives the dearest freshness deep down things...
> (Hopkins 84)

Because here we have a hint of something present in Tolkien and mostly absent in the Romantics: *hope*.

They were driven to worship nature somehow as *divine* in itself, and were lead to sadness (or Lermontov's unhealed nostalgia of a lost past) and eventually despair.

Tolkien instead would respect and honour nature as *given*, as *created*, which leads to something greater than itself: and this 'inner consistency of reality' leads to *hope*, to 'recovery, escape and consolation', 'the fulfilment of Creation'. Even for the nostalgic elves: the *Great Eucatastrophe*, as is told in *On Fairy-Stories*.

The Romantic writers' view seems well translated onto the canvas of painters such as John 'Warwick' Smith, Thomas Hearne, J.M.W. Turner, and many others: blurred, misty, soft nostalgic colours and forms, exceed. Similarly, feelings are sort of *stretched*, 'like butter that has been scraped over too much bread'.

Quite unlike Tolkien: his paintings are *sharp*; his mountains pointed, piercing the landscape. Even his mist and foam are not blurred (cf. Hebron; Hammond/Scull). As a clear example we have the description when Frodo (and Sam) arrived at Cerin Amroth, in Lothlorien:

> The others cast themselves down upon the fragrant grass, but Frodo stood awhile still lost in wonder. It seemed to him that he had stepped through a high window that looked on a vanished world. A light was upon it for which his language had no name. All that he saw was shapely, but the shape seemed at once clear cut, as if they had been first conceived and drawn at the uncovering of his

eyes, and ancient as if they had endured for ever. He saw no colour but those he knew, gold and white and blue and green, but they were fresh and poignant, as if he had at that moment first perceived them and made for them names new and wonderful...
He turned and saw that Sam was now standing beside him, looking round with a puzzled expression, and rubbing his eyes as if he was not sure that he was awake.' It's sunlight and bright day, right enough', he said. 'I thought that Elves were all for moon and stars: but this is more elvish than anything I ever heard tell of. I feel as I was inside a song, if you take my meaning'. (LotR 369)

Here, all is wrapped in clarity, in sharpness. The 'inner consistency of reality' is perceived as sunshine evidence, radiant and concrete. But no emphasis is needed: there is a kind, humble adhering to the given, as if from far depths comes up the realism of things *and* the perception of the same things. As G.K. Chesterton would said, 'stare at the familiar until it becomes strange', which is the same conviction, we believe, that underlines *Tree and Leaf* (cf. Spirito). This sobriety, this lack of emphasis, this simplicity, is a trait of Tolkien, but hardly of the Romantics.

Dostoevskij: Zosima & Aliosha

In Dostoevskij, the flow of the narration usually hides spaces, never lingering. It displays them so rarely that the rise of a landscape, however rapid, offers to the reader a meaning, a key to understand the vision *(Weltanschauung)* of who is involved (cf. Catteau 491.525).

It was a bright, warm, still, July night, a cool mist rose from the broad river, we could hear the plash of a fish, the birds were still, all was hushed and beautiful, everything praying to God. Only we two were not sleeping, the lad and I, and we talked of the beauty of this world of God's and of the great mystery of it... I saw the dear lad's heart was moved... "I know nothing better than to be in the forest," said he, "though all things are good." "Truly," I answered him, "all things are good and fair, because all is truth".
(Dostoevskij, *Brothers* 267)

Zosima views the world as did Adam when he awoke (or as Frodo, when his eyes were uncovered): everything is true and beautiful, the surrounding reality is given, and shows and introduces a greater mystery – the reality is *mystagogic* (as Karl Rahner used to say). Dostoevskij here, by virtue of his spiritual viewpoint, allows us to take a step forward: a few characters – *the heroes* (cf. ibid. XIII) – have the possibility to overcome the veil and arrive at a genuine mystical experience.

It is the case of Alexej, the youngest of the brothers Karamazov and Zosima's novice, which received the passing on of the spirit that belonged before to little Markel and after to his *starec*. The episode is described in the chapter 45 entitled *Cana in Galilee*. In the cell where the body of the dead *starec* Zosima rests, Aleksej, exhausted, tries to pray, while a monk reads the evangelical passage of the wedding at Cana of Galilee.

Half asleep, many thoughts cross the mind of the young man: 'The road is wide and straight and bright as crystal, and the sun is at the end of it', suddenly he saw the wedding feast, the guests and his beloved *starec* who indicates Christ. For the Russian orthodox hero *mystagogy*, veiled by the paradox of the smelly body of the saint, leaves space for a genuine mystical moment, this is where we enter the arena from the threshold (cf. Bakhtin 176). A genuine need to go out, to escape suffocation, to breathe in the openness (a rather typical Russian trait):

> But what's this, what's this? Why is the room growing wider? ... Ah, yes... It's the marriage, the wedding... yes, of course... But who is this? Who? Again the walls are receding. Who is getting up there from the great table? What! He here, too? But he's in the coffin... but he's here, too.   (Dostoevskij, Brothers 331)

> He did not stop on the steps either, but went quickly down; his soul, overflowing with rapture, yearned for freedom, space, openness. The vault of heaven, full of soft, shining stars, stretched vast and fathomless above him. The Milky Way ran in two pale streams from the zenith to the horizon. The fresh, motionless, still night enfolded the earth... The silence of earth seemed to melt into the silence of the heavens. The mystery of earth was one with the mystery of the stars... Alyosha stood, gazed, and suddenly threw himself down on the earth. He did not know why he embraced it. He could not have told why he longed so irresistibly to kiss it, to kiss it all. But he kissed it weeping, sobbing, and watering it with his tears, and vowed passionately to love it, to love it for ever and ever.   (332f)

The perception is clean, clear, without blurring of personal comments by the author, nor an explanation. Here Dostoevskij portrays and shows to the reader not his ecstasy, but the character, and lets him act according to what he had heard from his teacher Zosima – Alexej continues to be free to move between the inner and outer landscape. The whole thing belongs to the character and not to the author, there is on his part, in fact, no intervention, only two discrete notes: the reference to the inner abundance of the young man and his *investiture* – 'He had fallen on the earth a weak boy, but he rose up a resolute champion' (333).

Some distinctive features: If we dare say, using a rather oversimplification, *'misty'* (*both* for landscapes *and* the perception of them) could be a word to somehow describe the sentimental way of the Romantics. The *feelings* of things reshape the reality of landscapes.

And for Tolkien? Recently, Timothy Radcliffe OP – from Blackfriars, in Oxford – came to give a talk in our Theological Institute in Assisi. He is an old friend of the Tolkiens (he performed the marriage liturgy of Simon, Christopher's and Faith's son; he also was a disciple of the only Dominican, Gervase Matthew, who was one of the *Inklings*, and with him was present at Tolkien's funeral). So we asked him: 'Timothy, how would you describe, in a nutshell, Tolkien's perception of landscapes?' He answered: 'I would say that while reading any of Tolkien's descriptions of landscapes you feel thousands of tons of rocks under your feet.'

The *reality* of things shapes the feelings and descriptions of landscapes. When we read Tolkien's works, *the inner consistency of reality is more perceptible than any filter or frame through which he perceives or describes it.* With the Romantics is the other way around.

For Tolkien we may dare use *'rocky'*, then. When Timothy said that, the thought flew to *The Two Towers*:

> 'This is more to my liking', said the dwarf, stamping on the stones.
> 'Ever my heart rises as we draw near the mountains. There is good rock here. This country has tough bones. I felt them in my feet as we came up from the dike.' (LotR 555)

So spoke Gimli to Legolas at Helm's Deep. Almost the same words that Timothy Radcliffe used. Or, in Hopkins' words in *As Kingfishers Catch Fire*:

> Each mortal thing does one thing and the same:
> Deals out that being indoors each one dwells;
> Selves-goes its self; myself it speaks and spells,
> Crying What I do is me: for that I came.
> (Hopkins 88)

Indeed, we dare say Tolkien is closer to Hopkins – and even somehow to Dostoevskij – than to the Romantics.

Conclusion

We may come to an end of our brief journey. We leave behind the dread of dark places (*Borrow-Downs, House of the Dead*) as we leave, sadly, the Homes and Inns and bright places alike.

We expose ourselves to the 'romantic nostalgia' – a nostalgic feeling that perhaps our elvish side may partially recognize –, giving voice to Wordsworth, and imagining Gimli's answer to him:

> The dreary intercourse of daily life,
> Shall e'er prevail against us, or disturb
> Our cheerful faith that all which we behold
> Is full of blessings. Therefore let the moon
> Shine on thee in thy solitary walk;
> And let the misty mountain winds be free
> To blow against thee. And in after years,
> When these wild ecstasies shall be matured
> Into a sober pleasure, when thy mind
> Shall be a mansion for all lovely forms,
> Thy memory be as a dwelling-place
> For all sweet sounds and harmonies; Oh, then,
> If solitude, or fear, or pain, or grief,
> Should be thy portion, with what healing thoughts
> Of tender joy wilt thou remember me...
>
> (Wordsworth 72)

> 'May be', said Gimli; 'and I thank you for your words. True words doubtless; yet all such comfort is cold. Memory is not what the heart desires. That is only a mirror, be it clear as Kheled-zaram. Or so says the heart of Gimli the Dwarf. Elves may see things otherwise. Indeed I have heard that for them memory is more like to the waking word than to a dream. Not so for Dwarves.'
>
> (LotR 399)

Not for Men either, we daresay. With the good peace of the Romantics. And thanks to Tolkien...

We may imagine a dialogue between Faramir son of Denethor and Aliosha Karamazov: it may give us a final hint of hope, a glimpse of a natural and human world finally redeemed in which Inner and Outer Landscapes, blended together, will be fulfilled with everlasting brightness and joy. As Faramir said to Frodo while parting near the Cross-Roads:

'If ever beyond hope you return to the lands of the living and we retell our tales, sitting by a wall in the sun, laughing at old grief, you shall tell me then...' (LotR 720)

'Certainly we shall all rise again, certainly we shall see each other and shall tell each other with joy and gladness all that has happened!' Alyosha answered, half laughing, half enthusiastic.
'Ah, how splendid it will be!' broke from Kolya.
(Dostoevskij, *Brothers* 718)

Bibliography

Bakhtin, Mikhail. *Problems of Dostoevsky's Poetics*. Minneapolis: Minnesota University Press, 1984

Blades, John. *Wordsworth and Coleridge: Lyrical Ballads*. Basingstoke/New York: Palgrave Macmillan, 2004

Carpenter, Humphrey. *J.R.R. Tolkien. A Biography*. London: HarperCollins, 2002

---. *The Inklings*, London: HarperCollins, 1997

Catteau, Jacques. *La création littéraire chez Dostoievski*, Paris: Institut d'Études Slaves, 1978

Crane, Bruce. *Man is a mystery. It must be Unraveled... A Collection of Dostoyevsky's Thoughts on the Human Condition, from Anger to Youth*. New York: Writers Club Press, 2001

Dostoevskij, Fedor M. "Memorie dal sottosuolo". *Romanzi brevi*, vol. II. Milano: Mondadori, 2005

---. *Delitto e castigo*.Torino: Einaudi, 1993

---. *The Brothers Karamazov*. Dover: Mineola, 2005

Duriez, Colin. *Tolkien and C.S. Lewis. The Gift of Friendship*. Mahwah (NJ): Hidden Spring, 2003

Florenskij, Pavel. "La lezione di una lugna passeggiata". *L'Osservatore Romano* (26.03.2010): 4

Guardini, Romano. *L'opera d'arte*. Brescia: Morcelliana, 1998

Hammond, Wayne and Christina Scull. *J.R.R. Tolkien, Artist & Illustrator*. London: HarperCollins, 2004

Hebron, Stephen. *The Romantics and the British Landscape*. London: The British Library, 2006

Hopkins, Gerald Manley. *La freschezza più cara. Poesie scelte*. Milano: BUR, 2008

Lewis, Clive Staples. *The Four Loves*. London: HarperCollins, 2002

Mac Carthy, Fiona. *Byron. Life and Legend*. Croydon: Faber and Faber, 2002

O'Donahue, John. *Divine beauty. The Invisible Embrace*. London/New York/Toronto/Sidney/Auckland: Bantam Press, 2003

Sisman, Adam. *Wordsworth and Coleridge. The friendship*. London: HarperCollins, 2006

Spirito, Guglielmo. "The Influence of Holiness: The Healing Power of Tolkien's Narrative". *Tolkien's The Lord of the Rings. Sources of Inspiration*. Eds. Stratford Caldecott and Thomas Honegger. Zurich/Jena: Walking Tree Publishers, 2008

Tolkien, John Ronald Reuel. *Tree and Leaf*. London: HarperCollins, 2001

---. *The Lord of the Rings*. London: HarperCollins, 1991

Van Baak, Joost. *The House in Russian Literature. A Mythopoetic Exploration*. Amsterdam/New York: Rodopi, 2009

Wordsworth, William. *Poems/Poesie (1798-1807)*. Milano: Mursia, 1997

'Secondary Belief': Tolkien and the Revision of Romantic Notion of Poetic Faith

Eduardo Segura (Granada)

Myth, Language, and (Literary) Belief

The origin of language was maybe the most obvious interest among the concerns of the Inklings. They were all deeply interested in the origin of the world, and as far as the world is presented before our understanding as something 'told', 'breathed', 'worded', it can be assumed that the word and the world are both parts of a correlative reality: "To ask what is the origin of stories ... is to ask what is the origin of language and of the mind" (TL 20).[1] Actually, the essence of what George MacDonald and John Ronald Reuel Tolkien after him considered *sub-creation*, is the power of the artist to explore and dig into the potential of *this* world in order to imagine and give consistency to *other* worlds. Therefore, those *other* worlds, 'secondary worlds' in Tolkien's expression are a means to retell the essence of the Primary World. 'Retell' is the key notion here, and it deserves careful attention.

Tolkien showed the way language becomes the standpoint for the construction of a feasible, fully believable world in a radical perspective, as the adequate tool for *mythopoiea*, the art of story-making. Creating from language is the way a man becomes the right image of God. Language is the magic wand in the hands of the most natural of wizards: this supernatural creature called man.[2] Language reveals the multiplicity of meaning of this world by means of Art, and thus it shows the richness of being, that can be told in many ways (cf. Aristotle, *Metaphysics* VI, 1028a). And as far as Creation is only God's task, man's is sub-creation provided that this is not the only possible world. Moreover, the world is so rich in essence that it needs to be told in as many different ways as it could and should be – the gift well deserves the effort. Multiplicity of meaning requires equal richness in the many words that can approach the multifarious beauty of being.

---

[1] See also *John* 1, 1-18. The prologue to this gospel explicitly asserts that everything was created *in* the Logos [of God], and *by* the Logos who is God Himself. The Word of God is, so to speak, the creative means to grant ontological existence to the concept of the world as *kósmos*. And thus the Word eternally becomes Lógos and Verbum. I have explained more extensively the implication of these ideas with Tolkien's poetics in Segura, *viaje*, chapter 1, especially 70-78, and also in *Mitopoeia*, XIX-XXX of the Preface, and 43-136.
[2] On the notion of 'supernatural', see My 86f.

Now, this *re*-presentation actualizes the infinite modes of being, i.e., it is a mythic mode to tell the world, to say the truth, to recover the pristine view of Man on earth. In doing so, Tolkien was sure, a sub-creator becomes able to shed a new light on everyday 'reality'. However, what we call 'real world' is not in exact correspondence with what Tolkien deemed 'real'. Reality is wider a notion than the simple reference to what we perceive through our senses – our material senses.[3] Myth becomes the privileged path to access secondary belief because belief leads towards the accomplishment of secret, remote desires[4] linked to both our reason and heart, to our feelings and also to our affections, remembrances and convictions. In other words, Myth is another name for Truth: "History often resembles 'Myth', because they are both ultimately of the same stuff" (FS 30). That shared 'stuff' obviously implies a wider notion of 'truth': what happened in time ('real' events, history) became legend (from Latin *legenda*: 'what is to be read' as a recall of those real events), while time makes the rest turning those distant events into Myth, an echo from the past, the actual memory of how language provides the telling of truth, the construction of feasible versions of mere oral traditions, or heroic 'facts', or 'deeds'. Myth ultimately becomes a discovery of the magical, supernatural side of reality, which means that magic illuminates the dark sides of truth: the narrative dimension of human being, the animal who is mainly a story-teller.[5]

This outlook reveals an interesting connection between language and belief. At the same time, Tolkien's notion of sub-creation refers to the art of narrative not only as the principal mode of Art, but also as Art in a unique sense. To him other forms of art cannot be called 'sub-creative' since they have no capability to reproduce the inner consistency of reality – of the truth that inhabits reality.[6] Being another way to tell the truth, to reveal it, myth reveals an expression of human nature and so of human need for escape, recovery, and consolation, three of the many aspects that can be found in belief as far as believing mainly deals with confidence, and trust. Historically man and the divine have sealed their compromise through oaths, covenants, words.[7] The history of the relationship

---

3 The distinction 'material' senses is introduced here following Saint Bonaventure's doctrine of the six modes of knowledge that include faith as a means to penetrate reality in a wider, deeper perspective through interior senses, and the help of the supernatural light of God's revelation. (Cf. Bonaventure, part V, especially qq. 2-7)
4 On Tolkien's point of view on the close relationship between desire and knowledge: FS 41.
5 For a deeper explanation of this notion, see MacIntyre, chapter 15. See also Marín, mainly chapter 1.
6 This is not place to discuss in what way Cinema is also an adequate set to develop a consistent, feasible secondary world, or not. I'm just suggesting that in working with images Cinema loses part of the potential of meaning narrative has because image determines free applicability by paradoxically limiting imagination.
7 In Christian revelation, Christ is the Word that reveals the Father, and the Word that is revealed by Him.

between God and humankind is a history made of stories. It's a mythic telling, a story of how truth is progressively revealed to humankind:

> ... human consciousness, language, and myth are interdependent and mutually supportive, arising and existing in relation to one another. There is no myth without a language to express it, no language without a people who speak it, no people without a myth that describes their world to them. (Flieger, *Barfield* 51)

Myth provides not only a description of the surrounding world, but also of its meaning, an explanation of *significance*. 'Religare', to rejoin with the divine, becomes *the* radical need for everyone – whatever the 'divine' means, a personal God, or an idol carved in stone. Myth is a revelation of consciousness where seeking for truth becomes a story on how the natural world is the mirror of the unexplained, of Mystery as Gift. Myth is the best way to access Being, to sing Beauty, to tell – and re-tell – Truth. Myth is a shortcut for a better understanding of God as Narrator.[8]

Sub-creation according to Tolkien: Art as an Echo of Redemption

In what way these notions lead to a consideration of Tolkien as romantic is something that should be reconsidered. Two authors stay at the core of the study, Max Müller and Samuel Taylor Coleridge, especially the latter's notion of 'poetic faith' as an aim and result of creative imagination that leads, according to Wordsworth's *Prelude*, to that 'genuine freedom' that is a long for an inner redemption (cf. especially chant XII).

Tolkien considered sub-creation, and his own mythology, a complete design expressed in words through the 'invented' languages – from Latin *invenire*: 'to find'. Invention is thus a rational activity, and not only or mainly a fortuitous relation between a notion and a group of letters we call 'word'. To invent a language means, to Tolkien, to find a complete world whose coherence must be found in the stories that explain its history as a recall of the truth of the Primary World.

---

8 Jesus Christ was in fact a brilliant story-teller. It is pretty revealing He chose parables as the best way to lead His audience into a better understanding of the mysteries of the Kingdom.

Those linguistic inventions were the result of more than fifty-five years of work seeking a vision or artistic logos already glimpsed while fighting at the trenches in the Great War, in 1916. That logos turned into a philological comprehension of the relation between myth and imagination, the mind and the world, the sacred and a complete outlook on being. Tolkien used the power of words to *create* truth. With that power a writer has the capability of becoming a wizard: he is able to actualize the truth that is inherent to the world which is expressed by a language, underlining the *supernatural nature* of reality. In doing so, he made also possible 'secondary belief' beyond the 'willing suspension of disbelief' Coleridge claimed to be the highest privilege of Fantasy:

> It was agreed, that my endeavours should be directed to persons and characters supernatural, or at least romantic, yet so as to transfer from our inward nature a human interest and *a semblance of truth sufficient to procure for these shadows of imagination that willing suspension of disbelief for the moment, which constitutes poetic faith*. Mr. Wordsworth on the other hand was to propose to himself as his object, to give the charm of novelty to things of every day, and to excite a feeling analogous to the supernatural, by awakening the mind's attention from the lethargy of custom, and directing it to the loveliness and the wonders of the world before us.
> (*Biographia*, cap. 14, quoted after Jackson 314, my italics)

Tolkien's revision of this notion of 'poetic faith' leads far beyond. If polysemy points at a multiplicity of names to be called because the truth of this world is metaphorical, then only by naming the multiple essence of the world the writer becomes able to sing the polysemy of the *kósmos* in a fair, adequate way. 'Magic' is here a notion joined to one of the privileges of human creature: that of naming reality. The act of naming reveals the exact measure and proportion of knowledge of the world that acknowledges it as a miraculous gift.

Now, what was Tolkien's notion of *mythopoeia* as an artistic form, as a way to re-produce reality not only, or mainly in a mimetic mode? His opinions were modelled by the early reading of Owen Barfield's *Poetic Diction* (1928). Actually, Tolkien described the impression the book caused on him in terms of a new "linguistic philosophy" (L 22) that had radically changed his own poetics. It is revealing that Tolkien admitted the influence of this reading, and the conversations with Barfield and Lewis as a turning point in the formation of his own linguistic philosophy, as well as on the vision of language as the cornerstone of sub-creation, since he was reluctant to admit influences, or even to quote authoritative voices to support his opinions. What is, then, the core of *Poetic Diction*? To sum up, we should say Barfield talks on Mythology as "the ghost of concrete meaning" (Barfield 92). After reading Rudolf Steiner, Barfield...

> ...came to believe that the universe was the product of design and was suffused with meaning and, moreover, that imagination can be used quite as well as logic and reason to gain a better understanding of that universe and to comprehend the phenomena of the world around us. (Flieger, *Light* 36)

Tolkien also thought this world is the result of a plan, of a logos: *the Lógos*, to be exact: the Word made flesh that we are told about in the Gospel according to John. But the original meaning of Greek *lógos* also embraces the notion of *word*. So, *lógos* includes both the complete design and also the word in which everything else was made. Similarly, naming the world is a privileged means to recover the original meaning of the whole, of Creation as a plan designed by God, and plenty of the meaningful essence of the divine Lógos. In a fallen world the instrument to accomplish the task of an artist is metaphor. But in the beginning it was not so: poetic word was the way to speak the world since the vision of reality easily led to the recognition of it as a miracle.

After the Fall, poetry has become not only a chance for delight in beauty, but also a way for true *epistéme*: a path towards knowledge, and wisdom[9]. Multiplicity of this world's meaning witnesses the infinite beauty of truth. It is a chant to the glory of God. And so poets are ultimately prophets, the bards, or *vates* of a never-ending re-creation of a *kósmos* which is an expression of meaningful prime, or *plenitudo pulchri*.

If we accept Barfield's view on myth, language, and perception humankind once had as deeply connected realities – they were in fact inseparable (cf. Flieger, *Light* 37) –, then the aim and goal of sub-creation is not merely the inventive gathering of imaginary worlds, but the rediscovery of the essence of the Primary World by means of the multiple reflections of truth that we perceive especially through *mythopoeia*, inventing secondary worlds – the 'splintered light'. In doing so human being recovers the control of the world-dominion by creative acts,

> not his to worship the great Artefact,
> man, sub-creator, the refracted light
> through whom is splintered from a single White
> to many hues, and endlessly combined
> in living shapes that move from mind to mind.   (*My* 87)

---

9   *Poetic Diction* is "not merely a theory of poetic diction, but a theory of poetry: and not merely a theory of poetry, but a theory of knowledge" (Barfield 14). See also p. 47, where Barfield heads a chapter under the title "The effects of Poetry" with these notions: pleasure and knowledge. I have studied the influence of these ideas on Tolkien's poetics in Segura, *viaje* 47-75.

However, provided that to Tolkien sub-creation was rooted in linguistic invention, the power of words to turn meaning into something literal led him to this conclusion: words contain an enormous potential of significance, and so they literally *realize* meaning – they turn it real. There is an essential connection between words and reality, between perception and notions. If the multiplicity of significance that we call now metaphor was unknown to humankind before the Fall, then it is also true that in a redeemed world metaphor becomes a unique way – maybe the *only* way – to recover the complete image of the world that once was (cf. Flieger, *Light* 38). In this sense, Middle-earth widens the meaning of the world we call 'real' for lack of a better word. Simultaneously, we recover a more complete, quintessential image of Creation. By knowing a secondary world is made possible a better understanding of the universe around us, and also of our inner world.

Now, this stress on linguistic invention was not only the response as an artist to Tolkien's 'secret vice', but mainly the tool to turn those secondary inventions into primary, or *real* in its deepest, radical sense. Tolkien was aware that making possible 'secondary belief' implied inventing a world literally: to find a literary time and place where words meant exactly what they meant.[10] To Tolkien there was a time when a name could call and perfectly describe the essence, an ancient age now forgotten when grammar was mythical. So that Flieger asserts that what is metaphorical to us is literal in *The Lord of the Rings* (cf. 54).

What is the range of this literality? It is obviously *not* referred to the extramental existence of the object, but rather to the way metaphor is transformed into the right measure of a *vocatio* of imagined reality into a context that makes it coherent, feasible, and so believable. As far as image is desirable, Tolkien deems it part of the way in which secondary belief, or even poetic faith, surpasses willing suspension of disbelief. Therefore believing with literary faith is, from the point of view of reception, the right, adequate attitude before the richness of significance of reality that is itself an *excess*: since the measure of reality for an empiricist mind requires the limitation of imagination to the narrow borders of experience, so that it is the subject who becomes the measure of everything.

On the contrary, belief that comes from feasibility, from similarity with the truth of the world which is always deeper than mere empirical data, widens the world and shows that the gift of being is always bigger than singular entities. Mythopoeia makes present superabundance of significance in a way that only Art can do: as a fair outlook on a notion of reality which is wider than the result of experience according to the methods of experimental sciences.

---

[10] Gandalf's self-introduction when he first meets Bilbo Baggins is an example of this conception: "I *am* Gandalf, and Gandalf *means* me!" (H 16f, my italics)

Image and Imagination: Allegory vs. Free Applicability

Now, in what way is imagination valid as a source for art on its own right? As a legacy from 17th and 18th centuries' rationalism, pejorative consideration of imagination comes from a misleading understanding of imagination as something irrational, an activity beyond rationality as the source of images without the control of reason. Thus, imagination has eventually been taken as a synonym of lie, and deception – as mere *escapism*. The very trial of Romanticism to recover the positive value of imagination was presumably doomed to fail. Only a notion of mythopoeia where art and life were closely linked – a bridge between art and beauty and so, a path to truth – could overcome the shadow of distrust that hangs over the notion of imagination in a world increasingly dominated by limited notions of reason, rationality, and reality.

Now, it is at this point where the notion of sub-creation stands at all its potential. How can it be assumed that Tolkien was really meaning that man is the image of God when he invents secondary worlds, is a question that we should face by taking 'secondary' as a synonym of 'primary' but for the difference of actual existence. Tolkien deemed 'real' every coherent and credible fantasy of the mind – a world made out of words, of *lógoi*. Man, artist, writer becomes the image of God by (sub)creating according to a lógos, a conceptual design, since it is in the very design a word posses that a complete world lies.[11]

As Seeman has explained, it is this notion of sub-creation as a synthesis of both the power of creative imagination and fantasy what takes Tolkien's view a step forward with regards to Coleridge's, who somehow dismissed imagination by assigning it the mission of just causing the willing suspension of disbelief, i.e., the assent of the mind to what is *not* true since it lacks a straight connection with what we take for granted as 'real'. But to Tolkien it is precisely the power to overcome disbelief what takes art to a new standard, ontologically, as it points at the essence of Art as an echo of Redemption, a renewal of all things.

By stressing the power of words and languages as a means to discover the mythical core of the world, and so finding in it other worlds and histories by telling stories, Tolkien was rediscovering a path that Romanticism had also treaded with a different final destination. To him words have the potential of significance that set the reader free to apply meanings to his own life, history and circumstances. On the other hand, images tend to make fantasy not only

---

11 Tolkien can be compared to Aüle the Vala in his desire for creatures made on his own image. The very desire of the artist is to conceive and call to existence those creatures of the mind.

actual, but also factual, leading to a narrower interpretation of the sense or senses in a text. In Tolkien's words:

> Drama has, of its very nature, already attempted a kind of bogus, or shall I say at least substitute, magic: *the visible and audible presentation of imaginary men in a story*. That is in itself an attempt to counterfeit the magician's wand. (FS 51, italics by the author)

Pure story-making, Tolkien goes on saying, is focused on things and their potentialities, while drama takes those realities from the point of view of actions and plot – mainly as *práxeos mímesis*, in Aristotle's expression (*Poetics* 1451b). In doing so, drama and cinema tell stories in a completely different way, by underlining the power of image to induce a totally different kind of metaphor and believability. Iconic imagination will maybe feel attracted by such a view, but for a reader who feels the close connection between things and names, Tolkien's mythology provides a realm for free applicability in a way that visual arts cannot grant.

By taking words and language in the Platonic sense, being themselves images of the world, storytelling becomes an accurate way to find the significance of the world in the multiple choice of meanings that a linguistic metaphor provides. Inventing a world where trees talk and tell their names by telling stories, since their own names are always growing and alive, is far more believable than seeing them marching on a screen as the spectacular result of special effects, a shortcut to turn desires into immediate reality. That's part of Tolkien's reluctant vision of machinery as opposed to true magic, or wizardry – i.e., as wisdom.

Although it is commonly assumed that Tolkien's tales can be easily read as allegories since they are the work of a Christian, his dislike for allegory is well-known. Should we trust him when he wrote: "I cordially dislike allegory in all its manifestations, and always have done so since I grew old and wary enough to detect its presence" (LotR xvii)? In other words, Tolkien was true to himself when he wrote that he 'cordially' disliked allegory, because he was so deeply in love with "history, true or feigned, with its varied applicability to the thought and experience of the readers" (LotR xvii) that he simply dismissed 'inner meanings' just because they could easily become some sort of interference in the interpretation of the tale that readers are supposed to undertake – and so, erasing any shadow of cordiality at all.

A closer attention to his words, as well as to the notion of 'myth' Tolkien explored in his scholarly writings, letters, and works – both major and minor –, reveals that Tolkien's predilection for what he called 'free applicability' was rooted in his conviction that the relation between myth and truth derived from the splintering light Truth was to him, as a Catholic. This light can be found in legend as well as in history – and, thus, in the multiplicity of stories. The very notion of 'Myth' as multiple image of Truth provides a better understanding of the explanatory lines in the Foreword to *The Lord of the Rings*. They also clarify his, say, 'Catholic outlook' for a full comprehension of Aesthetics, and Art:

> I think that many confuse 'applicability' with 'allegory'; but the one resides in the freedom of the reader, and the other in the purposed domination of the author.[12]   (LotR xvii)

As a Catholic, the notion of Art that Tolkien had learnt and put into practice was closer to that of 'gift', and so of *gratia*, of 'grace', than to any kind of allegorical meaning that could be derived from an intentional, 'designed' architecture of a story, or even from some sort of strategy planned *a priori* by the author in order to 'convince', 'teach', or 'evangelize' the reader.[13] The Epilogue to *On Fairy-Stories* is devoted to explain how Redemption is the Eucatastrophe of the History of humankind (cf. FS 70-73) in terms of a totally undeserved present that mankind has been granted out of Love. According to this rationale, and provided that the history of Christ's Death and Resurrection had taken place in the Primary World – i.e., it was 'True' in the truest sense of the word –, *mythopoeia*, the art of making stories, or storytelling, was a unique way to retell the joy of the point of no return in the history of mankind. Therefore, the task of a mythmaker is that of a mediator between truth and the readers, because Truth shines itself as a light to become ultimately *evangelium* to any reader, believer or atheist (cf. FS 70f).[14]

From this perspective only a full respect for the freedom of the reader can preserve the essence of Art, which is a grace, a gift – an undeserved present. Pretending that a story *is* just an allegory becomes a sad impoverishment of its true meaning, which provides an expansion of the meaning of Creation, for this is not the only possible world – nor even the best one.[15] Allegorizing always involves minimizing both the meaning and the extent of sub-creative work because it devalues the essence of Creation, which is an excess of Love.

---

12 Accordingly, it can be deduced that Art is a fruit of freedom: the artist is free to create, and also the spectator / reader is free to receive the work of art and 'decode' it according to one's own aesthetic taste, preferences, experiences, and understanding.
13 It is revealing that Tolkien used the notion of 'myth' as a synonym of truth when he was asked by C.S. Lewis 'what have I to do with Christ?', paraphrasing Shippey's explanation of the stories of Fróda and Frodo as a 'reconstructed myth', in *The Road to Middle-earth*, chapter 6. To put it another way, Lewis wanted to know what was the *real* influence of Christ's death in his actual life and destiny. What we *do* know according to Carpenter's account is that Tolkien did *not* choose an apologetic approach.
14 The response to truth is not mainly, or not only, a question of 'religion', or 'beliefs'. It's the automatical answer to a deep anthropological concern.
15 Suárez and Leibniz questioned whether God had created the best of possible worlds or not. The question is of course related to the deeper philosophical problem of God's freedom, and omnipotence but does not ultimately illuminate the way *this* world is.

Therefore, a deeper answer to the question on what does to Tolkien mean to be a Catholic writer, and from what point of view his tales can be read as those of a Christian, must eventually endure this theological analysis: is redemption the *teleology* of Art, its main purpose and highest vocation? Is the task of any artist to recall the echo of that redemption? Tolkien did believe so:

> ... the 'consolation' of fairy-tales has another aspect than the imaginative satisfaction of ancient desires. Far more important is the Consolation of the Happy Ending. Almost I would venture to assert that all complete fairy-stories must have it ... – I will call it *Eucatastrophe*. The *eucatastrophic* tale is the true form of fairy-tale, and its highest function.　　　　　　　　(FS 68)[16]

If we accept that Redemption is a joyful gift, a gift that nobody deserves, and the kind of present no one is obliged to accept – again, it is literally a 'grace' –, then we must expand the notion of God not 'only' as Creator, but more precisely as *the* Sub-creator, so to say, the First and Only Artist, and thus consider Creation and Redemption as His Masterpieces. Under this light, Humphrey Carpenter's account of the conversation between Hugo Dyson, *Jack* Lewis, and Tolkien concerning myths and their value as real 'wisdom', becomes clearer. Similarly, the explanation Tolkien provided of Christ as *the* myth, the one in which every other story is finally redeemed and finds its truest meaning – the echo of ultimate Truth (cf. Carpenter, *Inklings* 42-44) – is also revealing of his conviction that History, Legend, and Myth were ultimately one and the same thing.

Now, how did Tolkien step forward from that notion of allegory to the wider, more adequate dimension of free applicability? First, Tolkien seems to have had in mind a notion of what the task of an artist is that can be described as closer to a certain 'priesthood', in the sense of 'mediation', than to the Aristotelian notion of the artist as a craftsman.[17] Every sub-creator, Tolkien says,

> wishes in some measure to be a real maker, or hopes that he is drawing on reality: hopes that the peculiar quality of this secondary world ... [is] derived from Reality, or [is] flowing into it ... The peculiar quality of the 'joy' in successful Fantasy can thus be explained as a sudden glimpse of *the underlying reality of truth*.

16　Accordingly, Tolkien points Tragedy as the true form of Drama.
17　However, Aristotle and Tolkien agree with regards to the core of the *Poetics*, that is, the construction of feasible worlds not only through the imitation of human actions (*mímesis práxeos*), but mainly on constructing worlds that participate of the inner consistency of truth, secondary worlds where the *téchné*, or skill of the author serves the highest purpose of literary art, *kátharsis* – or eucatastrophe. See Aristotle, *Poetics*, 49b27-28, 1451b, 1453b.

It is not only a 'consolation' for the sorrow of this world, but a satisfaction, and an answer to that question, 'Is it true?'.
(FS 71, my italics)

Therefore, if we accept that the main question Art is supposed to answer deals mainly with truth, with the way things *really* are – that is, with the world, and ultimately with Being[18] –, and not only – or mainly – with meaning, then true artistry becomes a search for the answer to philosophical, theological questions that lie deep in everyone's soul. These questions are linked to the existential core of our lives, and the more the questions gather, the more becomes Art a quest for significance. If we accept that life has a *télos*, then it can be argued that Art is the point where the questions about being – Metaphysics – and the questions about the ultimate destiny of every single person – Theology – finally meet. Art provides an explanation to those many loosing threads that seem to spread out.

But, would Tolkien have agreed this view? The author developed a true theology of Art, a notion of artistic work as a means of redemption, of Recovery of initial grace – the grace before the Fall –, and so, of Consolation in its deep, truest spiritual sense. It is this that I call his personal Aesthetics. According to these notions of Art and sub-creation, and from a teleological outlook, storytelling – and also reading and listening to stories, any kind of Art worth the name – becomes the exercise of a primordial human right: the right to Escape. This Escape is not escapism to Tolkien, since Escape provides a privileged access to knowledge, to true *epistéme*. From this almost existentialist perspective Tolkien points out Art as the threshold to avoid death, and so Art becomes the vehicle to the Great Escape[19] – escape from oblivion. Art provides an explanation to the meaning of life, and the world.

Moreover, Tolkien's theory of sub-creation suggests that imagination is able of re-presenting objects before our knowledge (or reason) so that the apprehension of universal ideas becomes more an intuition than the fruit of deduction or reasoning.[20] It is a path to wisdom through an almost straight understanding, and through almost no abstraction. 'Mythopoeia' is to Tolkien on one hand an 'art', a skill, a *téchné*. On the other hand, it is a gift, participation in creature of God's creative power; and so, an evidence of the narrative condition of human existence:

---

18 It is ultimately a Metaphysical answer.
19 See FS 68. Niggle escapes death and oblivion by means of his picture.
20 See Flieger, *Light* 33: "Tolkien's response to words, to their shape and sound and meaning, was closer to that of a musician than a grammarian, and *his response to language was instinctive and intuitive as well as intellectual*" (my italics).

> ... in God's kingdom ... redeemed Man is still man. Story, fantasy, still go on, and should go on. The Evangelium has not abrogated legends; it has hallowed them, especially the 'happy ending'. The Christian has still to work, with mind as well as body, to suffer, hope, and die; but he may now perceive that all his bents and faculties have a purpose, which can be redeemed. So great is the bounty with which he has been treated that he may now, perhaps, fairly dare to guess that in Fantasy he may actually assist in the effoliation and multiple enrichment of creation. (FS 73)

Storytellers are blessed not only because they, human beings, have been redeemed, but also because they retell the echo of the primordial Fairy Tale every time they build their little, consistent worlds so that Eucatastrophe may shine for ever. Creation hopes, it even needs the assistance of sub-creators so that it may be completed, filled with *other* truths, since God himself commanded Man to work and finish His task:[21]

> Blessed are the legend-makers with their rhyme
> of things not found within recorded time.
> ...
> (and counterfeit at that, machine-produced,
> bogus seduction of the twice seduced). (My 88)[22]

Therefore, the right to sub-create derives from the divine *lógos*, or 'primordial design' in which we were created:

> ... 'twas our right
> (used or misused). The right has not decayed.
> We make still by the law in which we're made. (My 87)

Why? Because the 'inner consistency of reality' is that of a saved world – and we are God's image. Man finally becomes the animal who tells stories, as Alasdair MacIntyre has pointed out (cf. footnote 5), an animal who is the image of a Creator – the Narrator – no matter "dis-graced he may be" because "yet is not dethroned, / and keeps the rags of lordship once he owned" (My 87). The tragedy of an illiterate society sadly underlines the fact that many people will

---

[21] See *Genesis* 2, *passim*, and especially verse 15.
[22] In Tolkien's mythology, Eru Ilúvatar counts on the Valar and the Maiar so that Arda can be embellished, complete. The original design is included in the initial Music.

not be able to understand themselves unless they turn their eyes to what they were, to what they are, by reading and writing myths:[23]

> The heart of man is not compound of lies,
> but draws some wisdom from the only Wise,
> *and still recalls him.* Though now long estranged,
> man is not wholly lost nor wholly changed.   (My 87, my italics)

Sub-creation becomes a recalling process of human essence. Art provides a way, by means of beauty, to learn and love wisdom, to exceed the immediacy of this world which is never enough.

Bibliography

Aristotle. *Metaphysics*. Cambridge: Harvard UP, 2003
---. *Poetics*. Cambridge: Harvard UP, 1995
Barfield, Owen. *Poetic Diction. A Study in Meaning*. Connecticut: Wesleyan UP, 1973
Bonaventure. Breviloquium itinerarium mentis in Deum. Opera Omnia, Vol. IV. Madrid: BAC, 1968
Carpenter, Humphrey (Ed. with assistance of Christopher Tolkien). *The Letters of J.R.R. Tolkien*. Boston: Houghton Mifflin, 2000
---. *The Inklings. C.S. Lewis, J.R.R. Tolkien, Charles Williams, and their friends*. London: HarperCollins, 1997
Flieger, Verlyn. *Splintered Light: Logos and Language in Tolkien's World*. Ohio: The Kent State UP, 2002
---. "Barfield, Owen (1898-1997)". *The J.R.R. Tolkien Encyclopaedia*. Ed. Michael C. Drout. New York: Routledge 2007, 51
Jackson, H.J. (Ed.). *Samuel Taylor Coleridge*. Oxford: Oxford UP, 1985
MacIntyre, Alasdair. *After Virtue. A Study in Moral Theory*. Indiana: The University of Notre Dame Press, 1981
Marín, Higinio. *De dominio público. Ensayos de teoría social y del hombre*. Pamplona: Eunsa, 1997
Seeman, Chris. "Tolkien's Revision of the Romantic Tradition". *Proceedings of the J.R.R. Tolkien Centenary Conference*. Eds. Patricia Reynolds & Glen GoodKnight. Oxford: The Tolkien Society, 1995, 73-83
Segura, Eduardo. *El viaje del Anillo*. Barcelona: Minotauro, 2004
---. *Mitopoeia y Mitología. Reflexiones bajo la luz refractada*. Vitoria: PortalEditions, 2008
Tolkien, John Ronald Reuel. *The Hobbit*. London: HarperCollins, 1993
---. *The Lord of the Rings*. London: HarperCollins, 1995
---. "Mythopoeia". *Tree and Leaf*. London: HarperCollins, 2001, 83-90
---. "On Fairy-Stories". *Tree and Leaf*. London: HarperCollins, 2001, 1-81
Wordsworth, William. *The Prelude*. Oxford: Clarendon Press, 1968

---

23 In this sense, it is eloquent the tremendous success and approval New Line movies have deserved. Leaving aside the mistakes in Peter Jackson's version, the epic tone of the tale is still there. Many spectators both Tolkien readers or not, understood the story not simply as 'fantasy' – it is not –, but as a mythical tale, and grasped in it the echo of a redeemed world – the eucatastrophe.

Beauty, Perfection, Sublime Terror
Some Thoughts on the Influence of Edmund Burke's *A Philosophical Enquiry into the Sublime and Beautiful* on Tolkien's Creation of Middle-earth

Stefanie Schult (Greifswald)

Introduction

Nature

The nature of things has always been of interest to mankind. It was an important matter in ancient philosophy, playing central roles in both Plato's theory of forms and Aristotle's writings on the beauty of goodness. In his theory of forms, Plato introduced categories that defined the aesthetic value of natural objects and scenery, particularly what is called 'beautiful itself', "which is beautiful in a way not relative to context or time or perspective" (Annas 84). Those who called themselves or were called Romantics put great emphasis on the importance of natural phenomena, so that nature reflects many important features and characteristics of Romanticism. From the sunset to extreme weather phenomena or stone formations and living beings, nothing is more diverse than the surrounding world and, according to the *Treaty on the Sublime* attributed to Longinus[1], bursts "out with a kind of fine madness and divine inspiration".

One can without doubt claim that, like many of their predecessors, contemporaries, and successors, both Edmund Burke and J.R.R. Tolkien were fascinated and inspired by the multiple facets of nature.

Burke and Nature

To Edmund Burke, nature was a source of both beauty and sublimity, as he discusses in detail in his pre-Romantic treatise *A Philosophical Enquiry into the Origin of our Ideas of the Sublime and Beautiful* (1757; second edition 1759). When he thought of the sublime, he saw William Shakespeare's King Lear wandering mad and aimless across the storm-swept heath. Burke saw before his inner eye high cliffs, majestic mountains, deep ravines, and misty bogs filled with will-o'-the-wisps. He also saw decaying buildings of former grandeur and gloomy, old forests where the wind created strange sounds in the gnarled boughs. But Edmund Burke recognized beauty in nature, as well:

---

1 The treatise is still attributed to Longinus, although the authorship is in question.

green meadows filled with the scent of wildflowers and bathed in sunlight or the bank of a river glittering in the sun right after a light rain in spring, the air smelling clean and sweet. One might say that he saw the typical medieval *locus amoenus*, the lovely place, as a fitting depiction of beauty in nature. And Burke, like Longinus, knew about the power that images of nature could evoke in writing.

Tolkien and Nature

Any direct influence of either Romanticism or Edmund Burke on John Ronald Reuel Tolkien's *Legendarium* is hard to detect, but as Chavkin (1) states:

> To understand properly some important twentieth-century writers of fiction, one must understand their connection with romanticism. Too often critics have examined these twentieth-century writers without looking at their roots in the literature of the previous century, with the result that the critics have presented simplified or distorted views of these writers.

And, like Burke, Tolkien was always fascinated by nature as well. He found particular delight in trees and growing things, as Humphrey Carpenter (38) points out in his biography:

> He was good at drawing too, particularly when the subject was a landscape or a tree. His mother taught him a great deal of botany, and he responded to this and soon became very knowledgeable. But again he was more interested in the shape and feel of a plant than in its botanical details. This was especially true of trees. And though he liked drawing trees he liked most of all to be with trees. He would climb them, lean against them, even talk to them.

Even the last picture taken of him shows him in front of his favourite pine tree in the premises of the Oxford Botanical Garden (Carpenter). In his short story *Leaf by Niggle* Tolkien depicts his own works as a large tree he is never able to finish, but which to him seems to symbolise all the beauty of things growing naturally.

Where, then, may traces of the sublime, as defined by Edmund Burke, be found in Tolkien's *Lord of the Rings*? In the following we will be looking at two different aspects of Burke's *Philosophical Enquiry*. In the first part Burke's idea of the sublime will be introduced and its workings in Tolkien's *Lord of the Rings* will be shown. This will be compared and contrasted with the beautiful in the second part.

The Sublime

Edmund Burke states in his influential *Philosophical Enquiry* that the sublime enforces great power. Through his treatise we come into contact with the classical theories of aesthetics, with Plato, Aristotle and Longinus, which became popular again from the seventeenth century onwards. Particularly the classical text ascribed to Longinus, which was rediscovered and translated into English in the sixteenth century, may be seen as a source of influence on Burke. It turned the sublime into a fashionable subject and may have prompted Edmund Burke to write the *Philosophical Enquiry*.

The literary creation of the sublime is one of the main aims of the so-called schools of horror or terror which flourished during the period of Romanticism, and later also of Victorian gothic fiction. Writers as well as other artists – like musicians, painters or even sculptors – tried to capture the mood of the age by evoking sublime images. So, what, according to Edmund Burke, defines and constitutes the sublime? Burke gives the following description of the sublime in his treatise:

> Whatever is fitted in any sort to excite the ideas of pain, and danger, that is to say, whatever is in any sort terrible, or is conversant about terrible objects, or operates in a manner analogous to terror, is a source of the *sublime*; that is, it is productive of the strongest emotion which the mind is capable of feeling. (Burke 86)

The sublime can also be called a *delightful horror*. It is a feeling both pleasant and terrifying at the same time, since it brings the reader/ audience close to dangerous objects and events without actually exposing him or her to it. The sublime is the most important cause of astonishment and awe in nature as well as in literature, offering "intimations of a great, if not divine, power" (Botting 39). "[A]stonishment is that state of the soul, in which all its motions are suspended, with some degree of horror" (Burke 101). It is this horror which is important to the evocation of a sublime feeling in literature. The fear of things and events in particular "robs the mind of all its powers of acting and reasoning" (Burke 101) so that we as an audience become subjected to "the great power of the sublime, that far from being produced by them, ... anticipates our reasonings, and hurries us on by an irresistible force" (Burke 101).

This *irresistible force* is the ultimate goal of an author. It is the means to captivate the reader's interest and imagination. "[T]he excitation of fear becomes one of the most significant enterprises a writer can undertake [and] fear is recognized as the primary means by which reason can be bypassed" (Punter 39f). The circumvention of reason is essential to bring a fantastic world like Tolkien's Middle-earth to life. If reasoning were to rule every thought, there would be no way we could enjoy reading *The Lord of the Rings* or other works of fantasy and science fiction. We encounter this view already in Longinus' *Treaty*, when he states that

> to believe or not is usually in our own power; but the Sublime, acting with an imperious and irresistible force, sways every reader whether he will or no... [A] sublime thought, if happily timed, illumines an entire subject with the vividness of a lightning-flash, and exhibits the whole power of the orator in a moment of time.

A sublime effect can be achieved via several different aspects, of which the most important are: power and magnificence, vastness, infinity, obscurity, and suddenness. We find an excellent example of those features in Tolkien's *Lord of the Rings* in the Fellowship's journey through the Mines of Moria: Although the halls of Dwarrowdelf are deserted, the group is still able to feel its former power and magnificence. Because of the darkness obscuring the Company's view it is impossible to judge the vastness of the dwarf city, which seems the stretch infinitely around them. Moria becomes even more terrifying and oppressive when the sudden booming noise of the Orc drums fills the Company with dread and forces them to make a stand in the Chamber of Mazarbul.

Still, there is a subtle but important difference in the sublime described by Edmund Burke and its original literary source ascribed to Longinus: while Longinus mainly saw the sublime in nature and natural phenomena, Edmund Burke included man-made objects in the definition as well. Particularly buildings like "soaring medieval cathedrals and rugged castle ruins" (Sanders 346) became the symbols of Romanticism, and inspired the movement called 'Graveyard Poetry' (Botting 32), which is a major part of pre-Romanticism (Baldick s.v. 'graveyard poetry'). To the poets of this movement nothing was more important than that

> poetical truth... lies beyond the bounds of a natural order [and that] poetry should indulge imagination and range in marvellous, magical and extraordinary worlds, worlds that are associated with forms of nature that evoke a sense of wonder. (Botting 38)

In Tolkien this development of the definition of the sublime gets even broader. First of all, he seems to use what may be distinguished as a 'good' and a 'dark' type of sublimity. All things natural that evoke some sense of awe may be perceived as a good kind of sublime, similar to what Longinus and Burke presented in their works. This includes landscapes and, for Tolkien as well, growing things which have been touched by the otherworldly realm of Faery and therefore are more than merely naturally beautiful, like for example Rivendell's flora or the golden woods of Lothlórien about which Legolas (LotR I 438) says:

> That is the fairest of all the dwellings of my people. There are no
> trees like the trees of that land. For in the autumn their leaves fall
> not, but turn to gold. Not till the spring comes and the new green
> opens do they fall, and then the boughs are laden with yellow flowers;
> and the floor of the wood is golden, and golden is the roof, and its
> pillars are of silver, for the bark of the trees is smooth and grey.

The creation of a dark type of the sublime[2], to be exact of images and events that evoke terror, has a long history before Tolkien. Homer, Ovid, Dante, the *Beowulf* poet, William Shakespeare, Mary Shelley or Bram Stoker, just to name a few, knew how to evoke dread and terror in their audience. Still, Tolkien connects the dark type of the sublime mainly with the intentional craving for power, which he first and foremost associates with the motif of the Biblical Fall. Furthermore, Tolkien includes creatures and, most important of all, artefacts, like the Palantiri or the One Ring, in this designation of the sublime.

One of the most profound and central questions of Tolkien's *Lord of the Rings* is undoubtedly: What is the Ring? Is it an object or does it have some sinister consciousness of its own? When Gandalf tells Frodo the story of the Ring he says that Sauron "let a great part of his own former power pass into it" (LotR I 68). All the magical rings are malicious because of their maker. The golden ring may look "bright and beautiful" (LotR I 70) in the sunlight, but it brings out the dark character of Smeagol who in his greed to gain it becomes a murderer. Here Tolkien clearly shows his dislike of unnatural artefacts of power. In a letter to Milton Waldman he describes them as the 'Machine' or Magic, which denotes

> all use of external plans or devices (apparatus) instead of develop-
> ments of the inherent inner powers or talents or even the use of
> these talents with the corrupted motive of dominating: bulldozing
> the real world, or coercing other wills.   (L 146)

Just like its master the One Ring has sinister abilities of its own that highlight its terrifying, sublime nature. "A Ring of Power looks after itself," says Gandalf (LotR I 73). "*It* may slip off treacherously, but its keeper never abandons it... It was ... the Ring itself that decided things." The One Ring has a consciousness of its own, most likely because it is a part of Sauron's malicious soul[3].

---

2   For some impressions on the workings of the dark sublime as well as general informa-
    tion about Romanticism in England and continental Europe see Jürgen Klein, *Schwarze
    Romantik. Studien zur englischen Literatur im europäischen Kontext.* Frankfurt am Main:
    Peter Lang, 2005.
3   This may be compared to the function of the Horcruxes in J.K. Rowling's *Harry Potter*-
    series. Here, the dark lord Voldemort hides parts he ripped out of his soul so that he
    cannot be killed when his physical form is destroyed.

Hence, the 'dark sublime' is characterized by a deceptive nature. A ring is usually just that: a ring. It may be small or big, cheap or unbelievably expensive, made of silver, gold or any other kind of metal. In fantastic literature it may become anything: the vessel of a soul or even a malicious, conscient creature, while on the outside it keeps its beautiful appearance. It becomes an object of the dark sublime, a machine which exceeds its own nature in power and is thus both dangerous and impossible to grasp with rational thought.

Apart from these artefacts or 'Machines' of power Tolkien manifests the sublime in the classical sense as well, by creating vast and impressive settings. With this he follows the typical romantic trend, which meant that

> Natural scenery ... was being perceived differently. Mountains, once considered as ugly blemishes, deformities disfiguring the proportions of a world that ideally should be uniform, flat and symmetrical, began to be seen with eyes pleased by their irregularity, diversity and scale. The pleasure arose from the range of intense and uplifting emotions that mountainous scenery evoked in the viewer. Wonder, awe, horror and joy were the emotions believed to expand or elevate the soul and the imagination with a sense of power and infinity. Mountains were the foremost objects of the natural sublime. (Botting 38)

Apparently, Tolkien felt intrigued by mountain ranges as well, since he prompts Bilbo Baggins to say: "I want to see mountains again, Gandalf – mountains" (LotR I 42) before he leaves for Rivendell. Tolkien had some distinct memories of his own tour to Switzerland right after school, which surely inspired his shaping of Middle-earth's great mountain ranges. He gives the following account of his trip:

> I left the view of the Jungfrau with deep regret, and the Silberhorn sharp against dark blue... One day we went on a long march with guides up the Aletsch glacier – when I came near to perishing... [At] noon we were strung out in file along a narrow track with a snow-slope on the right going up to the horizon, and on the left a plunge down into a ravine. The summer of that year had melted away much snow, and stones and boulders were exposed that (I suppose) were normally covered. The heat of the day continued the melting and we were alarmed to see many of them starting to roll down the slope at gathering speed ... They were whizzing across our path and plunging into the ravine... I remember the party in front of me (an elderly schoolmistress) gave a sudden squeak and jumped forward as a large lump of rock shot between us. About a foot at most before my unmanly knees. (Carpenter 1977, 75f)

Tolkien clearly recalls this experience in *The Lord of the Rings*, when the Company tries to pass the Redhorn Gate:

> Caradhras rose before them, a mighty peak, tipped with snow like silver, but with sheer naked sides, dull red as if stained with blood. (LotR I 376)
> The narrow path now wound under a sheer wall of cliffs to the left, above which the grim flanks of Caradhras towered up invisible in the gloom; on the right was a gulf of darkness where the land fell suddenly into a deep ravine. (LotR I 378)
> The Company halted suddenly, as if they had come to an agreement without words being spoken. They heard eerie noises in the darkness round them. It may have been only a trick of the wind in the cracks and gullies of the rocky wall, but the sounds were those of shrill cries, and wild howls of laughter. Stones began to fall from the mountain-side, whistling over their heads, or crashing on the path beside them. Every now and then they heard a dull rumble, as a great boulder rolled down from hidden heights above.
> (LotR I 379)

It is easily possible to deduce from these passages that Tolkien knew very well how to evoke awesome and terrifying scenery – in this scene also emphasized by the involvement of uncanny and fantastic supernatural powers – before the mind's eye of his readers, so that he could captivate them with his tales.

So what about the Elves? Are they sublime creatures or did Tolkien fashion them otherwise? Again, J.R.R. Tolkien's letter to Milton Waldman provides helpful insights for this sting of arguments. First of all, the Elves are immortal beings. This is definitely in accordance with the sublime aspect of infinity. Furthermore, they appear to be much more powerful, in comparison to the humans, dwarves or hobbits. But then, Tolkien states that "[the] doom of the Elves is to be immortal, to love the beauty of the world, to bring it to full flower with their gifts of delicacy and perfection" (L 147). Accordingly, it is just their different nature which, from the perspective of other peoples like Hobbits, Men or Dwarves, makes them appear so perfect and, as long as they are true to their nature and not corrupted by power, they represent the beautiful instead of the sublime.

The Beautiful

To Burke beauty meant "that quality or those qualities in bodies by which they cause love, or some passion similar to it" (Burke 128). Aspects or characteristics that evoke such emotions are "smallness, smoothness, delicacy, and gradual variation" (Botting 39). Edmund Burke very decidedly distinguishes love from desire and lust, which he considers to be inferior emotions. Tolkien follows this view in his *Lord of the Rings*, associating desire and lust with the craving for power and ultimately with the dark sublime, as the following example shows.

A most important, and from a Postmodern view quite controversial, fact is that Edmund Burke saw sublimity and beauty as mutually exclusive. To him everything extreme or intense is sublime, while all the normal shades in between can be beautiful. With this Burke contrasts the classical notion of the aesthetic quality of beauty which Plato distinguished in his so-called 'theory of forms'[4] from ugliness as the source of intense emotions instead of the sublime. (Annas 84)

Burke (157) also writes that the beautiful and the sublime can exist in one object at the same time, which may highlight the strange nature of the respective object or being, but which definitely weakens the effect of both aesthetic concepts. With Tolkien we get the impression that the combination of beauty and the natural sublime in one object or being rather increases the sensations that they evoke.

Once again it is possible to divide the perception and use of beauty in Tolkien's *Lord of the Rings* into two varieties: On the one hand anything the Hobbits love and take pleasure in is essentially beautiful. This is an absolute down-to-earth kind of beauty, which may be hidden behind a rugged exterior or even a naïve mind. On the other hand there are the Elves with their ineffably superior lore and skill. They are Tolkien's master sub-creators, gifted in making delicate as well as intriguing and perilously fair objects. Because of this their abilities also make them vulnerable. They are always on the brink of the Fall, which could instantly turn them from beautiful craftsmen following their nature's call to produce art into sublime creatures craving power or mindless minions with genetically enhanced abilities and powers, like, for example, Saruman's Uruk-hai. Still, this Elvish kind of beauty is touched by the realm of Faery and is elevated from the 'ordinary' sphere of the lands of Middle-earth.

The Elves seem to come close to perfection in their ways, but Burke clearly emphasizes in his *Philosophical Enquiry* that perfection is not a cause of beauty (Burke 144). Particularly women who show weakness and imperfection are much more amiable and beautiful than those who are perfect. As a result, Tolkien's character of Galadriel through her perfection and strange intuitive powers seems to inspire fear and superstition in Boromir of Gondor. She is the keeper of Nenya, one of the Great Rings (LotR I 61f), and knows the taste of desire and greatness, something she has to resist at all times. When Frodo offers the One Ring to her, Galadriel illustrates that giving in to the temptation would

---

4 For further information on Plato's definition of beauty and aesthetic 'theory of forms' see for example Kraut.

destroy her: she would fall and lose herself and thus become like the cruel faery queen from John Keats's poem *La Belle Dame Sans Merci*[5]:

> In place of the Dark Lord you will set up a Queen. And I shall not be dark, but beautiful and terrible as the Morning and the Night! Fair as the Sea and the Sun and the Snow upon the Mountain! Dreadful as the Storm and the Lightning! Stronger than the foundations of the earth. All shall love me and despair!
> (LotR I 480)

Conclusion

Although Tolkien may have read and known Burke's *Philosophical Enquiry*, it is impossible to ascertain that Tolkien was influenced directly from it in his creation of sublime and beautiful elements in his *Lord of the Rings*. It can without doubt be claimed that Edmund Burke's pre-Romantic *Philosophical Enquiry* touched a nerve in the arising Romantic Movement and had quite an impact on the development of gothic tales of horror and terror in Britain. Thus, he indirectly influences Tolkien through the large body of romantic and gothic literature from the 18th and 19th century, which Tolkien grew up with. That he made use of the aesthetic qualities and created terrifying elements on purpose can be inferred from the following statement Tolkien makes in one of his letters to Stanley Unwin:

> Evidently I have managed to make the horror really horrible, and that is a great comfort; for every romance that takes things seriously must have a warp of fear and horror, if however remotely or representatively it is to resemble reality, and not be the merest escapism.
> (L 120)

Furthermore, we have seen that for Tolkien beautiful and sublime objects are not always that easy to distinguish, if such a distinction is even necessary or wanted. What, after all, is the difference between the sublime and the beautiful? Are they oppositions? Can beautiful things not also invoke a sublime feeling? Are sublime things not also beautiful, both in Burke's aesthetic understanding of as well as the everyday meaning of the term? The silhouette of the Misty Mountains in the rising sun or the unearthly music of the apparently timeless Elves is without doubt beautiful as well as sublime, while beautiful things like

---

5   Cf. Allott 500-506. For a concise commentary on the inspiring effect of both the poet as well as the poem on Tolkien see Shippey 193-194, 282.

the Hobbits' gardens are not sublime, because they do not produce the necessary element of fear and awe. It is hard to find a clear distinction at all times. For Tolkien there exists merely a clear distinction of the good/natural and the dark/unnatural sublime. He always associates the latter with delusions of grandeur, the biblical fall and decay.

In the end, both beauty and the sublime bring pleasure to the reader. Beauty delights through the love and tenderness that it evokes and the sublime because of its intensity and suddenness which assault all senses and overwhelm them. Essentially one can claim that in beautiful things it is the heart that is moved and in sublime things it is the spirit that is elevated.

Bibliography

Allott, Miriam (Ed.). *The Poems of John Keats*. London/New York: Longman, 1970

Annas, Julia. *Ancient Philosophy. A very short Introduction*. Oxford: Oxford University Press, 2000

Baldick, Chris. *Oxford Concise Dictionary of Literary Terms*. Oxford: Oxford University Press, 2004

Botting, Fred. *Gothic*. London/New York: Routledge, 1996

Burke, Edmund. *A Philosophical Enquiry into the Origin of our Ideas oft he Sublime and Beautiful* [1757/1759]. London/New York: Penguin, 2004

Carpenter, Humphrey. *J.R.R. Tolkien – A Biography*. London: HarperCollins, 2002

---. Ed. with assistance of Christopher Tolkien. *J.R.R. Tolkien – The Letters of J.R.R. Tolkien*. London: HarperCollins, 2006

Chavkin, Allan (Ed.). "Introduction." *English Romanticism and Modern Fiction. A Collection of Critical Essays*. New York: AMS Press, 1993, 1-6

Kraut, Richard (Ed.). *The Cambridge Companion to Plato*. Cambridge: CUP, 1992

Punter, David. *The literature of terror: a history of gothic fictions from 1765 to the present day*. Harlow/New York: Longman, 1996

Sanders, Andrew. *The Short Oxford History of English Literature*. Oxford/New York: Oxford University Press, 2004

Shippey, Tom. *The Road to Middle-earth. How J.R.R. Tolkien Created a Mythology*. Boston/New York: Houghton Mifflin, 2003

Tolkien, J.R.R. *The Lord of the Rings 1 – The Fellowship of the Ring*. London: HarperCollins, 19997

Reading J.R.R. Tolkien's Work in the Light of Victor Hugo's Notions of the Sublime and the Grotesque

Marguerite Mouton (Paris)

Critics, it seems, tend to analyse the meaning of Tolkien's work more willingly than its style. The rare studies devoted to its style generally ponder its archaism, comparing it for instance to Shakespeare's writing. Michael Drout for example suggested similarities between the two authors' use of English grammar. Indeed, all the stylistic surveys tend to concentrate on very precise linguistic use and pay little or no attention to the meaning conveyed by the text[1].

My object here is to propose an analysis of Tolkien's style in *The Lord of the Rings* and to restore a link between this writing style and a world-view.

To that end, Victor Hugo provides useful tools in the preface to *Cromwell*, a manifesto of French romanticism. There he describes the sublime and the grotesque as both aesthetic and ethical notions. The new "drama" as well as the "real", he argues, "resul[t] from the wholly natural combination of two types, the sublime and the grotesque, which meet in the drama, as they meet in life and in creation"[2]. Central to Hugo's conception of the sublime and the grotesque, lies a principle of contrast between contraries which is the same in life and art and therefore implies a link between style and the interpretation of the world, between aesthetics and ethics.

I will use the word *ethics* to refer to the way individuals see the world, to their image of the world. I am merely extending the traditional meaning of the rhetorical category of *ethos*, which refers to the image of something that is conveyed by a text. I will try to show how the tool devised by Hugo allows an interesting description of the relationship between Tolkien and romanticism that helps us fathom both Tolkien's style (I), and the link within his work between aesthetics and ethics (II).

---

[1] Brian Rosebury's remark in 1992 is still up-to-date (65-72, 80); we must yet acknowledge the exception of Isabelle Pantin's recent book, which makes a start towards an analysis of Tolkien's style.
[2] "le caractère du drame est le réel; le réel résulte de la combinaison toute naturelle de deux types, le sublime et le grotesque, qui se croisent dans le drame, comme ils se croisent dans la vie et dans la creation." (Hugo, Œuvres 16f)

I. The Aesthetics of Contrast

The aesthetics of contrast is a productive principle of Tolkien's writing. His work does not confine itself to a simplistic opposition that would identify goodness, beauty and light on the one hand, and evil, ugliness and darkness on the other hand. On the contrary, it provides a dramatic pattern of contrasts at once visual (by the juxtaposition of beautiful and monstrous items), rhythmical and tonal (by the alternation of serious and light scenes). In Hugo's terms, such contrasts are to be opposed to the "monotony" and the limitation of effects that are central to classic minds[3]. On the contrary, contrast offers both dramatic dynamism and variety.

1. Contrast as a Means of Dramatisation

First, Tolkien uses contrast as a means of intensifying the dramatic aspect of particularly important passages (cf. Ferré 179). Chapter I, 2 of *The Lord of the Rings* ("The Shadow of the past") juxtaposes the tale of the dark history of the ring and a finale where curtains are opened and admit sunshine, Gandalf laughs, and Sam cries "Hooray!" (LotR I 63) at the prospect of seeing elves[4].

This pattern of contrast between a negative scene and its positive ending should not be overstated. Even within dark episodes, contrast plays a dynamic part, and positive endings are sometimes a mere trampoline that leads the reader towards other dark scenes. This is the case, for example, in the chapter "The Black gate is closed". The chapter builds up two successive scenes of anxiety (LotR II 629-633) contrasting in every possible way with one another and also with the comic ending towards the end of the chapter. The whole passage

---

3   "The universal beauty which the ancients poured out solemnly over everything, was not without monotony; the same impression repeated again and again may prove tiring at last. It is difficult to produce a contrast by piling sublime upon sublime, and we need a break from everything, even the beautiful. On the other hand, the grotesque seems to be a halting-place, a mean term, a starting-point whence one rises toward the beautiful with a fresher and keener perception. The salamander gives relief to the water-sprite; the gnome heightens the charm of the sylph." ["Cette beauté universelle que l'antiquité répandait solennellement sur tout n'était pas sans monotonie; la même impression, toujours répétée, peut fatiguer à la longue. Le sublime sur le sublime produit malaisément un contraste, et l'on a besoin de se reposer de tout, même du beau. Il semble, au contraire, que le grotesque soit un temps d'arrêt, un terme de comparaison, un point de départ d'où l'on s'élève vers le beau avec une perception plus fraîche et plus excitée. La salamandre fait ressortir l'ondine; le gnome embellit le sylphe." (Hugo, Œuvres 11f)]

4   The principle of contrast is not unconnected to the notion of "eucatastrophe" forged by Tolkien: it plays upon the narrative effect of a clash between an "apparently" sad yet eventually happy ending that produces a distinctive emotion and allows the revelation of a superior truth, namely that the Gospel is the only true story (L 100).

is placed under the shadow of the terrifying name of "Cirith Ungol, a name of dreadful rumour", and of prostrated characters, reduced to a silent, supine, "insect-like" position. First, the characters are "alone" and the sky "empty": no bird can see from it nor be seen in it. Then, black riders come into the picture, producing a "warning fear" and a "helpless horror". They are followed by troupes of men from the South, representing "a new fear". Expectation, immobility and loneliness are replaced by a space that gradually fills up, as frightening as the empty one, and gives rise to irrational fear: "It leaped into all their minds that the Black Wings had spied them and had sent armed soldiers to seize them: no speed seemed too great for these terrible servants of Sauron." Aggressive sounds fill the auditory space ("The voices and the clink of weapons and harness were very close.") and ugly characters the visual field. Gollum talks of "very cruel wicked Men", "Almost as bad as Orcs, and much bigger". Gollum even evokes the menace that the space will eventually be saturated with all the people of Middle-earth, when he says: "Always more people coming to Mordor. One day all the peoples will be inside."

To these dramatic elements (the anxiety conjured up by the name of Cirith Ungol that opens the passage; the prostration of the characters; the emptiness or saturation of space), the end of the chapter opposes Sam's standing position, his playful use of speech, and the evocation of an exotic place and a fabulous name and animal: the Oliphaunt. The text reads as follows: "Sam stood up, putting his hands behind his back (as he always did when 'speaking poetry'), and began". Sam's intervention produces a double effect on Frodo: his song relieves the tension and, from a dynamic point of view, the scene helps Frodo make up his mind and decide to go to Cirith Ungol. Symbolically, Frodo rises: "Frodo stood up. He had laughed in the midst of all his cares ..., and the laugh had released him from hesitation." The fearful name of Cirith Ungol is replaced by that of the Oliphaunt, in a playful game that alleviates the dramatic and psychological tension and allows the resolution of the expectation. But Gollum has the last word in the chapter. He invites the Hobbits to be "soft and quick as shadows": the narrative does not end on a positive note, and the decision that was made by Frodo while laughing will lead him to Shelob's sinister lair.

As these two examples show, Hobbits have a special gift for relieving tension and making the action go on. But contrast does more than shape the linear progression of the text: it comes into play at every level and multiplies images.

2. Contrast as a Means of Diversification

Throughout the text, Tolkien uses techniques of variation to produce an effect analogous to Hugo's notion of combining "two types, the sublime and the grotesque", in order to represent the totality of being in a work of art. Thus *Notre-Dame de Paris* stages a type of characters defined as *grotesque*. We may for instance mention Quasimodo, the cathedral itself, and even La

Esmeralda. Their portraits and destinies are ruled by paradox. Quasimodo is the best example, with his "sublime grimace" and the twisted but yet existing logic of his nature lying in a clash between various possible descriptions, which are made visible in a monstrous character who synthesises them without producing harmony. Quasimodo challenges both the writer's talent and the reader's imagination:

> We shall not try to give the reader an idea of that tetrahedral nose, that horseshoe mouth; that little left eye obstructed with a red, bushy, bristling eyebrow, while the right eye disappeared entirely beneath an enormous wart; of those teeth in disarray, broken here and there, like the embattled parapet of a fortress; of that callous lip, upon which one of these teeth encroached, like the tusk of an elephant; of that forked chin; and above all, of the expression spread over the whole; of that mixture of malice, amazement, and sadness. Let the reader dream of this whole, if he can[5].

Through the intricacy of the grotesque and the sublime various contradictory descriptions can coexist within one character and passage. To represent the totality of being, Tolkien uses two such techniques: that of multiplying points of view and that of synthesising images.

Tolkien often contrasts a hard situation with light behaviour by showing it from various points of view. Thus, Merry and Pippin manage to escape the Orcs while they are attacked by the Rohirrim only to find themselves caught between the battle field and the frightening forest of Fangorn. But their reaction consists paradoxically in talking gaily together. The contrast between the situation into which the Hobbits are thrown and their behaviour makes the whole passage difficult to understand and Tolkien in fact provides several interpretations of it. First, after the scene is reported through the Hobbit's dialogue, the narrator, in one of his rare intrusions, stresses the discrepancy between the characters' behaviour and the normal reaction that would be expected by the reader: "No listener would have guessed from their words that they had suffered cruelly". He assigns this gap to a way of being specific to Hobbits, who can talk "lightly in hobbit-fashion" (LotR II 448). Then, thirty pages later, "the three hunters", Aragorn, Gimli, and Legolas, provide new interpretations of what has happened. Each of the three interpretations proposed by the three friends multiplies the

---

5   "Nous n'essaierons pas de donner au lecteur une idée de ce nez tétraèdre, de cette bouche en fer à cheval, de ce petit œil gauche obstrué d'un sourcil roux en broussailles tandis que l'œil droit disparaissait entièrement sous une énorme verrue, de ces dents désordonnées, ébréchées çà et là, comme les créneaux d'une forteresse, de cette lèvre calleuse sur laquelle une de ces dents empiétait comme la défense d'un éléphant, de ce menton fourchu, et surtout de la physionomie répandue sur tout cela, de ce mélange de malice, d'étonnement et de tristesse. Qu'on rêve, si l'on peut, cet ensemble." (Hugo, *Notre-Dame* I, 5, 119)

episode's possibilities and thus furthers the romantic enterprise of representing the totality of being in a work of art.

Legolas develops a humorous interpretation of the scene which appears to be "the strangest riddle that we have yet found!": "A bound prisoner escapes both from the Orcs and from the surrounding horsemen. He then stops, while still in the open, and cuts his bonds... Being pleased with his skill, he then sat down and quietly ate some waybread! That at least is enough to show that he was a Hobbit" (LotR II 478). The scene's comical aspect is conveyed by a progressive change in the subject of the sentences. The first subject is defined by his situation of being "a bound prisoner". This implies a given kind of behaviour. Then, the subject position is filled by a pronoun in the third person, linked to a series of actions that are at odds with the behaviour required by the circumstances. The contrast is emphasized by remarks such as "while still in the open", "being pleased with his skill", or "quietly". Finally, the subject is defined anew in view of this contrast between situation and behaviour: the "bound prisoner" of the beginning is changed into "a Hobbit" through the use of the less precise pronoun "he".

Seen from Gimli's point of view, the interpretation shifts from humour to fear of something that seems irrational – "'There was sorcery here right enough,' said Gimli" – while Aragorn's reading of the episode goes in the opposite direction. He "smiles" and offers a rational explanation thanks to "some other signs near at hand that you have not considered" (LotR II 478).

Tolkien also realizes the romantic enterprise of representing the totality of being in a work of art through another stylistic means, by synthesising or contrasting images through the mediation of a character who interprets these images as simultaneous. While, for example, enemies are flocking to the walls of Minas Tirith and while, inside it, Denethor denies the return of the king and falls into folly, Pippin observes Gandalf, who starts laughing all of a sudden, instead of showing anger:

> Pippin glanced in some wonder at the face now close beside his own, for the sound of that laugh had been gay and merry. Yet in the wizard's face he saw at first only lines of care and sorrow; though as he looked more intently he perceived that under all there was a great joy: a fountain of mirth enough to set a kingdom laughing. (LotR III 742)

The mediation of Pippin's point of view, characterised by "wonder", provides a means of synthesising sounds ("the sound of that laugh"), images (introduced through the use of the verbs "saw", "looked"), and maybe even less sensory but rather cognitive impressions (introduced by the word "perceived"). These various impressions are set in opposition through the use of "yet" or "though".

Their coexistence is intimated either by succession (expressed by "at first"), or by superposition ("under all"). The text represents the totality of being in the various possible links between Pippin's perceptions.

The contrast that Hugo identified as central to the romantic theory of the sublime and the grotesque provides Tolkien with a principle for dramatising the text and lending it dynamism, but it likewise multiplies images and thereby helps realize the romantic enterprise of representing the totality of being in a work of art.

II. A Link between Aesthetics and Ethics

The preface to *Cromwell* insists on the way the notions of the sublime and the grotesque lie at the crossroads of a stylistic principle of drama and a description of the world[6], of aesthetics and ethics. If a consideration of the complexity of being in reality gives rise to a stylistics of contrast, the same principle of aesthetic clash questions any univocal or monolithic interpretation and therefore determines the ethics of a text, the way it should be interpreted.

As we saw earlier, Romantic aesthetics tends towards a representation of the totality of being. From an ethical point of view, this aesthetics leads to two distinct ideas about the structure of a text: either the text is shaped by a dialectical pattern in pursuit of an end and it integrates negative elements, or it is open to a multiplicity of interpretations. I will now examine these possibilities.

1. Dialectics or Multiplicity?

The dynamic of contrast I have already discussed here can be interpreted as the integration of negative elements by a dialectics directed towards an end. For instance, the gift of Galadriel to Sam makes the Shire flourish more than ever after the damage caused by Saruman's men. An exceptional tree replaces the party tree: "the only *mallorn* west of the Mountains and east of the Sea, and one of the finest in the world." The year 1420 is said to be "a marvellous year", and possess "a gleam of a beauty beyond that of mortal summers" (LotR III 1000). This positive dialectics opens a path to an interpretation of the text as a redemption story leading eventually to something like a heavenly state.

---

6 "[Drama:] Is it, in truth, anything other than that everyday contrast that struggle every moment, between two opposing principles which are always present in life, and which vie for possession of man from the cradle to the grave?" ["[Le drame,] est-ce autre chose en effet que ce contraste de tous les jours, que cette lutte de tous les instants entre deux principes opposés qui sont toujours en présence dans la vie, et qui se disputent l'homme depuis le berceau jusqu'à la tombe?" (Hugo, Œuvres 16)]

But this positive dialectics, this target-oriented progression is questioned in the very same passage through the mention of a later period with regard to which the present appears to be superior. Such a notion counters the idea of progress towards a stable heavenly state: "the beer of 1420 malt was long remembered and became a byword. Indeed a generation later one might hear an old gaffer in an inn ... put down his mug with a sigh: 'Ah! that was proper fourteen-twenty, that was!'" (1000f).

The following section evokes Frodo's irremediable loss, as he expresses it during his illness: "'It is gone for ever,' he said, 'and now all is dark and empty.' But the fit passed" (1001). The text stages the illusion of a positive dialectics through the character of Sam who is absent while Frodo is ill and therefore not fully aware of the negative effects of the quest. The cyclic aspect of Frodo's illness, together with the succession of a variety of tones from one paragraph to another within the same scene is suggestive less of a positive dialectics than it is of a pattern of eternal return, or of a variety of possibilities that cannot be integrated into one teleological movement.

2. The Romantic Theory of Participation

In the midst of all these contradictions, how can we choose between interpretations rather than accepting all of them on an equal footing? Hugo's *Notre-Dame de Paris* gives an insight into the way of reading that is favoured by the author. Traditionally, the relationship between aesthetics and meaning is conceived as allegorical. But Hugo deals with this kind of univocal understanding of a text with irony in Book One, on the occasion of a Mystery Play that Gringoire performs before the Parisians at the beginning of the book. Whereas the characters of the play are marked out by obvious signs clarifying their functions in the story, the narrator adds: "in order to help sluggish minds which would not have seen clearly through the transparency of these attributes, there was to be read, in large, black letters, on the hem of the robe of brocade, MY NAME IS NOBILITY[7]". The exaggeration and the paradox surrounding the themes of clarity and vision debunk a theatrical genre that multiplies signs and forbids freedom of interpretation.

Such a search for a univocal meaning is staged in Book Seven: Hugo proposes an analogy between the reckless deciphering of a text and judicial violence. Referring to the trial of a man accused of sorcery and who is believed to know

---

[7] "pour aider les intelligences paresseuses qui n'auraient pas vu clair à travers la transparence de ces attributs, on pouvait lire en grosses lettres noires brodées, au bas de la robe de brocart, JE M'APPELLE NOBLESSE" (Hugo, *Notre-Dame* I, 2, 89).

the secret of the making of gold, the King's doctor, Master Jacques Coictier, says: "That man is a stone. We might have him boiled in the Marché aux Pourceaux, before he would say anything. Nevertheless, we are sparing nothing for the sake of getting at the truth; he is already thoroughly dislocated[8]". The recurrence of the theme of the search for truth allows an analogy between the judicial system and a certain way of reading: the meaning is forced from a work of art exactly as a confession is from a culprit, even though it implies doing violence to a text or a person and extorting a meaning that may not tally with the facts.

Running counter to this allegorical reading and unreasonable search for a meaning, Book Two invites the reader to adopt an aesthetic conception of a text, whose meaning is ultimately withheld and therefore open to various interpretations. A night scene replaces the day transparency of the scene of the Mystery Play performed at the law courts. Gringoire, lost in the streets of Paris, follows the gipsy La Esmeralda who is singing: "The words which she sang were in a tongue unknown to Gringoire, and which seemed to him to be unknown to herself, so little relation did the expression which she imparted to her song bear to the sense of the words[9]." The meaning is no longer immediate as it was in the case of allegory; it is shattered into several viewpoints introducing in the text the possibility of multiple interpretations. Gringoire does not know the language in which La Esmeralda sings; but she does not understand her own words. Among these points of view another voice appears which is difficult to attribute to any definite body (since Gringoire does not know the language, he is not in a position to perceive such a gap), but through which the narrator can mention a discrepancy between the phrases and the sense of the words.

Hugo's text opposes two types of reading: one insisting on the aesthetic dimension of a work of art and the other looking for a "hidden sense" in it. The latter being tinted with irony, the reader is invited to go beyond a conception of the text as univocal and to recognise its irreducible opaqueness. Here lies precisely the definition of the *symbolic* favoured by the Romantics[10]. Far from being a one-to-one relationship between aesthetic items and elements of signification, the symbol implies a global link between them and a resistance of the aesthetic individual, which cannot be fully elucidated. Such a concep-

---

8 "Cet homme est un caillou. Nous le ferons bouillir au Marché-aux-Pourceaux, avant qu'il ait rien dit. Cependant nous n'épargnons rien pour arriver à la vérité. Il est déjà tout disloqué." (Hugo, *Notre-Dame* VII, 5, 408)
9 "Les paroles qu'elle chantait étaient d'une langue inconnue à Gringoire, et qui paraissait lui être inconnue à elle-même, tant l'expression qu'elle donnait au chant se rapportait peu au sens des paroles." (Hugo, *Notre-Dame de Paris* II, 3, 139)
10 For a detailed analysis, see Marie-Christine Bellosta and Myriam Roman, Les Misérables, *roman pensif*, 142f.

tion of the *symbolic* relies on the romantic theory of participation as defined by Tzvetan Todorov.

> The symbolic is the exemplary, the typical, what one may legitimately consider as the manifestation of a general law. This confirms the worth of the relation of participation for the romantic aesthetics, as opposed to the relation of resemblance that had reigned unchallenged on classical doctrines.[11]

Tzvetan Todorov distinguishes between the classical interpretation of the common points that we perceive between objects of the world as resemblances, and the Romantic interpretation of these common points as evidence that all the objects of the world belong to a common universe where everything enters into correspondences with everything else since everything is ruled by the same laws. In such a universe, ethical and aesthetic dimensions are linked to each other.

Such a theory provides us with a guideline to read Tolkien's work. Indeed, the notion of eternal return already explored, as well as the generalisation of the principle of contrast, suggest the existence of recurrent structures like contrast or repetition. Within Hugo's conception, these recurrences, built up by the principle of contrast itself, show that the various items belong to a common universe. Indeed, the same principle of contrast produces dynamism and variety in both ethical and aesthetic spheres.

From this point of view, aesthetics and ethics work in the same way and share the same motifs within the text. A notion of writing that unites aesthetics and ethics is precisely the definition of the romantic *symbolic*. Todorov identifies it as the tool specific to romanticism, synthesising ethical meaning and aesthetic presence within the same piece of writing. This *symbolic* writing allows one to interpret style and meaning according to the same categories and criteria and it also resists any attempt at univocal interpretation and opens up other possible readings, as long as they reflect the rules of the textual motif they interpret. It is not a matter of the direct application of an interpretation to the text but of *applicability*[12], to take up a notion dear to Tolkien and of which the romantic theory of participation provides a subtler understanding.

The notion of contrast which is central to the sublime and the grotesque gives shape to both style and meaning. Aesthetics and ethics work in the same way. Both in Hugo's theory and in Tolkien's work, contrast helps shape and

---
11 "Le symbolique est l'exemplaire, le typique, ce qui permet d'être considéré comme la manifestation d'une loi générale. Par là se confirme la valeur de la relation de participation pour l'esthétique romantique, au détriment de la relation de ressemblance, qui avait régné sans conteste sur les doctrines classiques" (Todorov, 238).
12 See the author's foreword to the 1966 edition of *The Lord of the Rings*.

understand narrative progression as well as suggesting the possibility and desirability of representing the totality of being in a work of art. The notion of the "symbolic" synthesises the link between aesthetics and ethics, insofar as it suggests that writing develops stylistic motifs to which some interpretations are *applicable* without their ever exhausting every potentiality of the motif. The motif is indeed irreducible to any univocal interpretation. Tolkien's work, like Hugo's, does not give precedence to ethics over aesthetics and is less dialectical, be it positively or negatively, than it is interested in the multiplication of possibilities that allow various interpretations to coexist.

Bibliography

Bellosta, Marie-Christine and Myriam Roman. Les Misérables, *roman pensif*. Paris: Belin, 1995

Drout, Michael C. "Tolkien's Prose Style and Its Literary and Rhetorical Effects". *Tolkien Studies* 1 (2004): 137-162

Ferré, Vincent. *Tolkien. Sur les rivages de la Terre du Milieu*. Paris: Christian Bourgois Éditeur, 2001

Hugo, Victor. "Critique". *Œuvres complètes*. Paris: Robert Laffont, 1985

---. *Notre-Dame de Paris* [1831-1832]. Paris: Librairie générale française, 1999

Pantin, Isabelle. *Tolkien et ses légendes. Une expérience en fiction*. Paris: CNRS Editions, 2009

Rosebury, Brian. *Tolkien. A Critical Assessment*. Basingstoke: Palgrave Macmillan, 1992

Todorov, Tzvetan. *Théories du symbole*. Paris: Seuil, 1977

Tolkien, John Ronald Reuel. *The Letters of J.R.R. Tolkien* [1981]. London: HarperCollins, 2006

---. *The Lord of the Rings* [1954-1955]. London: HarperCollins, 2002

Tolkien, Newman und das Oxford Movement

Thomas Fornet-Ponse (Bonn)

Wer sich den Artikel »Romantik« der deutschsprachigen *Wikipedia* durchliest – was natürlich nur mit der gebotenen Vorsicht allen Quellen gegenüber geschehen darf –, dem wird als Vertreter der Romantik unter dem Stichwort »Religion« nur ein Name begegnen: »John Henry Newman als Mitbegründer der Oxford-Bewegung« (Stand: 2.10.2010). Nun hatte Tolkien bekanntlich nach dem Tod seines Vaters mit Father Francis Morgan einen Priester jenes Oratoriums zum Vormund, das Newman (1801-1890) nach seiner Konversion zur Katholischen Kirche (1845) in Birmingham gegründet hatte. Was also liegt näher, als sich der Fragestellung unseres Seminars aus theologischer Sicht zu nähern, indem genau diese Beziehung zwischen dem Oxford Movement, Newman als dessen Hauptvertreter und Tolkien untersucht werden soll?

Angesichts der sehr mageren Forschungslage zu dieser Thematik soll dies exemplarisch erfolgen, indem zunächst die ambivalente Stellung Newmans und des Oxford Movement zur Romantik herausgestellt wird. In Anbetracht der anderen Seminarbeiträge zu Tolkiens Verständnis der Imagination etc. soll nach einer kurzen Skizze der Newman'schen Konzeption des Gewissens, in der sich wichtige Einzelmotive seines Denkens niederschlagen (und die besonders mit dem intuitiven Charakter des *moral sense* Anklänge an romantische Überzeugungen aufweisen dürfte), an einschlägigen Situationen in Tolkiens narrativem Werk untersucht werden, ob und inwiefern sich in diesen ein ähnliches Verständnis des Gewissens zeigt.

Newman und das Oxford Movement – eine romantische Bewegung?

Der Beginn des Oxford Movement wird von Newman selbst in der am 14.7.1833 in der Universitätskirche St Mary the Virgin von John Keble gehaltenen Predigt *On National Apostasy* gesehen. Der faktische Auslöser waren wohl eher Newmans im Anschluss an die so genannte »Hadleigh Conference« veröffentlichten *Tracts for the Times* (1833-1841), wonach auch von den »Tractarians« die Rede ist. Es ist eine hochkirchliche Bewegung der Anglikanischen Kirche, die im Kampf gegen staatliche Eingriffe entstand und die Kirche als göttliche Institution ausweisen wollte. Dazu wird der protestantische Charakter der Church of England bestritten und sie als ein Zweig der geschichtlichen katholischen Kirche – neben der Römisch-Katholischen und den Orthodoxen Kirchen – gesehen. Dementsprechend werden die apostolische Sukzession

(Bischöfe), die verbindliche Lehre aus Schrift und Tradition (Kirchenväter), das sakramentale Prinzip sowie die tradierte Liturgie betont. Unterschiede zur sonstigen High Church des Anglikanismus bestehen im religiösen Ernst ihrer Praxis, der poetischen Sprache sowie ihrer Kritik an der staatskirchlichen Verfassung. Kritik kam vor allem gegen Newmans katholische Deutung der 39 Glaubensartikel auf, und mit seiner Konversion am 9.10.1845 endete das Oxford Movement im engeren Sinn, stabilisierte sich aber unter Führung der den anderen Hauptvertreter (Keble und Pusey) und führte zur Bildung des modernen Anglokatholizismus (vgl. Chadwick, Klausnitzer 52-59, Nockles).

Was die inhaltlichen Nähen des Oxford Movement zur Romantik betrifft, ist ein differenziertes Urteil abzugeben. Newman kann die Dichter der Romantik als Wegbereiter ansehen, gleichwohl das Oxford Movement nicht aus ihr komme[1], sich aber auch sehr kritisch über romantische Ideen äußern. In der Forschung hat sich ein Sowohl-als-auch eingebürgert. So behauptet Coulson, die Oxford-Bewegung habe in einer Hinsicht für England das gleiche getan wie Schleiermacher für Deutschland: »it provides the theological programme of Romanticism, if we interpret Romanticism as restoring a conception of Nature, not as dead and exploitable, but as a divine sacramental language« (35).[2] Auf der anderen Seite bestehen wichtige Differenzen zwischen Newman (und dem Oxford Movement) und der Romantik. Nach Beer habe Newman zwar seinen Platz in der romantischen Tradition der nach Dauer strebenden Sensibilität, andererseits aber wenig übrig gehabt für eine andere Tradition der Romantik, »more vitalistic in tendency, which, seeing man as a child of the earth and an involuntary disciple of his own imagination, sought to use resources for the renewal of humanity« (213f). Deutlich schärfer äußert sich Pattison, nach dem das Oxford Movement sich gegen zentrale Ideen der Romantik wie die religiöse Ehrfurcht der Individualität, des sakramentalen Wertes der Kunst oder der göttlichen Inspiration individueller Vision richtet; substantiell habe Newman mit der Romantik nichts gemeinsam gehabt (vgl. 44f). Auch Berger spricht von Kontinuität und Diskontinuität zwischen Oxford Movement und Romantik, da nicht einfach romantische Prinzipien in einen kirchlich-religiösen Kontext übersetzt würden. Besonders wichtig sei dies für die Liturgie, aber es bestünden auch Affinitäten in den theologischen Grundüberzeugungen. Als erste nennt sie die Interpretation der Wirklichkeit, wonach die sichtbare Welt als quasi-sakramentale Größe gilt (vor allem bei der Lake School). »Die Oxford Bewegung partizipiert an diesem romantischen Lebensgefühl, distanziert sich allerdings

---

1 »These writers, however, are to be noticed far more as indications of what was secretly going on in the minds of men, than as causes of it.« (Newman, *Prospects* 269.) »The Oxford Movement was a religious flowering of the English Romantic movement: as we have seen, an inheritor of the ›poetic‹ tension of head and heart so typical of Wordsworth and Coleridge.« (Prickett 170)
2 So ist nach Chadwick »that symbolic and sacramental consciousness ... the deepest link, perhaps the only true and valid link, between Romanticism and Catholicism« (53).

kategorisch von allen pantheistischen Tendenzen« (51). Deswegen zeigen ihre Vertreter ein ambivalentes Verhältnis, weil sie zwar einerseits einige Elemente wie die antirationalistische Ausrichtung der Naturschauung (entsprechend ihrem Kampf gegen den Rationalismus) positiv werten, andererseits sie als Ganzes eher ablehnen. Die Ablehnung erfolgte möglicherweise, weil sie eine gefühlsgetragene Spiritualität ablehnen und einen asketisch-strengen Moralbegriff betonen, was sie beides nicht in der Romantik fanden. Auch die in ihren Werken durchgängig präsente sakramentale Weltanschauung wird von ihnen nicht auf die Romantik zurückgeführt, sondern »durch den Verweis auf die Kirchenväter, die biblischen Schriften und auch Butlers *Analogy*« (52, mit Belegen) legitimiert; die Romantik habe dieser fundamentalen Wahrheit nur wieder Geltung verschafft.[3] Weitere Entsprechungen zwischen Romantik und Oxford Movement sind die Orientierung an einer (idealisierten) früheren Epoche bzw. die Wiederentdeckung des Wertes und der Autorität der Geschichte – in der Romantik vor allem das Mittelalter, im Oxford Movement vor allem die Alte Kirche – sowie der ausgeprägte Individualismus: »two and two only absolute and luminously self-evident beings, myself and my Creator« (Newman, *Apologia* 4).[4]

An Unterschieden nennt Berger das sozialrevolutionäre Gedankengut der Romantik, die Sympathie mit unteren Gesellschaftsschichten sowie die Suche nach Extremsituationen der Erfahrung. Kontinuität und Diskontinuität bestehen, weil das Oxford Movement zwar einerseits auf dem Nährboden romantischer Anschauungen entstanden sei, aber die übernommenen Ansätze anders gefüllt wurden und zudem die Distanz zu mit ihren Grundpositionen nicht zu vereinbarenden Tendenzen gewahrt wurde (vgl. 53f).

Auf dieser Basis erscheint die eingangs genannte Einordnung Newmans in die Romantik durch die deutschsprachige *Wikipedia* als ein wenig vereinfachend oder nur eine Sondermeinung der Forschung repräsentierend.[5] Denn auch wenn Newman durchaus Individualität, Kunst und individuelle Vision zuweilen wertschätzte, erfolgte dies aus einer anderen Perspektive als derjenigen der ursprünglichen Autoren, verwendet er ein voraufklärerisches, spezifisch theologisches Vokabular für solche Phänomene und unterminiert die Verschmelzung der imaginativen und religiösen Perspektiven, die für die offeneren Christian

---

3   Keller-Hüschemenger sieht zwar die engen Beziehungen zwischen Oxford Movement und Romantik, aber die eigentlichen Wurzeln des Oxford Movement »eindeutig im kirchlich-religiösen und theologie-geistlichen Bereich« (14). Prickett betont die engen Beziehungen zwischen Theologie und Literaturkritik im 19. Jh. und meint: »The idea of poetic ›creativity‹ developed by Coleridge, Wordsworth, and their successors in Victorian England, which is usually seen in purely aesthetic terms, was in fact a re-discovery and a re-application of a much older Judeo-Christian way of thinking about religious experience.« (7)
4   »In religious inquiry each of us can speak only for himself, and for himself he has a right to speak.« (Newman, *Grammar* 292)
5   Der Vollständigkeit halber: In der zuletzt betrachteten Version des Romantik-Artikels (22. Febr. 2011) ist der Abschnitt über die Vertreter der Romantik entfernt; und auch der Artikel ›Liste der Romantiker‹ nennt Newman und das Oxford Movement nicht mehr.

Romantics charakteristisch waren. »Despite these incongruities, however, we will find that Newman's efforts to ground his own subjectivity rest upon and often parallel the progress of German Idealism from Kant through Hegel« (Goslee 81, vgl. 88ff). So teile Newman die implizite und pragmatische Annahme der Englischen Romantiker, wonach Subjektivität kein philosophisches Recht sei, sondern ein Sieg inspirierter Äußerung – also Resultat des andauernden Dialogs des Selbst mit Gott, in dem die Identitäten beider immer wieder neu verhandelt werden. »As both Romantic and anti-Romantic, Newman escapes subsequent efforts to reduce Romantic claims into their psychological or sociological counterparts; he also anticipates some of the more recent post-structuralist challenges to these same claims« (Goslee 81).

Wie Goslees Analyse der Äußerungen Newmans zur Romantik zeigt, interpretiert er ihre Anliegen immer schon aus theologischer Perspektive, was zu seiner teilweise sehr scharfen Kritik führt (vgl. *Sermons* 288; *Discussions* 233), scheint sich allerdings nicht sehr intensiv mit ihr beschäftigt zu haben. Goslee sieht den zentralen Unterschied zu Schleiermacher in der Differenz zwischen einer liberalen und einer doktrinalen Theologie und zu Coleridge zwischen einer Theologie, die Religion und subjektive Ästhetik verbinden, und einer, die beides trennen will (vgl. 86). Zu Coleridge äußert Newman sich ab 1835 häufiger und nennt ihn z.B.

> a very original thinker, who, while he indulged a liberty of speculation, which no Christian can tolerate, and advocated conclusions which were often heathen rather than Christian, yet after all instilled a higher philosophy into inquiring minds, than they had hitherto been accustomed to accept. In this way he made trial of his age, and succeeded in interesting its genius in the cause of Catholic truth. (*Apologia* 97)

Dementsprechend verteidigt er in Predigten die orthodoxe Selbst-Transzendenz, in der das Subjekt seine Individualität aufgibt, um eine engere Einheit mit Gott zu erreichen, gegenüber einer romantischen Selbst-Erhöhung, in der das Subjekt sich fast mit der Gottheit identifiziert. Dennoch bestehen große Ähnlichkeiten, weil seine Visionen letztlich doch das exklusive Vorrecht des Auserwählten sind, womit Newman faktisch doch eine romantische Selbst-Instantiierung vertritt, wenngleich die Visionen seine radikalsten Versuche verkörpern, einer romantischen Subjektivität zu entkommen.[6] Insofern Newman in ihnen einen dialektischen Prozess gegenseitiger und andauernder Neudefinition von Selbst

---

6 Nach Rule legt eine Lektüre der Biographien Coleridges und Newmans, ihrer Schriften über Kirche und Staat sowie über den Glauben nahe »that everything they wrote springs from and returns to a conviction that the human person can rise, under the direction of conscience or moral self-consciousness, to a level of self-transcendence that enables the person, aided by faith, to come to the new cognitive horizon that is God« (3).

und Gott sieht, kann er als implizit romantisch angesehen werden. So kann in seinen Schriften als Anglikaner eine dialogische Romantik ausgemacht werden, die seine Vorstellungen persönlicher Identität, spiritueller Auserwählung, von Selbst- wie Kultur- und Sozialkritik ausweitet.

Im Laufe der Zeit bricht diese Synthese allerdings zusammen. »In trying to baptize phenomena usually associated with gothic, satanic, sublime, or ironic Romanticism, Newman sought to encompass them within a more capacious image of God«[7] (Goslee 11f). Dadurch wird dieser Gott aber zu einer bedrohenden Präsenz, die innerhalb einer institutionellen Kirche beschränkt werden muss. Da er in der anglikanischen Kirche keine dafür ausreichende spirituelle Kraft sah, konvertierte er deswegen zur katholischen Kirche.[8] Damit löst er die Verbindung zu seinen vorherigen Mitstreitern, aber »remained emotionally and aesthetically within the tradition which had brought him *to* Catholicism – the world embraced by the Anglican sensibility of Coleridge and Keble« (Prickett 170) – und skeptisch gegenüber der Rationalität der in der katholischen Kirche vorherrschenden Neuscholastik.[9] Auch wenn Newman mit der Konversion die Autorität der katholischen Kirche und z.B. ihres Lehramtes anerkennt, bedeutet dies keine einfache Unterwerfung der so hoch geschätzten Subjektivität, wie am Beispiel seiner Gewissenskonzeption deutlich wird.

Newmans Gewissenskonzeption als Zusammenfassung seiner Theologie

ich in diesem Kontext auf Newmans Gewissenskonzeption zu konzentrieren, bietet sich aus zwei Gründen an: Zum einen nimmt Newman mit ihr eine sehr eigene Position in der Theologie ein, was es ermöglicht, nach spezifischem Newman'schen Gedankengut bei Tolkien zu fragen, und die Gefahr vermeidet, solches mit allgemeinen römisch-katholischen Überzeugungen zu vermischen.

---

7 »For Newman, as for Coleridge, there is no clear break psychologically and empirically between natural and supernatural: they may pull in opposite directions, but they are no less mutually dependent.« (Prickett 202)
8 »Newman's conversion can be seen as the removal from a faith under which his sense of reality had gradually been undermined to a faith which restored it.« (Beer 201f)
9 Vgl. Rule 145. »From the cultivation of sensibility he had endeavoured to remove all self-indulgence from an exclusive concentration on personal relationships within an ordered social network. ... He had sought for truth, but had rejected the idea that one could find an ultimate truth in nature, or any symbol of truth in the human mind, apart from revelation« (Beer 217f). Chadwick zählt zu den großen Verdiensten Newmans, »to make at home in modern English religion two interwoven ideas: the indwelling of God in His world, as that idea is found in Wordsworth and others of the romantics; and Catholic sacramentalism, with all its consequences for an attitude to the material world« (315). Nachdem er einige Unterschiede zwischen Coleridge und Newman genannt hat, betont Rule eine »striking similarity«: »Both insisted on the primacy of the moral order and the corollary that morality and religion are inseperable« (29).

Zum anderen bündeln sich in ihr zentrale Linien der Theologie Newmans, weswegen die im vorherigen Abschnitt genannte Ambivalenz gegenüber der Romantik sich auch darin niederschlägt.

Indem Newmans Gewissenslehre wichtige Einzelmotive seines Denkens – Theorie der formlosen Folgerung, Differenzierung zwischen dem persönlichen Wissen des *real assent* (man stimmt der Wahrheit einer Aussage über Konkretes zu) und dem *notionol assent* (man stimmt der Wahrheit einer Aussage über Abstraktes zu), die Unterscheidung zwischen objektiver und subjektiver Gewissheit etc. – vereint und diese in der *Grammar of Assent* (1870) und im Brief an den Herzog von Norfolk (1875) ausführt, kann diese als biographische Theologie angesehen werden: »eine nachträgliche Reflexion auf das eigene intellektuelle Ringen, das Newman in jeder Phase seiner Entstehung als Unterwerfung unter die stufenweise erfasste Wahrheit deutet« (Schockenhoff 123). Zu den Grundüberzeugungen gehört, jeder Mensch verfüge von Geburt an über ein Gewissen; er setzt das in jedem Menschen vorhandene Gefühl dessen, was wir gutes oder schlechtes Gewissen nennen, als allgemeine Erfahrungstatsache, eine anthropologische Grunderfahrung voraus. Newman betrachtet dieses jedem Menschen vertraute Phänomen in doppelter Hinsicht:

> Es ist einerseits ein moralisches Sensorium allgemeiner Art, durch das wir die sittlichen Werte erfassen und unser Handeln im Licht der Unterscheidung von gut und böse beurteilen (*moral sense*). Andererseits zeigt sich das Gewissen für Newman als Pflichtgefühl und als Wissen um die Unbedingtheit des sittlichen Anspruchs, der hinter seinen einzelnen Urteilen steht (*sense of duty*).
> (Schockenhoff 125; vgl. Lackner 152f)

Auch wenn Newman in seinen Schriften verschiedene Formulierungen und Akzentsetzungen für diese Unterscheidung verwendet und nicht eindeutig gesagt werden kann, ob *moral sense* und praktische Vernunft identisch sind (wie Lackner 165ff meint), lässt er in *Grammar of assent* keinen Zweifel daran, dass sie keine nach- oder nebeneinander tätigen unterschiedlichen Gewissensformen oder distinkte Seelenvermögen sind. Vielmehr ist der eine Gewissensakt unteilbar, kann aber in seinen zwei Aspekten betrachtet werden. »Thus conscience has both a critical and a judicial office« (Newman, *Grammar* 81; vgl. *Letter* 255f), wobei sich der *moral sense* auf den materialen Aspekt, d.h. den Inhalt der sittlichen Verpflichtung bezieht (ich fühle, ob ein Akt moralisch verwerflich ist oder nicht bzw. was in der konkreten Situation ethisch richtig oder falsch ist), der *sense of duty* auf den formalen Aspekt, d.h. den Sollenscharakter (ich fühle, das Gute sei zu tun und das Böse zu lassen).[10] Stark vereinfacht können

---

10 »Im Befehlscharakter liegt der Grund für die innige Beziehung des Gewissens zu Gefühl und Gemütsbewegung. Eine ganze Bandbreite von Gefühlen wird angesprochen: Ehrfurcht,

der *moral sense* als eine instinkthaft-intuitive Erfassung sittlicher Werte dem Verständnis des Gewissens als natürliche Anlage und der *sense of duty* eher demjenigen des Gewissens als Stimme Gottes zugeordnet werden. Zum *moral sense* gehört wesentlich ein inneres Gespür, ein Instinkt, eine Intuition für das sittlich Richtige und Falsche, das die notwendige Erfahrungsbasis für das schlussfolgernde Denken der Vernunft bereitstellt und diesem voraus liegt. Entsprechend der Erkenntnis alltäglicher Dinge verläuft die Erkenntnis aus vielfältigen Einzelerlebnissen unter der Führung des *moral sense* hin zu allgemeinen moralischen Normen. Diese induktive Vorgehensweise relativiert nach Newman nicht den Wahrheitsanspruch der moralischen Normen, sondern das instinkthafte Erfassen des sittlich Richtigen führt dazu, die Wahrheit des allgemeinen sittlichen Gesetzes begrifflich zu verstehen.

> Even one act of cruelty, ingratitude, generosity, or justice reveals to us at once *intensivè* the immutable distinction between those qualities and their contraries; that is, in that particular instance and *pro hac vice*. From such experience – an experience which is ever recurring – we proceed to abstract and generalize; and thus the abstract proposition »There is a right and a wrong,« as representing an act of inference, is received by the mind with a notional, not a real assent. (*Grammar* 50)

Das konkrete Gewissenserleben des *moral sense* wird also mit dem voranschreitenden begrifflichen Verständnis des allgemeinen Sittengesetzes verbunden. Deswegen kann Newman den *moral sense* auch als »the principle of ethics« (Grammar 84) bezeichnen, weil er unser natürliches Wissen um gut und böse von seinen ersten Erfahrungen bis hin zu einem allgemeinen ethischen System führt.[11] Der *sense of duty* hingegen ist »the creative principle of religion« (ebd.) bzw. »a connecting principle between the creature and his Creator« (89). Denn beide Prinzipien besitzen zwar eine analoge Funktion in ihrem jeweiligen Bereich, sind aber nicht gleichrangig. Es besteht eine Asymmetrie, da der *sense of duty* dem *moral sense* gegenüber vorrangig ist. »The natural voice of Conscience is far more imperative in testifying and enforcing a rule of duty, than successful in determining that duty in particular cases« (*Development* 361; vgl. *Dispositions* 64). Wegen der möglichen Undeutlichkeit bzw. Unklarheit des Gewissensspruches ist auch ein irrendes Gewissen möglich, allerdings irrt es nicht in den Prinzipien, sondern im Detail. Newman ist wie Thomas der Meinung, auch dieses sei bindend, denn im Fall des irrenden Gewissens

---

Scheu, Hoffnung, Furcht, Qual, Scham, Selbstvorwürfe, unaufhörliche Gewissensbisse, Schuld und Entmutigung, aber auch Selbstbilligung und innerer Friede.« (Siebenrock 306)

[11] »Like Coleridge, Newman sees conscience, that is, moral self-consciousness, as prior in nature to all other forms of human knowing in that it grounds them and orchestrates all cognitive activity.« (Rule 57)

ist man von der Richtigkeit seines Handelns subjektiv überzeugt, muss dem unbedingten Anspruch dieser Überzeugung gehorchen und handelt insofern in sittlich guter Gesinnung, obwohl das Handeln objektiv falsch ist. Um solche Entscheidungen aber zu vermeiden, ist das Gewissen als *moral sense* auch mit Hilfe der Kirche und ihres Lehramtes zu bilden (vgl. Grave 91-130; Lackner 177-180. 228-233).[12]

Der Unterschied des Gewissens als *sense of duty* zu anderen menschlichen Instinkten besteht in der besonderen Art der Gefühlsbetontheit, die auch den intellektuellen Sinnen (Menschenverstand, praktische Vernünftigkeit, sogar dem moralischen Sinn) nicht eigen ist. Diese besondere Qualität erklärt Newman durch den Bezug moralischer Handlungen auf Personen, durch den und das Gefühl der Verpflichtung bzw. Verantwortlichkeit das Gewissen über sich hinaus verweist und als Stimme bzw. »echo of a voice« (*Grammar* 82) wahrgenommen wird. »If, as is the case, we feel responsibility, are ashamed, are frightened, at transgressing the voice of conscience, this implies that there is One to whom we are responsible, before whom we are ashamed, whose claims upon us we fear« (83). Dies bezieht Newman zwar zunächst auf den zwischenmenschlichen Bereich, dehnt dies aber weiter aus, weil jeder natürliche Erklärungsversuch die Gewissensregung nicht vollständig auflösen kann, womit »Newman die Gegenwart der Gottesidee in der moralischen Gewissenserfahrung« (Schockenhoff 132) erschließt – und die Kennzeichnung des *sense of duty* als »creative principle of religion« geklärt ist.[13] Die Gewissenserfahrung erzeugt nicht die Gottesidee, bewirkt aber, dass der Mensch ansprechbar ist und nach einer göttlichen Offenbarung Ausschau hält. Newman geht es mithin nicht um einen moralischen Gottesbeweis, sondern um die Vernunftgemäßheit des Glaubens.[14] Aus der Gewissenserfahrung gehen drei Voraussetzungen für den Glauben hervor – der Mensch vernimmt eine autoritative Stimme, der Gewissensspruch ist hinsichtlich konkreter Anweisungen oft nicht klar und der Mensch erfährt seine eigene sittliche Unvollkommenheit. Je mehr er sich auf den Anspruch des Gewissens einlässt, desto klarer und unzweideutiger wird er ein festes Prinzip vernehmen, das ihn auf die Gerechtigkeit und Liebe Gottes verweist.[15]

---

12 Das Gewissen als sense of duty setzt nicht die persönliche Autonomie voraus. »It does not prompt us to attach any significance to a moral opinion as being our own. Its dictate requires us to do the thing we see as right.« (Grave 61)

13 »If the cause of these emotions does not belong to this visible world, the Object to which his perception is directed must be Supernatural and Divine; and thus the phenomena of Conscience, as a dictate, avail to impress the imagination with the picture of a Supreme Governor, a Judge, holy, just, powerful, all-seeing, retributive, and is the creative principle of religion, as the Moral Sense is the principle of ethics.« (*Grammar* 84)

14 Rule sieht darin eine enge Beziehung zwischen Coleridge und Newman: »Each left, incomplete and unpublished, what is in substance a working paper on an ›argument‹ for a personal God from the consciousness of conscience.« (2)

15 »[I]n proportion as we listen to that Word, and use it, not only do we learn more from it, not only do its dictates become clearer, and at its lessons broader, and its principles more consistent, but its very tone is louder and more authoritative and constraining.

Newmans besondere Leistung hinsichtlich der theologischen Gewissensdeutung liegt darin, die beiden wichtigsten theologischen Interpretamente des Gewissens zu vereinen: das Gewissen als Stimme Gottes (Augustinus) und das Gewissen als natürliche Anlage (Thomas von Aquin). Sein eigenständiger Beitrag besteht vor allem darin, die religiöse Dimension des Gewissens aufzuweisen, die intuitive, vorrationale Tiefenschicht der sittlichen Erfahrung ernst zu nehmen und sich darum zu bemühen, den personalen Charakter der Verpflichtung durch das Gewissens herauszustellen, ohne damit die objektive Wahrheitsbindung abzuschwächen. Newman setzt somit »bei der ursprünglichen Selbstgegebenheit des menschlichen Geistes [an], in der die Urgewissheit der je eigenen Existenz gründet« (Schockenhoff 136; vgl. Siebenrock 314).

Dieser Ansatz ermöglicht ihm die Verbindung beider Traditionen, weil einerseits das Gewissen als natürliche Anlage oder geistiges Urerlebnis ausgewiesen wird, das jedem Menschen eigen ist. Andererseits verweist diese natürliche Gewissenserfahrung über sich hinaus und wird erst in der Anerkennung Gottes erfüllt. Der Gewissensspruch darf aber nicht unmittelbar mit der Stimme Gottes identifiziert werden, als ob Gott direkt zum Menschen spräche, sondern ist deren »Echo«. Die Handlungen sind aber nicht deswegen gesollt, weil sie von außen als göttlicher Befehl autorisiert werden, sondern um ihretwillen, weil das sittlich Gute in sich wertvoll ist.

Sicherlich wird man das Newman'sche Gewissensverständnis nicht einfach als romantisch bezeichnen können und wird auch die Betonung der Subjektivität und des Individuums sich nicht rein romantischen Einflüssen verdanken, sondern kann sich auch auf die theologische Tradition stützen. Gleichwohl zeigen gerade der Aspekt des *moral sense* und die allgemeine Betonung des Gewissens durchaus Nähen.

Gewissen bei Tolkien

Im Blick auf Tolkien stellt sich nun die Frage, ob in seinen narrativen Werken eine ähnliche Konzeption des Gewissens präsentiert wird bzw. eine solche Gewissenskonzeption zumindest einen geeigneten Rahmen abgibt, um die in Tolkiens Werk auftauchenden Situationen moralischer Dilemmata plausibel zu erklären.

And thus it is, that to those who use what they have, more is given; for, beginning with obedience, they go on to the intimate perception and belief of one God. His voice within them witnesses to Him, and they believe His own witness about Himself. They believe in His existence, not because others say it, not in the word of man merely, but with a personal apprehension of its truth.« (*Dispositions* 65f)

The Hobbit

Eine sehr bekannte und aus moralphilosophischer Sicht alles andere als einfach zu bewertende Stelle ist sicherlich Bilbos Umgang mit dem Arkenstein. An dieser Stelle kann ich auf die diversen Probleme nicht weiter eingehen (vgl. Fornet-Ponse 108f, Sternberg) und muss mich damit begnügen, Bilbos subjektive Entscheidung zu untersuchen. Als Bilbo den Arkenstein im Drachenhort sieht und einsteckt, ohne den Zwergen anschließend davon zu berichten, heißt es: »he had an uncomfortable feeling that the picking and choosing had not really been meant to include this marvellous gem« (H 293). Das braucht nicht mehr als eine bloße Vorahnung sein, kann aber auch als Ausdruck seines *moral sense* verstanden werden, der ihm signalisiert, dass das, was er da gerade tut, eben doch nicht sittlich gut ist – auch wenn er sich dazu auf den Vertragstext berufen kann. Ähnlich unbequem reagiert er auf die Frage Bards: »But how is it yours to give?« (331), antwortet aber, er möge vielleicht ein Dieb sein, aber er hofft, ein mehr oder weniger ehrlicher zu sein – was er bei der Verabschiedung vom Elvenking auf der Rückreise bestätigt, als er ihm das Halsband schenkt und sagt: »I mean even a burglar has his feelings« (353). Offensichtlich sieht er es als geboten (oder zumindest als sittlich gut) an, den Konflikt dadurch zu lösen, dass er Bard das Einzige in die Hand gibt, was Thorin zu gewissen Zugeständnissen bewegen kann. Auch erscheint es ihm als geboten, zu seinen Freunden zurückzukehren – zumal er Bombur versprochen hat, ihn zu wecken. Er wertet die Rückkehr und das Einhalten eines Versprechens also nicht nur als sittlich gut, sondern sieht sich dadurch auch aufgefordert, dies zu tun und nicht dem Rat des Elvenking zu folgen. Auch sein Gefühl, den Dank Komburs kaum verdient zu haben, kann als Ausdruck seines *moral sense* verstanden werden (vgl. 332).

Der *sense of duty*, eine einmal eingegangene Verpflichtung einzuhalten, wird in Bilbos Selbstgespräch auf dem Weg zu Smaug deutlich, nachdem er schon vorher gegenüber Thorin zwar auf seine außervertraglichen Leistungen hingewiesen hat, aber dennoch nicht zurückstehen will: »You went and put your foot right in it that night of the party, and now you have got to pull it out and pay for it!« (269) Er bezeichnet sich zwar selbst als »fool« und wünscht sich nach Hause, lässt sich aber nicht seine Handlungen bestimmen.

Ein ähnliches Gefühl der Verpflichtung oder der Verantwortung gegenüber den Zwergen zeigt Bilbo auch schon während der Reise. So legt die Formulierung »obviously he had first of all to look for his friends« (208), nachdem er die erste Spinne im Düsterwald getötet hat, eine selbstverständliche Verpflichtung den Zwergen gegenüber nahe, zumal er an die Hilfeschreie der Zwerge in der Nacht denkt. Nach der Gefangennahme der Zwerge durch die Waldelben zögert er zwar etwas, entschließt sich aber dann doch, sie nicht zu verlassen – hier ist der Verpflichtungscharakter weniger deutlich. Die verschiedenen Gelegenheiten, in denen er die Höhlen verlassen kann, nutzt er nicht, wobei nicht klar ist, ob hier zwei verschiedene Motive genannt werden oder das eine nur eine erläuternde Anmerkung des Erzählers ist: »He did not wish to desert the dwarves, and indeed he did not know where in the world to go without them« (226). Umgekehrt fühlten sich aber auch die Zwerge verpflichtet, ihm bei den Trollen zu helfen, ohne einen besonderen Grund zur Dankbarkeit ihm gegenüber zu haben. Dies wird später betont, als sich außer Balin niemand bereit erklärt, ihn in den Berg zu begleiten (vgl. 268).

Ein anderes Beispiel, das den Verpflichtungscharakter des als Gut erkannten oder gewussten illustriert, ist das Rätselspiel. Denn: »the riddle-game was sacred and of immense antiquity, and even wicked creatures were afraid to cheat when they played at it« (127). Der materiale Gehalt der Regeln verdankt sich zwar keinem *moral sense*, aber die Heiligkeit und das Alter des Rätselspiels bekräftigen sehr effektiv den *sense of duty*, sie nicht zu brechen.

Hinsichtlich der Frage der Gewissensbildung ist die Passage nach der Flucht von den Waldelben aussagekräftig, weil sie einen Einstellungswandel Bilbos aufgrund von Gewöhnung attestiert: »He no longer thought twice about picking up a supper uninvited if he got the chance, he had been obliged to do it for so long, and he knew now only too well what it was to be really hungry« (238).

Lässt sich im *Hobbit* zwar auch nicht eindeutig ein an Newman orientiertes Gewissensverständnis feststellen, haben sich doch gewisse Nähen gezeigt bzw. hat sich die Unterscheidung zwischen *moral sense* und *sense of duty* als hilfreich erwiesen.

The Lord of the Rings

Der schon im *Hobbit* deutlich gewordene unbedingte Sollenscharakter des als Gut Erkannten, der vom Subjekt erfahren wird, zeigt sich auch in *The Lord of the Rings*. Er kann zu den Grundvoraussetzungen gezählt werden, da er den Kampf gegen Sauron – und Gandalfs Absage an die Vorschläge Sarumans – ermöglicht. Gerade darin zeigt sich aber auch ein *moral sense*, weil auch Sauron es als gut wertet, Melkor zu dienen. Tolkien selber betont, Sauron habe noch Relikte guter Absichten gehabt, »that descended from the good of the nature in which he began« (MR 396), besonders seine Liebe zu Ordnung und Koordination. Auch Sarumans Vorschlag, sich mit Sauron zu verbünden, verdankt sich seiner Einsicht, es sei das Beste für Mittelerde, wenn sie dies täten: »But we must have power, power to order all things as we will, for that good which only the Wise can see« (LotR 252). Dieses Gute spezifiziert er: »the high and ultimate purpose: Knowledge, Rule, Order« (253). Gandalf hingegen bewertet die Freiheit der Bewohner Mittelerdes höher als das von den Weisen erkannte Gut, das gewaltsam durchgesetzt wird, und sieht sich dementsprechend (und entsprechend ihrer ursprünglichen Sendung als Istari) dazu verpflichtet, dafür einzutreten.[16] Noch prägnanter wird dies in verschiedenen Einzelsituationen:

In den Hügelgräberhöhen überlegt Frodo zunächst, ob er mit Hilfe des Rings entkommen könnte und meint, Gandalf müsste zugeben, er hätte nichts für seine Freunde tun können. Daraus spricht sein Gefühl, auch in Situationen eigener Gefährdung ihnen gegenüber zur Hilfe verpflichtet zu sein. Sein erwachter Mut schließlich ermöglicht es ihm, diesem Anspruch gemäß zu handeln (vgl. 138). Weil er sich für seine Freunde verantwortlich fühlt, weigert er sich auch zunächst, mit Glorfindels Pferd zu fliehen (vgl. 206), und viel später auch, sein Versprechen gegenüber Gollum zu brechen (vgl. 676). Vergleichbar sehen es Legolas, Gimli und Aragorn in Emyn Muil als treulos an, wenn sie Frodo nun verließen, obwohl sie in Rivendell nicht versprochen haben, ihn bis zum Ende zu begleiten und selber dafür plädieren, nach Minas Tirith zu gehen (vgl. 393).

In Lothlórien berichtet jeder der Gefährten von der Begegnung mit Galadriel, er sei vor eine Wahl gestellt worden »between a shadow full of fear that lay ahead, and something that he greatly desired« (349), wozu er lediglich umkehren müsse. Boromir betont, es sei nicht nötig zu sagen, er habe abgelehnt zu hören; die Männer aus Minas Tirith stünden zu ihrem Wort. Er setzt damit wie selbstverständlich voraus, es sei gut und daher geboten, zu seinem Wort zu stehen. Interessanterweise wird die Diskussion durch Pippins Frage an Sam ausgelöst, wieso er errötet sei. »Anyone would have thought you had a guilty conscience.«[17] (348) Diese Reaktion Sams auf das gefühlte Angebot Galadriels könnte auf seinen *moral sense* hindeuten, der ihn schon das Bedenken des Angebots als moralisch fragwürdig empfinden lässt.

Bei der Entscheidung Aragorns, ob sie versuchen sollen, Frodo und Sam zu folgen oder Merry und Pippin zu befreien, will er »a right choice« treffen, was deutlich seinen Wunsch ausdrückt, sein Handeln am objektiv Guten auszurichten und nicht nur seinen Neigungen zu folgen. Denn wenn er nun Frodo in der Wildnis sucht, überlässt er die beiden anderen Folter und Tod. Die Entscheidung fällt er allerdings in Berufung auf ein Gefühl: »My heart speaks clearly at last: the fate of the Bearer is in my hands no longer. The Company has played its part. Yet we that remain cannot forsake our companions while we have strength left« (409).

Die Ausrichtung am objektiv Guten wird auch in der Begegnung mit Éomer deutlich, denn dieser fragt sich, wie in diesen Zeiten ein Mensch entscheiden soll – worauf Aragorn antwortet: Wie immer. »Good and ill have not changed since yesteryear; nor are they one thing among Elves and Dwarves and another

---

16 Dies wird deutlich in seiner Begegnung mit Théoden, weil er ihn eindeutig vor die Wahl stellt: »Do you ask for help? ... Yet counsel I could give, and words I could speak to you. Will you hear them?« (503)
17 Dies ist meiner Kenntnis nach die einzige Verwendung von »conscience« in LotR.

among Men. It is a man's part to discern them, as much in the Golden Wood as in his own house«[18] (428). Aragorn betont damit nicht nur, Gut und Böse seien objektive und unveränderliche Größen, sondern betont auch die Bedeutung des Gewissens bzw. die Notwendigkeit, beide zu unterscheiden. Obwohl er es nicht explizit sagt, dürfte es keine Überinterpretation sein, anzunehmen, er gehe dabei auch von der unbedingten Verpflichtung aus, das Gute sei zu tun bzw. das Böse zu lassen. Denn andernfalls wäre ihre Unterscheidung irrelevant. Ohne damit die Subjektivität völlig negieren zu wollen, bekennt sich Tolkien zu einem Wertobjektivismus, denn das Gute soll getan werden, weil es gut ist – und ist nicht gut, weil es gewollt wird. Das aber ist eine Voraussetzung, um überhaupt sinnvoll von Gewissensentscheidungen sprechen zu können.

Einen sehr ausführlichen Bericht über einen Entscheidungsprozess bietet Tolkien uns bei Sam in Cirith Ungol, der einerseits bei Frodo bleiben und andererseits ihre Queste nicht aufgeben will. Zunächst sieht er es als nötig an, allein weiterzugehen, weswegen er den Ring (und andere Sachen) an sich nimmt. Wichtig dabei ist, dass er nicht fragt, was er tun will, sondern, was er tun soll bzw. zu tun hat: »Go on? Is that what I've got to do?« (714). Das spricht deutlich für das Gewissen als erfahrbare autoritative Stimme. Tolkien betont aber auch, er habe sich vielleicht entschieden, aber »what he was doing was altogether against the grain of his nature« (716), weswegen er letztlich doch geht. Aber er ist sich bewusst, die moralisch gebotene Tat nicht tun zu können (vgl. 718). Dies verändert sich, als er erfährt, dass Frodo noch lebt: »He no longer had any doubt about his duty: he must rescue his master or perish in the attempt« (877). Aber auch wenn sich der Inhalt dessen verändert, was Sam als seine Pflicht ansieht, verändert sich nicht der Verpflichtungscharakter. Dies zeigt sich auch kurz bevor sie zum Schicksalsberg kommen, als er sich Gedanken darüber macht, dass ihr Proviant nicht mehr für einen Rückweg reicht: »to help Mr. Frodo to the last step and then die with him? Well, if that is the job then I must do it« (913).

Schließlich kann auch überlegt werden, ob die mehrfache Verschonung Gollums sich nicht nur »pity« oder »mercy« oder dem Gefühl verdankt, er habe noch eine Rolle zu spielen (vgl. 58, 601), sondern auch einem *moral sense*, der besonders bei Sam deutlich wird, weil es nur gerecht, mehrfach verdient und die einzig sichere Sache wäre, Gollum zu töten. »But deep in his heart there was something that restrained him: he could not strike this thing lying in the dust, forlorn, ruinous, utterly wretched« (923).

---

18 Die objektive Gültigkeit zeigt sich auch bei Gollums/Sméagols Selbstgespräch, weil selbst Gollum den Verrat bzw. den Bruch des Versprechens als sittlich schlecht anerkennt und versucht zu verteidigen bzw. umzuinterpretieren (vgl. 618f, 709).

Schluss

Schon in der Beschränkung auf zwei narrative Werke Tolkiens wurden die Nähen zum Newman'schen Gewissenverständnis deutlich, da auch Tolkien neben dem Festhalten an der Objektivität von Gut und Böse deutlich die subjektive Dimension des Handelnden hervorhebt. Die Berichte über Entscheidungsfindungen enthalten darüber hinaus oft nicht nur rationale Erwägungen, sondern auch Gefühle – was die Deutung in Richtung eines *moral sense* sehr nahelegt. Schließlich tritt auch bei Tolkien der unbedingte Verpflichtungscharakter des als gut Erkannten hervor.

Indem gerade die Betonung der Sensibilität ein Bindeglied zwischen Newman und der Romantik war, kann dies auch hinsichtlich Tolkiens gelten – ohne damit notwendig behaupten zu müssen, dies sei ihm (ausschließlich) durch Newman und seine Kindheit am Oratorium in Birmingham vermittelt.

Bibliographie

Anderson, Douglas A. *The Annotated Hobbit. Revised and expanded edition.* London: HarperCollins, 2003

Beer, John. "Newman and the Romantic Sensibility". *The English Mind: Studies in the English Moralists Presented to Basil Willey.* Cambridge: Cambridge UP, 1964, 193-218

Berger, Teresa. *Liturgie – Spiegel der Kirche. Eine systematisch-theologische Analyse des liturgischen Gedankenguts im Traktarianismus.* Göttingen: Vandenhoeck & Ruprecht, 1986

Chadwick, Owen. *The Spirit of the Oxford Movement. Tractarian Essays.* Cambridge: Cambridge UP, 1992

Coulson, John. *Religion and Imagination.* Oxford: Clarendon, 1981

Fornet-Ponse, Thomas. »Der Zwerg lebt nicht vom Gold allein. Vom Umgang mit Reichtum im *Hobbit*.« *Hither Shore* 5 (2008): 106-120

Goslee, David. *Romanticism and the Anglican Newman.* Athens: Ohio UP, 1996

Grave, Selwyn Alfred. *Conscience in Newman's Thought.* Oxford: Clarendon, 1989

James, D.G. *The Romantic Comedy.* London: Oxford UP, 1948

Keller-Hüschemenger, Max. *Die Lehre der Kirche in der Oxford Bewegung. Struktur und Funktion.* Gütersloh: Gütersloher Verlagshaus, 1974

Klausnitzer, Wolfgang. *Päpstliche Unfehlbarkeit bei Newman und Döllinger. Ein historisch-systematischer Vergleich.* Innsbruck: Tyrolia, 1980

Lackner, Bernhard. *Segnung und Gebot. John Henry Newmans Entwurf des christlichen Ethos.* Frankfurt: Peter Lang, 1994

Newman, John Henry. "Prospects of the Anglican Church". *Essays. Critical and Historical. Vol. I.* London: Longmans, Green, 1907, 262-308

---. *Apologia pro vita sua. Being a History of his Religious Opinions. With an Introduction by Basil Willey.* London: Oxford UP, 1964

---. *An Essay on the Development of Christian Doctrine.* London: Longmans, Green, 1909

---. *An Essay in Aid of a Grammar of Assent.* London: Longmans, Green, 1947

---. "Dispositions for Faith". *Sermons Preached on Various Occasions.* London: Longmans, Green, 1908. 60-74

---. "A Letter Addressed to the Duke of Norfolk on Occasion of Mr. Gladstone's Recent Expostulation". *Certain Difficulties Felt by Anglicans in Catholic Teaching. Vol. II.* London: Longmans, Green, 1900. 179-378

---. *Discussions and Arguments on Various Subjects.* London: Longmans, Green, 1907

---. *Parochial and Plain Sermons. Vol II.* London: Longmans, Green, 1908

Nockles, Peter Benedict. *The Oxford Movement in Context. Anglican Church Highmanship. 1760-1857.* Cambridge: Cambridge UP, 1994

Pattison, Robert. *The Great Dissent: John Henry Newman and the Liberal Heresy.* New York: Oxford UP, 1991

Prickett, Stephen. *Romanticism and Religion. The Tradition of Coleridge and Wordsworth in the Victorian Church.* Cambridge: Cambridge UP, 1976

Rule, Philip C. *Coleridge and Newman. The Centrality of Conscience.* New York: Fordham UP, 2004

Schockenhoff, Eberhard. *Wie gewiss ist das Gewissen? Eine ethische Orientierung.* Freiburg: Herder, 2003

Siebenrock, Roman. *Wahrheit, Gewissen und Geschichte. Eine systematisch-theologische Rekonstruktion des Wirkens John Henry Kardinal Newmans.* Sigmaringendorf: Regio, 1996

Sternberg, Martin. "The Treasure of my House: The Arkenstone as Symbol of Kingship and Seat of Royal Luck in *The Hobbit*." Hither Shore 5 (2008): 121-133

Tolkien, John Ronald Reuel. *The Lord of the Rings.* London: HarperCollins, 1995

---. *Morgoth's Ring. The History of Middle-earth X.* London: HarperCollins, 1994

Tolkien, the Philistine, and the Politics of Creativity

Martin G.E. Sternberg (Bonn)

> And why beholdest thou the mote that is in thy brother's eye,
> but considerest not that beam that is in your own eye?
> Mt. 7.3

When Tolkien subscribed to the Romantic notion of man as sub-creator and the pivotal role of imagination, he not only took up a concept, but also a conflict. Imaginative sub-creation is rarely the chief activity in a society, a society in which the artist has to exist and fit in: to make a living, to find an audience, and to gain a following even in the political sense of that word: for many romantic poets did want to make a political impact. In the famous words of Shelley, poets were the "unacknowledged legislators of the world" whose imagination shaped the thoughts and ideas of whole peoples and directed societies to a (hopefully brighter) future (Dawson 3f).

This exalted status as unacknowledged legislator however remained mostly just that: unacknowledged by society at large. The romantic artists thus started to define themselves in opposition to what they saw as the main exponent of that society: the philistine. They contrasted their own creative imagination, intensity of feeling, love of risk and adventure with those who attribute everything wonderful to ordinary causes, judge everything by its materialistic usefulness and avoid all extreme experiences which might shatter or transform their drab selves. German Romanticism called people of such disposition *Philister*, philistines (cf. Safranski 199-203). Looking up the word *philistinism* in the *Oxford English Dictionary*, one encounters among the earliest entries Matthew Arnold's of 1869, defining philistinism as "respectability with its thousand gigs."

This definition begs the questions with which the following paper deals: What does it mean that with the hobbits, a people whose chief virtue of respectability is a philistine one takes centre stage in the work of the supposedly romantic Tolkien? Does this have any political ramifications? Finally, what conclusions are to be drawn from this on the political role to which artists and poets lay claim on behalf of their capacity for imagination?

I have to make a qualification beforehand. In this paper, Romanticism means imagination-centred Romanticism. I agree if somebody says that this reduces and distorts Romanticism in general, but I do not claim to deal with Tolkien and

Romanticism in general, which is notoriously difficult to define. I choose this focus because Tolkien made a link with creativity-based Romanticism explicitly in *On Fairy-Stories* (cf. TL 52; Flieger, *Light* 22-25), and implicitly in *Mythopoeia* and *Leaf by Niggle*. Approaching the problem of creative imagination not by tracing Tolkien's thinking on this issue itself but by looking at its enemy, its Other, is simply due to the fact that philistine characters feature large in Tolkien's work, a fact which ultimately will reveal a stance on creative imagination very different from the one proposed in texts that deal with it openly.

The terms *philistinism* and *philistine* were not in use among the English romantics. Yet another entry in the OED by Matthew Arnold may apply here: "Perhaps we do not have the word because we have so much of the thing." For while the *terms* philistine and philistinism were concepts imposed by German students and later artists on their more prosaic contemporaries, the *values* of philistinism were self-assuredly proposed and shared by many in 17th and 18th century England, including members of the intellectual establishment. People were adverse to any kind of enthusiasm and private fancies, and not only because these were opposites of enlightened reason. From Hobbes onward, private fancies and enthusiasm, especially in religious matters, were seen as causes of revolution and civil war (Rohloff 100-103). In his *Satyre against Wit* from 1700, Sir Richard Blackmore levels this charge even at wit, a concept central to classicist poetics:

> The Mob of Wits is up to storm the Town
> To pull all Virtue and right Reason down
> Quite to subvert Religion's sacred fence,
> To set up Wit, and pull down common sense.
> (quoted after Rohloff 107)

The real focus thus was not adherence to reason, but social conformity: Joseph Addison spoke of "foolish singularity" and told a tale of a person who, by always following the dictates of reason, became so estranged from his fellow men that he was deemed insane (cf. Rohloff 103). Ultimately, the aim of this kind of common sense is being predictable: precisely what the Hobbit notion of respectability is all about.

For people of such disposition, Clemens Brentano's satire *Der Philister in und vor der Geschichte* (The Philistine in and before history) would have been both a vindication of their views and the realization of their worst nightmares. Brentano depicts the philistine as the enemy of all genius, all enthusiasm and all free divine creation. Instead, the philistine prefers the decent, traditional and comfortable. He is so tied to the present and "comfortably dead" that he has lost all sight of anything primeval and eternal (Brentano 3f). According to Brentano, thinkers and believers know that the world is but a thought of God, and that the death of something reveals what it was intended to be. The philistine in contrast has forgotten his divine origin (4). Brentano traces the philistine's ancestry back to Lucifer who, as "a No who just wants to be itself" fell out of the unity with the Yes in the Idea. The human philistine too wants just to be himself, wants only to mean himself, and thus renounces God (6f). Philistinism as a desire for things staying the same is therefore a deviation from the divine order and thus theologically reprehensible.

The only kind of change the philistine can abide is the one to greater uniformity, which in Brentano's time meant emulating the French model. The philistine destroys any remnants of the past and what makes up the individuality of his country. The catch here is that he does so mainly because he wants to wipe out all traces of the individuality of the geniuses of the past (21) – so that what he attacks is not tradition as such, but as a trace of the creativity of other minds. His own indulgences are of a minor sort: He is fond of tobacco and his pipe, probably knowing some poem in their praise. His preferred drink is coffee: no risk of intoxication here. He is also particularly attached to his nightcap (as garment, not as drink, 15): again something that prevents a minor discomfort, that of catching a cold.

The opposites of the philistine are all students in the original sense of the Latin verb *studere*: to strain for, to desire: All those who crave for the Eternal, for God, all who adore the Idea (13). This includes heroes and martyrs among whom Samson is deemed to be the most excellent because he build his tomb with the bodies of his enemies when he made the palace of the Philistine king collapse (11).

Brentano closes his essay with a toast that contains the lines:

> Flamme Gottes in dem Sieger!
> Flamme Gottes in dem Krieger!
> Flamme Gottes in dem Richter!
> In dem Schöpfer, im Vernichter.[1] (24)

Three points can be drawn from Brentano's essay. Philistinism as a desire for things staying the same is not just cultural or personal failure but a sin: it is a fall from God's nature of creative change and from man's destiny to partake in

---

1 God's flame in the victor! God's flame in the warrior! God's flame in the judge! God's flame in the creator, in the destroyer (translation MS).

it. Philistinism is thus not just a set of specific ideas or forms, but a *disposition of desire*. Second, philistines are the embodiment of this principle of rigidity, conservatism and sameness and may thus appear on any social level: even kings can be philistines. Third, the opposite of philistines are artists, poets, warriors and martyrs, who are *not* unlikely bedfellows: For they share the willingness to take risks, to serve an idea, to sacrifice and let go. Destruction and self-destruction are emphatically endorsed: the flame of God burns in the creator *and* the destroyer.

This link between the artist and the warrior is especially important from the point of literary tradition because it was also made in a work which influenced English medievalism and the renaissance of chivalry in Victorian and Edwardian Britain up to World War I: Kenelm Digby's *Broad Stone of Honour*. Here, Digby defines chivalry as "only a name for that general spirit or state of mind which disposes men to heroic and generous actions, and keeps them conversant with all that is beautiful and sublime in the moral and intellectual world" (quoted after Girouard 62). For Digby as for Brentano, aesthetic sensibility and military valour go together. This connection, independent of all questions of literary tradition, and Brentano's idea of philistinism as a disposition of desire that is a fall from God, makes Brentano's concept of the philistine a useful torch to throw some light on the evolution of philistine characters in Tolkien's work and the political aspects of creativity.

The Cosmos as Philistine: Mythopoeia

Let us start the search for philistines with *Mythopoeia*. The materialistic-scientific worldview which carelessly and coldly denotes "this and that by this and that" could be equated with the philistine's habit of pulling down anything wonderful to his narrow set of concepts. This view however is not depicted as parochial and limited, but as fatalistic and intimidating, for the real horror in Mythopoeia is sameness. A star is just "some matter in a ball, compelled to course on mathematical/ amid the regimented, cold, Inane/ where destined atoms are each moment slain" (TL 97). Tolkien abhors "the world immutable wherein no part/ the maker has with maker's art", and progress is resented because it "ceaselessly revolve[s] the same/ unfruitful course with changing of a name" (100). Although there is criticism of "lotus isles of economic bliss", what is strangely absent are the destructive effects of technical and economic progress. Tolkien was of course intensely aware of them, as *On Fairy-Stories* and the poem *Progress in Bimble Bay* (Anderson 254) testify. But they pale in comparison to the vast, cold, immutable universe – whose existence is not denied: for blessed as legend makers are, their rhymes speak of things really "not found within recorded time". The Universe is the supreme philistine due to the immutability of the laws of observable nature. The Iron Crown before which the poet refuses to bow is borne by the Universe itself. The often-quoted lines on man as sub-creator make this explicit:

> Disgraced he may be, yet is not dethroned,
> and keeps the rags of lordship once he owned,
> his world-dominion by creative act:
> not his to worship the great Artefact
> man, sub-creator, the refracted light,
> through whom is splintered from a single White
> to many hues, and endlessly combined
> in living shapes that move from mind to mind.
> (TL 98f)

In concordance with 18th century diction, great Artefact here refers not to a machine constructed by humans, but to the created universe. The human capacity for imagination and sub-creation means not only that man has the power to dominate the world and clad this cold universe with ideas and images that make it habitable for his soul. This world-dominion enables him to detach himself from that world, for creating a secondary reality entails by necessity a certain detachment from primary reality – something philistines are unable to do.

Refraining from changing and modifying the world by imagination does not only mean to defect from man's divinely ordained role as sub-creator, it ultimately means worshipping the world. As with Brentano, accommodating oneself in an unchanging world means apostasy. For this reason, *Mythopoeia* depicts sub-creation not so much as an embellishment of creation but as worship: the minting of the image of a distant king, the weaving of the banners of a lord unseen. This has to be done in hiding as if by the persecuted faithful, bringing Brentano's motif of martyrdom to mind. In paradise however the suppressed poets will have flames upon their heads: they will be vessels of the Holy Ghost like the apostles on Pentecost.[2]

Because sub-creation is worship, and only God must be worshipped, refraining from sub-creational activity means in turn worshipping the world and thus violating the first commandment. Sub-creation is a transcending activity commanded by the transcendent God, and transcending by necessity always

---

2   Poets are meant to function as leaders even before the coming of Christ: Poets "oft to victory have turned the lyre / and kindled hearts with legendary fire / illuminating Now and dark Hath Been / with light of suns as yet by no man seen" (TL 100). This combination of illuminating imagination and kindling the appropriate emotions is found also with Shelley, s. Dawson 213.

entails leaving behind. All this the philistine is unable to do, and succumbs to a Universe as cold and dead as himself. As with Brentano, the rejection of the philistine love of sameness has a theological foundation and includes a detachment from things already existing, and subordinating them to things to be created (which ultimately means to treat them as raw materials for creative endeavours, of which more later).

Visiting Dragons

Moving from *Mythopoeia* to the poem *The Dragon's Visit* is a move from cosmic to petty philistinism. Here, in the seaside town of Bimble Bay, a dragon is resting on flowering cherry trees until their owner tries to drive him away with a garden hose. The dragon mistakes this as a kindness and starts singing to return the favour. After the local fire-brigade, headed by a captain George, has been unsuccessful in making the dragon fly away as well, people start poking the dragon with poles. This finally rouses the dragon's wrath. He destroys the town and kills his opponents, whom however he shows his respect by burying them atop a cliff and singing them a dirge – something which reminds of Beowulf (lines 3150-60). He reflects on the folk of Bimble Bay:

> They did not have the wit to admire
> A dragon's song or colour
> Nor heart to kill him brave and quick
> The world is getting duller. (Anderson 311)

As with Brentano and Digby, a lack of artistic sensibility goes hand in hand with a lack of military prowess.

The Dragon's words already contain what could be called the blueprint for Bilbo how he was originally conceived – as a hobbit overcoming his hobbitishness. That the hobbits' chief virtue of respectability and their aversion to adventures in general are philistine characteristics has already been mentioned. Their penchant for comfort fits in too, and the philistine's chief pleasures of tobacco, coffee and nightcap are echoed amazingly well in Bilbo's love of tobacco, tea and his need of handkerchiefs. As a rural population, the Hobbits are however depicted in more sympathetic terms, "good natured faces" and "deep fruity laughs" (H 14) betray no hatred of philistines here.

Nevertheless, they represent a way of life which Bilbo was meant to leave far behind. In plot notes B and C, Bilbo was intended to slay Smaug, to bathe, like Siegfried, in the dragon's blood to become "hard and strong" and distinguish himself in a final battle with the orcs in the Anduin valley. All this was connected to a heightened aesthetic sensibility, for he was fascinated by the Gem of Girion (which became the Arkenstone later on) while the dwarves saw in this excellent jewel nothing more than the means for paying Bilbo his promised fourteenth share in a transportable form. This fascination motivated Bilbo to heroic deeds: "Bilbo keeps on looking at his gem. He must earn it. He goes in and kills dragon as it sleeps ... with a spear" (HH I 364). In the end, Bilbo was meant to return to the Shire with the Gem of Girion and a golden dinner service to live a quiet hobbit life – with two exceptions: he would turn to writing poetry, and would daily look at the gem (HH I 364 f, II 495 f).

Allan Turner has shown the great weight that is given to desire as a central theme in *The Hobbit* on two levels: within the story as the (potentially possessive) desire of the hearts of dwarves, and on the level of the reader as the desire, the *Sehnsucht* for the wonders of the world, with parallels in German Romanticism (cf. Turner 83f, 89f). Bilbo's reaction to the dwarf-song (cf. H 25f) shows the linked germination of the aesthetic and the heroic as an evolving disposition of desire in almost minute detail: It *starts* with him feeling the love of beautiful things made by hand, which *then* wakes up something Tookish inside him, *leading* to the desire to see the high mountains – and to wear a sword instead of a walking stick. It is a move from the beautiful to the sublime to danger and violence.

In turn, the dwarves were initially shown as incompetent both aesthetically and in matters of war and the dangers of the Wild: they were unable to appreciate the Gem of Girion in other terms than money, had to be rescued by Bilbo time and again, and were described as "calculating folk with a great idea of the value of money; some are tricky and treacherous and a pretty bad lot, some are not, but are decent people like Thorin and Company, if you don't expect too much" (H 204).

Through successive drafts and plot notes up to the published text, this relation between the aesthetic and the military is maintained, yet their distribution between the dwarves and Bilbo changes. Bilbo's fighting prowess and accomplishments are reduced (no killing the dragon, no prominent part in battle), and his fascination by the Arkenstone is diminished to the point where he is able to give it up, though not without a glance of longing, for a peaceful winding up of affairs. With the dwarves and especially Thorin, this fascination is increased until Thorin is obsessed by it – and also heroic enough for his last sortie.

In the final chapters of *The Hobbit*, Bilbo is increasingly motivated by philistine desires for comfort, food, drink and an end to his adventure. The way he tries to gain these by disposing of the Arkenstone could be called good statesmanship, but for Brentano, statesmanship (Staatsklugheit) was a main character trait of philistines and always tied to malice and betrayal (cf. Brentano 12).

It is only with these changes to the fabric of Bilbo's desires from the heroic to the philistine that hobbits *as* hobbits become accepted in Middle-earth. This development takes place not only in dissociation from older concepts of heroism and honour, but also from a specifically artistic behaviour, the possessive fascination by the aesthetically exceptional object.

This critique was nothing new to Tolkien, if we think of Fëanor and the Silmarils. What was new however was the development of an alternative, and this alternative did not take the shape of an ethically faultless artist or warrior, but a character with many philistine traits. We have also to take into account that the grand heroic gesture is the more dramatic, gripping, and aesthetic one, even if in a terrifying way. Establishing a character who does not perform such acts thus has in itself aesthetic consequences.

The thesis that Bilbo the hobbit is developed not only against traditional concepts of the hero but also the artist can be underpinned by another passage. Of Bilbo's stay in Rivendell is said: "Now it is a strange thing, but things that are good to have and days that are good to spend are soon told about, and not much to listen to, while things that are uncomfortable, palpitating, even gruesome, may make a good tale, and take a deal of telling anyway" (H 58). This means nothing less than that the *artistic* requirements of narrativity, of telling a story effectively, distort the representation not only of reality, but also the *desirability* of things and events itself. Ultimately, when stories start working on minds, they may distort human desire itself.[3]

It is significant that *Leaf by Niggle*, written after *The Hobbit*, shows a rebalancing of the bias between artist and philistine. In essence, it repeats the theme of *Mythopoeia* of the artist as divine agent and prophet: When turned from secondary to primary reality in the afterlife, Niggle's picture is not only a good resting place for other souls, "working wonders" in some cases, but also for many "the best introduction to the Mountains" (TL 95), which may easily be regarded as a region of greater closeness to God. The Mountains had already been present in the background of Niggle' picture, and a mountain peak and a spray of leaves are what the teacher Atkins finds as its sole remnant and cannot get out of his mind (94): the artist provides glimpses of a higher reality.

---

3 An example of such distorting effects of poetry could be Torhthelm, a minstrel's son, and Beorhtnoth himself, in Tolkien's poem *The Homecoming of Beorhtnoth*, see for this Shippey, Homecoming, 326-332.

Again as in *Mythopoeia*, the prophet is persecuted by philistines, most notably by counsellor Tomkins who adheres strictly to the philistine criterion of worldly usefulness. His idea of the use of painting is a telling poster, and he demands of schoolmasters like Atkins to turn "useless people" like Niggle into a "serviceable cog of some sort" (94). He talks everything down to his own narrow notions of usefulness: Flowers are genital organs of plants, and the journey everyone has to undertake, i.e. death, is to him just "pushing somebody through the tunnel on the big Rubbish Heap" (94). He is greedy as well, acquiring Niggle's house after his departure.

Transferring the conflict between artist and philistine from the mythic timelessness of *Mythopoeia* to the contemporary setting of *Leaf by Niggle* means however that proposing the values of change and variation is no longer the prerogative of the artist. It is Tomkins who praises "bold young men not afraid of new ideas and new methods" whereas Niggle's painting to him is old-fashioned (94). Tolkien starts facing the problem that his view of the poet in *Mythopoeia* and the modernist progressive are both hooked on innovation, and the line between good artistic innovation and a progress of "ceaselessly revolving the same" may be more difficult to draw than presumed in *Mythopoeia*.

This may be one reason for the appearance of Parish, the positive non-artistic person. Niggle recognizes that the most characteristic examples of his style were created in collaboration with Parish, and this collaboration must have consisted in Parish's interruptions like his admonition on weeds in Niggle's garden. Parish helps Niggle by supplying him with knowledge about plants and gardening: the real world which provides the artist's raw material.

The interruptions may have been contributions in themselves because they prevented the artist from being carried away by his imagination[4]. Shippey has pointed to just such a remark in the *Notion Club Papers* where Lowdham criticizes that when inventing languages, and the inventor's whim is law, he is bound to be forever niggling and changing things all over again, never finishing his work – just what Niggle does with his picture (Shippey, *Road* 332f).

What at any rate separates Parish from the aggressive philistine Tomkins is not his attitude to Niggle's art – he calls it "daubing" or "nonsense" (TL 93). It is rather a certain backwardness – as a gardener, he is from Tomkins' point of view probably as old-fashioned as Niggle the painter. It is also his limitedness: unlike

---

4 There may be a romantic precedent here in Coleridge being interrupted in composing his poem *Kubla Khan* by "a person on business from Woking", an incursion which could be called beneficial because it meant detaching oneself from the pleasures of an intensive, but also deficient creative vision (Rohloff 191).

Tomkins, he has no higher ideas like progress or service to society from which he could form an idea of his own on the uses of art. Also unlike Tomkins, who is a member of the city council, he has no formal powers over Niggle, only his claims for compassion as a lame man. Philistinism is more acceptable with modest people in rural settings, and such philistines may possess in their very limitedness of outlook and ambition an antidote to the failings of the artist.

In the *Lord of the Rings*, the additional information given on hobbits supports the view that they are rural philistines, and not just rustic characters with some philistine traits. Their idea of a book is that it is filled with things that they already know, set out fair and square with no contradictions (LotR I 26) – quite the opposite of an inspired work of art. Their mistrust of anything unusual or outlandish does not begin at the Shire's borders. The inhabitants of the different regions are distrustful of each other: Sam "had a natural mistrust of inhabitants of other parts of the Shire" (131), Farmer Maggot, the object of his suspicions, calls the people of Hobbiton "queer" (133), who in turn have the same view of the Bucklanders (41).

Tolkien wrote in a letter how tiring hobbits could be in their narrow outlooks, and called Sam the prime example for their cocksureness and their habit, in a way typical of philistines, to measure everything against a very limited set of proverbial wisdom (cf. L 329), of which Sam's confrontation with Faramir is a prime example. In this letter of 1963, Tolkien explicitly makes the connection between aesthetic sensibility and a capacity for heroism: "We only meet exceptional hobbits in close companionship – those who had a grace or gift. A vision of beauty, and a reverence for things nobler than themselves, at war with their rustic self-satisfaction" (L 329). This leads to another question: Hobbits are generally held to be humble, but are they really? They are surely not grand, splendid or heroic, and they are not ambitious. However, calling the king of Rohan a fine old and polite fellow betrays no humility, and it is only towards the end of their development that Merry and Pippin recognize in the Houses of Healing that there are people higher than them, who deserve to be honoured (cf. LotR III 173f). Humility and even modesty always entail an element of self-deprecation that the hobbits lack. A better word would be self-sufficiency, both physical and mental. They are comfortable with themselves and their surroundings, and they can do so because their desires are limited, as is their imagination that could make them want more or different things.

Even their "deep friendship with the earth" veers more to the philistine predilection of comfort than the romantic love of untamed nature. The Shire is above all an agri*cultural* landscape. Even in its uncultivated parts it is without extremes. Bilbo makes this explicit when he contrasts his wish to see the "wild country again ... and the Mountains" with Frodo who "is still in love with the Shire, with woods and fields and little rivers" (LotR I 55): two opposing landscapes, two opposing desires. And finally the sea: for the Romantics the essence of the sublime, for Tolkien abode of remnants of the music of creation (S 6f) – and for the hobbits a word of fear and a token of death (LotR I 25). Perhaps nothing symbolizes the hobbits' philistinism better than their fear of drowning in the bottomless, ever-changing, ever-singing water.

Unsurprisingly, philistinism as explicit hostility to change is a recurring theme. Already in the Shire, Gildor points out to the hobbits the transience of this seeming epitome of safety and static stability: "But it is not your own Shire. Others dwelt here before hobbits were, and others will dwell here again when hobbits are no more. The wide world is all about you: you can fence yourself in, but you cannot for ever fence it out" (LotR I 120). Another example is Hamfast Gamgee who "can't abide changes ... and least of all changes for the worst" (344), by which he means merely the Sackville Bagginses being the new owners of Bag End. This aspect of philistinism is not limited to hobbits: Faramir attributes the decay of Gondor to the hunger of "endless life unchanging" (LotR II 357), and its supreme embodiment is the One Ring itself, which saves its bearer from physical death and yet takes all life from him. Verlyn Flieger even thinks that the message of Tolkien's mythology is "not to keep hold but to let go" (*Music* 142).

Parallel to this however, an opposing view is established. Frodo had at times thought the inhabitants of the Shire "too stupid and dull for words" and had "felt that an earthquake or an invasion of dragons might be good for them," but faced with the possibility of its destruction he wants to save it (LotR I 92). After the destruction of the Ring, Gandalf describes Aragorn's task at the beginning of the Fourth Age "to order its beginnings and preserve what may be preserved" (LotR III 302). It is telling that Aragorn's rule begins with the establishing of what are effectively conservation areas: Aragorn gives the Forest of Druadan to the Wild Men, and no man shall enter it without their leave (307). The Shire men must not enter at all, an order that Aragorn takes so seriously that he himself does not enter it, but meets his companions at the Brandywine Bridge (475f). Gildor had told the hobbits that they could not fence out wide world out. Now the most powerful Kingdom of the West tries to do just that and to secure the Shire's provinciality.

The four hobbits of course are far from provincial. They undergo an "ennoblement" through their experiences, as Tolkien called it, and the War of the Ring leads the hobbits at large to explore their past and to write down their hitherto mainly oral traditions. Libraries are built up, and the greater families even collect news of events in the kingdom at large and study its ancient histories and legends. This is something new in the Shire, but these intellectual endeavours are mainly antiquarian or encyclopaedic in nature, like Merry's herb-lore, and not flights of creative imagination. In a way, the hobbits allow Tolkien to have his cake and eat it, for their antiquarianism and philological activity are at the same time a change from their formerly historically benighted existence.

So the desire for separation and preservation that Tolkien criticised so often is rehabilitated in the end. It is precisely the limitedness of the hobbits' desires and imagination which makes them so suited to being ringbearers, for power becomes the more desirable the more ends for its use can be imagined. This is as trivial as it is fundamental. It is one reason why the ring gives power according to the stature of its bearer. Smëagol desired to spy on others and to hurt them, and such powers the ring gave him. Gandalf fears to be tempted by the Ring through his wish to do good with it. Galadriel imagines transforming herself into someone sublime whom everyone will love and despair. When Sam is tempted by the Ring, he imagines making Mordor into a garden. The stronger and more creative the imagination, the greater is the wish for power to turn one's visions into reality.

For this reason, it takes philistines to save Middle-earth. Bilbo, Frodo and Sam show a pattern in their character that could best be described as: the Took carries the Baggins to the theatre of action. A Tookish love of adventure and a desire to see extraordinary things and beings is what draws Bilbo and Sam beyond into the wide world (Frodo is to a large part also motivated by duty), but it is their hobbit qualities, their limited desires which are required out there, in Bilbo's handling of the Arkenstone and Frodo's and Sam's handling of the Ring.

Tolkien thus re-evaluates and rehabilitates the philistine disposition of desire. The question remains why. The first reason is probably a personal one. It is quite impossible to engage in the kind of philology that was Tolkien's occupation without the philistine desire to save things just for their own sake. The fact that Tolkien's philology informed his creativity has been proven time and again by Tom Shippey, yet philology was for Tolkien very much an end in itself, and what could be more antiquarian than creating asterisk words to fill gaps in the remnants of dead languages, almost a kind of "Jurassic Park" with pen and paper. Without the desire to preserve, to defy time, there would be no texts for philologists to work on, and at the end of *The Lord of the Rings*, Tolkien has need of a mindset that encourages preservation. It is telling that in the manuscript tradition constructed in *The Lord of the Rings*, the *Red Book of Westmarch* is not any source of the War of the Ring, but *the* source, and also contains with Bilbo's translations from the Elvish the history of the Elder Days. Moreover, "only here in the Shire were to be found extensive materials for the history of

Numenor and the arising of Sauron" (LotR I 36) – which means that much was preserved there that perished with the men in Gondor and elsewhere. The elves, criticised by Tolkien for their desire for an unchanging frozen perfection (Flieger, *Question* 112-115), were also the memory of Middle-earth, and with their departure, the hobbits, who have a similar aversion against change, take over their role.

The second and much more fundamental reason is that there exists an intricate relationship between the artist, especially the romantic artist, power, and, ultimately, modernity. To start with, many English and German romantics were admirers not only of the French Revolution, but practiced for a long time a cult of Napoleon as a genius and the creator of a new world order (cf. Safranski 187, Rohloff 173f). But it was in the 20th century that the connection between the artist and absolute power became especially close and the artistic and the political genius were seen as one.

In her book *Geniewahn: Hitler und die Kunst*, Birgit Schwarz has extensively demonstrated how much Hitler's view of himself *as a politician* was that of an artist (cf. Schwarz 88-93).

Hitler's rejection by the Academy in Vienna did not hinder this, for he saw himself not as a *failed* artist but as a *misunderstood* artist. It was commonplace in the 19th century biographies of painters to be initially rejected by a philistine audience, which actually proved their genius. This notion was so strong that such a rejection was made up when none had taken place (54f).

Hitler subscribed to the widespread idea that a politician of genius must also be an artist, and accordingly was repeatedly represented as an artist by Nazi Propaganda. His artistic creativity was seen as the fundament of his political and military "genius", calling him on occasion the first leader and the first artist of the Third Reich (129).

And Nazism was no exception. In the Soviet Union as well, the idea of art as politics and politics as art, and of an artistic redesign of world and society were elements of the Avantgarde, the October Revolution and later Stalinism (Groys 11, 14, 76f). All these cases illustrate that for the creative genius, things as well as people are just raw materials with which to realize his visions. As Josef Goebbels put it bluntly: "Geniuses consume people. It is just that way" (Schwarz 88).

Totalitarianism formulated in the terms of art and artist may however just be an extreme expression of a strong tendency of modernity. When an exhibition of modern French painting in New York in 1913 drew large crowds and intense criticism, a committed supporter of the new art, the lawyer Arthur Jerome Eddy, answered this criticism:

> We are all Impressionists or Futurist sometimes in our lives. But
> ... how progressive we may be on some issues, we may be stubbornly conservative on others. The man who laughs about a cubist painting may be a cubist – that means, be an innovator – in his profession or business. (Daniels 58f, transl. MS)

It is not the philistine, but the romantic artist with his predilection for innovation, for breaking rules and conventions that has become the role model for the economically active bourgeois. The issues on which he is conservative have become less and less, and so we get new magazines like *Business Punk*.

On its cover, Richard Branson shows his tongue (of course in imitation of the genius Einstein) and pronounces as his rule "I break rules". The magazine is filled with articles on interfaces of business with sport, music and the arts. Anyone who has read business papers and magazines in the run-up to the financial crisis knows how much the cult of the business genius and financial wizard, and the rhetoric of unconventionality and creativity, were all-pervading. Today, even bankers are bohemians, with matching results.

But what has Tolkien to do with these excesses of the cult of the genius? Although evil in Arda has its beginnings in Melkor's wish for autonomous creativity, is its real root not creativity but hubris? Did Tolkien not depict in Fëanor an in this case elf-consuming genius? And is the hobbits' real virtue not the limitedness of their desires and imagination, but their humility?

Tolkien has indeed given much thought to the connection between art and power, and tried to separate the artist from the technician and magician (see e. g. TL 49f). Although his thoughts on this subject require a much more detailed discussion, there remains the possibility that it is, as Boris Groys put it, impossible to separate art from power. Art is always connected with power: artworks adorn and serve the powerful, the artist's wish to shape his material according to his own designs by necessity is a will to power, and the politician shaping his country is the artist's alter ego (Groys 11-16). Tolkien's effort to distinguish art and power collapses when he leaves the realm of reflection, be it in essays or the opinions of his characters, and it comes to the old scriptwriter's adage of *show, don't tell*: when the word must become flesh. The puzzling example here is Saruman. On the one hand, he is the exponent of technology, having a mind of "metal and wheels", as Treebeard puts it, and he talks like a progressive politician (Shippey, *Road* 135f, 194f), and yet it is he who explicitly takes up the central image of *Mythopoeia* of splintering light into many colours. It is he who wears the multi-hued coat of the unfixed and changeable romantic subject – and gets rebuked by Gandalf for it (LotR I 338f). Saruman exposes the central image of *Mythopoeia* as a self-deception, for there is no such thing as a single white from which creativity of any kind, including that of the most power-averse artist, can draw its materials by refraction, but only concrete things and beings which are broken as concept, image and quite often body before recombination can take place.

The dangers of creativity-based Romanticism show up with other romantic concepts in Tolkien as well. Julian Eilmann has pointed in this volume to romantic nostalgia in Tolkien's work, a desire which directs humans ultimately out of this world. Tolkien gave as the reason for men's propensity for evil their "quick satiety with good" (L 344) – does this mean that the transcendent longings of man can also be a source of evil? After all, boredom, ennui, and satiety are the shadow of the romantic emphasis on creativity and change. Once something is accomplished, it is dead, and must be left behind (cf. Berlin 114). Finally, there is Tolkien's "theology of death" in which death is a necessary passage to greater perfection (Fornet-Ponse 181f, 183). This is however not only good Christian thinking, but fits in beautifully with Joseph Alois Schumpeter's thesis of the creative destructivity of capitalism.

Following the path of creativity-based Romanticism thus means walking a very thin line, and the pitfalls on both sides make the virtue of humility so central.[5] The problem here is that humility as a virtue conflicts with Romanticism precisely because it is a virtue. For a virtue is a predisposition of the will, a *habitus* that lets the virtuous person do the ethically approved deed[6]: it is a disposition of desire. As such, it clashes with the romantic desire for the new and intense. "Denn das ist der Philister-Schlendrian" wrote Clemens Brentano, "zu glauben, was einem gerade genüge, sei einem genug"[7] (Brentano 18). In romanticism, there is a specific kind of greed, not for gold and gems, but for emotions, experiences and creative activity as such, a greed which can easily become as harmful as the former kind. With such a disposition of desire, humility can never exist as contentment, only as repression and frustration, which in the long run makes the destructive eruption of the frustrated desires inevitable.

In the end, there is no denying the fact that modernity in its obsession with creativity, change and variety is, as Isaiah Berlin put it, a strongly romantic affair (Berlin 145f). That Tolkien ultimately moved away from this disposition

---

5 The Inklings in general were acutely aware that any attempt to turn the visions of their "political romanticism" into reality by revolutionary measures would mean violence and accumulations of power which would lead to evil (cf. Coulombe 53), a view also held by Shelley (cf. Dawson 6).
6 See for this Thomas I-II, qu. 49-54, esp. 49 art. 3 and 51 art. 1, p 217, 219.
7 "For this is the philistine sloppiness: to believe that what is just sufficient for oneself is enough for oneself", transl. MS.

of desire that is at the heart of creativity-based Romanticism is therefore neither surprising nor cause for regret. Today, the paradigm of innovation and creativity is firmly embedded everywhere. So what point is there in pouring artistic gasoline on an already roaring fire of change? There is rather need of fire fighters. Even if they are only four feet tall.

Bibliography

Anderson, Douglas A. *The Annotated Hobbit*. Revised and expanded edition. London: HarperCollins, 2003

Berlin, Isaiah. *The Roots of Romanticism*. Princeton (NJ): Princeton University Press, 1999

Brentano, Clemens. *Der Philister in, vor und nach der Geschichte*. Berlin: Ernst Freusdorff, 1905

Business Punk. G + J Wirtschaftsmedien & Co. KG, Hamburg. No. 1/2009

Coulombe, Charles A. "Romantic Conservatives. The Inklings in their Political Context". *The Ring Goes Ever On. Proceedings of the Tolkien 2005 Conference*. Ed. Sarah Wells. Coventry: The Tolkien Society, 2008. Vol. I, 52-65

Daniels, Dieter. *Duchamp und die anderen*. Köln: DuMont Buchverlag, 1992

Dawson, P.M.S. *The Unacknowledged Legislator*. Oxford: Clarendon Press, 1980

Flieger, Verlyn. *A Question of Time*. Kent: Kent State University Press, 2001

---. *Interrupted Music*. Kent/London: The Kent State University Press, 2005

---. *Splintered Light. Logos and Language in Tolkien's World*. Kent/London. Kent State University Press, 2002

Fornet-Ponse, Thomas. »Tolkiens Theologie des Todes«. *Hither Shore* 2 (2005): 157-184

Girouard, Mark. *The Return to Camelot. Chivalry and the English Gentleman*. New Haven/London: Yale University Press, 1981

Groys, Boris. *Gesamtkunstwerk Stalin*. München/Wien: Carl Hanser Verlag, 1996

Rateliffe, John D. *The History of the Hobbit*. 2 Vols. London: HarperCollins, 2007

Rohloff, Heide N. *Poesie und Politik. Studien zur englischen Romantik*. Essen: Verlag die Blaue Eule, 1995

Safranski, Rüdiger. *Romantik. Eine deutsche Affaire*. München: Carl Hanser Verlag, 2007

Schwarz, Birgit. *Geniewahn. Hitler und die Kunst*. Wien/Köln/Weimar: Böhlau, 2009

Shippey, Tom. *The Road to Middle-earth*. Revised and expanded edition. London: HarperCollins, 2005

---. "Tolkien and 'The Homecoming of Beorthnoth'". *Roots and Branches. Selected papers by Tom Shippey*. Zurich/Berne: Walking Tree Publishers, 2007, 323-339

Thomas Aquinas. *Summa Theologica*. Ed. Petrus Caramellus. Turin/Rome: Marietti, 1952

Tolkien, John Ronald Reuel. *The Hobbit*. London: Unwin Paperbacks, 1984

---. *The Letters of J.R.R. Tolkien*. Ed. Humphrey Carpenter. London: Allen & Unwin, 1981

---. *The Lord of the Rings*. 4th ed. London: Unwin Hyman, 1988

---. *The Silmarillion*. Ed. Christopher Tolkien. Boston/New York: Houghton Mifflin, 2004

---. *Tree and Leaf*. 2nd edition. London: Unwin Hyman, 1988

Turner, Allan. "The Hobbit and Desire". *Hither Shore* 5 (2008): 83-92

Falsche Harmonie
oder: Darf man nach Auschwitz noch vom Auenland träumen?

Fabian Geier (Bamberg)

Hier geht es um ein heikles Thema. Und da ich noch weit davon entfernt bin, dass meine Urteile darin bereits zur Ruhe gekommen wären, hoffe ich auf nachsichtige Leser. Fragen im Umfeld kritischer Gesellschaftstheorie sind leider von jeher stark aufgeladen. Ich will nicht sagen ideologisch. Aber die hier gewählte Thematik berührt Diskurse, die meist mit viel Wut, Verachtung, mitunter viel Prätention, und immer sehr humorlos geführt werden.

Humorlosigkeit liegt freilich auch in der Natur der Sache. Auch für weniger feine Gemüter wirkt Lachen in Anbetracht des Grauens berechtigterweise blasphemisch. Und das allein gibt auch schon einen Hinweis auf Adornos Denkweise. Man soll nicht über Auschwitz lachen, seine negative Heiligkeit, die Unfassbarkeit des systematischen, millionenfachen Mordes inmitten einer modernen Gesellschaft nicht durch gedankenlose Rekontextualisierung beschädigen und zu einer scheinbaren Kontingenz herabsetzen.

In dieser Perspektive ist jedoch nicht nur das Lachen sondern auch vieles andere unmöglich, unglaubwürdig und falsch geworden. Nach Adorno gilt das für jede Form unmittelbarer Positivität. Wenn man, wie Adorno sagt, kein Gedicht mehr nach Auschwitz schreiben kann, stellt sich zwangsläufig auch die Frage, ob man auch sonst noch harmonisch, archaisierend und bürgerlich schreiben, und solche Erzeugnisse und mit unbekümmerter Freude lesen kann. Das ist die Grundfrage des folgenden Texts. Dabei werde ich mich primär auf Tolkiens *Herrn der Ringe* beziehen, da dieses Werk weit mehr beglückte Leser gefunden hat als seine anderen Schriften – und vielleicht auch mehr als andere den süßlichen Geist atmet, der Kritikern bestimmter Couleur so viel Schrecken einjagt.[1]

---

1 Ein Vorwurf gegen das vorgestellte Thema war, dass Auschwitz nie als Provokation missbraucht werden dürfe. Der Punkt ist berechtigt. Aber es ist auch zu sagen, dass es bereits Adornos Provokation ist. Und zwar eine Provokation, die offensichtlich genau solche Werke wie die Tolkiens betrifft, und die mich als Leser derselben betroffen macht. Um diese Problematik in all ihrer Schärfe zu diskutieren, sehe ich kaum einen geeigneteren Ort als die einschlägige Gelehrtengemeinschaft, zumal wenn diese zu überschaubar ist, als dass man von Provokationen persönlichen Nutzen erwarten könnte.

Intaktes und Gebrochenes

Tolkiens Werk entspricht nicht den intellektuellen Hauptströmungen seiner Zeit. Während Schönberg und Picasso, Gropius und Beckett die Form- und Harmonieprinzipien ihrer Künste auseinanderreißen, schreibt Tolkien Abenteuergeschichten über Feen und fröhliche Kleinbürger. Tatsächlich nennt sich Tolkien selbst ein »reaktionäres Fossil« (L Nr. 53) und stellt sich in *Leaf by Niggle* folgendes Zeugnis aus: »Es gibt haufenweise Möglichkeiten für kühne junge Männer, die sich nicht vor neuen Ideen und neuen Methoden fürchten. Aber für dieses altmodische Zeug nicht. Heimlicher Träumer... Immer bloß mit Blättern und Blumen herumspielen. Ich fragte ihn einmal, warum. Er sagte, er finde sie hübsch. Können Sie sich das vorstellen? Hübsch sagte er! ›Was, Verdauungs- und Geschlechtsorgane von Pflanzen?‹, fragte ich ihn; und darauf wusste er nichts zu antworten. Alberner Fummler« (LN 158f). Das aber bedeutet: Tolkien ist kein Unwissender, sondern, wenn schon, ein Unverbesserlicher.

Ganz anders Adorno: Zunächst Kompositionsschüler von Alban Berg, wurde er nach Abbruch seiner musikalischen Karriere Angehöriger der neomarxistischen Frankfurter Schule und bekämpfte reaktionäre Kulturformen, wo er sie fand. Und auch wenn er Tolkien nicht gelesen hat: Es ist schwer vorstellbar, dass sein Urteil nicht vernichtend gewesen wäre.[2] Denn es geht hier um zwei fundamental verschiedene künstlerische Klimata: Schönheit, Harmonie und die Signatur des Bürgerlichen gegen eine Ästhetik der Verstörung, die im Lichte des Schreckens des Zeitalters als einzig legitime erscheint.

Romantik nach Auschwitz

Adorno ist vor allem berühmt für sein Diktum, dass man nach Auschwitz kein Gedicht mehr schreiben könne (Adorno, *Kulturkritik* 30). Weniger bekannt ist, dass er diesen Satz mehrmals relativiert hat[3]. Ich will ihn aber als

---

2   Wenn es auch methodologisch hoch problematisch ist, über Urteile von Geistesgrößen zu spekulieren, so liegt auch ein sachlicher Grund darin: Man transferiert die als relevant anerkannten Geltungsansprüche eines Textes auf einen anderen Gegenstand. Diese sind, selbst wenn sie immer auch an Standards historischer Adäquatheit zu messen sind, in einem wichtigen Sinne unabhängig von der Person und ihrem Werk, oder von hermeneutischen Fehlern bei Erschließung derselben.

3   »Das perennierende Leiden hat soviel Recht auf Ausdruck wie der Gemarterte zu brüllen; darum mag falsch gewesen sein, nach Auschwitz ließe kein Gedicht mehr sich schreiben. Nicht falsch aber ist die minder kulturelle Frage, ob nach Auschwitz noch sich leben lasse, ob vollends es dürfe, wer zufällig entrann und rechtens hätte umgebracht werden müssen. Sein Weiterleben bedarf schon der Kälte, des Grundprinzips der bürgerlichen Subjektivität, ohne das Auschwitz nicht möglich gewesen wäre: drastische Schuld des Verschonten.« (Adorno, Negative Dialektik 355f; vgl. Kulturkritik 452f, Noten 603)

Aufhänger nehmen, weil er treffend zuspitzt, wie Adorno insgesamt denkt: Dass man nach Auschwitz nur noch ohnmächtig im Angesicht des Schreckens schreiben dürfe, während alles Positive als »barbarisch« zu gelten hatte.

Die ursprüngliche Behauptung taucht in der Schlusspassage des Aufsatzes *Kulturkritik und Gesellschaft* auf. Dort kritisiert Adorno diejenigen, die sich durch eine Fundamentalkritik an Kultur deren Rationalität enthoben meinen. Der berühmte Satz soll am Ende illustrieren, dass es unmöglich ist, eine Perspektive einzunehmen, die sich unabhängig von den kritisierten Zuständen ist. Das betrifft die Lyrik deswegen besonders, insofern sie grundsätzlich das Medium der scheinbar isolierten Innerlichkeit sei. Daran lässt erkennen, dass Adorno Lyrik spezifisch romantisch versteht: Lyrik als Ausdruck individueller Erfahrung – Ausdrucksform eines in sich gekehrten Subjekts in Abgrenzung von Welt und Gesellschaft (vgl. auch Adorno, *Noten* 53).

Inwiefern lassen sich solche Gedanken auf Tolkien anwenden? Immerhin schreibt er ja nicht primär Lyrik. Er ist außerdem in vielen seiner Motive und Techniken gerade kein Romantiker – wie mehrere Autoren im vorliegenden Band zeigen. In einigen der wichtigsten Motive, selbst im Zugang zur Natur, ist er viel mehr mittelalterlich als modern. Und das geniehafte, einsame Ich ist ihm fremd. »Romantik« bezeichnet allerdings, wie jeder Epochenbegriff, ein Konglomerat von familienähnlichen Beispielen mit verschiedenen Charakteristika. Und unter diesen gibt es eines, dem Tolkien durchaus nahe steht: Er teilt mit der Romantik eine Art des Zugangs zur Empfindung: Ungebrochene, ungebremste und unmittelbare ästhetische Erfahrung; das vorbehaltlose sich Einlassen des Subjekts auf das, wovon es fasziniert ist. Und genau in dieser Haltung liegt etwas, das nach den Katastrophen des 20. Jahrhunderts verdächtig wurde.[4]

Irritationen

Wer nun den *Herrn der Ringe* mit uneingeschränkter Faszination liest, der empfindet angesichts solcher Vorwürfe zumeist große Irritation. Darf man sich etwa nicht daran freuen? Wäre das nicht völlig harmlos? Warum soll man nicht Tolkien genießen, so wie man auch ältere Epen genießen kann? Und

---

4 Man könnte im Übrigen auch sagen, *Der Herr der Ringe* (geschrieben von 1937 bis 1949) sei eigentlich gar kein Werk nach Auschwitz. Aber ich will es mir so leicht nicht machen, denn wir lesen ihn ja immer noch. Desgleichen für den Hinweis, dass Tolkien als Engländer nicht in der gleichen Weise mit seinen Traditionen habe brechen müssen wie deutsche Literaten – denn das Buch wird auch hierzulande gelesen. Tatsächlich schreibt Tolkien sogar selbst einmal, dass „[Hitler] den edlen nordischen Geist, jenen vortrefflichen Beitrag zu Europa, den ich immer geliebt und in seinem wahren Lichte zu zeigen versucht habe, ruiniert, missbraucht und verdorben hat, sodass er nun für immer verflucht ist." (L Nr. 45). Doch das bleibt für sein Werk folgenlos.

wenn die rezeptive Freude an altem Material erlaubt ist – warum dann nicht auch die schöpferische? Und meine heimliche Frage wäre: Steckt in derartigen Irritationen nicht, auch, ein Körnchen Wahrheit?

Wenn ja, dann doch nur ein Körnchen. Denn die Gefahr ist groß, wenn man nur irgendein Schlupfloch findet, dass man gleich die ganze Kritik erleichtert vom Tisch wischt. Doch ebenso wenig wie ein Hinweis auf die Fehler in Guido Schwarz' *Jungfrauen im Nachthemd* reicht, um jegliche Rassismuskritik an Tolkien ad acta zu legen, reicht der Verweis auf mögliche Harmlosigkeit, um das hier vorliegende Problem zu erfassen. Viel mehr käme es darauf an, die Wahrheit in Adornos Kritik zu suchen.

Adorno plausibel machen: Präliminarien

Normative Momente

Adornos Kritik enthält einerseits ein *ästhetisches Verbot*, dass man Bestimmtes nicht mehr schön finden dürfe, und ein *ethisches Verbot*, d.h. dass, wenn man es schön findet, man sich schuldig mache. Adorno scheint also zu verbieten, was vielen ganz selbstverständlich erscheint: Dass die Wahl der Literatur eine private, nicht diskutable »Geschmacksfrage« sei. Mir gefällt es eben – ob ich ein guter Mensch bin, ist eine andere Frage?

Den Wert von Literatur auf diese Weise ins Subjektive zu verabsolutieren, das würden immerhin beide Autoren ablehnen (auch wenn das nur ein argumentum ad hominem ist). Sowohl Adorno als auch Tolkien beharren darauf, dass Literatur Wahrheit transportieren könne. Und wenn dem so ist, dann kann die Wahrheit durch Literatur auch korrumpiert werden. Falschheit in der Literatur wird allerdings von Tolkien nie thematisiert. Adorno dagegen spricht vor allem davon.

Muss aber jede Literatur an ihrer Wahrheit gemessen werden? Behauptete man, dass Tolkiens Werk nicht als Literatur durchgehen könne, weil es nicht auf der Höhe der historischen Wahrheit sei, wäre das Tolkien und vielen Lesern herzlich gleichgültig, denn sein Werk hat keinen derartigen Anspruch. Was bedeutete schon so ein Etikett, wenn es beliebig wäre, ein Werk darunter zu subsumieren?

Die bessere Antwort ist daher: Wenn man in einer bestimmten Weise nicht schreiben »darf«, dann weil man es *nicht kann*. Die Falschheit von Literatur ist keine Frage externer Verbote. Die Frage ist vielmehr, ob es möglich bleibt, ein solches Werk zu schreiben oder zu lesen. De facto möglich ist es natürlich. Aber kann man es auch dann ohne schlechtes Gewissen, wenn man für soziale und historische Querverbindungen sensibel wird? Und wenn nein: Kann man das auch von anderen einfordern?

Perspektive: Literatur und Gesellschaft

Zentral für Adorno ist: Ästhetische Erfahrungen sind nie frei schwebend, sondern immer mit vorherrschenden Denkmustern und politischen Zuständen verwoben. Tolkien dagegen, und viele seiner Leser, behandeln Literatur gerade so: entweder als privates Vergnügen oder, wo ihr höhere Bedeutung zukommt, als losgelöst von den jetzigen gesellschaftlichen Zuständen oder gar bewusst gegen diese. Denn wenn Tolkien von Wahrheit in der Literatur spricht, dann meint er nie gesellschaftlich bedingte, sondern zeitlose Ideen.

Das jedoch ist erst die nachträgliche reflexive Form, Tolkiens Literaturtheorie, wie sie z.B. in *On Fairy-Stories* ausgedrückt ist. Sowohl beim Schreiben als auch beim Lesen hält er sich an die Perspektive der immanenten Faszination. Bei Adorno lesen wir: »Innerlichkeit, die subjektiv beschränkte Gestalt der Wahrheit, war stets schon den äußeren Herren mehr als sie ahnte untertan« (Adorno/Horkheimer, *Dialektik der Aufklärung* 166). Und hierin liegt nun der sachliche Grund, warum Literatur nicht einfach Geschmackssache ist: Es ist kein Zufall, wovon man fasziniert ist, sondern hat gesellschaftliche Bedingungen. Daher muss man sich die Frage stellen: Was für einer bin ich, dass ich genau diesen Geschmack habe?

Modus: Historisches Denken

Aus dem Gesagten ergibt sich, warum Adornos Urteile nicht zeitlos sind. Denn wer gesellschaftlich denkt, muss auch historisch denken. Die Möglichkeit, bestimmte Erfahrungen zu machen, insbesondere ästhetische Erfahrungen, hängt davon ab, was man erlebt hat. Vom Erwachsenwerden kennt man solche Phänomene: Lego Bionicles faszinieren (normalerweise) mit Dreißig auch weniger als mit Acht. Ebenso existentielle Erfahrungen: Nach radikalen Veränderungen der Lebensumstände, oder dem Tod einer nahestehenden Person, kann man auch viele Freuden und Nöte nicht mehr in der gleichen Weise erleben. Der Holocaust ist für Adorno eine solche Erfahrung, nur auf gesellschaftlicher Ebene. Und es stellt sich die Frage, wie wir angesichts dieser historischen Situation Literatur erleben können und dürfen. Deswegen kann nach Auschwitz etwas unmöglich sein, das z.B. in Eichendorffs Gedichten oder Homers *Ilias* noch möglich war.

Grundfiguren der Affirmation

Grundsätzlich kritisiert Adorno Kunstwerke und Ausdrucksformen, wenn sie affirmativ sind: also falsche Zustände und Denkweisen bestärken. Im Hinblick auf Literatur kann man mehrere affirmative Momente beschreiben.

1.) *Affirmation durch Anwesenheit*. Falsche Überzeugungen (z.B. Rassismus oder entwürdigende Frauenbilder) sind in einer Weise im Text enthalten, die Zustimmung signalisiert oder hervorruft.

2.) *Affirmation durch Abwesenheit.* Der Text ist deswegen falsch, weil er von den entscheidenden Dingen *nicht* spricht. Dadurch, dass er vorhandenes Grauen, Ungerechtigkeit und Unterdrückung nicht anspricht, entsteht z.b. der Eindruck, die von ihm beschriebenen Lebensweisen verhielten sich zu derartigen Dingen kontingent. Dadurch, dass er unzureichend universale Konzepte benutzt um Personen und Situationen zu beschreiben, wird konkretes Leiden und Erleben übergangen und umso unausdrückbarer gemacht, je mehr das Gefühl entsteht, mit den vorhandenen Kategorien sei alles gesagt[5].

Es ist von daher verständlich, dass Adorno letztlich einen prinzipiellen Verdacht gegen *alles* Bestätigende, Abgeschlossene und sich selbst Genügende hat. Generell hält er jede Darstellung für gefährlich, die es erlaubt, es sich in den gegebenen Kategorien bequem zu machen, weil schon diese Bequemlichkeit ein Ignorieren aller Andersheit (des »Nichtidentischen«) bedeutet. Kunst hat daher immer die Aufgabe, das Denken in einen fluiden Zustand an den Bruchstellen der vorherrschenden Denkschemata zu bringen. Und weil für Adorno alles Fixierende latent faschistisch ist, ist diese Aufgabe ein moralischer Imperativ. Plakativ für die genannten Punkte ist folgende Stelle:

> Es gibt nichts Harmloses mehr. Die kleinen Freuden, die Äußerungen des Lebens, die von der Verantwortung des Gedankens ausgenommen scheinen, haben nicht nur ein Moment der trotzigen Albernheit, des hartherzigen sich blind Machens, sondern treten unmittelbar in den Dienst ihres äußersten Gegensatzes. Noch der Baum, der blüht, lügt in dem Augenblick, in welchem man sein Blühen ohne den Schatten des Entsetzens wahrnimmt; noch das unschuldige ›Wie schön‹ wird zur Ausrede für die Schmach des Daseins, das anders ist, und es ist keine Schönheit und kein Trost mehr außer in dem Blick, der aufs Grauen geht, ihm standhält und im ungemilderten Bewußtsein der Negativität die Möglichkeit des Besseren festhält. (Adorno, *Minima Moralia* §5)

Unmittelbarkeit: Falschheit und Sehnsucht

Ein komplementärer Aspekt der Kritik ist die Unmittelbarkeit, die in ihren harmonischen, mythischen und archaischen Formen in Tolkiens Werk so charakteristisch ist. Unmittelbarkeit bezeichnet das direkte Erleben, im Unterschied zu Reflexion und Verbegrifflichung. Analog zu den genannten normativen Momenten gibt es zwei Formen: Ästhetische Unmittelbarkeit (»Ach, wie schön!«)

---

5 Einsichtige Argumentationen dieser Art finden sich z.B. auch in W.G. Sebalds *Luftkrieg und Literatur*.

und ethische Unmittelbarkeit, d.h. die direkte, intuitive Anerkennung eines Werts oder Ereignisses als gut und richtig.
Der Herr der Ringe bietet viel davon: Unkompromittierte Weisheit und Altruismus. Ein fragloser Schöpfergott als Garant des ebenso fraglos Guten. Keine letzten Zweifel, keine Subjektivität – alles trägt den objektivistischen Charakter der Weltenschöpfung. Verstärkt wird diese Tendenz dadurch, dass es bei Tolkien Ästhetik und Moral immer parallel laufen: Alles, was als schön erfahren wird, ist gut, alles Schlechte schon von Weitem als hässlich und angsteinflößend erkennbar (vgl. Honegger et al. 67-88). Dazu passt gut, dass Tolkien sagt, mythisches Denken vertrage an den wesentlichen Stellen keine Ironie (FS 114).

Was ist nun falsch an Unmittelbarkeit? Falsch ist zunächst, dass nicht anerkannt wird, dass es »nichts [gibt], das nicht vermittelt wäre« (Adorno, *Negative Dialektik* 173). Der Fehler liegt in mangelnder Einsicht in die Herkunft und gesellschaftliche Bedingtheit der eigenen Erfahrungskategorien, und womöglich damit verbundenen heimlichen normativen Überzeugungen, die gar nicht so harmlos sind wie der ästhetische Genuss, den sie ermöglichen. Gefährlich wird das vor allem, wenn es mit der (romantischen) Tendenz zusammentritt, das unmittelbar Erfahrene für notwendig, natürlich und unhintergehbar zu halten. Das Problem ist also der mangelnde reflexive Abstand, der gerade im faszinierten Bewusstsein enthalten ist: Die schiere Bewunderung des Schönen und Guten als etwas Letztem und Fraglosen.
Aber dennoch will Adorno Unmittelbarkeit auch nicht eliminieren und sich bloß noch reflexiv zu den Dingen verhalten. Und zwar deswegen, weil die Abstraktion der Reflexion ein ebenso gefährliches Defizit aufweist. Dafür steht Adornos Erfahrungsbegriff[6]. Adorno versucht gerade, den Reichtum der Erfahrung vor ihrer »Verstellung durch Begriffe«, vor der Welt der kalten Abstraktion zu retten. Er sieht, dass authentische Erfahrung uns dann entkommt, wenn wir sie in feste Prinzipien fassen, entweder als Begriffe oder als Habitus. Doch er weiß gleichzeitig auch, dass ohne begriffliche Strukturen gar nichts erlebt werden kann. Das Beste, was nach ihm daher zu erreichen ist, ist ein Zustand der Negativität: Das augenblickshafte Hinaustreiben über die Grenzen der bisherigen Begriffswelt. Aus diesen Gründen ist das bruchlos romantische Bewusstsein, mit dem Tolkien schreibt, für Adorno Sehnsucht und Unmöglichkeit zugleich.[7]

---

6   Vgl. dazu Adorno, Negative Dialektik 13-66; exemplarisch sind z.B. die Bemerkungen zur Romantik, Dialektik der Aufklärung 147, oder zu Beethoven, Negative Dialektik 390.
7   Es gibt womöglich auch eine biographische Komponente in dieser Sehnsucht, die interessanterweise Adorno und Tolkien gemeinsam haben: Beide stehen unter dem Eindruck einer glücklichen Kindheit. Tolkiens Sarehole hat durchaus eine ähnliche Funktion wie Adornos Amorbach. Und auch wenn solche Psychologisierungen heikel sind, scheint es

Konkretionen von Unmittelbarkeit

Die skizzierte Kritik bleibt aber selbst abstrakt, wenn wir sie nicht an verschiedenen Aspekten von Tolkiens Werk durchführen.

Mythos

Die erste Frage wäre natürlich: Kann man heute noch Mythen schreiben? Zunächst müssen wir uns dafür über den Begriff ›Mythos‹ verständigen, der ja auch viele Facetten hat und mitunter einen inflationären Gebrauch erlebt. Mir geht es hier vor allem um das wahrscheinlich auf Max Weber zurückgehende und von Adorno betonte Moment, dass Mythen von der Unmittelbarkeit eines schlechthin Individuellen leben (Adorno/Horkheimer, *Dialektik der Aufklärung* 25ff). Elendils Schwert, der Schicksalsberg oder der Eine Ring sind gute Beispiele. Im Gegensatz zu modernen Denkweisen sind mythische Gegenstände, Personen und Orte nicht beliebig austauschbar und instrumentalisierbar. Wichtig ist vielmehr, dass es genau *dieses*, *hier* und *jetzt* ist. Davon lebt auch die Magie Tolkiens. Entsprechend birgt jedoch ein Rückgriff auf mythisches Denken die Gefahr eines Rückfalls hinter die Errungenschaft der Aufklärung[8]: Den forschenden Geist, der Kontingenzen durchschaut, neu evaluiert und rekonfiguriert, im Gegensatz zu einer in Ehrfurcht erstarrten Bewusstseinsform. Mythisches Denken müsste man dann als das Aufgeben einer autonomen Vernunft zugunsten eines blinden, unbewusst auf Dogmen fixierten Lebens sehen, das die Bereitschaft zur Reflexion der eigenen Fundamente lähmt.

Archaismen

Ähnlich gelagert wäre der mögliche Vorwurf gegenüber der Verwendung archaischer Kategorien und Darstellungsformen. Adorno könnte sagen, Tolkien lasse möglich erscheinen, was unmöglich ist: Einen unwiederbringlich verlorenen und vergangenen Bewusstseinszustand.[9]

---

doch nicht ganz unplausibel, dass bei beiden das Glück der Kindheit der Fluchtpunkt Ihres Denkens ist. Die Werke beider verweisen stark auf die Ahnung eines verlorenen Zustandes des unmittelbar-naiven, versöhnten Zugangs zur Welt. Während aber für Adorno der Zugang zum Guten und Schönen schlechthin unmöglich wird, empfindet Tolkien den Verlust nicht als epistemisches sondern als empirisches Faktum. Daher bleibt Tolkien, anders als Adorno, dem mythischen Denken verbunden, auch wenn er der Ungreifbarkeit desselben auf seine eigene Weise Rechnung trägt.

8 Vgl. Adorno, Kulturkritik 17, die Bemerkungen über Okkultismus in Minima Moralia §151, sowie zu den »Märchenträumen, die so eifrig sich auf das Kind im Manne berufen« in Minima Moralia §131.

9 Zum komplizierten Verhältnis von Adorno zum Vergangenen vgl. z.B. Ästhetische Theorie 31, 100-102, 243f. Erhellend dazu: auch die verstreuten Bemerkungen zum Jugendstil.

Entgegnen könnte man, dass die neue Verwendung alter Elemente natürlich nicht das mittelalterliche Bewusstsein reproduziert – und auch nicht diesen Anspruch hat. Nach Tolkiens eigenen Maßstäben reicht es ja aus, dass wir als moderne Wesen von diesen Elementen fasziniert sein können, und mag diese Faszination vom mittelalterlichen Lebensgefühl auch noch so verschieden sein. Tolkien schreibt ja auch nicht konsistent archaisch, sondern nur archaisierend, und zudem in verschiedenen Ebenen von Archaizität und Moderne (vgl. L Nr. 171). Wenn man sehr nett sein wollte, könnte sagen: Tolkiens Werk atmet Archaisches, ohne es zu prätendieren.

Doch der Punkt hinter Adornos Kritik ist subtiler. Es geht nicht um die archaischen Formen, sondern die bruchlose Einstellung, mit der sie verwendet, und die Bewusstseinshaltungen, die damit transportiert werden. Tatsächlich sind nicht nur die Form der Queste, nordische Sprachelemente oder der technische Entwicklungsstand von Tolkiens Welt mittelalterlich. Vor allem sind Tolkiens Charaktere vormodern. Sie sind eingebettet in einen objektiven Horizont von Werten und gesellschaftlichen Funktionen – und gerade keine modernen, krisenhaften, gebrochenen Subjekte. Diese Abwesenheit einer umfassenden subjektiven Negation objektiver Denkformen, gepaart mit scheinbar völliger Subjektivität (»privates Vergnügen«) auf Seiten von Autor oder Rezipient ist das, was uns auf den Kardinalvorwurf der falschen Unmittelbarkeit zurückführt.[10]

Naturschönheit

Warum lügt der blühende Baum? Weil er ein unmittelbares Verhältnis zu einem begrenzten Gegenstand herstellt, und die darin liegende Faszination als in sich geschlossen und unabhängig von allem anderen erfahren wird, so als könnte sie jeder zu jeder Zeit empfinden[11].

---

10 Sowohl Tolkien als auch Adorno waren im übrigen Fossilien: »Man spricht manchmal von kompromittierenden Formen seines Verhaltens. Ich glaube, über diese Formen ist dasselbe zu sagen. Sie haben seiner Radikalität nicht das Geringste angetan. Ich sehe in ihnen die bewusste Aufrechterhaltung von Formen einer vergangenen Kultur und zwar – vielleicht – aus Schutz vor der aufdringlichen, brutalen, falsch-egalitären Vertraulichkeit des Bestehenden; ein Pathos der Distanz, Formen der Höflichkeit, Formen der Härte, die vielleicht auch Angst bekunden vor zu großem Mitleid mit dem, was den Menschen angetan wurde – Mitleid, das vielleicht die notwendige Rücksichtslosigkeit der Kritik beeinträchtigen könnte. Mir jedenfalls waren diese aristokratischen Formen seines Verhaltens immer besonders liebenswert« Hier spricht nicht das Geringste von Tolkiens Freunden, sondern Herbert Marcuse über Adorno (Schweppenhäuser, zum Gedächtnis).
11 Zu diesem und den folgenden Punkten vgl. Adorno, Kulturkritik 26: »Die Ideologie, der gesellschaftlich notwendige Schein, ist heute die reale Gesellschaft selber, insofern deren integrale Macht und Unausweichlichkeit, ihr überwältigendes Dasein an sich, den Sinn surrogiert, welchen jenes Dasein ausgerottet hat. Die Wahl eines ihrem Bann entzogenen Standpunkts ist so fiktiv wie nur je die Konstruktion abstrakter Utopien. Daher sieht sich die transzendente Kritik der Kultur, ganz ähnlich der bürgerlichen Kulturkritik, zum Rückgriff verhalten und beschwört jenes Ideal des Natürlichen, das selber ein Kernstück der bürgerlichen Ideologie bildet. Der transzendente Angriff auf die Kultur spricht regel-

Im Naturbezug liegt außerdem die besondere Gefahr, und zwar wegen der Doppeldeutigkeit des Naturbegriffs: Natur beschreibt einerseits die biologische Sphäre, also Wald und Wiesen. Andererseits aber beschreibt sie auch das Ursprüngliche, Eigentliche, Wesenhafte einer Sache. Und in dieser zweiten Bedeutung enthält sie einen versteckten Imperativ: Dass die Sache in ihrem ursprünglichen Zustand besser ist als im veränderten. Und damit stehen wir wieder vor dem grundlegenden Fehler, Kontingenzen für Unabänderlichkeiten zu halten.

Der zweite problematische Aspekt der Naturbetrachtung ist, dass sie eine Rückzugsbewegung ist – was uns zu Tolkiens eigener Kritik bringt.

Tolkiens Gesellschaftskritik

Tolkien ist weder als Person noch in seinem Werk völlig unkritisch. Zwar verwehrt er sich gegen allegorische Lesarten seiner Texte, erlaubt aber die, wie er es nennt, »Anwendung« derselben auf gesellschaftliche Phänomene[12]. Von den Briefen an seinen Sohn Christopher zur Zeit des Zweiten Weltkriegs bis zum Kapitel »The Scouring of the Shire« des *Herrn der Ringe* spricht Tolkien eine Sprache, die sich vor allem gegen jede Form von physischer und geistiger Mechanisierung, Brutalisierung und Macht, und die Zerstörung von Natur und traditionellen Lebensformen richtet.

Tolkiens Kritik ist allerdings zutiefst resignativ. Zwar hat es eine gewisse Ironie, das im Zusammenhang mit Adorno anzusprechen, aber genau in dieser Resignation liegt für Adorno eine Unzulänglichkeit, die Tolkiens Kritik selbst ein affirmatives Moment gibt. Tolkien sieht, gut katholisch, das Gute als zeitlose Möglichkeit für jedes einzelne Subjekt und erkennt, dass es de facto heute nicht zu haben ist, ohne dass er sich näher mit den historischen und sozialen Gründen befassen würde. Dieses Eingeständnis der Machtlosigkeit ist aber selbst eine Form der Affirmation, weil sie dazu beiträgt, Fehlentwicklungen für ebenso zufällige wie unüberwindliche Mächte zu halten.

Fiktion und Eskapismus

Diese Rückzugsbewegung spiegelt sich auch in Tolkiens Werk selbst. Das, was Tolkiens Entwürfe so faszinierend macht – dass er eine eigene Welt errichtet – kann ihm auch den Vorwurf eintragen, uns weiter von der Realität zu entfernen. Zwar erlauben all die fremdartigen Dinge in Tolkiens Universum eine ganz eigene

---

mäßig die Sprache des falschen Ausbruchs, die des Naturburschen. Er verachtet den Geist: die geistigen Gebilde, die ja doch nur gemacht sein, nur das natürliche Leben überdecken sollen, lassen um solcher vorgeblichen Nichtigkeit willen beliebig sich hantieren und für Herrschaftszwecke verwerten.«

12 Der Unterschied ist hier die Reihenfolge. Tolkien wehrt sich gegen den Gestus, mit der Allegorese den eigentlichen Kern zu entdecken. Primär bleibt für ihn auch hier: die unmittelbare Faszination für die geschaffenen Fiktionen. Alles andere kommt danach.

ästhetische Erfahrung, und unsere Welt wäre definitiv ärmer ohne sie. Aber natürlich wird der mögliche Vorwurf umso schlimmer, je weniger die verwendeten Kategorien auf unser Leben passen – weil man z.b. von Heroen träumt, statt von den Problemen unserer Gesellschaft. Kann solche Faszination nicht betäubende Wirkung haben, sodass wir das Falsche unserer eigenen Realität eher tolerieren – einfach weil wir uns weniger damit beschäftigen? Und trägt das nicht auch zur Anerkennung der absoluten Trennung zwischen Arbeit und Freizeit bei, in der letztere nur als Kompensation der ersteren dient und beide ihren Sinn verlieren? (vgl. Adorno, *Noten* 599; *Minima Moralia* §84)

Doch ist Tolkien tatsächlich so wenig anschlussfähig? Immerhin geht es auch in fiktiven Welten um menschliche Kategorien und Erfahrungen. Tolkien macht nicht umsonst eine ganze Theorie aus der »Zweitschöpfung« und der »Anwendbarkeit« seiner Konstruktionen: Wenn fiktionale Gebilde gelungen sind, dann deswegen, weil sie allgemeine Ideen spiegeln und daher auch allgemeinen Erkenntniswert für uns besitzen. Und wenn in klassischer Literatur fiktive Handlungsstränge einen eigenen Wert für die menschliche Bildung haben können, dann spricht nichts dagegen, dass auch fiktive Welten ähnliches – und doch unterschiedliches in ihrer besonderen Weise leisten können, und sei es zur Not nur als Mahnung, die Kontingenzen unserer eigenen Welt besser zu erkennen. Fiktive Welten ähneln in diesem Sinne vielleicht Utopien, sind aber wesentlich reicher, weil sie nicht dafür geschaffen werden, ein einzelnes Prinzip zu extrapolieren. Das heißt natürlich nicht, dass man das als Leser bemerken muss.

Happy End im Auenland

Der Herr der Ringe konfrontiert uns auch mit einer Lebensform, die fast wie das Gegenteil aller Weltfluchtfantasien wirkt: Die kleinbürgerliche Gesellschaft der Hobbits. Und Tolkiens positive, fast sehnsüchtige Haltung dieser Lebensform gegenüber ist auch dann deutlich erkennbar, wenn man nicht um seine Biographie und die Liebe zum ländlichen England weiß. Und den Wert seiner Erzählung sah er gerade auch darin, dass eben nicht die Starken und Weisen, sondern die kleinen, bürgerlich geerdeten Hobbits am besten in der Lage scheinen, aller Korruption durch Macht und Größe zu entgehen. Das Heil kommt also von den Hobbits? So hat beispielsweise Purtill Tolkien gelesen (vgl. Honegger, *Grammatik* 13). Man könnte leicht auf den Gedanken kommen, dass alles in Ordnung sei, wenn wir alle nur ungestört kleinbürgerlich leben könnten.

Doch man darf auch nicht zu genau hinsehen, wenn man dieser Ansicht bleiben will. Denn die Gesellschaft des Auenlandes ist bei Tolkien in keiner Weise moralisch besser als andere, und außerdem in ihrer eigenen charakteristischen Weise deutlich defizitär, wie man unschwer an den Sackheim-Beutlins, den Wirtshausgesprächen, oder auch Bilbos Ruf erkennt. Am Ende erweist sich diese Gesellschaft auch nicht als resistenter gegen Korruption als die stolzen Reiche der »großen Menschen«, und selbst Frodo versagt am Ende vor der Macht des Rings. Deutlich sind auch Gildors Bemerkungen, der gegenüber Sams Heimatliebe auf die historische Kontingenz seines Landes hinweist – zumal angesichts der Tatsache, dass das Auenland nur von Gnaden der Dunedain ungestört existieren konnte, ohne dass man diese dort überhaupt kannte.

Das Auenland ist also allenfalls kleiner und bodenständiger, im Guten wie im Schlechten. Das ändert nichts daran, dass Tolkien hierin ein Element erblickt, das er selbst wiederum für gut hält, und dass er bestimmte Individuen, die aus einem solchen Horizont kommen, ihre eigene Art des Guten finden lässt. Doch insgesamt ist der Wert des Auenlandes wohl in Gandalfs Haltung gegenüber den Hobbits am klarsten erfasst: in einer charakteristischen Mischung aus Wut und Liebe, angesichts der teilweise eklatanten Naivetäten. Das ist nicht gerade die Darstellung einer Glücksideals.

Bliebe noch die Sache mit dem Happy End. Denn wenn nicht nur alle Bösen fallen und alle guten Hauptcharaktere überleben[13], sondern auch noch ihre Heimat in alter Form wieder hergestellt wird und selbst Mithrilhemd und Lieblingsschwert gerettet werden, dann steht das in scharfem Kontrast zu dem, was man sonst aus ernstzunehmender Literatur kennt. (Und das ist umso prekärer, als die noch sentimentalere Variante des Schlusses erst auf Betreiben der Inklings von Tolkien gestrichen wurde).

Die Antwort darauf könnte zweierlei sein: Einerseits könnte man darauf hinweisen, dass selbst im *Herrn der Ringe* nicht alles glücklich und geheilt endet. Für den geistig gereiften Frodo, für Bilbo, und Gandalf und die Elben sowieso, gibt es kein gutes Ende im Diesseits. Wenn, kann man daraus wieder einen Eskapismusvorwurf machen, nicht aber die Affirmation kleinbürgerlicher Ideen des Angekommenseins. Die andere Möglichkeit wäre, die *Eucatastrophe* selbst als etwas zu sehen, das seinen eigenen Wert hat – wie Tolkien es in *On Fairy-Stories* versucht.

Mainstream und Kunst

Es bleibt noch ein weiterer Punkt: Als leicht lesbares und leicht fesselndes Buch gehört *Der Herr der Ringe* zum Mainstream. Und damit bewegt er sich in dem Bereich, den Adorno als »Kulturindustrie« fundamental kritisiert (Adorno/Horkheimer, *Dialektik der Aufklärung* 141ff).

---

13 Vgl. Adornos Bemerkung, dass das »Märchen ... immer schon dem Unrecht diente, und läßt in den gemaßregelten Bösewichtern das Antlitz derer dämmern, welche die integrale Gesellschaft verurteilt und welche zu verurteilen von je der Traum der Vergesellschaftung war.« (Minima Moralia § 131)

Tolkiens Werk steht allerdings seltsam quer zur Unterscheidung von Mainstream und hoher Literatur. In seiner Motivation und im inneren Aufbau hat es nicht alle Merkmale, die Adorno als Kulturindustrie geißelt: Weder gibt es einen klaren Schematismus aus immergleichen Stereotypen, noch haben marktstrategische Überlegungen in das Werk eingegriffen. Die Dispute über die Länge des Texts zwischen Tolkien und seinen Verlagen zeugen davon: Tolkiens Werk trägt stark idiosynkratische Züge und war weder als Bestseller noch als dezidiertes Kunstwerk konzipiert.

Das allerdings ist scheinbar noch schlimmer. Denn die Vermischung von hoher und niedriger Kultur bekämpfte Adorno rigoros. Werke, die in ihrer Anlage und Herkunft zur Volkskunst gehören, aber dann in halber Weise zum Anspruchsvollen tendieren, waren für Adorno »ein Jahrmarkt, erkrankt an Kultur« (Adorno/Horkheimer, *Dialektik der Aufklärung* 180) – oder eben ein »Kinderbuch, das irgendwie außer Kontrolle geraten ist, weil der Autor, statt dabei an ein jugendliches Publikum zu denken, seiner Fantasie um ihrer selbst willen freien Lauf gegeben hat«, wie ein Rezensent des Herr der Ringe 1956 schrieb. Doch muss ein gutes Buch immer ein Minimum an intellektueller Widerständigkeit bieten? Oder zeigt sich an diesem Punkt nicht auch Adornos zu einfache Einteilung von Kultur-, Faszinations- und Denkformen?

Ausblick

Zu sagen, Adornos Kritiklinien gälten für Tolkien in all ihrer Wucht, ist falsch – und trüge auch der jeweiligen Zeit- und Ortsgebundenheit nicht angemessen Rechnung. Also: teilweise interessant, aber ein bisschen zu radikal? Dies liefe Gefahr, den Gewinn zu verspielen – falls man Kritik dann nur soweit gelten lässt, wie sie den Kern der eigenen Ideen und Vorlieben nicht beschädigt. Doch Adornos Verdienst liegt gerade darin, weitere und subtilere Zusammenhänge von gesellschaftlichen Zuständen und Ästhetik zu erkunden, als man gewöhnlich annimmt. Anders gesagt: Adorno ist gerade da von Wert, wo er wehtut.

Dennoch ist Adornos Kritik in ihrer Radikalität auch eine Sackgasse. Denn sie verfällt zu oft einem negativen Holismus, in dem jeder denkbare Gegenstand unterschiedslos zum Repräsentanten des Unheils wird. Diese Haltung nivelliert – gegen ihren eigenen Anspruch – viele Unterschiede und negiert in charakteristischer Weise das ihren Kategorien nicht Gemäße. Daher darf man vielleicht froh sein, dass es nicht bloß die Traditionsstränge Kritischer Theorie und avantgardistischer Kunst gibt. Zweifellos mangelt es in Tolkiens Werk an manchen sozialkritischen Dimensionen und so wirkt es gefährlich affirmativ. Doch nicht immer wird, wie oben gezeigt wurde, diese Gefahr eingelöst. Tolkien kann vielleicht sogar der einen oder anderen Anforderung Adornos standhalten. Mit einem kleinen Augenzwinkern könnte man daher auch fragen: Hat Tolkien womöglich sogar progressives Potential? Oder, wo er das nicht hat, vielleicht sogar seine »eigene kleine Wahrheit« (vgl. L Nr. 113)?

Tolkien war sicher gerade in seiner Rückwärtsgewandtheit eine untypische Gestalt für seine Zeit. Sehr selten nur ging er so weit, daraus eine Position zu formulieren, wie gegen den »Provinzialismus des Zeitgemäßen« im Brief an Hugh Brogan (L Nr. 171). John Garth jedoch schreibt über Tolkien: »[He is the] most dissident of twentieth-century writers. Unlike many others shocked by the explosion of 1914-18, he did not discard the old ways of writing, the classicism or medievalism championed by Lord Tennyson and William Morris. In his hands these traditions were invigorated so that they remain powerfully alive for readers today« (Garth 41).

Natürlich wäre es vollkommener Unsinn, Tolkien wegen der Wahl seiner Stilmittel zum nonkonformistischen Helden machen zu wollen. Tolkien ist kein Dissident in einem noch so entfernt politischen Sinne, dafür fehlt es ihm schlicht an gesellschafts- oder literaturpolitischem Willen. Vielmehr fand er sich gleichsam zufällig, nach privater Verfolgung seiner eigenen Interessen, in der Position des Außenseiters vor, was er aber nie vollständig zu einem bewussten Programm oder Ziel kondensieren ließ.

Richtig an Garths Punkt ist jedoch der Hinweis auf die Außenseiterrolle und Tolkiens unbeirrt idiosynkratische Anknüpfung an ältere Traditionen. Und auch wenn das Konglomerat aus katholischer Ästhetik, ländlicher Idylle, linguistischer Einflüsse und literarischer Anglophilie nicht ohne soziale Hintergründe auskommt, sollte man nicht für die Möglichkeit individueller Zufälle und Akzente gar keinen Raum mehr lassen. Und diese Selbständigkeit Tolkiens hat vielleicht auch ihren Wert.

Man könnte aber auch versuchen, im Werk selbst Elemente von Negativität im Sinne Adornos zu suchen. Immerhin: Tolkien macht es uns nicht immer behaglich. Nicht nur beschreibt er immer wieder Korruptionsformen des Guten, die Brutalität einer absoluten Gerechtigkeit in Gandalfs, und die absoluter Schönheit in Galadriels Visionen, bis hin zur Aporie der christlichen Demut- und Mitleidsethik im letzten Gespräch mit Saruman, von der Tolkiens Werk sonst so zehrt (vgl. Honegger et al. 102ff). Auch die selbstgefällige Unzulänglichkeit auenländischer Naivetäten ist augenfällig, während in der elbischen Kunst und dem entrückten Segensreich eine Ahnung der Versöhnung von Natur und Kultur aufscheint, die Adorno vielleicht gar nicht so fremd hätte sein müssen.

Tatsächlich gibt es eine sehr eigene Vermittlung von Mythos und Aufklärung in Mittelerde. Tolkiens Welt ist in hohem Maße nicht verdinglichend und ebenso wenig driftet er ins Irrationale oder Vernunftfeindliche[14]. Sowohl in der Behandlung von Magie als auch in dem Bezug auf ältere Legenden ist der Zugriff

---

14 Auch darin ist Tolkien ganz mittelalterlich. Der Mythos geht Hand in Hand mit rationaler Begründung und ist nicht, wie in der Romantik, deren Widerpart und Aufhebung.

nicht positivistisch, sondern immer historisch und ästhetisch. Ein maßgebliches Gestaltungselement ist das Ungefähre und die bewusste Lehrstelle. Dadurch wird vieles nicht festgeschrieben und so kann die mittelirdische Metaphysik auch keinen abschließenden Charakter haben.

Zudem wird der Ausblick auf das Gute und Schöne wiederum gebrochen im Fall derer, die es zu ergreifen und in ewig gleicher Gestalt festzuhalten suchen: Der Untergang von Numenor zeugt davon, aber auch der Vergangenheitskult von Gondor, wie die konservatorische Tendenz der Elben – um den Preis, dass sie in der Welt der Gegenwart keine aktive Rolle mehr spielen. Tolkien nennt sie deswegen auch »Balsamierer« (L Nr. 154).

Derartige Fäden könnte man verfolgen, wenn man Tolkien kritisches Potential zusprechen wollte. Aber man kann auch sagen: Allzu weit ist es damit nicht her. In vielen Passagen bleibt *Der Herr der Ringe* doch recht behaglich, und sperrt sich deswegen auch nicht so sehr gegen affirmativere Lesarten. Wenn überhaupt, sind die aufgezeigten Punkte Ansätze, die eine Aburteilung Tolkiens brechen können, nicht aber dieses Urteil aufheben.

Keines der genannten Elemente erlaubt es, Tolkien umfassend zum Gesellschaftskritiker zu machen. Aber wenn ich mich nicht irre, liegt vielleicht auch darin ein Wert. Dann wäre die zweite mögliche Strategie, Tolkiens Darstellung von bruchlosen Verwirklichungen des Guten und Schönen selbst als Negation solcher Negationen zu lesen – und sei es nur als leises Indiz davon, was eine Literatur unter Adornoschen Vorzeichen bei all ihrer berechtigten Zeitkritik zu verschütten droht. Für Adorno war die Idee des Guten und Schönen, bei ihm charakterisiert als »Versöhnung«, nur noch im Gebrochenen augenblickshaft zu erhaschen. Damit aber wird sie selbst ein abstraktes, leeres Regulativ. Wenn das stimmt, wäre die Kritische Theorie tatsächlich selbst der subtilste aller Eskapismen. Und davon droht ihrerseits eine resignative Gefahr: dass jede Handlung so gut und schlecht sei wie jede andere, da es ohnehin, nach einem anderen berühmten Diktum, »kein richtiges Leben im Falschen« gibt (Adorno, *Minima Moralia* §18).

Mittelerde ist zwar in vieler Hinsicht entrückt, aber in ethischer Hinsicht ist Tolkiens Welt gerade nicht realen Geltungsansprüchen enthoben. Seine Fantasien sind auf das Gute ausgerichtet und das ist gegenüber einem negativen Holismus deswegen von Wert, weil es den Gedanken bewahrt, dass es einen Unterschied macht, wie man handelt. Darin liegt potentiell eine Gefahr (nämlich das Gute für abgeschlossen zu halten), aber auch eine Stärke: die Stärke, mit der manche auch im Angesicht von unüberwindbarer Ungerechtigkeit noch handeln, an einzelnen Schicksalen Anteil nehmen oder gar lachen können. Die Moral des *Herrn der Ringe* ist unmittelbar, aber sie muss deswegen nicht selbstgefällig sein. Viel mehr bringt sie in ihrer Unmittelbarkeit die notwendige Bedingung mit, dass das Gute jemals wirklich sein kann, bevor der Tag der Versöhnung da ist: als einzelne, letztlich einfache Tat in einer egal wie schlechten Welt. Honegger spricht dabei zu Recht von einer »Banalität des Guten« (Honegger et al. 13). Darauf aufbauend würde ich die These wagen, dass Tolkien gerade wo er naiv ist auch einen Wert hat[15]. So kann die Differenz, die Tolkiens Werk in seiner besonderen Weise zu den avantgardistischen Strömungen der Literatur herstellt, wieder etwas Neues befruchten. Das jedenfalls wäre ein Lehrstück von Dialektik:

> Vielleicht wird Kunst, einmal ohne Verrat, jenes Gebot außer Kraft setzen, so wie Brecht es empfunden haben mag, als er die Verse niederschrieb: ›Was sind das für Zeiten, wo/Ein Gespräch über Bäume fast ein Verbrechen ist/Weil es ein Schweigen über so viele Untaten einschließt!‹. Kunst verklagt die überflüssige Armut durch die freiwillige eigene; aber sie verklagt auch die Askese und kann sie nicht simpel als ihre Norm aufrichten.
> (Adorno, *Ästhetische Theorie* 65-66)

Tolkien ist darauf nicht die Antwort. Aber er illustriert die Frage.

Bibliographie

Adorno, Theodor W. *Ästhetische Theorie*. Frankfurt: Suhrkamp, 1970
---. *Minima Moralia. Reflexionen aus dem beschädigten Leben*. Frankfurt: Suhrkamp, 1951
---. *Kulturkritik und Gesellschaft I/II. Prismen. Ohne Leitbild. Eingriffe. Stichworte*. Frankfurt: Suhrkamp, 1977
---. *Negative Dialektik*. Frankfurt: Suhrkamp, 1970

---

15 Ich würde für Tolkien in Anspruch nehmen, was Adorno, mit Blick auf Homer, in Über epische Naivetät schreibt: »Die epische Naivetät ist nicht nur Lüge, um die allgemeine Besinnung von der blinden Anschauung des Besonderen fernzuhalten. Wie sie, als antimythologische Anstrengung, aus dem aufklärerischen, gleichsam positivistischen Bestreben hervorgeht, treu und unverstellt was einmal war so festzuhalten, wie es war, und damit den Zauber, den das Gewesene ausübt, den Mythos im eigentlichen Sinn zu sprengen, bleibt ihr in der Beschränkung aufs Einmalige ein Zug eigentümlich, der Beschränkung transzendiert. Denn das Einmalige ist nicht bloß der trotzige Rückstand gegen die umfassende Allgemeinheit des Gedankens, sondern auch dessen innerste Sehnsucht, die logische Form eines Wirklichen, das nicht mehr von der gesellschaftlichen Herrschaft und dem ihr nachgebildeten klassifizierenden Gedanken umfaßt wäre; der Begriff, der sich versöhnt mit seiner Sache. In der epischen Naivetät lebt die Kritik der bürgerlichen Vernunft. Sie hält jene Möglichkeit von Erfahrung fest, welche zerstört wird von der bürgerlichen Vernunft, die sie gerade zu begründen vorgibt.« (Adorno, Noten 36)

---. *Noten zur Literatur.* Frankfurt: Suhrkamp, 1974

---/Horkheimer, Max. *Dialektik der Aufklärung.* Frankfurt: Fischer, 1969

Carpenter, Humphrey. *The Letters of J.R.R. Tolkien.* London: HarperCollins, 1995

Garth, John. *Tolkien and the Great War. The Threshold of Middle-Earth.* London: HarperCollins, 2003

Honegger, Thomas/ Andrew Johnston/Friedhelm Schneidewind/Frank Weinreich. *Eine Grammatik der Ethik.* Saarbrücken: Villa Fledermaus, 2005

Marcuse, Herbert. »Reflexion zu Theodor W. Adorno –Aus einem Gespräch mit Michaela Seiffe«. *Theodor W. Adorno Zum Gedächtnis: Eine Sammlung.* Hg. Hermann Schweppenhäuser. Frankfurt: Suhrkamp, 1971, 47-51

Schwarz, Guido. *Jungfrauen im Nachthemd - Blonde Krieger aus dem Westen.* Würzburg: Königshausen & Neumann, 2003

Sebald, Winfried G. *Luftkrieg und Literatur.* Frankfurt: Fischer, 2002

Tolkien, J.R.R. "Leaf by Niggle". *Tales from the Perilous Realm.* London: HarperCollins, 2002, 119-144

---. "On Fairy-Stories". *The Monsters and the Critics and Other Essays.* Ed. Christopher Tolkien. London: Allen & Unwin, 1983, 109-161

---. *The Lord of the Rings.* London: Allen & Unwin, 1981

Zusammenfassungen der englischen Beiträge

»Sterne über einem dunklen Felsen«: Tolkien und Romantik
Anna Slack

Als tiefgehender Wandel in den westlichen Einstellungen zu Kunst und menschlicher Kreativität legte die Romantik den Akzent auf die Freiheit des Selbstausdrucks: Dies fand seinen Höhepunkt im Jubel über die Spontaneität und Originalität der individuellen Vorstellungskraft. Diese Vorstellungskraft sollte den Status quo der zeitgenössischen Literatur durchbrechen und den romantischen Stift zu Mythen und Legenden und den transzendenten Qualitäten der Natur und einer erneuerten Beziehung mit der Sprache zurückwenden. Ob sie die erhabene Begeisterung der kreativen Vorstellungskraft des Poeten feierten, den Exzessen der Sinnlichkeit nachgaben oder die neuen Bewegungen des Gothic losließen, waren die Romantiker eine Kraft der Erneuerung in der Literatur des späten 18. und frühen 19. Jahrhunderts. Wie viele Schriftsteller seitdem sah sich auch Tolkien mit dem literarischen Erbe der Romantiker arbeiten.

Dieser Beitrag gibt einen allgemeinen Überblick über Romantik und untersucht, mit besonderer Berücksichtigung des *Lord of the Rings*, unter welchen Hinsichten Tolkiens Schriften als Werke eines romantischen Autors angesehen werden können. Diese Untersuchung erlaubt ihrerseits eine detaillierte Betrachtung, wie Tolkien den romantischen Impuls sowohl verwendete als auch umarbeitete.

Romantik, Symbolismus und Onomastik in Tolkiens *Legendarium*
Annie Birks

E.B. Burgum schrieb einmal in der *Kenyon Review* (1941): »Derjenige, der versucht, Romantik zu definieren, betritt ein gefährliches Gebiet, das schon viele Opfer gefordert hat.« Gleichwohl kann nicht bestritten werden, dass Empfindsamkeit zu den Hinweisen gehört, über die Konsens besteht. Bei der Auseinandersetzung mit den Motiven Tolkiens, die der Entfaltung seines *Legendariums* zugrunde liegen, kann ebenso wenig bestritten werden, dass seine von ihm selbst behauptete extreme Sensitivität für Wörter und Sprachen nicht nur ein Hinweis ist, sondern an der Wurzel seines gesamten Schreibprozesses liegt. Solch innere Faszination für die Schönheit und Musikalität von Wörtern kann in Etymologie und Symbolismus der Personen- und Ortsnamen in ganz Mittelerde gefunden werden. Als Beitrag zur Untersuchung der Romantik in Tolkiens Werk untersucht dieser Aufsatz die möglichen Charakteristika dieser komplexen Bewegung, die ein Echo in der onomastischen Zweitschöpfung des Autors und in deren Beziehung zu den Charakteren, Orten und Objekten in Mittelerde finden.

›Die Vergangenheit ist ein anderes Land‹ – Romantik, Tolkien und das Mittelalter
Thomas Honegger

Das Mittelalter bildet für J.R.R. Tolkien als auch für zahlreiche Vertreter der Romantik den Hintergrund, vor dem sich die Handlung ihrer Werke entfaltet. Aber weder die Romantiker noch Tolkien fühlen sich verpflichtet, die Epoche archäologisch-historisch korrekt darzustellen. Anhand eines Vergleichs der Verwendung dieses ›konzeptuellen‹ Mittelalters in zwei ›typischen‹ Werken der Romantik (*Ivanhoe* und *Heinrich von Ofterdingen*) und im *Herrn der Ringe* wird aufgezeigt, inwiefern Tolkien und die Romantik sich in ihrem Bezug auf das Mittelalter gleichen wie auch unterscheiden.

Allen gemeinsam ist die Sehnsucht nach einem ›goldenen Zeitalter‹, das die destruktiven Auswirkungen der politischen, naturwissenschaftlich-kulturellen und industriellen Umwälzungen seit 1789 nicht kennt und das sie in einem idealisierten ›konzeptuellen‹ Mittelalter ansiedeln. Tolkien unterscheidet sich von den Romantikern jedoch insofern, als dass er nicht so sehr rückwärts schaut, sondern oftmals eine organische Fort- und Weiterentwicklung einer ursprünglichen mittelalterlichen Gesellschaftsform entwirft.

Entzaubert mit ihrer Epoche: Die große Flucht von Keats, Morris und Tolkien
Marie-Noëlle Biemer

In diesem Artikel soll die inhärent romantische Idee einer Flucht aus einer eintönigen modernen Zeit, die ihres Zaubers und der Schönheit beraubt wurde, hin zu einer nostalgischen besseren Fantasiewelt im *Oeuvre* von drei Autoren erörtert werden. Um die Lücke zwischen dem Romantiker John Keats und J.R.R. Tolkien, der das moderne Fantasy-Genre wohl am meisten geprägt hat, zu schließen, betrachten wir das Multi-Talent William Morris. Dessen Werke wurden massiv von Keats beeinflusst, und er selbst hat einen tiefen Eindruck bei Tolkien hinterlassen.

Alle drei Autoren, jeweils als Vertreter desselben Phänomens in ihrer Zeit, waren von ihrer Gegenwart desillusioniert, vor allem von der fortschreitenden Industrialisierung, der daraus resultierenden Umweltverschmutzung und dem Verlust von Traditionen. Sie alle »flüchteten« in eigene fantastische Welten, die Ausdruck in verschiedenen Kunstformen fanden. Keats' nach innen gerichtete Ästhetik zeigt dabei eine Diskrepanz zwischen realer Welt und Fiktion, als wolle er damit eine Armut im Leben kompensieren. Die verschiedenen Stadien im Werk von William Morris spiegeln seine schwindende Hoffnung auf eine Veränderung der Realität durch die Romantische Revolution wider. Das führte ihn zu seinem politischen Engagement als Sozialist und, gegen Ende seines Lebens, zum Schreiben seiner Prosaromanzen, die oft als erste »echte« Fantasy bezeichnet werden. Zwei Jahrzehnte später begann J.R.R. Tolkien mit der Schaffung des sorgfältig ausgearbeiteten mythologischen Hintergrunds für seine von Morris inspirierten Geschichten aus Mittelerde.

Verschiedene Formen von Eskapismus werden somit in diesem Artikel betrachtet. Dazu werden einige biografische Informationen über die Autoren herangezogen und Vergleiche in den Werken der Autoren selbst angestellt.

Keltische Einflüsse und die Suche nach nationaler Identität
Doreen Triebel

Tolkien schuf sein literarisches Werk in einer Zeit, die von einem weit reichenden sozialen und kulturellen Wandel geprägt war, der sich u.a. in zeitgenössischer Kunst, Musik, Architektur, Theologie, den sozialen Strukturen und der Literatur widerspiegelte. Auf letzterem Gebiet experimentierten in England Autoren wie V. Woolf, J. Joyce, H.G. Wells und D.H. Lawrence mit innovativen Handlungselementen und neuen narrativen Techniken, um die Werte der vergangenen Epoche in Frage zu stellen und die Innenwelt ihrer Charaktere sowie die menschliche Natur zu beleuchten. Bekanntermaßen stand Tolkien wie zahlreiche seiner Zeitgenossen industriellem Fortschritt, Materialismus und dem, was er als sklavische Anerkennung der Fakten bezeichnete, skeptisch gegenüber. Jedoch war sein kreativer Blick, im Gegensatz zu dem vieler anderer Autoren seiner Zeit, nicht vornehmlich auf die Zukunft oder die Gegenwart gerichtet, sondern auf eine frühe anglo-keltische Vergangenheit.

Er bedauerte das Fehlen eines literarischen Erbes in England, das vergleichbar mit dem der Brüder Grimm in Deutschland oder Elias Lönnrots *Kalevala* in Finnland den Grundstein für die Ausbildung eines nationalen Identitätsgefühls legen konnte, das sich entscheidend von einem gesamtbritischen unterschied. Aus diesem Grund beschloss er, diese Mythologie selbst zu schaffen. Aber trotz des anfänglichen Ziels, eine Sammlung von zusammenhängenden Geschichten zu schreiben, die in erster Linie auf rein englische Wurzeln zurückgehen, und trotz zahlreicher Äußerungen, in denen er eine Abneigung gegenüber dem Keltischen zum Ausdruck brachte, wurde er besonders in der Repräsentation der Elben und der Anderswelt beträchtlich von der keltischen Tradition beeinflusst.

Jedoch war Tolkien keineswegs der einzige britische Autor, dessen Blick sich in seiner Suche nach nationaler Identität auf die keltische Vergangenheit seines Landes richtete. Indem er sich von dieser inspirieren und Elemente jener Tradition kreativ in sein Werk einfließen ließ, folgte er anderen Autoren, die absichtsvoll keltische Komponenten oder lediglich romantische Rekonstruktionen dieser in ihre literarischen Kreationen einfügten, um ein wachsendes Gefühl nationaler Identität herauszustellen. In diesem Kontext lieferten z.B. Macphersons ossianische Verse ungeachtet ihrer kontroversen Entstehungsgeschichte zahlreichen romantischen Autoren eine fruchtbare Quelle der Inspiration, ein Bild der Andersartigkeit und eine scheinbar historische Verkörperung romantischer Ideale. Während jedoch Macpherson, Wordsworth oder Keats diese Motive bewusst nutzen, um ihren Unmut über die englische Kolonialpolitik zum Ausdruck zu bringen, deuten vergleichbare Einflüsse in Tolkiens Werk trotz gegenteiliger Äußerungen darauf hin, dass er, wie er es in *English and Welsh* formulierte, »britisch im Herzen« war.

Äußere und innere Landschaften bei J.R.R. Tolkien: Zwischen Wordsworth, Coleridge und Dostojewski
Emanuele Rimoli und Guglielmo Spirito

Die Romantiker beschritten neue Wege, indem sie die Wirkungen von Landschaften auf den Geist, das Gedächtnis und die Emotionen untersuchten und dabei zeigten, wie diese durch die Vorstellungskraft transformiert werden konnten. Unter anderen können William Wordsworth und Samuel Taylor Coleridge gemeinsam mit Fjodor Dostojewski (der über die russischen Romantiker hinausgehend einen guten Kontrast und eine gute Entsprechung bietet) einige Elemente anbieten, um Tolkiens innere und äußere Landschaften neu zu entdecken.

»Sekundärglaube«: Tolkien und die Revision des romantischen Verständnisses poetischen Glaubens

Eduardo Segura

John Ronald Reuel Tolkien wird normalerweise lediglich als ein »Fantasy«-Autor angesehen, d.h. vor allem als ein Prosaautor. In diesem Beitrag wird diese allgemein akzeptierte Vorstellung diskutiert, aber ebenso auch die Wurzeln des Verständnisses von Tolkien als einem Prosaautor, besser einem Mythenmacher, oder einem Mythopoeten, ebenso wie die Implikationen dieses Zugangs zur Mythopoesie als Zweitschöpfung. Dies ist ein erster Versuch, seine Mythologie als ein Echo auf die romantische Lösung, eine neue Ästhetik zu finden, zu verstehen und ein Porträt von Tolkien als einem Poeten aus dem Blickwinkel der Themen und des Tons seiner frühen Gedichte, dem frühen *Silmarillion* und dem Logos des gesamten literarischen Designs zu entwerfen. Ebenso wird die pejorative Bedeutung untersucht, die »Fantasy« besonders seit dem 17. Jahrhundert erhielt, und Tolkiens tiefe Re-Evaluation der Ansichten Max Müllers und Coleridges über Mythologie und den rationalen, kreativen Gebrauch der Imagination.

Der letzte Teil des Beitrags besteht aus einer Reflexion über die Konsequenzen der Zweitschöpfung aus dem Blickwinkel der Rezeption, vor allem des Gegensatzes, den Tolkien zwischen Allegorie und freier Anwendbarkeit sieht. Indem er den Bereich der ung auf die Mythopoeia einschränkt, unterstreicht Tolkien die Kraft der Wörter, Sekundärglauben zu erzeugen und auf diese Weise Fantasy im vollen Sinne glaubwürdig zu machen. Gleichzeitig betont er die Begrenzungen der Bilder, glaubwürdig zu werden, besonders im Versuch, Fantasy in die Primärwelt einzuführen, der paradoxerweise die Kraft der Metapher im Versuch selbst, Fantasy präsent zu machen, einschränkt. In diesem Sinne können wir Tolkien als ein ganz eigenes Beispiel in der Tradition der Romantik ansehen.

Schönheit, Vollendung, erhabener Schrecken: Einige Gedanken über den Einfluss Edmund Burkes *A Philosophical Enquiry into the Sublime and Beautiful* auf Tolkiens Schöpfung Mittelerdes

Stephanie Schult

Die ästhetischen Formen des Erhabenen und des Schönen, so wie sie Edmund Burke in seiner Prä-Romantischen Schrift beschrieb (basierend auf dem Longinus zugeschriebenen Werk über das Erhabene, das im 16. Jh. wiederentdeckt und ins Englische übersetzt wurde), spielen in J.R.R. Tolkiens *Lord of the Rings* zwar keine herausragende, aber indirekt dennoch eine wichtige

Rolle. Da sich die Romantik in ihrer Symbolik häufig der Natur bedient, finden wir zwangsläufig eine romantische Ästhetik in der Natur wieder. Dabei unterscheidet Burke zwischen dem Erhabenen, einer göttlich, und daher übernatürlich, anmutenden Ästhetik und dem Schönen, das sich in kleinen, filigranen oder zarten natürlichen Dingen verbirgt. In Tolkiens Werk lässt sich zusätzlich zu dieser bestehenden Unterscheidung noch eine Untergliederung des Erhabenen in eine gute und eine dunkle Variante erkennen: Die gute Variante bezieht sich in der Tradition von Longinus oder Burke auf sublime Anblicke wie beispielsweise Berge oder gigantische Bauten, während die dunkle Variante finstere Intentionen sowie das Streben nach Macht in den Vordergrund stellt – und, gerade in Bezug auf die Elben und die Benutzung von mächtigen Artefakten wie dem Einen Ring, das Motiv des biblischen Falls aufgreift.

Als stilistisches Mittel kommen sowohl das Erhabene als auch das Schöne in Tolkiens Werk vielfach zum Einsatz. Diese erschaffen die Authentizität und Intensität einer fiktiven Welt, die besonders durch den fesselnden, unwiderstehlichen Effekt des Erhabenen geprägt sind, der den Leser quasi in diese Welt »entführt«.

Von besonderer Bedeutung ist im Bezug auf einen Vergleich von Edmund Burkes Schrift und Tolkiens Werk letztlich die Unterscheidung des Erhabenen und des Schönen an sich, die im Grunde stets im Auge des Betrachters liegt und auf ein subjektives Urteil gründet. So können sich schöne Dinge auf den zweiten Blick ebenso als sublim herausstellen, wie erhabene Dinge schön sein können.

Eine Lektüre des Werkes Tolkiens im Lichte von Victor Hugos Konzepten des *Sublimen* und des *Grotesken*
Marguerite Mouton

In diesem Beitrag wird die Ansicht vertreten, dass die Konzepte des *Sublimen* und des *Grotesken*, die Victor Hugo im Vorwort zu *Cromwell* ausführte und in *Notre-Dame de Paris* illustrierte, effektive Mittel bereitstellen, um zu verstehen, wie Tolkien mit seinem Schreiben umging.

Hugo identifiziert den ästhetischen Kontrast zwischen den Konzepten des *Sublimen* und des *Grotesken* als das für die Romantik spezifische Schreibprinzip im Unterschied zur auf dem Prinzip der kultivierenden Harmonie basierenden klassischen Literatur. Hugos ästhetische Theorie des Kontrastes ist unlösbar mit einer ontologischen Behauptung verbunden: Beim Bemühen, das Sein in einem dialektischen Muster zu totalisieren, versucht der romantische Autor, die konfligierenden Elemente, die durch klassisches Denken verdunkelt wurden, sowohl in der Literatur als auch in der Welt wieder zu etablieren. Diese Ästhetik des Kontrastes ist ebenso ein produktives Prinzip der Tolkien'schen Schriften. Sein Werk beschränkt sich nicht auf die vereinfachende Gegenüberstellung von gut, schön und Licht auf der einen Seite und böse, Hässlichkeit und Dunkelheit auf der anderen Seite. Im Gegensatz stellt es ein dramatisches Muster visueller (Nebeneinanderstellung schöner und monströser Dinge), rhythmischer und tonaler (Abwechslung von ernsten und leichten Szenen) Kontraste. Unter der Voraussetzung, dass Hugos ästhetische Theorie wesentlich mit ethischen Überlegungen verbunden ist, führt uns die Analogie zwischen Hugos und Tolkiens Schreibprinzipien dazu, über die Möglichkeit einer entsprechenden Ähnlichkeit ihrer Weltverständnisse zu reflektieren. Ist Tolkiens Werk durch irgendeine romantisch totalisierende Dialektik organisiert, die negative Elemente integriert?

Eine solche Frage zu stellen, darf uns nicht vergessen lassen, was der wohl wichtigste Beitrag der Theorie Hugos zur Untersuchung des Werkes Tolkiens ist. Tatsächlich liegt dieser nicht in der Analogie ihrer jeweiligen ästhetischen und ethischen Konzeptionen, sondern in der durch den romantischen Schriftsteller etablierten Verbindung zwischen beiden Arten der Konzeptionen. Hugos Theorie beleuchtet die ästhetische Arbeitsweise des Textes und warnt uns vor einer Tendenz, Tolkiens Werk als reinen Ausdruck eines Weltverständnisses zu lesen denn als ein literarisches Objekt.

Summaries of the German Essays

Middle-earth as an Expression of Romantic Creativity and Yearning
Oliver Bidlo

Next to yearning, the term creativity defines Romanticism as an intellectual trend as well as a mindset, playing an important part in all definitions. Contemplating both terms, we find that there is an *essential* link between them. Creativity stems from yearning for unselfconscious and freely unfolding fantasising. Tolkien's idea of creation and the design of Middle-earth are expressions of the Romantic process of the power of the creator as well as the yearning for the design of a world created by the power of imagination.

The Romantic mind-set does indeed not aim at depicting or representing reality. The Romantic poet instead wants to create an entirely new world flowing from his own creativity, driven by introspective yearning. The connotations of the new and the creative are also at the basis of the definition of the term *creativity*, which describes the ability to create something new. This paper demonstrates the relation between creativity and yearning during the period of Romanticism and then goes on to show that Tolkien's underlying concept of Middle-earth as evidenced in his entire body of work can be read and understood as the result of such a Romantic process and of the interplay between creativity and yearning. This also shows that Romantic elements are not restricted to the world as such. Indeed, there are numerous set-pieces of Romantic thinking right in the text of, for instance, *The Lord of the Rings* or *The Silmarillion*.

At the same time, the interplay between author, work, and reader creates a world that has to be understood as the result of a Romantic process of creativity. This process, in turn, can be traced back to the Romantic mind-set of the author. *Because of* this Romantic mindset on the part of the author, the overall conception of Middle-earth in its final form is the result of a Romantic process. This leaves us with a substantiated way of reading Tolkien's Middle-earth related works in general, and *The Lord of the Rings* in particular.

J.R.R. Tolkien and Romantic Nostalgia
Julian Tim Morton Eilmann

This article clarifies that the topos of nostalgia, which is of importance for the literature and philosophy of German Romanticism (1790–1850) is also essential for mythology of Tolkien's Middle-earth. By analysing Tolkien's specific use of nostalgic topoi in his texts in context of Romantic nostalgia, we will get a better understanding of Tolkien as an author. Three forms of nostalgia are present in Middle-earth.

First, there is the psychological phenomenon of an individual setting out on a journey into the unknown and suffering from agonising homesickness to return to his safe and beloved home. The typical representatives of this form of local nostalgia in Tolkien's novels are the hobbits, especially Frodo and Sam, who are confronted with deprivation and death on their way to Mount Doom, and thus cling to the concept of the Shire as a lost idyllic and peaceful paradise.

For an understanding of Tolkien's use of nostalgia in context of the Romantic tradition, the second form of historical nostalgic longing in Tolkien's work is more important. Concurring with the longing for an idealised distant age that is a recurrent topos in Romantic novels, individuals in Middle-earth also contrast their prosaic present with a poetic past. This yearning for the idealised "Elder Days" (LotR 308) is not only an elegiac rapture, but can also be understood as a political statement because the nostalgic attitude of some individuals and people is linked with political claims.

According to this, the *Song of Durin* (ibid.), which Gimli takes up in Moria, not only presents Durin's reign as a lost Golden Age, but formulates the certainty of the dwarves that their great king once will return and renew their glory. In a similar manner, the nostalgic longing for a poetic past is expressed in Tolkien's mostly ignored *Kortirion*-poems.

It is the third form of nostalgia in Tolkien's work, the existential longing and homesickness of Men, that is especially in line with Romantic philosophy. In the *Athrabeth Finrod ah Andreth*, Tolkien introduces the idea that Men in Arda suffer from an existential homelessness, while the physical world reminds Men of something they once knew but have lost. The idea that Men love the beauty of the surrounding world not for itself, but because all things act as symbols for "some other dearer thing" (MR 316) and thus remind Men of a transcendent home is crucial for Romantic philosophy and present in many novels of the Romantic Age.

'There and back again' – a Romantic Walk?
A Critical Consideration of J.R.R. Tolkien's *The Hobbit* in the Perspective of Romanticism
Thomas Scholz

The question if Tolkien's texts – in this case *The Hobbit* – are (a rather late) part of the Romantic Movement can only be answered when there is a concise definition of what Romanticism is. However, this problem has kept literary scholars busy for more than a century. The latest agreement is that the era we label as Romantic and the artistic products we deem to be representative for that time are all a reaction to the "ever-accelerating modernization of European Society", as Christoph Bode put it. Therefore, if either Tolkien's book resembles the original literary reactions of this time or if it is a new form of reaction to that same acceleration, we might consider it as Romantic.

However, there are very few similarities between *The Hobbit* and Romantic texts. The individual is not as important as it should be for an even remotely Romantic work. Nature is not the inspiration for true feelings, but a source of danger. Love and religion have no part in the voyage "there and back again" at all. Only the past, the Middle Ages, have a significant value in Middle-earth – but unfortunately a rather different one compared to the Romantic Era. In the end, the only possibility to deem *The* Hobbit as Romantic, is to read it as a reaction to the cultural changes that influenced the Romantic poets. But more than a century after the first point of Romantic culmination, Tolkien's time can hardly be considered to be the same as the early 19th century. His writing can therefore scarcely be seen to react to circumstances which did not exist at his time. Therefore, *The Hobbit* cannot be considered to belong to Romanticism.

Tolkien, Newman, and the Oxford Movement
Thomas Fornet-Ponse

This article analyses the relationships between Romanticism and the Oxford Movement (and John Henry Newman as one of its proponents) on the one hand, and Newman (who founded the Birmingham Oratory) and Tolkien on the other hand. This allows us to deal with the question of Romanticism and Tolkien from a theological perspective. Although there are some very important similarities between Romanticism and the Oxford Movement (e.g., restoring a conception of nature), there are fundamental differences as well (e.g., in regard to the pantheistic tendencies of Romanticism). Continuity and discontinuity are due to the Oxford Movement having developed on the soil of Romantic views but interpreting the adopted conceptions in a totally different way.

The same is valid for Newman's personal view on Romanticism – he can be regarded as both Romantic and anti-Romantic. This is reflected in his conception of conscience, which combines the main lines of his philosophical and theological thinking and is a very important stage in the intellectual history of this idea. Newman distinguishes between a "moral sense" (a general sensorium of judging acts as good or evil) and a "sense of duty" (knowing that one has to do the act one believes to be right). While it is not implausible to see a clear reference to romantic ideas in the moral sense, the sense of duty reflects the Augustinian conception of conscience as the voice of God, which is quite incompatible with Romanticism and its individualism.

Without claiming that Tolkien consciously employed this conception of conscience in his narrative works, the differentiation between an instinctively felt moral sense and a sense of duty as a compelling force provides a helpful tool for interpreting relevant passages, such as Bilbo's handling of the Arkenstone, his duties to the dwarves, the choices of Aragorn or Samwise, etc.

False Harmony
Or: Is it possible after Auschwitz to dream of the Shire?
Fabian Geier

The topic of this essay is a very German one, even though I do not believe its relevance is confined to the German borders. I want to discuss a possible criticism of Tolkien's works which I find in the writings of Theodor W. Adorno, a member of the Neo-Marxist Frankfurt School. I am pretty sure that Adorno never read Tolkien. But when I read Adorno, I cannot help but see that what he says might also apply to Tolkien. And what he has to say is indeed highly disturbing.

One of Adorno's most well-known claims is that no poem could be written after Auschwitz. This claim extrapolates his general suspicion about any kind of art, that depicts things as immediately beautiful and good, that relies on the symmetry and harmony of traditional forms, in short: Any kind of art that is not inherently broken or scarred. For Adorno, such art is not just old-fashioned and bourgeois. In the face of a historic situation of unspeakable atrocities having happened in the middle of society, he finds a mindset that revels in such things downright dangerous.

One might say: "Tolkien does not write about society. He creates his own world, a world of sheer beauty". But this makes things just worse: For, according to Adorno, this is the very weakness of what I will call a "romantic consciousness": that it retreats to the inner self, and considers the inner world to be disconnected from a society it ignores or even loathes – while it does not recognise how at the same time it cannot escape from its categories. And by not seeing this, such a consciousness fosters and affirms their wrongness and could even be said to participate in all its wrongdoings.

Such, at least, is the outline of Adorno's thought. The question is: Inhowfar is it plausible? And what are the consequences? Should something like *The Lord of the Rings* better not have been written the way Tolkien did, and better not be read and enjoyed for what it is?

Reviews / Rezensionen

Lothar Mikos, Susanne Eichner, Elizabeth Prommer, Michael Wedel: Die »Herr der Ringe«-Trilogie – Attraktion und Faszination eines populärkulturellen Phänomens

Konstanz: UVK Verlagsgesellschaft, 2007, 299 Seiten, Paperback

Peter Jacksons Filmtrilogie *Der Herr der Ringe* hat in den Jahren seit ihrem Erscheinen große mediale Aufmerksamkeit erfahren. Dass es sich bei Jacksons Trilogie insbesondere in den Augen derjenigen, die sich als Filmemacher oder -kritiker professionell mit dem Medium Film beschäftigen, um ein filmhistorisch epochales Werk mit langfristiger Bedeutung für das Kino handelt, wird u.a. daran ablesbar, dass *Der Herr der Ringe* in zahlreichen renommierten Best-of-Listen der letzten Jahre erscheint oder diese sogar anführt.

Angesichts der Tatsche, dass ein Großteil des Publikums, der Filmschaffenden und -kritiker den *Herrn der Ringe* als eines *der* wichtigsten Kinoerlebnisse ihres Lebens empfindet, enttäuscht die bisherige (film-)wissenschaftliche Auseinandersetzung mit der Filmtrilogie. Dabei erstaunt es wenig, dass vonseiten der traditionell literarisch-philologisch orientierten Tolkienistik nur wenig Fundiertes zu den Filmen vorgelegt wurde, lehnen zahlreiche Tolkienwissenschaftler und -fans Jacksons Adaption doch wegen der inhaltlichen Abweichungen von der literarischen Vorlage ab. Für ein vertieftes Verständnis von Jacksons *Herrn der Ringe* als genuinem Filmkunstwerk und seiner filmästhetischen Qualitäten sind solche Ressentiments jedoch hinderlich.

Vor diesem Hintergrund ist es umso erfreulicher, dass mit dem Buch *Die »Herr der Ringe« Trilogie – Attraktion und Faszination eines populärkulturellen Phänomens* ein dezidiert film- und medienwissenschaftlicher Beitrag vorgelegt wurde, der die Ergebnisse eines Forschungsprojekts der Berliner Hochschule für Film und Fernsehen Konrad Wolf präsentiert. Wie der Titel des Buches bereits deutlich macht, geht es Mikos und seinen Mitautoren darum, Jacksons Filme nicht nur isoliert als eine dreiteilige Spielfilmreihe zu betrachten. Vielmehr verfolgen die Autoren das Ziel, die durch die Filme konstituierten medialen Kontexte in die Analyse mit einzubeziehen. Grundsätzlich erweist sich dieses methodische Vorgehen als zielführend. Denn es gelingt den Autoren, deutlich zu machen, wie sich die verschiedenen medialen Ausformungen des *Herrn der Ringe* (Romanvorlage, Kinofilme, DVD-Extended-Version, Computerspiel, Internetpräsenz, Fanforendiskussionen usw.) wechselseitig bedingen, was die Grundlage dafür bildet, dass ein aus verschiedenen medialen Angeboten bestehendes »Phänomen« der (Pop)-Kultur entstehen kann. Als gänzlich neu erweist sich eine solche Betrachtungsweise sicherlich nicht, hat doch nicht zuletzt Kristin Thompson in ihrer umfassenden Studie *The Frodo Franchise: The Lord of the Rings and Modern Hollywood* hierzu ein Standardwerk vorgelegt.

Angesichts der Tatsache, dass sich die zentrale These der hier diskutierten Berliner Studie im internationalen Vergleich als nicht besonders innovativ und neuartig erweist, läge es nahe, den Forschungswert des Buches als gering einzuschätzen. Aber auch wenn die Berührungspunkte zu Thompsons Studie groß sind, würde man Mikos und seinen Mitautoren mit einer ablehnenden Einschätzung nicht gerecht, überzeugt ihre Arbeit doch in den zahlreichen interessanten Untersuchungsergebnissen der einzelnen Kapitel und aufgrund der zugrunde liegenden statistischen Daten zur Rezeption der Filme (s.u.); und dies macht das Buch insgesamt dennoch zu einem sinnvollen und lesenswerten Werk, das dazu beiträgt die medienübergreifenden Rezeptionsstrukturen infolge der Filmtrilogie besser zu verstehen.

Die terminologische Grundlage der Berliner Studie bilden die Begriffe »transmediale Erzählung« und »konvergente Medienprodukte« (10). Als transmedial erweist sich das »Medienphänomen« (ebd.) *Der Herr der Ringe*, da es aus einer Vielzahl medialer Angebote besteht, die der Rezipient nutzen kann. Aus diesem Grund plädieren die Autoren zu Recht dafür, dass eine allein auf die Kinofilme beschränkte Analyse die gesellschaftliche Bedeutung des Tolkien-Franchise-Universums (vgl. 153) nicht hinreichend erklären kann. Dementsprechend machen sie sich Henry Jenkins Konvergenzbegriff zunutze, um die vielschichtigen Überschneidungen und Wechselbezüge der Tolkien-Medienprodukte aufzuzeigen. Als Methode für die Analyse eines solchen Medienphänomens haben die Autoren einen interdisziplinären Zugriff gewählt, der auf dem von Mikos und Prommer entwickelten so genannten »Babelsberger Modell« (11) basiert. Dessen »Multiperspektivität« (ebd.) unterscheidet sich jedoch meiner Einschätzung nach nicht grundlegend von anderen interdisziplinären Vorgehensweisen.

Die Berliner Studie nimmt für sich in Anspruch, die Ergebnisse einer empirischen internationalen Rezeptionsstudie zu verwenden, die 2003 im Rahmen der Premiere des letzten Teils der Kinotrilogie *Die Rückkehr des Königs* durchgeführt wurde. Neben einer Telefonbefragung und einer standardisierten Befragung mit offenen und geschlossenen Fragen an die Kinogänger im Premierenvorfeld wurden von den Autoren auch verschiedene Fangruppierungen in Gruppendiskussionen befragt. Ziel war es hierbei, die unterschiedlichen Rezeptionsinteressen verschiedener von den Autoren kategorisierter Zuschauergruppen zu evaluieren. Die Ergebnisse der Rezeptionsstudie werden am Ende des Buches in aller Ausführlichkeit auf knapp 100 Seiten dargestellt.

Grundsätzlich erweist sich die Masse an statistischen Informationen als sinnvoll, ist es doch sehr zu begrüßen, dass nun wissenschaftlich ermittelte quantitative und qualitative Daten zum Rezeptionsverhalten der »*Herr der Ringe*«-Zuschauer vorliegen. Auf die vielen Einzelergebnisse der Studie zum Rezeptionsverhalten verschiedener von den Autoren zusammengestellter Zuschauergruppen (z.B. »Filmsozialisierte«, »technikaffine Gamer« (13), Kenner der literarischen Vorlage, Frauen) und Länder kann an dieser Stelle nicht eingegangen werden. Fraglich im Hinblick auf die durchgeführten qualitativen Gruppendiskussionen ist es, inwiefern die Aussagen einer sehr kleinen Gruppe von Zuschauern bzw. Fans repräsentativ für die hypothetischen Publikumskategorien sein können. Ob darüber hinaus durch Gruppen wie »Hardcore-Gamer« (209) und »Leseratten« (ebd.) die wesentlichen Teile des Publikums tatsächlich erfasst wurden, kann durchaus angezweifelt werden.

Insgesamt sind die Aussagen der interviewten Personen jedoch interessant und belegen zusammen mit den quantitativ erhobenen Daten die sehr positive Einschätzung, die die Kinozuschauer weltweit den »*Herr der Ringe*«-Filmen entgegenbringen. Die Berliner Studie liefert demnach empirische Belege für die übermäßig hohe internationale und geschlechterübergreifende Zuschauerbegeisterung für die Jackson-Filmtrilogie. Diese wertvollen Daten sollten die Grundlage für zukünftige Untersuchungen bilden, um Erklärungsansätze für dieses umfassende breite Zuschauerinteresses zu finden.

Neben der Präsentation und (ersten) Auswertung der begrüßenswerten statistischen Daten liegen die Stärken des Buches in jenen Kapiteln, in denen die Autoren die verschiedenen Facetten des *Herrn der Ringe* »als konvergente[m] Medienprodukt« (5) aufzeigen und deren Bedeutung für das Gesamtphänomen analysieren. Auch im Falle der Einzelaspekte, die im Buch angesprochen werden, liegen bereits von anderen (vor allem amerikanischen) Autoren (u.a. Jonathan Gray, Craig Hight, Ernest Mathijs) Einzeluntersuchungen vor, so z.B. zur Frage, welche Konsequenzen das Nebeneinander von Kinofilmen und den DVD-Langfassungen für die Filmrezeption selbst hat.

Auf Grundlage dieser Studien lenken die Autoren u.a. das Augenmerk darauf, dass sich im Falle des *Herrn der Ringe* durch die exzessive Nutzung des Mediums DVD zahlreiche Spiegelungen zwischen den Spielfilmen und dem Produktionskontext ergeben. Durch die in den DVD-Dokumentationen vorgenommene Inszenierung von Peter Jackson und seinem Produktionsteam als heroischer

›Gefährtengruppe‹, die bei der Produktion der Filme scheinbar ein episches Abenteuer in Analogie zur Ringgemeinschaft erlebt, überträgt sich die mythische Aura der Filmtrilogie auf den Produktionsprozess selbst. Obwohl Mikos und seine Mitautoren sich bei der Behandlung solcher Fragestellungen stark auf bereits vorliegende Arbeiten stützen, gelingt es ihnen dennoch in Übereinstimmung mit Thompson, überzeugend nachzuweisen, dass die »ästhetische[n] Konvergenzen« (131) zwischen verschiedenen medialen »Texten«, z.b. die verschiedenen Filmfassungen (Kino, DVD), die PC- und Videospiele sowie weitere Merchandisingprodukte ein in sich geschlossenes »Franchise-Universum« (153) generieren, in dem der Rezipient aus verschiedenen Textangeboten wählen kann. Dass im Zuge der »*Herr der Ringe*«-Spielfilmtrilogie ein transmediales Gesamtkonstrukt zu Tolkiens Mittelerde-Mythologie entstanden ist, das die Wahrnehmung all derjenigen beeinflusst, die sich mit Tolkien auseinandersetzen, erweist sich als überaus wichtig für unser Verständnis von Tolkiens Werk und dessen Rezeption in der Gegenwart.

Darüber hinaus finden sich in dem Buch lesenswerte Kapitel zur Inszenierung Mittelerdes in den Filmen, zur Figurenzeichnung und Erzählperspektive und den damit verbundenen Intentionen der Filmemacher. Zwar stößt man auch in diesen Kapiteln auf manches, was man anderswo schon einmal ähnlich gelesen hat, dennoch bringen die Autoren auch beachtenswerte eigene Beobachtungen ein: z.B. die gelungene Analyse, wie mit filmischen und dramaturgischen Mitteln (exzessive Kamerafahrten, Massenszenen, Landschaftspanoramen, visuelle Effekte, Emotionalisierung von Figuren und Szenen) konsequent eine Ästhetik der Überwältigung zum Einsatz kommt, die für die von vielen Zuschauern wahrgenommene »epische Wirkung der Filme« (129) verantwortlich ist. Auch die von den Autoren vorgenommene Untersuchung des deutschen Diskurses über die Filmtrilogie in Printmedien und im Internet ist willkommen, wobei man hier noch sehr viel mehr in die Tiefe gehen könnte.

Insgesamt bleibt festzuhalten, dass sich die hier vorgelegte Analyse der Jackson-Spielfilme im Kontext eines Tolkien-Franchise-Universums im Vergleich mit Kristin Thompson und anderen Untersuchungen als keineswegs innovativ erweist. Ungeachtet dessen liegt der Gewinn der Berliner Studie in den erhobenen empirischen Daten zum Rezeptionsverhalten des Spielfilmpublikums und in den zahlreichen aufschlussreichen Deutungsansätzen zu verschiedensten Einzelaspekten der Filmtrilogie.

Julian Tim Morton Eilmann

Cécile van Zon (ed.):
Tolkien in Poetry and Song
Lembas Extra 2009. Tolkien Genootschap Unquendor,
88 pp., Softcover

As explained in the preface, this journal differs from the previous ones in the occasional series published by the Dutch Tolkien Society in that it is not the proceedings of a conference, but is a collection built specially around a special topic. Therefore in addition to six articles it also contains three Tolkien-inspired poems.

One of the articles is a significant contribution by Tom Shippey to the growing discussion on Tolkien's alliterative poetry. This short but highly concentrated appraisal traces Tolkien's development in adapting the complex formal requirements of Old English metre to the modern English language. Although the early *Lay of the Children of Húrin* has a monumental and often moving quality, Shippey points out that the individual lines lack variation and are sometimes metrically questionable because of the frequency of short syllables in today's language. In this he is following up a point made in his review of *The Legend of Sigurd and Gudrún* in the *Times Literary Supplement*, that Tolkien underlined the revelation of Sigurd's breaking of faith by a deliberate, jarring fault in the metre. However, the whole question of resolution in modern alliterative verse is a difficult one, since syllable length alone is not a significant parameter in the prosody of modern English. Also vowel length is not phonemic as it was on Old English. This is a problem that also arises in the modern reproduction of classical metres, which were based on quantity rather than stress. Tolkien may indeed have attempted to apply the traditional rules for syllable length, but this is something that few readers are likely to feel, even if they have absorbed the relatively easy rhythmic forms of the half-lines purely as stress patterns. Perhaps this is just one stage too far on the re-creative journey.

Renée Vink finds echoes of Tolkien's *Mythopoeia* in the post-modern pastiche *The Garden of Proserpina* from A.S. Byatt's novel *Possession*. From other references in Byatt's works she concludes that the author certainly has a knowledge of Tolkien, and therefore concludes that a deliberate intertextual reference is not impossible. Of course there can be no proof of such a thesis, and the argument wanders in places, but it is heartening to see Tolkien scholarship drawing together strands from such diverse writers as Sidney and Vico.

Marion Kippers gives an introduction to the legend of St. Brendan and the Irish genre of the *imram*. She traces the motif of sailing to an unknown land in several of Tolkien's poems and prose works, particularly the poem *Imram*, which developed from the uncompleted *Notion Club Papers* but was eventually published as a stand-alone piece, albeit with a reference to Tolkien's own mythology, thus linking it with Irish myth.

Sjoerd van der Weide gives an overview of *The Adventures of Tom Bombadil*, in the form of a running commentary on individual poems rather than an analysis of the collection in general. Its major weakness is that for the most part it maintains a viewpoint within Tolkien's secondary world and makes no reference to the actual origin of the poems.

Ben Koolen's *The Song of Durin* also remains within the text-world. He catalogues the dwarf songs in *The Hobbit* and *The Lord of the Rings* and places them within a history and mythology of the Dwarves which is essentially a paraphrase of material from the Appendices.

Middle-earth Language Training by Frits Burger is a meditation on what various sections of *The Lord of the Rings* have to say about the human language impulse. It concludes with an appeal for us all to touch "the source of language which is the Logos", illustrated by a poem in this author's own "Elvish", which bears little relation to Tolkien's. Other original poetic items are *Lhûn* by Dorine Ratulangie and *A Fading Voice – a Song of Maglor* by Renée Vink.

This is a very mixed bag, containing a number of items which will be of interest mostly to enthusiasts. However, it can be recommended for the more analytical article by Vink, and above all Shippey's expert views on Tolkien's increasing understanding of the techniques of writing alliterative verse.

Allan Turner

Isabelle Pantin: Tolkien et ses légendes. Une expérience en fiction.
Paris: CNRS Éditions, 2009, 320 pp., Softcover

The recent book by Isabelle Pantin, first publication of the CNRS new collec-tion entitled *Médiévalisme(s)*, comes as an event in the Tolkien criticism. Following the track of Vincent Ferré's *Tolkien: sur les rivages de la Terre du Milieu* (Paris, Christian Bourgois Éditeur, 2001), the author takes up the same challenge of considering J.R.R. Tolkien's work as a literary construction to be studied in the context of the literary production and the history of its own century; and she extends this question to the whole of the *Legendarium*, demonstrating a great knowledge of Tolkien's complete works.

Isabelle Pantin addresses the myth of a "Tolkien exception", according to which the historical and literary contexts would not be relevant to understand a work considered to be anachronistic since its subject matter belongs to some kind of Middle Ages. She strives to assess in fairness Tolkien's originality without attributing to his work a mysterious, even "magical" (p. 6), a-temporality. In a book entitled "Tolkien and his legends", the author denounces the "legends" conveyed by the critics, offering instead a detailed and literary analysis of the *Legendarium*, Tolkien's own "legends".

In this effort to identify where Tolkien's *Legendarium* stands in the history of literature, Isabelle Pantin, Professor at the École Normale Supérieure and specialist of the relationship between 16th century literature, philosophy, history and cosmology, takes an eager interest in the question of time in and around Tolkien's work. She offers a very powerful reflection on this issue which underlies the whole book, although it can be regretted that the author does not always make explicit the hidden link between the various developments and leaves it to the reader to make out the thread she is following.

The first aspect of time which is investigated lies in the historical and literary contexts in which Tolkien wrote. Pantin dedicates two chapters to a well-informed and subtle overview of the relationship between the books, the two World Wars, and the literary background and environment of the Professor (the Inklings, the question of the folklorist tradition...). She also provides a critical assessment of the main lines of interpretation suggested so far by Tolkien scholars, addressing for example the issues of fascism or racism. The link to the literary heritage is further developed in the third chapter which focuses on the manifold ways in which memory and time work within the fiction itself (including the texts of the *Legendarium* but also *The Lost Road* and *The Notion Club Papers*) and draws comparisons with an unusual selection of material: she brings into her study some other works of the 20th century (Marcel Proust, Julien Gracq...) in which she identifies the question of time as a common point, developed under the influence of Bergson.

Pantin justifies this highly contextualised analysis by a reflection on Tolkien's conception of literature. A study of C.S. Lewis' theoretical works shows how some books, like Tolkien's, should not be defined according to the genre to which they belong, but rather according to the experience they provide for the reader. The theoretical input of the fourth chapter allows for the definition of "poetical realism" which Isabelle Pantin offers in chapter 5 as Tolkien's own aesthetics. She examines for instance how the level and specificity of the character's speeches contribute to the building of a sense of realism within the text.

From chapters 6 to 10, Pantin explores the link between time and narrative on the one hand, time and geography on the other hand. After introducing the reader to the whole *Legendarium* and its complex history and development, she endeavours to define its precise relationship with *The Lord of the Rings*. She describes the writing of the *Silmarillion* and of the main part of *The History of Middle-earth* as a process expressing both a universal movement of eternal return and the destiny of literature itself throughout time: the invention of stories, their transformation and eventual loss or revival. Such texts constitute an unfinished mythology underlying the masterpiece of 1954-1955; indeed, *The Lord of the Rings* should not be understood as the conclusion of this great movement but as the "resolution", giving sense to the whole – maintain-ing an hesitation between the notion of Christian Providence and the idea that time always brings separation and decline.

The narrative thus developed through time takes place in a world whose geography itself constantly undergoes change and evolution. Pantin draws upon her vast knowledge of 16th century cosmology and scientific revolutions to offer an outstanding study of the double aspect of Tolkien's imagination, both mythical and astronomical. She offers a first-rate analysis of Tolkien's maps, with their various stages, and of the traditional interpretations and symbolism attached to the natural areas where the actions take place.

With the same precise attention to the matter of the *Legendarium*, Pantin eventually gives a number of appendices (in the purest Tolkien tradition), among which we find useful chronologies and presentations of *The Silmarillion* and the stories of Kullervo and Völsung.

Isabelle Pantin's book offers a collection of reflections convincingly setting Tolkien's work into its context. Yet, it is not quite clear whether *Tolkien et ses légendes* is meant for a public of specialists or not. Her helpful summaries of the main stories and critical issues, although often subtle and insightful, do not always open new tracks. In this respect, the last section – studying maps in detail – is probably the most useful to the scholar. Nevertheless, the whole book is one of the best publications in French, and its fight for the demystification and literary recognition of Tolkien's work will undoubtedly be appreciated by anyone interested in the Professor's sub-creation.   *Marguerite Mouton*

Elizabeth Solopova: Languages, Myths and History. An Introduction to the Linguistic and Literary Background of J.R.R. Tolkien's Fiction

New York: North Landing Books, 2009, 108 pp., Paperback

Dr. Elizabeth Solopova, of *Keys to Middle-earth* (2005 – together with Stuart Lee) fame, has written a very accessible introduction to some of Tolkien's most important ideas, as well as more specialist aspects of his fiction, such as its grounding in linguistics and medieval culture. The study opens with a brief introductory chapter, which sketches the structure of the book, which is followed by a succinct summary of Tolkien's life (focussing on his academic career). She then builds on this groundwork and discusses in chapters three to six the most important 'primary world languages' (Old Norse, Old English, Finnish, and Gothic) and the contribution of their individual literary and cultural heritages to the development of the Tolkien's works.

Solopova manages to present the most important aspects of Old Norse literature and mythology on a dozen pages without necessarily oversimplifying matters. This applies to the other chapters as well. They are all clearly written, avoid jargon and provide an excellent first informed (though, of course, selective) access to the themes under discussion. Each of the chapters devoted to the 'primary world languages' focuses on a specific central theme, such as the Northern Heroic Spirit, the Nature of Courage, Predestination and Free Will. A selection of relevant publications under the heading 'Further Reading' points the interested reader to complementary studies on the topic. The seventh chapter, on Gothic, is with 23 pages almost twice as long as the preceding ones. This is mainly due to Solopova's decision to include some lengthy passages (in Modern English translation) from Jordanes's *Getica*. Such a step may be justified by the fact that the 'Gothic' influence on Tolkien's fiction has, as yet, been less prominently treated (in contrast to that of Old English, Old Norse or Finnish literature). A brief survey of Tolkien's invented languages concludes the book, which features also an index.

The book is essential reading for students of literature and anyone with an interest in Tolkien as a writer. It makes an excellent introduction for all those who have just begun to explore Tolkien – and even I, as an old hand in the business, found some new and inspiring ideas. *Thomas Honegger*

Steve Walker: The Power of Tolkien's Prose: Middle-Earth's Magical Style
New York: Palgrave Macmillan, 2009, 213 pp.

The title of this book promises a great deal, since a detailed analysis of Tolkien's style has long been a major desideratum in Tolkien studies. The standard critical works by Shippey and Rosebury contain valuable sections on style, which only serve to whet the appetite for a whole book devoted to the close stylistic analysis of a highly distinctive author. Unfortunately this book, for all its plethora of detail, is unlikely to satisfy those who are looking for depth as well as breadth.

The research for Walker's book appears to have been begun early and continued over a long period of time, since although the bibliography contains a variety of books and articles published during the last ten years, nevertheless the analysis draws much more heavily on critical works from the sixties and seventies than would be likely in the case of a project begun recently. As a result of the author's familiarity with this large corpus, he is able to quote extensively, demonstrating many times over how different critics have come to totally opposite conclusions about points of Tolkien's style, often without any firmer basis than their subjective reactions. The negative side of this potential virtue is that in places Walker's text relies to such an extent on a mosaic of quoted scraps, often with four or more in a sentence, each consisting of only three or four words without any indication of context, that the argument threatens to become lost in a flood of detail, or else lapses into mere assertion by quotation.

In spite of the title, the first four chapters out of six are concerned not so much with style as with the structure and motifs of the narrative, since Walker sets himself the task of explaining what makes Tolkien's writing so accessible and attractive to a wide readership. It is justifiable that he confines his attention to *The Hobbit* and *The Lord of the Rings*, since these two titles form the basis of his reputation, while *The Silmarillion* poses a different set of stylistic questions anyway. The underlying thesis is that Tolkien deliberately wrote in such a way that his descriptions, though detailed in some respects, nevertheless avoid precision of a type that would permit a complete visualisation of the scene. This degree of open-endedness encourages readers to supply the gaps from their own imagination, and therefore draws them into the narrative world in a way that a more precise realisation would not. This is a thought-provoking claim in itself, although a dangerous one too, since it suggests the theory presented by C.S. Lewis in his essay *Different Tastes in Literature*, that inexperienced readers are satisfied by inferior art because their own superior imagination allows them to see what the work might have been rather than what it actually is.[1]

Ultimately Walker fails to convince because the book lacks a clear theoretical basis and consistent terminology, so that it misses the chance to rise above a useful but frustrating wealth of examples. Even a limited amount of exact linguistic description would be an improvement on certain passages of hazily impressionistic, polysyllabic fine writing. One example of a lost opportunity is his analysis of Tolkien's anthropomorphic descriptions of mountains with their "animate anatomy: 'feet' and 'knees' and 'naked sides' and 'shoulders' and 'heads' and 'thick hair'" (43). It is all very well for us to learn that through this linguistic usage "[w]e see clear to the 'heart' of the mountain" (ibid.), but it would be methodologically sounder, and also allow a closer understanding

---

1   In C.S. Lewis: *On Stories and Other Essays on Literature*. Orlando, FL: Harcourt, 1982, 119-125.

of Tolkien's art, to point out that the effect comes through a use of metaphors, some of which have become fully lexicalised in English, and others only partially or not at all. It should have provided an opportunity to link Tolkien's vision with the methods of cognitive linguistics, or to trace the possible influence of Owen Barfield with his theory that literal and metaphorical meaning developed parallel to one another in the human consciousness. As it is, we are left with just one more decontextualised example.

For all its claim to textual detail, the book shows many inaccuracies of reading. Several quotations are attributed to the wrong character; for example, it is said to be Frodo instead of Aragorn who experiences a "shudder" at the re-appearance of Gandalf in III/5 (137). Isildur regularly appears as *Isuldur*. Once again we are told that *The Lord of the Rings* was "primarily linguistic in inspiration" (142), whereas the phrase in Tolkien's foreword clearly refers to the *Silmarillion* material. Walker occasionally has difficulty in distinguishing between different strata of language: he mixes archaic or merely rare expressions (the obsolete measure *ell*, still in use in the 19th century, and the perennial favourite *eyot*, well known to anyone who has lived near the Thames) with Old English forms such as *éored* (153), and even confuses real with invented language in claiming that "[t]he formal term for *galenas* is *nicotania* [sic]" (152).

This book is worth perusing for anyone interested in how Tolkien gains his literary effects, purely for the profusion of ideas and examples. There is no doubt that it represents the distillation of one person's thoughts over a long period of time. Unfortunately, though, its shortcomings detract from its usefulness. The much-needed book on Tolkien's style has yet to make its appearance.

Allan Turner

Fastitocalon.
Studies in Fantasticism Ancient to Modern.
Vol I-1 (2010): Immortals and the Undead
Trier: WVT, 2010, 90 pp.

Mit diesem Band liegt der erste Teil der doppelbändigen Startausgabe einer von Thomas Honegger und Fanfan Chen ins Leben gerufenen neuen Zeitschrift zur epochenübergreifenden Forschung zur Phantastik vor. Die Zeitschrift trägt den aus Tolkiens Werk bekannten Namen *Fastitocalon* (nach dem gleichnamigen Gedicht aus *Adventures of Tom Bombadil* über die Schildkröte, die für eine Insel gehalten wird). Ihr Konzept besteht darin, die einzelnen

Ausgaben entweder primär einem bestimmten Autoren oder Werk oder einem enger umgrenzten, für die Phantastik relevanten Thema zu widmen. Wenngleich zu jeder Ausgabe ein Call for Papers veröffentlicht wird, werden die eingesandten Beiträge zusätzlich noch einer anonymen und externen Begutachtung unterzogen, was ein bewährtes Mittel der Qualitätssicherung ist.

Den Anfang bildet im Band I-1 die Thematik der Unsterblichen und Untoten, deren literarische, poetische, kulturelle und historische Aspekte untersucht werden. Nach einer kleinen Einführung ins Thema seitens der Herausgeber gibt Dirk Vanderbeke einen Überblick über die verschiedenen folkloristischen und literarischen Quellen über Vampire und macht ihre Entwicklung und Veränderungen deutlich. Es folgt ein Beitrag von Eugenio Olivares Merino, der sich anhand englischer Quellen aus dem 12. Jahrhundert über Wiedergänger der Frage der Entstehung früher englischer Vampirtraditionen widmet.

Anschließend folgen zwei Beiträge, die einzelne Werke behandeln: Siobhán Ní Chonaill untersucht die »politischen« Konsequenzen der Unsterblichkeit, wie sie William Godwin in seinem Roman *St Leon* deutlich macht, und kontrastiert dies mit Überlegungen Godwins zur Unsterblichkeit in seinem früheren Werk *Political Justice*. Françoise Dupeyron-Lafay setzt sich mit viktorianischer Gothic Fiction auseinander und zeigt unter Rekurs auf Swedenborg auf, wie in Joseph Sheridan Le Fanu's *Uncle Silas* das Thema Unsterblichkeit/Untote mit Fragen der Identität, des Selbst und des Geistes verbunden sind.

Schließlich folgt der Beitrag von Amy Amendt-Raduege, die sich den Tolkien'schen Ringgeistern widmet und dabei nicht nur Bezüge zur Folklore und Tolkiens eigenen Überlegungen zu Tod und Unsterblichkeit herstellt. Dementsprechend betont sie, wie das Nicht-Sterben der Ringgeister ihre Menschlichkeit vernichtet. Der Band wird abgerundet durch einen kleineren Beitrag von Douglas Anderson, in dem er verschiedene weitgehend in Vergessenheit geratene phantastische Schriftsteller vorstellt – in diesem Fall mit Bezug zur Thematik, d.h. die Werke der hier Vorgestellten behandeln explizit das Thema der Untoten und/oder der Unsterblichkeit.

Zusammenfassend kann gesagt werden, dass es sich um eine sehr gelungene Startausgabe einer Zeitschrift handelt, die nicht nur mit einem überzeugenden Konzept aufwarten kann, sondern auch eine Forschungslücke füllt.

Thomas Fornet-Ponse

Heidi Steimel and Friedhelm Schneidewind (eds.): Music in Middle-earth

Zurich/Jena: Walking Tree Publishers, 2010, 311 pp., Softcover

The essay collection under review takes the name *Music in Middle-earth* – a name in itself more musical, in its rhythm and alliteration, than most scholarly volumes! The name is also vague (perhaps striking through the omission of the name "Tolkien"): it might be taken to refer to music as described in Tolkien's texts, or the music used in Peter Jackson's film adaptations, or indeed settings of Tolkien or music that makes reference (in one way or other) to the world he created. One might also be tempted to examine the "musical" aspects of his poetry and prose: several authors have previously mentioned the rhythm and flow of Tolkien's narrative patterns and the ingenuity of his poems.[1] The breadth of subject-matter presented in Steimel's and Schneidewind's volume is accordingly large and varied, demonstrating approaches to the theme that range from the metaphysical to the scientific to the creative. Authors include practising musicians, musicologists, scientists, instrument makers and philosophers, promising a wealth of ideas and viewpoints that will give almost every reader something new to think about.

Of course there is one fundamental issue with the discussion of music in Middle-earth, and it is one that many of the authors in the present volume allude to. As long as we stay within the confines of Tolkien's secondary world, we do not actually *have* any music – all we have is Tolkien's words describing music and (more often) its effects on its listeners. The Appendices to *The Lord of the Rings* and the many volumes of the *History of Middle-earth* contain tables, maps, drawings – but no musical notation. We are given instructions on how to pronounce Sindarin, but not told what musical mode might have been preferred by the Grey-elves, or given a tune. This means that when discussing the possible development of music in Middle-earth and the ways in which the peoples of Middle-earth might have expressed themselves musically, these discussions must remain a hypothesis. Indeed, in his short piece *Embodying the Voices: Documentation of a Failure* that forms the volume's conclusion Schneidewind with refreshing honesty admits that his original idea to examine the possible voice ranges of Tolkien's non-human peoples became impossible, given the lack

---

[1] For just some examples of this: Jenny Turner discusses narrative rhythm in *Reasons for Liking Tolkien*, Rosebury analyses the cadences and rhythm of certain *Silmarillion* passages in *Tolkien: A Cultural Phenomenon* (107), and Russom discusses poetic structures in *Tolkien's Versecraft in* The Hobbit *and* The Lord of the Rings.

of concrete information and the physical differences possible within Tolkien's fantastic world – drawing conclusions from our world simply was not sufficient. Steimel sums the problem up accurately: "All that we can do today is to compare a secondary world to our own, explaining in our languages and concepts music that could have been completely different" (104).

This does not mean to say, however, that the discussion of music in and inspired by Middle-earth must remain purely abstract and indeed, this volume proves otherwise. I found myself wondering whether music in Middle-earth might be an inspiring topic precisely because of the dearth of concrete information, along the line of Keats's "Heard melodies are sweet, but those unheard / Are sweeter" (344).[2] The creative inspiration Tolkien's songs in particular have provided for many musicians would seem to confirm that his words invite further "musical sub-creation", as the editors call it – and in their afterword they state that they hope these essays inspire readers to engage in this activity (cf. 311).

I, for one, remember being delighted by the songs in *The Lord of the Rings* when I first read it as a twelve-year-old, and I made up my own tunes, which seemed to me to come almost directly from the text, without any conscious attempt at composition on my part. The inherent musicality of Tolkien's lyrics – the regular rhythm, the cunning rhyme schemes, the richness of alliteration and assonance (something I realised later as an undergraduate he had learnt from Victorian poetry) – immediately appealed to me as it had to many readers before (and after) me. I later found out my father had done exactly the same and had even sent some of his settings to the Professor himself![3] To use the example of just one musician who has been inspired by Tolkien, the harper Asni (Astrid Nielsch), she writes that "To me, the whole point of engaging with music that has been buried by time is to eventually create something new. Often, particularly with very old music, there is so little knowledge left that there are vast spaces to be filled by the imagination. It is a play with possibilities, all of them equally valid, rather than an attempt to arrive at one 'correct' version of a tune fit to be displayed in a museum" (*Travels in Middle-earth* CD booklet).[4]

Certainly the theme of music in Middle-earth has inspired a wide range of responses in the form of essays in the present collection. Faced with a large variety of approaches to the theme, Steimel and Schneidewind have sensibly divided the volume into four parts: Creation and Music (different interpreta-

---

2   Geier touches on this in his essay in the present volume: "We can only read a depiction of how a character experiences music which cannot be heard by the reader. However, precisely this provides literature with possibilities that go beyond real music" (286).
3   Tolkien sent a brief letter thanking my father for these settings. This was in 1965, before the "authorised" settings of Swann; Tolkien writes: "I am unable to read music, and my wife is no longer able to play. I shall have to wait for some time until my daughter returns before I can make any judgement on your settings: she sings and plays."
4   Please visit Asni's website *asni.net* for more information on her Middle-earth inspired art and music.

tions and explanations of the Music of the Ainur); Music in Tolkien's World (several articles that "hypothesise" about the development and performance of music in Middle-earth); Influences of Our World on Tolkien's Music (ways in which music and music theory might have influenced the way Tolkien writes about music); Interpretations of Tolkien's Music in Our World (music in the films, the radio play and settings by various musicians).

The first section, Creation and Music, starts with a bang – more specifically, the Big Bang. The role played by sound in the evolution and physical shape of the universe is the focus of Kristine Larsen's "'Behold Your Music!': The Themes of Ilúvatar, the Song of Aslan, and the Real Music of the Spheres". Larsen's essay discusses parallels between creation myths, the tales of Tolkien and C.S. Lewis, and scientific theories regarding the origins of the universe in a way that is interesting and informative as well as accessible a scientific layperson like myself – no mean feat. The focus remains on the Music of the Ainur in Reuven Naveh's "Tonality, Atonality and the Ainulindalë". This article examines the Music of the Ainur not from the much-touted Boethian perspective, instead using traditional sonata form and Schenkerian analysis to try and understand the heavenly music's function and symbolism. The essay also contains a pertinent comparison of Schoenbergian atonality and Melkor's music. Overall, I was impressed how relevant the techniques of musical analysis could be shown to be to literary analysis. A further challenge to Boethian and Pythagorean "music of the spheres" is presented by Jonathan McIntosh's "Ainulindalë: Tolkien, St. Thomas, and the Metaphysics of the Music", which builds a convincing argument based (as the title suggests) on Thomist philosophy. Here the actuality of Ëa is seen not as a flawed or less pure (because material) version of the Music: rather, Ëa is the Music's ultimate, perfected realisation.

In the second section, Music in Tolkien's World, we find three articles that consider possible developments of music in Arda, based on the snippets of information provided by Tolkien and assuming parallels in development between language and music. The first of these articles is Steven Linden's "Speculative History of the Music of Arda". This article is exactly what it says it is: speculation. Linden states it is "irresistibly tempting to try to fill [the gaps in Arda's music history]" (75), and his take on how music might have evolved is highly interesting and logical, although with the dearth of concrete information it is hard to come to many conclusions. I liked the idea presented that the songs of the Rohirrim may have sounded like calls of horns, their favoured instrument. Heidi Steimel discusses the instruments of Middle-earth in more detail in her article "'Bring out the Instruments!' Instrumental Music in Middle-earth". Much of this article reads as a list, with no great depth of interpretation – at some points I would have welcomed further discussion by the author. Two points in particular I found striking: Steimel mentions gender differences in music, such as the fact that female Elves appear to play instruments, whereas male Elves build instruments and compose music (here I found myself wondering whether Lúthien composed her own songs?); further, she touches on the link between heirloom weapons and heirloom instruments such as Merry's horn. Perhaps the author could be encouraged to produce a further paper elaborating on these points? The final article in this section focuses on one specific instrument: the harp. Norbert Maier, harpist and harp-builder, discusses "The Harp in Middle-earth". This is a really interesting and informed article, covering music history, musical analysis and interpretation. Maier discusses both the harp as an instrument in the primary world and its traditional associations, as well as how Tolkien uses the harp as a distinctive literary device. Interestingly, some of his thoughts find parallels in those of Asni, who also considers different kinds of harps in the booklet of her CD *Travels in Middle-earth*.

The third section examines the influences of our world and its music on Tolkien. Gregory Martin examines "Music, Myth and Literary Depth in the 'Land ohne Musik'" in a very intriguing article focusing on links between Tolkien's aim to (re)create a native tradition and the aspirations of composers such as Vaughan Williams and Butterworth, who drew on folk music and an English national idiom in their compositions. Especially interesting are the speculations Martin makes based upon Vaughan Williams's theory that the origins of music lie in speech patterns: Martin considers the possible implications of this for Elvish music (a comparison to mediaeval Welsh music, for example, is made). Martin also draws a link between Tolkien's recorded performance of *Namarië* and the tradition of Finnish rune-singers. After this tour-de-force I found Bradford Lee Eden's article on "Strains of Elvish Song and Voices" somewhat disappointing. The author states he will discuss the Victorian poets Tennyson, Swinburne and Morris and their musical style and symbolism; however, while long quotes with (some) musical references are given, no further analysis or discussion follows and these quotes are not compared explicitly to Tolkien. While I personally agree with Eden that there are influences on Tolkien by the poets mentioned, I would have liked to see some close analysis of rhyme, rhythm, and all the other literary devices that create musical poetic language in order to see this influence made more explicit. The points Eden makes about the contrast between the role of music in the early versions of the mythology and its role in *The Silmarillion* were certainly interesting, though. Julian Eilmann creates a clear and convincing argument in the following article, "Sleeps a Song in Things Abounding: J.R.R. Tolkien and the German Romantic Tradition". Eilmann shows how Tolkien's theory of sub-creation and especially its elements of recovery and re-enchantment are in line with the ideology of German Romanticism. The final paper in this section is Murray Smith's "'They Began to Hum Softly': Some Soldiers' Songs of World Wars I and II and of Middle-earth Compared and Contrasted". As stated in the article's title, an interesting comparison is drawn between world war songs and songs in Middle-earth. The hobbits' songs about material comforts (such as food and drink) parallel some soldiers' songs, though Murray points out a notable absence of ribaldry and (perhaps more remarkably) patriotism – this is of course linked to Tolkien's own lack of patriotism.

The final section of the book is devoted to various interpretations of Tolkien's music in our world by a number of different artists. Michael Cunningham's fascinating essay "An Impenetrable Darkness: An Examination of the Influence of J.R.R. Tolkien on Black Metal Music" demonstrates how the vividness of Tolkien's depictions of evil become attractive for counter-cultures such as Black Metal. I found particularly interesting the links established between Tolkien's darkness and the darkness inherent in and associated with Norse and Viking cultures. The next essay, Paul Smith's "Microphones in Middle-earth", discusses the music of the BBC radio play version of *The Lord of the Rings*. Composer Stephen Oliver's use of various idioms to express "Englishness" is commended – the score contains references to folk music, the pastoral school of (for example) Vaughan Williams, Purcell and baroque music, and modern composers such as Britten. Smith ends his essay with a spirited plea to finally publish Oliver's music to enable a wider audience to enjoy it. Mira Sommer considers how to represent the otherworldly Elves in her essay "Elven Music in Our Times". She provides an overview of the different melodies, tonalities, instruments and voices used to represent Elvish music. A thorough discussion of Howard Shore's music in Jackson's *Lord of the Rings* films is followed by a consideration of other Tolkien-themed "Elvish" music. Sommer's study ranges here from the *Tolkien Ensemble* to the metal band *Battlelore* who use Tolkienian subject-matter in their songs, singing in their native Finnish (which is of course similar to Quenya). Fabian Geier provides the final essay in this section where he discusses his own "musical fan fiction", his attempts to find an appropriate musical tone for the songs in Tolkien's *Lord of the Rings*. As such, Geier's essay and his music can also be seen as speculation or hypothesis – as all musical settings must be – but it is interesting to gain insight into one individual's compositional struggles and the amount of intellectual consideration that must go into setting these kinds of texts.

Overall, I found this volume fascinating and I enjoyed reading every single essay, as each one gave me new ideas and thoughts to consider, even where I did not find myself wholly convinced by the author's point of view. There are the usual small quibbles with typos and mistakes, but in days where even the big academic presses do not employ proof-readers and their publications are riddled with errors, it seems unfair to make much of them here. I would also like to comment on the fact that a special discussion forum has been set up for this book (the editors refer readers to it in their afterword). I have followed the discussions of the essays on the forum and have been impressed by the level of the exchanges and criticism (both positive and negative). I think it would be a great idea if every such publication had a forum space dedicated to it!

Margaret Hiley

Other works cited:

Asni. *Travels in Middle-earth*. Wellington, NZ: Harp and Hobbit Records, 2007
Keats, John. *The Complete Poems*. London: Penguin, 1973
Rosebury, Brian. *Tolkien: A Cultural Phenomenon*. Basingstoke: Palgrave Macmillan, 2003
Russom, Geoffrey. "Tolkien's Versecraft in *The Hobbit* and *The Lord of the Rings*".
    J.R.R. *Tolkien and His Literary Resonances*. G. Clarke and D. Timmons. Westport, CT: Greenwood Press, 2000, 53-69
Tolkien, J.R.R. Unpublished letter of 30 September 1965 (author's own)
Turner, Jenny. "Reasons for liking Tolkien". *London Review of Books* Vol. 23, No. 22 (2001): 15-24

Martha Sammons: War of the Fantasy Worlds: C.S. Lewis and J.R.R. Tolkien on Art and Imagination
Santa Barbara/Denver/Oxford: Praeger, 2010, 237 pp., Hardcover

War of the Fantasy Worlds is not intended as a critical analysis of Tolkien's *The Lord of the Rings* and Lewis's *Chronicles of Narnia* but rather as an examination of elements relating to the writers' views about imagination, fantasy, and creativity. For this purpose, the author relies heavily on Tolkien's published *Letters* and his essay *On Fairy-Stories*, and several essays by Lewis, as well as their fictional works. Although some literary theories and concepts are sketched and explained, the argument mostly follows the writers' own statements, which are more often than not taken at face value, with little regard to the situations that occasioned them and their rhetorical strategies.

The study is divided into seven thematic, partially overlapping chapters. "The Artist" provides concise biographical sketches up to the mid-Fifties, concentrating on the genesis of the literary works and the two writers' different approaches to writing, Tolkien working slowly from a preliminary outline and from names and objects, Lewis much more rapidly from images that sprang up in his mind. "Art", the second chapter, depicts their differing definitions of and attitude towards fairy-stories, a term which Tolkien takes more or less as synonymous with "fantasy" in his very own concept of the writer as a lesser creator in the image of God who created Man. Lewis, on the other hand, is seen writing as an adult to children and using fairy-stories as the form that fits best what he wants to say, in particular in moral terms. The author also summarizes Tolkien's didactic poem *Mythopoeia*, but provides no deeper interpretation. *Mythopoeia* is characterized as an essentially Platonic concept. On the other hand, Tolkien's fantasy is seen as the epitome of an Aristotelian approach, for its love of detail and its derivation from elements of the created world. In contrast, Lewis is characterized as a Platonist, which may have some justification with regard to the Narnia books and their concept of earth as "Shadowlands" of the true world, although he, too, pleads for a "realism of presentation" (in *An Experiment in Criticism*). Both writers are viewed as influenced by medieval concepts, such as the Music of the Spheres or the Great Chain of Being, which are sketched summarily in the chapter "Art Theory and Metaphors", as well as by the Romanticism of Coleridge and George Macdonald. The same chapter also lists as ethical metaphors various motives such as light, which in Tolkien's writings is rather a permeating force unfolding in time, whereas Lewis also holds up the concept of reflection more in a line with a Platonic view.

The other theme that is followed by the line of argumentation revolves around "Applications", "Allegory and Applicability", and "Advantages of Fantasy", that is to say the uses of creativity. The first of these three chapters gives summaries of various works and also tries to deal with the depiction of evil, resulting, among else, in a strange statement that "Tolkien believes that evil in fantasy teaches us that we have an eternal element" (p. 59); he actually said that about literature (cf. L 106).

In general, the author makes a rather unscholarly use of documentation. In some paragraphs, almost each sentence is bolstered up with a reference, often from the same source. Then again, there are sentences which are obviously very close paraphrases but which are not documented at all. For instance, MacDonald's explanation of "Fancy" and "imagination" (sic!) on page 72 is almost verbally lifted from the same context as the immediately preceding quotation but to the undiscerning reader it appears as an authorial comment. In between, there are cases of undocumented sentences in which a reader should have liked to know where the idea actually came from.

It is sometimes difficult to pinpoint what is exactly wrong with the text, since the sentences are mostly so short and unconnected that they read like apodictic statements lacking for context. In the description of Tolkien's Elves from *The*

Silmarillion on page 48, for instance, most of the statements are correct by themselves and just appear jumbled. But then, somewhere in between, there is a puzzling claim that seems simply wrong, for it is said about the Noldor elves, "because they love machinery, science, and technology, they can produce things that can be used for evil". Following up the reference at the end of the sentence, the reader is directed to *The Silmarillion*, page 190. Actually, the reference is to *Letters*, page 190, where a much more subtle statement is given, namely that the Noldor elves "were always on the side of 'science and technology', as we should call it" (note the inverted commas and the qualification), and that the "'desire'" for such knowledge among the Elves of Eregion is said to be "an 'allegory', if you like it of a love of machinery and technical devices". Here, as often, one wonders if the author has simply done injustice to the original thought by reducing the argument, or just missed the meaning.

Again, a sentence such as "Sauron, another angelic spirit, becomes Aule's servant and later instigates a revolt in Númenor" (p. 49) is factually correct, but without the intermediate state of Sauron becoming Morgoth's servant simply fails to make sense. In addition, there are several glaring mistakes, from harmless ones – *The Lord of the Rings* was not published in 1950 (p. 7) – to blunders – Mary Renault (p. 32) was no science fiction author – to serious misrepresentations – Tolkien certainly does not say that "the Norse gods ... are really allegories" (p. 22) but stresses their dual personal and representative nature (in *On Fairy-Stories*).

The title of the study presumably paraphrases H.G. Wells' *War of the Worlds*, but the implied antagonism of Tolkien's and Lewis's concepts and creations rather seems to have been anything from an amicable coexistence to a slightly jealous rivalry rather than an outright war. The final chapter on "Advantages of Fantasy" clearly shows that they were not that far apart in their conviction that fairy-stories, myth, and fantasy are modes of conveying a higher truth – or Truth in the sense of the Christian gospel. An attitude the author seems to endorse fully.

Hopefully, the author cannot be held responsible either for the title or the cover (with "WAR" in capital letters). Nevertheless, she must take the blame for a study which asks the right questions but fails to give trustworthy answers. Trying to defend Tolkien and Lewis in their own words, adopted by the critic himself, is more typical of early writings about these writers, which is why the study feels curiously old-fashioned. Although the author takes some later studies into account, these references, often at the end of the chapters, are peripheral to the argument. An obtuse and at times inept language and unreliable documentation further obscure any potential value this study might have had. In this "war", the major casualty is the reader.

Helmut W. Pesch

Publishing about Tolkien
Polemic Musings about New Developments by an Old Hand in the Business
Thomas Honegger (Jena)

Rayner Unwin, in his memoirs (*George Allen & Unwin: A Remembrancer.* Ludlow: Merlin Unwin Books, 1999), has two chapters on 'Publishing Tolkien' in which he gives some insight into the publication history of, among others, *The Hobbit* and *The Lord of the Rings*. The 'publishing Tolkien' story is still going on – thanks to the endeavours of Christopher Tolkien and some few chosen scholars who have been allowed to work on a selection of the unpublished manuscripts. However, in this brief essay I would like to focus on another topic, namely the state of things in 'publishing about Tolkien'.

The original inspiration for such a survey goes back to my dissatisfaction with some of the new publications on the Professor's work. Let me take the most recent one, Martha C. Sammons' *War of the Fantasy Worlds. C.S. Lewis and J.R.R. Tolkien on Art and Imagination* (Santa Barbara, CA: Praeger, 2010). The first impression is mostly positive. The book is bound in black cloth, has an index, and the text is without spelling mistakes and set in a reader-friendly font – but this is about all that can be said in favour of the book.

The list of negative points starts with the artwork on the dust jacket, which sports a woman in a business-outfit holding a sword, and a fire-breathing dragon hovering above. The picture has, of course, nothing to do with either Tolkien or Lewis and the 'cover-artist' seems to see his/her work in the tradition of all those infamous cover-illustrations that avoid reflecting the content and are a glaring testimony to the bad taste of the 'artist'. This 'theme' is continued in the choice of the title – which again is, to put it mildly, misleading. The book tries to provide a 'contrastive' discussion of Tolkien's and Lewis' take on art and imagination, but has nothing to do with 'war' at all. The content, then, is trivial and riddled with factual mistakes and misunderstandings of Tolkien's concepts. Since Helmut Pesch's in-depth review of this work can be found in the review-section of this volume, I will not go into any further details.

The shocking thing is not so much the disparity between content and form (pace 'cover-illustration'), but that this monograph has been published by a big 'respectable' company: Praeger, which is part of the Greenwood publishing group. I know, of course, that the great publishers are run like any other profit-oriented business and that the times are long gone when book-typescripts were proofread, criticised and polished by series-editors who were actually knowledgeable about literature rather than marketing. So unless publishers have a good peer-review scheme with expert outside readers in operation (as is the case, e.g., with Palgrave Macmillan), no one involved in the production process will spot the factual mistakes or the overall lack of quality in a study such as *War of the Fantasy Worlds*. Spell-checker programmes will produce a text free of spelling mistakes, and a layout programme will provide a reader-friendly format – yet there is nobody to pay special and knowledgeable attention to the actual content.

What, then, is the situation at the other end of the 'publishing house' scale, i.e. how are the small and micro-publishers handling things? Since the advent of desktop publishing and 'print on demand', publishing books is, in theory, open to everybody. All you need is a computer, some text-processing software, and an internet-link to one of the printers offering their services. Some texts never see a printing press and are distributed electronically and quite a few of the big publishers also use the advantages of the new technologies (esp. print on demand). It is, however, predominantly the smaller ones that are thus able to keep their costs low – which is not always reflected in the public prices of their products.

Theresia Mardhany's *Motives behind Four Characters' Decision Makings which Reveal Their Good and Evil Actions in J.R.R. Tolkien's The Lord of the Ring* [sic] (Lambert Academic Publishing, 2009) comes at the proud price of 49 Euro – for a study of merely 55 text pages. Lambert Academic Publishing, an imprint of Verlag Dr. Müller (VDM), both with their home-base in Saarbrücken, Germany, seems to keyword-search university-archives and other publicly accessible databases for 'suitable' BA or MA theses. They then contact the prospective author and offer to publish his/her study (at no cost to the author). The proofreading, layouting etc., however, has all to be done by the author himself/herself and it is very questionable whether anyone else but the author has ever taken a look at the text during the entire process. The 'published' results are therefore accordingly: if the author has written a brilliant thesis, the 'book' will be worth reading. If not, then we have yet another study on Tolkien we do not need. The same is more or less true for other publishers with impressive-sounding names, such as Cambridge Scholars Publishing (based in reality in Newcastle upon Tyne and with no connection to Cambridge University at all).

What Tolkien studies therefore need is a quality management on all levels. Ideally, this begins with a critical evaluation of the submitted typescript by (hopefully) knowledgeable series editors, who then pass it on (in case of a primary positive evaluation by the series editors) to one of the internationally acknowledged Tolkien experts who serve as peer-reviewers on a Board of Academic Advisors, and to a general reader whose task it is to comment on the 'readability' of the study from an informed lay-person perspective. These readers/reviewers assess the typescript and provide a detailed feedback and comments, which are passed on to the author in anonymised form and s/he, together with the series editors, decide on the necessary revisions and changes. Upon successfully completing the reviewing process, the author and the publisher sign a contract regulating the copyright, honorarium etc. The publisher, in addition to the author, proofreads the revised typescript and creates a professional layout (there are other programmes than Word!) and provides, in agreement with the author and in co-operation with acknowledged visual artists, a suitable (custom-made) cover-illustration and cover-layout. The publisher also takes care of an appropriate distribution of the book in Europe and the USA at an attractive and competitive price.

Am I being too idealistic? Maybe, but the general thrust of my argument is valid and such 'measures' are all the more necessary in a world where the rapid spread of new technologies has done away with many elements of the former 'quality management'. I am not advocating a new form of censorship but rather hope for the emergence of a new 'minimal standard' that is to the advantage of both reader and author.

Thomas Honegger

Note: I have based my comments and discussions upon original research, e-mail-interviews/questionnaires with/sent to authors, editors and publishers – if they were willing to co-operate, that is. Some of the publishers refused to discuss the elements of their 'editorial policies', probably because they don't have any beyond the expected profitability of a publication.

Unsere Autoren und Autorinnen

Oliver Bidlo, Dr. phil., Studium der Kommunikationswissenschaft, Germanistik, Soziologie und Philosophie; arbeitet als wissenschaftlicher Mitarbeiter am Institut für Kommunikationswissenschaft der Universität Duisburg-Essen, ist Dozent u.a. für Kriminologie und Soziologie an der Ruhr-Universität Bochum und der Universität Duisburg-Essen; seit 2006 selbstständiger Verleger (*Oldib Verlag*) und Herausgeber einer Fachzeitschrift für Theater und Theaterpädagogik (*Thepakos*).
www.oldib-verlag.de

Marie-Noëlle Biemer studierte Englisch, Russisch und Wirtschaftswissenschaften an der Justus-Liebig-Universität in Gießen und Business Studies an der University of Bradford, UK. In ihrer Diplomarbeit *William Morris's Prose Romances and Their Influence on Tolkien* untersuchte sie Morris' späte phantastische Romanzen und einige auffallende Gemeinsamkeiten zu Tolkiens Werken über Mittelerde. Gegenwärtig arbeitet sie als Nachrichtenredakteurin, ist 2. Vorsitzende der Deutschen Tolkien Gesellschaft und Redakteurin des *Flammifer of Westernis*.
canamarth@yahoo.co.uk

Annie Birks lehrt Englische Sprache und Literatur an der Katholischen Universität des Westens in Angers (Frankreich). Sie erwarb kürzlich ihr Doktorat an der Sorbonne über *Vergeltung in den Werken J.R.R. Tolkiens*. Ihre gegenwärtigen Forschungsinteressen fokussieren im Wesentlichen die theologischen Perspektiven der Schriften Tolkiens.
annie.birks@neuf.fr

Julian Tim Morton Eilmann studierte in Aachen und Nottingham Geschichte, Germanistik und Kunstgeschichte und ist gegenwärtig Referendar für das Gymnasiallehramt. Neben seinen akademischen Arbeiten ist er seit drei Jahren bei einer Film- und TV-Produktion als Autor von Reportagen und historischen Dokumentation tätig und darüber hinaus Inhaber einer Kunstgalerie und Kurator einer Künstlerstiftung. Schwerpunkte seiner Tolkien-Forschungen sind Tolkiens Lieder und Gedichte sowie die Filmadaption von Peter Jackson.
julianeilmann@aol.com

Thomas Fornet-Ponse, Dr. theol., studierte Katholische Theologie, Philosophie und Alte Geschichte in Bonn und Jerusalem, war 2006/07 Studienleiter beim Theologischen Studienjahr in Jerusalem und promovierte in Fundamentaltheologie und Ökumene. Er veröffentlichte zahlreiche Aufsätze zu Tolkien,

Pratchett und Lewis, war bis 2009 Beisitzer im Vorstand der Deutschen Tolkien Gesellschaft und ist inhaltlicher Koordinator des Tolkien Seminars wie von *Hither Shore*.
thomas.fornet-ponse@tolkiengesellschaft.de

Fabian Geier, Dr. phil., arbeitet gegenwärtig als Hochschulassistent für Philosophie an der Universität Bamberg. Vorher hatte er verschiedene Lehraufträge an unterschiedlichen Institutionen in Heidelberg, Mannheim, Witten/Herdecke und Duisburg/Essen inne. Seine Dissertation behandelte den Zufall als Individuationsproblem. Er ist Autor einer Monographie über Tolkien (bei Rowohlt erschienen) und diverser Aufsätze.
fabian.geier@philosophie.de

Margaret Hiley erwarb ihren Doktor in Glasgow mit einer Arbeit über die Inklings und ihre kontroverse Beziehung zur literarischen Moderne (wird bei *Walking Tree Publishers* erscheinen). Sie hat über verschiedene Aspekte der Fantasy und Science Fiction vorgetragen und publiziert, an den Universitäten Glasgow und Regensburg unterrichtet und arbeitet gegenwärtig als Dozentin für Englisch am University Centre Peterborough, wo sie zudem die Studiengänge in Arts und Sciences koordiniert.
margaret.hiley@peterborough.ac.uk.

Thomas Honegger, Prof. Dr. phil, hat in Zürich promoviert und zahlreiche Bände zu Tolkien, mittelalterlicher Sprache und Literatur herausgegeben und verschiedene Beiträge zu Chaucer, Shakespeare und mittelalterlichen Romanzen publiziert. Seit 2002 lehrt er als Professor für Mediävistik an der Friedrich-Schiller-Universität Jena.
www2.uni-jena.de/fsu/anglistik/homepage/Honegger3.htm

Marguerite Mouton erwarb ihre *Agrégation* in Moderner Literatur und einen Magister in Politikwissenschaften in Paris und verfolgt gegenwärtig ein Magisterstudium in Vergleichender Literaturwissenschaft an der Université Paris 13.
marguerite.mouton@laposte.net

Helmut W. Pesch, Dr. phil., hat in Köln über Fantasy-Literatur promoviert und arbeitet seitdem in diesem Gebiet als Kritiker, Autor, Übersetzer und Künstler. Ferner arbeitet er als Lektor beim Bastei-Lübbe-Verlag, Bergisch Gladbach.
www.helmutwpesch.de

Emanuele Rimoli OFM Conv., ist Franziskaner-Konventuale aus Kalabrien und beendet sein Studium der anthropologischen Theologie in Rom. Er ist Gastdozent an der Theologischen Fakultät von Sankt Bonaventura *Seraphicum*

in Rom und am Theologischen Institut von Assisi sowie Koautor dreier Bücher über Literatur und Spiritualität. Sein Forschungsgebiet sind russische Autoren, besonders Dostojewski.
emanuelerimoli@yahoo.it

Thomas Scholz, arbeitet als Journalist und Literaturkritiker für Tageszeitungen, unter anderem für die *Frankfurter Allgemeine Zeitung*. Seine erste Monographie *Weit entfernte Wunder* zu Tolkiens *The Hobbit* wurde als vierter Band von Professor Elmar Schenkels Reihe *ALPH: Arbeiten zur literarischen Phantastik* veröffentlicht.
t.scholz@pandora-solutions.de

Stefanie Schult studierte Biologie und Englisch (1. Staatsexamen) und arbeitet gegenwärtig an ihrer Dissertation in Englischer Literatur in Greifswald (bei Prof. Jürgen Klein). Ihre Forschungsinteressen fokussieren die Aspekte und Funktionen der Sub-creation in moderner und postmoderner Fantasyliteratur. Weiterhin lehrt sie Englische Literatur und Didaktik an der Ernst-Moritz-Arndt-Universität Greifswald.
kokuyochan@aol.com

Eduardo Segura, Dr. phil., ist Professor für Ästhetik, Politische Philosophie und Literatur und Philosophie im Christlichen Europa am Institut Edith Stein in Granada. Er war Berater für die Verfilmung des *Herrn der Ringe* durch New Line Cinema und hat mehrere Bücher über Tolkien geschrieben und herausgegeben.
edusegura@yahoo.es

Anna Slack erhielt ihren MA in Cambridge im März 2009. Zwischen 2006 und 2008 arbeitete sie als Lehrerin für Englisch als Fremdsprache an einer privaten Sprachschule in Palermo, Sizilien. Gegenwärtig unterrichtet sie Englische Sprache und Literatur an der St. Gabriel's School, ist die englische Chefredakteurin von PortalEditions, wofür sie einen Aufsatzband zu C.S. Lewis herausgibt und die Autorin verschiedener Artikel zu Tolkien.
AnnaSlack@cantab.net

Guglielmo Spirito OFM Conv., Prof. Dr. theol., studierte vor seinem Eintritt in den Franziskanerorden Philosophie und Ägyptologie, erwarb in Rom sein theologisches Lizenziat am Camillianum und sein Doktorat (mit der Spezialisierung in Spiritualität) am Antonianum. Seit 1994 ist er Professor für Patristik, Franziskanische Spiritualität und Literatur (vor allem Tolkien) am Theologischen Institut Assisi und an der Päpstlichen Fakultät des Heiligen Bonaventura in Rom. Er lehrte auch in Kroatien, Rumänien, Russland, Mexiko, England, Kanada,

Armenien und Ägypten. Über Tolkien hat er verschiedene Essays, Aufsätze und Bücher publiziert; er ist auch Mitglied der Italienischen Tolkiengesellschaft.
fraguspi@gmail.com

Martin G.E. Sternberg hat von 1990 bis 1996 Alte Geschichte, Mittlere Geschichte, Kunstgeschichte und Rechtswissenschaften studiert. Er arbeitet als Referent bei einer Bundesbehörde. Ein Schwerpunkt seines Geschichts- und Philosophiestudiums lag in der Spätantike und im frühen Christentum.
lasgalen@web.de

Doreen Triebel studierte Englische und Amerikanische Literatur und Sprache, Psychologie und Deutsch als Fremdsprache an der Friedrich-Schiller-Universität Jena, der University of Nottingham und der Illinois State University. Gegenwärtig verfolgt sie ein Dissertationsprojekt in Englischer Literatur und lehrt an der Universität Jena.
Doreen-T@gmx.de

Allan Turner, Ph.D., studierte Deutsche Philosophie, Mediävistik and Allgemeine Linguistik. Seine Dissertation in Übersetzungswissenschaften untersucht die inhärenten Probleme bei der Übersetzung philologischer Elemente in *The Lord of the Rings*. Sein Interessenschwerpunkt liegt gegenwärtig auf dem Stil der Werke Tolkiens. Er unterrichtet Englische Sprachpraxis und British Cultural Studies an der Friedrich-Schiller-Universität Jena.
allangturner@aol.com

Our Authors

Oliver Bidlo, Dr. phil., studied Science of Communication, German Studies, Sociology and Philosophy. He is working as an assistant professor at the Institute of Communication Science at the University of Duisburg-Essen and teaches also Criminology and Sociology at Bochum University. Since 2006, he is independent publisher (*Oldib Verlag*) and Editor of a Journal for theatre and theatre pedagogics (*Thepakos*).
www.oldib-verlag.de

Marie-Noëlle Biemer studied English, Russian and Business at the Justus Liebig University, Giessen, and Business Studies at the University of Bradford, UK. She wrote her diploma thesis on *William Morris's Prose Romances and Their Influence on Tolkien*, taking a look at Morris's late fantastic romances and some striking similarities that can be found in Tolkien's works on Middle-earth. She now works as a news editor in Frankfurt. As a member of the board of the German Tolkien Society, she spends her free time organising events for Tolkien enthusiasts and is an editor of the society's magazine *Der Flammifer von Westernis*.
canamarth@yahoo.co.uk

Annie Birks teaches English Language and Literature at the Université Catholique de l'Ouest, in Angers, France. She has recently received a doctorate from the Sorbonne on *Reward and Punishment in the Works of J.R.R. Tolkien*. Her current research interests focus essentially on the theological perspectives of Tolkien's writings.
annie.birks@neuf.fr

Julian Tim Morton Eilmann studied History, German Philology, and History of Arts at Aachen and Nottingham, UK, and is currently working as student teacher. Furthermore, since three years he is working as a journalist and author of films and TV productions, and as a developer of historical TV documentation. In addition, he is fulfilling the functions of gallery owner and conservator for an artists' foundation. His works on Tolkien focus an Tolkien's songs and poems and the adaptation by Peter Jackson.
julianeilmann@aol.com

Thomas Fornet-Ponse, Dr. theol., studied Catholic Theology, Philosophy, and Ancient History at Bonn and Jerusalem. He worked as an inspector of Studies at Theologisches Studienjahr Jerusalem and has recently finished his doctorate studies in Fundamental Theology and Ecumenics in Salzburg. He was a committee member of the German Tolkien Society and has been charged with conceptually coordinating the Tolkien Seminars as well as *Hither Shore*.
thomas.fornet-ponse@tolkiengesellschaft.de

Fabian Geier, Dr. phil., is currently assistant professor (Hochschulassistent) for Philosophy at the University of Bamberg. Before that he taught courses at various institutions in Heidelberg, Mannheim, Witten/Herdecke, Duisburg/Essen and wrote a monography on Tolkien in the *Rowohlt Monographien* Series, a book on chance, and some articles.
fabian.geier@philosophie.de

Margaret Hiley holds a Ph.D. from the University of Glasgow dealing with the Inklings and their controversial relationship to literary modernism (to be published by *Walking Tree Publishers*). She has published and lectured on various aspects of fantasy and science fiction. She has taught at the Universities of Glasgow and Regensburg and now is Lecturer in English at the University Centre Peterborough, where she also coordinates the degrees in the Arts and Sciences.
margaret.hiley@peterborough.ac.uk.

Thomas Honegger holds a Ph.D. from the University of Zurich. He edited several volumes on Tolkien, medieval language and literature, and published papers on Chaucer, Shakespeare, and mediaeval romance. He teaches, since 2002, as Professor for Mediaeval Studies at the Friedrich Schiller University Jena.
www2.uni-jena.de/fsu/anglistik/homepage/Honegger3.htm

Marguerite Mouton has the *Agrégation* of Modern Literature, an MA in Political Sciences (Sciences-Po Paris), and is currently an MA student in Comparative Literature (Université Paris 13).
marguerite.mouton@laposte.net

Helmut W. Pesch holds a Ph.D. from Cologne University. He wrote his doctoral dissertation on fantasy literature and has been working in this field as a critic, writer, translator, and artist. He is a full-time editor with *Luebbe Publishers*, Bergisch Gladbach (Germany).
www.helmutwpesch.de

Emanuele Rimoli is a Conventual Franciscan from Calabria (Italy) and is finishing his degree in Anthropological Theology at Rome. He started teaching as guest professor in the Theological Faculty of Saint Bonaventure *Seraphicum* in Rome and in the Theological Institute of Assisi. He is the co-author of three books on literature and spirituality. His field are the Russian writers, especially Fedor Dostoevsky.
emanuelerimoli@yahoo.it

Thomas Scholz works as a journalist and literary critic for various newspapers, including the *Frankfurter Allgemeine Zeitung*. His first monograph *Weit entfernte Wunder* on Tolkien's *The Hobbit* has just been published as volume four of Professor Elmar Schenkel's series *ALPH: Arbeiten zur literarischen Phantastik*.
t.scholz@pandora-solutions.de

Stefanie Schult recently finished her degree in Biology and English with the *1. Staatsexamen*. At present she works on her Ph.D. in English Literature under the supervision of Professor Dr. Jürgen Klein at the University of Greifswald. Her research interests are focussed on the aspects and functions of Sub-creation in modern and post-modern fantasy literature. Since the beginning of 2010, she teaches both English literature and didactics as a teaching assistant at Ernst Moritz Arndt University Greifswald (Germany).
kokuyochan@aol.com

Eduardo Segura, Dr. phil., is professor for Aesthetics, Political Philosophy and Literature and Philosophy in Christian Europe at the Institute Edith Stein in Granada. He was consultant for the New Line Cinema adaptation of The Lord of the Rings and published several books on Tolkien.
edusegura@yahoo.es

Anna Slack was awarded her MA Cantab in March, 2009. Between 2006 and 2008 she worked as a teacher of English as a Foreign Language at a private language school in Palermo, Sicily. She currently teaches English Language and Literature at St. Gabriel's School, is the General English Editor of *PortalEditions*, for whom she is editing a volume of essays on C.S. Lewis and the author of various papers on Tolkien.
AnnaSlack@cantab.net

Guglielmo Spirito OFM Conv., Prof. Dr. theol., studied Philosophy and Egyptology before joining the Order of Saint Francis in the 1980s. In Rome he obtained the Degree (Licenza) in Pastoral Theology of Health Care at the Camillianum and the Doctorate in Theology with specialitation in Spirituality at the Pontifical Ateneum Antonianum. Since 1994 he is professor of Patristic and Franciscan Spirituality and of Theology and Literature (especially J.R.R. Tolkien) at the Theological Institute of Assisi and at the Pontifical Faculty of Saint Bonaventure in Rome. He gave courses in Croacia, Romania, Russia and Mexico, and lectures in England and Canada, Armenia and Egypt. On Tolkien he had published essays, articles and books. He is also a member of the *Società Tolkieniana Italiana*.
fraguspi@gmail.com

Martin Sternberg studied Ancient History, Mediaeval History, History of Arts, and Law at Münster from 1990 to 1996. He is currently working in a federal authority. During his studies, he specialised in Late Antiquity and Early Christianity.
lasgalen@web.de

Doreen Triebel studied English and American Literature and Linguistics, Psychology and German as a Foreign Language at Friedrich Schiller University Jena, the University of Nottingham and Illinois State University. She is currently pursuing a Ph.D. in English Literature and teaches at the University of Jena.
Doreen-T@gmx.de

Allan Turner, Ph.D., studied German Philology, Mediaeval Studies, and General Linguistics. His Ph.D. thesis in translation studies examines the problems inherent in translating the philological elements in *The Lord of the Rings*. His main focus of interest is currently on the stylistics of Tolkien's works. He teaches English Language Skills and British Cultural Studies at Friedrich Schiller University of Jena.
allangturner@aol.com

Siglenverzeichnis

Die Schriften von J.R.R. Tolkien werden im Text jeweils ohne Angabe des Verfassernamens mit den folgenden Siglen zitiert. Die jeweils benutzte Ausgabe findet sich im Literaturverzeichnis.

AI:	The Lay of Aotrou and Itroun
ATB:	The Adventures of Tom Bombadil and other Verses from the Red Book / Die Abenteuer des Tom Bombadil und andere Gedichte aus dem Roten Buch
AW:	Ancrene Wisse and Hali Meiðhad
B:	Die Briefe von J.R.R. Tolkien
BA:	Bilbos Abschiedslied
BB:	Baum und Blatt
BGH:	Bauer Giles von Ham
BLS:	Bilbo's Last Song
BMC:	Beowulf: The Monster and the Critics
BT:	Blatt von Tüftler
BUK:	Beowulf: Die Ungeheuer und ihre Kritiker
BW:	Die Briefe vom Weihnachtsmann
CH:	The Children of Húrin
CP:	Chaucer as a Philologist
EA:	The End of the Third Age (History of Middle-earth 9). Auszug
EW:	English and Welsh / Englisch und Walisisch
FC:	Letters from Father Christmas
FGH:	Farmer Giles of Ham
FH:	Finn and Hengest
FS:	On Fairy-Stories
GD:	Gute Drachen sind rar
GN:	Guide to the Names in the Lord of the Rings
GPO:	Sir Gawain and the Green Knight, Pearl, and Sir Orfeo
H:	The Hobbit / Der Hobbit / Der kleine Hobbit
HB:	The Homecoming of Beorhtnoth Beorhthelm's Son
HdR:	Der Herr der Ringe
HdR I:	Der Herr der Ringe. Bd. 1. Die Gefährten
HdR II:	Der Herr der Ringe. Bd. 2. Die Zwei Türme
HdR III:	Der Herr der Ringe. Bd. 3. Die Rückkehr des Königs / Die Wiederkehr des Königs
HdR A:	Der Herr der Ringe. Anhänge
HG:	Herr Glück
HH I/II:	The History of the Hobbit
HL:	Ein heimliches Laster
KH:	Die Kinder Húrins
L:	The Letters of J.R.R. Tolkien
LB:	The Lays of Beleriand (History of Middle-earth 3)
LN:	Leaf by Niggle

Siglenverzeichnis

LotR:	The Lord of the Rings
LotR I:	The Fellowship of the Ring. Being the first part of The Lord of the Rings
LotR II:	The Two Towers. Being the second part of The Lord of the Rings
LotR III:	The Return of the King. Being the third part of The Lord of the Rings
LotR A:	The Lord of the Rings. Appendices
LR:	The Lost Road and other Writings (History of Middle-earth 5)
LSG:	The Legend of Sigurd and Gudrún
LT 1:	The Book of Lost Tales 1 (History of Middle-earth 1)
LT 2:	The Book of Lost Tales 2 (History of Middle-earth 2)
MB:	Mr. Bliss
MC:	The Monsters and the Critics and Other Essays
ME:	A Middle English Vocabulary
MR:	Morgoth's Ring (History of Middle-earth 10)
My:	Mythopoeia
NM:	Nachrichten aus Mittelerde
OE:	The Old English Exodus
OK:	Ósanwe-Kenta
P:	Pictures by J.R.R. Tolkien
PM:	The Peoples of Middle-earth (History of Middle-earth 12)
R:	Roverandom
RBG:	The Rivers and Beacon-hills of Gondor
RGEO:	The Road Goes Ever On (with Donald Swann)
RS:	The Return of the Shadow (History of Middle-earth 6)
S:	Silmarillion
SD:	The Sauron Defeated (History of Middle-earth 9)
SG:	Der Schmied von Großholzingen
SGG:	Sir Gawain and the Green Knight / Sir Gawain und der Grüne Ritter (Essay)
SM:	The Shaping of Middle-earth (History of Middle-earth 4)
SP:	Songs for the Philologists
SV:	A Secret Vice
SWM:	Smith of Wootton Major
SWME:	Smith of Wootton Major Essay
TB:	On Translating Beowulf
TI:	The Treason of Isengard (History of Middle-earth 7)
TL:	Tree and Leaf
ÜB:	Zur Übersetzung des Beowulf
ÜM:	Über Märchen
UK:	Die Ungeheuer und ihre Kritiker. Gesammelte Aufsätze
UT:	Unfinished Tales
VA:	Valedictory Address
VG 1:	Das Buch der Verschollenen Geschichten 1
VG 2:	Das Buch der Verschollenen Geschichten 2
WJ:	The War of the Jewels (History of Middle-earth 11)
WR:	The War of the Ring (History of Middle-earth 8)

Index

Adorno, Theodor W.	204-219, 232f
Aragorn/Elessar	23, 29, 37, 41, 51, 102f, 165f, 183,184, 198, 232, 244
Archaism (Geschichtlichkeit)	162, 211
Aristoteles/Aristotle	138, 145, 147, 152, 154, 252
Art (Kunst)/Artist/Artistic	8, 11f, 14, 42, 49, 54f, 61, 63-66, 69, 73, 162, 164, 166f, 169, 171, 188f, 191, 193, 195-197, 200-203, 231, 232, 243, 251f
Auenland (Shire)	40, 98, 115, 118, 204, 214f
Aufklärung (Enlightenment)	16, 36, 208, 210f, 215, 217
Baumbart	→ Treebeard
Beauty (Schönheit)	8, 14, 19-25, 27f, 52, 64, 66, 69, 71, 85, 89, 120, 132, 138, 140, 142, 144, 150, 152f, 158f, 161, 163, 167, 230, 233
Beren	24f, 36f, 41, 103
Bilbo	13, 88, 99, 114-116, 126, 143, 157, 181f, 193-195, 197, 199, 215, 232
Blake, William	9-12, 25, 36, 79, 110
Brentano, Clemens	189-193, 195, 202
Burke, Edmund	152-155, 158-160, 226f
Byron, Lord	9, 20, 36, 60, 65, 79, 110, 113, 122
Carpenter, Humphrey	18f, 38, 45, 63, 122, 125 ,130, 146f, 153, 157
Cirith Ungol	12, 128, 164, 184
Coleridge, Samuel Taylor	9f, 20, 24, 29, 36, 49, 65, 79, 110,120f, 124f, 140f, 144, 173-179, 196, 225f, 252
Denethor	28, 56, 135, 166
Disenchanted (entzaubert)	60, 62
Dostoevskij, Fedor M.	120-128, 132-136, 225
Eichendorff, Joseph von	97f, 208
Elben	41, 43f, 103-108, 112f, 181f, 215, 218, 225, 227
Elves	19-25, 28, 66, 70, 72, 87-90, 103-105, 107, 114, 131f, 135, 158-160, 163, 183, 200, 246, 249f, 252f
Empfindsamkeit (Sensitivity)	222
Enlightenment (Aufklärung)	27, 29, 49, 52f, 69, 189
Entzaubert (disenchanted)	104, 223
Eskapismus	118, 213, 215, 218, 224
Escapism/Escapist	10, 15, 60-67, 73, 84, 144, 148, 160
Eucatastrophe	9, 11-15, 67, 131, 146-150, 163, 215
Faerie/Faery/Faërie	26f, 67, 70-73, 83-85, 87-90, 155, 159f
Faith (Glaube)	17, 134-135, 138-143, 175f, 238
Fëanor	21, 23, 26-28, 195, 201
Ferré, Vincent	163, 239
Flieger, Verlyn	73, 140, 142f, 148, 189, 198, 200
Frodo	13f, 16, 21, 28, 40, 42, 56, 63, 100, 127-135, 146, 156, 159, 164, 168, 183f, 198f, 215, 230, 235, 244

Galadriel	16, 23, 27f, 71f, 159, 167, 183, 199, 217
Gandalf	27, 29, 51, 53, 70, 104, 111, 143, 156f, 163, 166, 182f, 198-200, 215, 217, 244
Garth, John	217
Geschichtlichkeit/Archaizität	38, 210, 212
Gewissen	172, 176-185, 207
Gimli	24, 53f, 68, 100f, 103, 134f, 165f, 183, 230
Glaube (Faith)	175, 179, 226
God	55, 113, 131f, 138ff, 142, 144, 146-149, 175f, 179f, 190ff, 195, 232, 252
Golden Age(s)	40, 96, 98, 101f, 223
Goldenes Zeitalter	48, 66ff, 231
Gott	36ff, 44, 107, 175f, 178ff, 190, 210
Heimat	38, 54, 96, 99f, 106ff, 115, 215
Hobbits	15f, 28, 48, 56, 63, 66, 99f, 103, 111ff, 127, 129, 158f, 160, 188, 193, 195, 197-201, 214f, 230, 250
Hoffmann, E.T.A.	73
Honegger, Thomas	39, 54, 57, 86, 210, 214, 217, 219, 244
Hugo, Viktor	162-165, 167-171, 227f
Humankind (Menschheit)	140, 142f, 146
Imagination (Vorstellungskraft)	8-20, 28, 61, 73, 77, 82, 124, 139-145, 148, 154f, 157, 165, 173, 179, 188f, 192, 196f, 199, 201, 229, 241, 243, 247, 251f, 254,
Industrialisation	48, 52ff, 56f, 61f, 69
Industrialisierung	34, 39, 41, 224
Keats, John	9, 24, 36, 60-73, 83ff, 88, 90, 110, 113, 118, 160, 223f, 225, 247
Kreativität/Schöpfungskraft	32ff, 37, 40, 43f, 46, 223
Kunst (Art)	34ff, 41, 43ff, 98, 101, 116f, 173f, 208f, 215-219, 223f, 234
Legolas	24, 68, 134, 155, 165f, 183
Lewis, C.S.	10f, 52, 121f, 125, 141, 146f, 240, 243, 248, 251-254
Lúthien Tinúviel	22, 24f, 37, 41, 64, 249
Melkor	26, 68, 182, 201, 248
Menschen/Menschheit (Humankind)	36, 44, 46, 97ff, 102, 106ff, 177, 179f
Middle Ages (Mittelalter)	48-53, 56f, 231, 240
Minas Tirith	166, 183
Mittelalter (Middle Ages)	35-41, 102, 113ff, 119, 212, 223
Morgoth	25, 64, 253
Moria/Dwarrowdelf	27, 68, 100f, 155, 231
Morris, William	42, 60-69, 73, 217, 223f, 249
Müller, Max	140, 226
Mythopoeia/Mythopoesie/mythopoetisch	10, 38, 141-144, 146f, 189, 191ff, 195f, 201, 226, 238, 252
Mythos	34, 37f, 45, 211, 217, 219, 222, 226
Myth	9, 77, 89, 138-142, 145ff, 150, 196, 237, 239, 241, 248f, 253
Natur(-verbundenheit)	35ff, 39, 41, 98f, 107f, 112f, 115-119, 174, 206, 212f, 217, 222, 227
Nature	9, 19-22, 24f, 28, 51, 53f, 62f, 66f, 69f, 73, 82, 89, 121f, 124f, 129, 131, 152-157, 173, 197, 231

Newman, John Henry	172-185, 231f
Niggle	10ff, 148, 153, 189, 195ff, 205
Nostalgia	24, 27f, 61, 66f, 83, 85, 131, 135, 202, 230
Nostalgie	94-108
Novalis	37, 49-56, 97f, 102f, 107f
Past (Vergangenheit)	27, 48ff, 63, 68, 76, 80f, 85f, 131, 139, 190, 198, 230f
Pippin	56, 165ff, 182f, 197
Phantasie/Imagination/Vorstellungskraft	34, 36f, 39ff, 43-46, 172, 222, 225, 227
Quest	21, 26, 54, 76, 116f, 148, 168
Queste	40, 184, 212
Rohirrim	28, 57, 165, 248
Sam(wise Gamgee)	14, 28, 232
Saruman	29, 39, 52f, 104, 130, 159, 182, 201, 217
Sauron	25, 27, 56, 69, 156, 164, 182, 200, 253
Shelley, Percy	8f, 17, 25-28, 36, 110, 113, 122, 188, 192, 202
(the) Sublime	152-165, 167, 170, 176, 191, 194, 198, 226
Schlegel, Friedrich	36
Scott, Walter	49-57, 79, 83
Schönheit (Beauty)	38, 105f, 108, 112, 205, 209, 217, 223, 226
Sehnsucht	32-38, 40-44, 46, 95f, 99f, 102f, 104, 108, 194, 209f, 219, 223
Sensitivity (Empfindsamkeit)	18ff
Shippey, Tom	26, 69, 146, 160, 195f, 199f, 238f, 242
Shire (Auenland)	48, 52f, 56f, 63, 129f, 167, 194, 197ff, 213, 230, 232
Sub-creation/Sub-creator	10ff, 18ff, 53, 57, 63f, 73, 121f, 138-150, 159, 188, 192, 241, 247, 249
Thorin	21, 111f, 114f, 181, 194
Todorov, Tzvetan	170
Treebeard	70, 201
Vergangenheit (Past)	37, 95f, 99-104, 108, 113, 117f, 218, 223, 225
Wordsworth, William	9, 16, 19ff, 29, 62, 79, 82f, 90, 110f, 116, 120ff, 124f, 130, 135, 140f, 173f, 225
Zweitschöpfung/-schöpfer (sub-creation)	34, 43f, 46, 117, 214, 223, 226

www.ingramcontent.com/pod-product-compliance
Lightning Source LLC
Chambersburg PA
CBHW051806230426
43672CB00012B/2648